Snow White
with the Red Hair

SORATA AKIDUKI

The Straw Millionaire Version

This piece of straw will somehow win me your mansion, so let's cut to the chase.

You can't just skip the whole trading sequence like that.

THE END

THE STORY

Shirayuki was born with beautiful hair as red as apples, but when her rare hair earns her unwanted attention from the notorious prince Raj, she's forced to flee her home. A young man named Zen helps her in the forest of the neighboring kingdom, Clarines, and it turns out he is that kingdom's second prince! Shirayuki decides to accompany Zen back to Wistal, the capital city of Clarines.

Shirayuki has met all manner of people since becoming a court herbalist, and her relationship with Zen continues to grow, as the two have finally made their feelings known to each other.

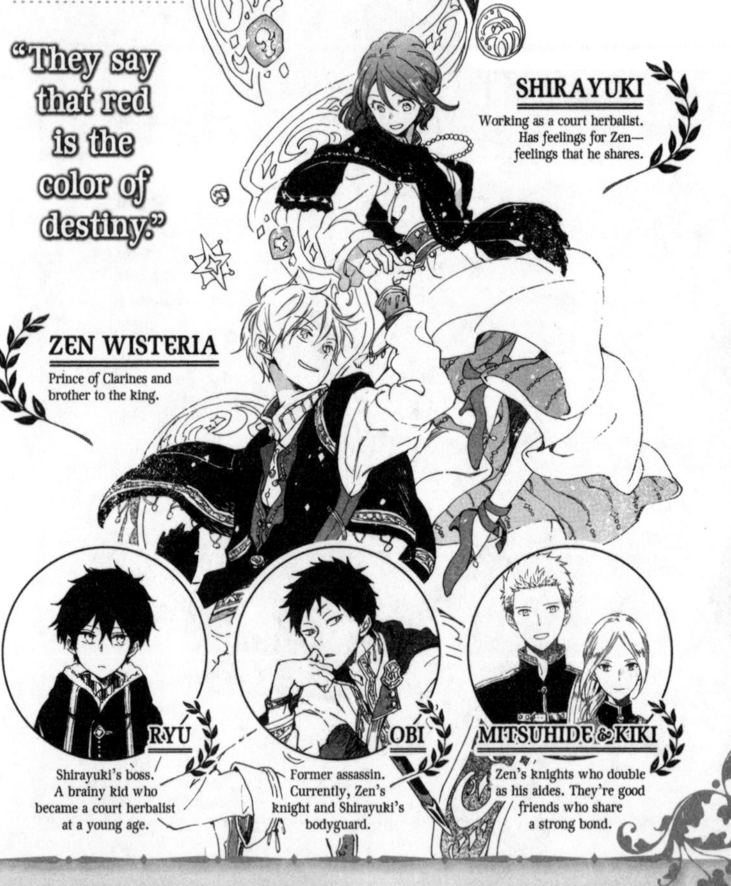
"They say that red is the color of destiny."
SHIRAYUKI
Working as a court herbalist. Has feelings for Zen—feelings that he shares.
ZEN WISTERIA
Prince of Clarines and brother to the king.
RYU
Shirayuki's boss. A brainy kid who became a court herbalist at a young age.
OBI
Former assassin. Currently, Zen's knight and Shirayuki's bodyguard.
MITSUHIDE & KIKI
Zen's knights who double as his aides. They're good friends who share a strong bond.

After becoming a full-fledged court herbalist, Shirayuki takes a work trip to the northern city of Lilias with her boss, Ryu. When a mysterious illness starts spreading, they put their skills to use and figure out what's causing it.

Once back in Wistal, Shirayuki and Ryu are ordered to return to Lilias by the newly crowned king Izana. But this time, it's no mere business trip—it's a personnel transfer for two whole years. After arriving, the pair endeavor to bolster their herbalism skills and knowledge as they work with colleagues to neutralize the toxin of the glowing orimmallys—the same plant that caused the mysterious illness earlier. Their stunning success brings an end to that chapter.

...WILL WORK AS HERBALISTS AND RESEARCHERS IN LILIAS.

Meanwhile, during a stay at Sereg, Zen is caught up in a plot by Toka Bergat to wrench authority over the northern lands away from the crown. When Zen's very life is threatened, Mitsuhide defeats Toka in a duel, foiling the would-be usurper's ambitions.

THIS MATTER WILL BE BROUGHT TO AN END WHEN THE ASSASSIN'S BLADE SINKS INTO HIS HIGHNESS'S FLESH.

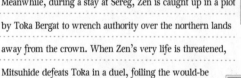

With the plot behind them, Zen and the others take a well-deserved break. Zen joins Shirayuki and Obi for a vacation in Lilias, and Mitsuhide attends a harvest festival in Kiki's home region. Kiki finally proposes to Mitsuhide, but he turns her down, citing his lifelong desire to serve as Zen's protector.

Despite this rejection, Kiki is understanding.

I'M ZEN WISTERIA.
I'M JUST TAGGING ALONG WITH THESE TWO DURING MY TIME OFF.
HE'S MY MASTER.

I LOVE YOU...
...AND I WANT US TO BE TOGETHER.

BUT KIKI...
I CAN'T GIVE YOU THAT.
I'M FINE...
...WITH THIS REJECTION.

VOLUME 20
TABLE of CONTENTS

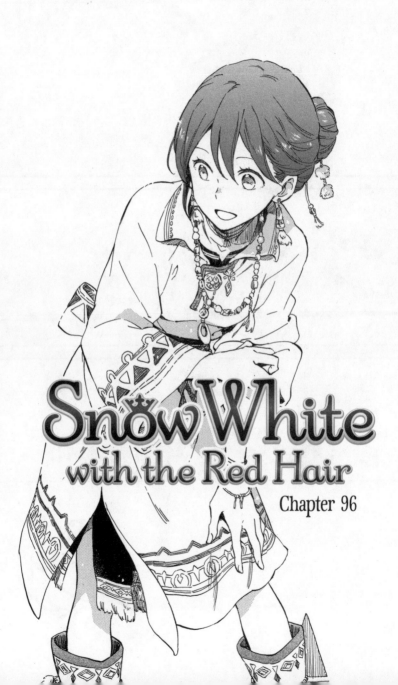

Snow White
with the Red Hair
Chapter 96

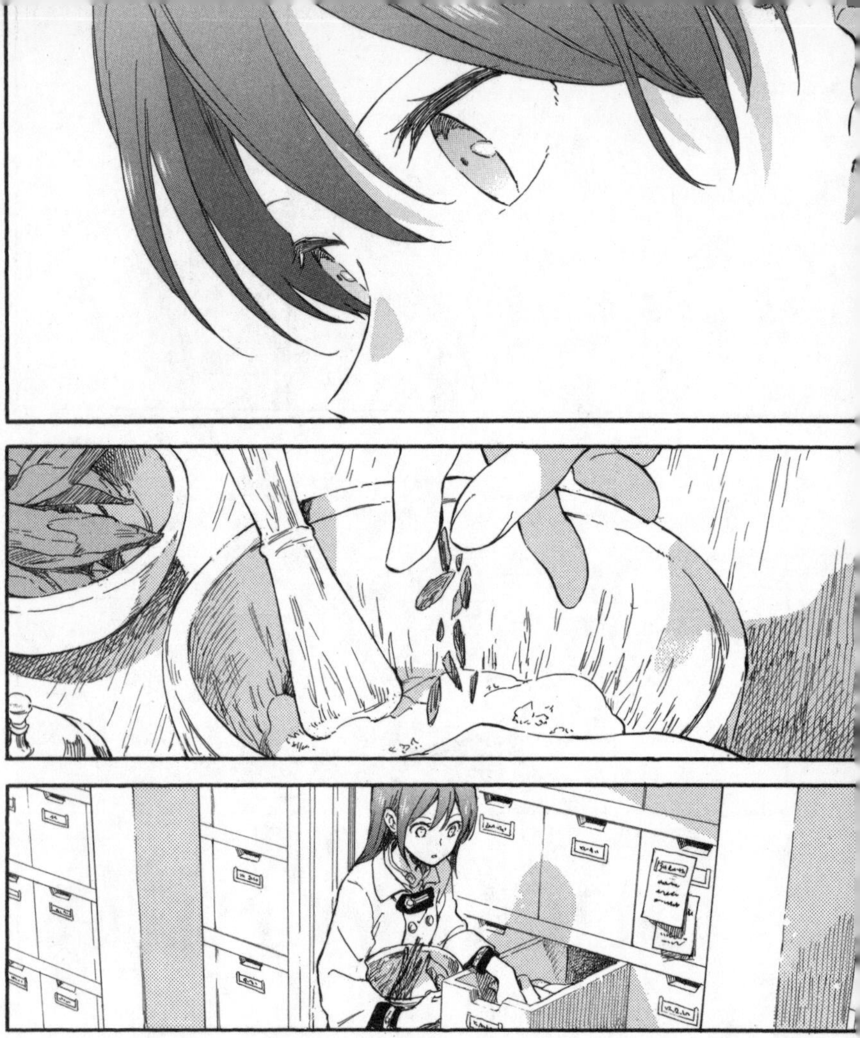

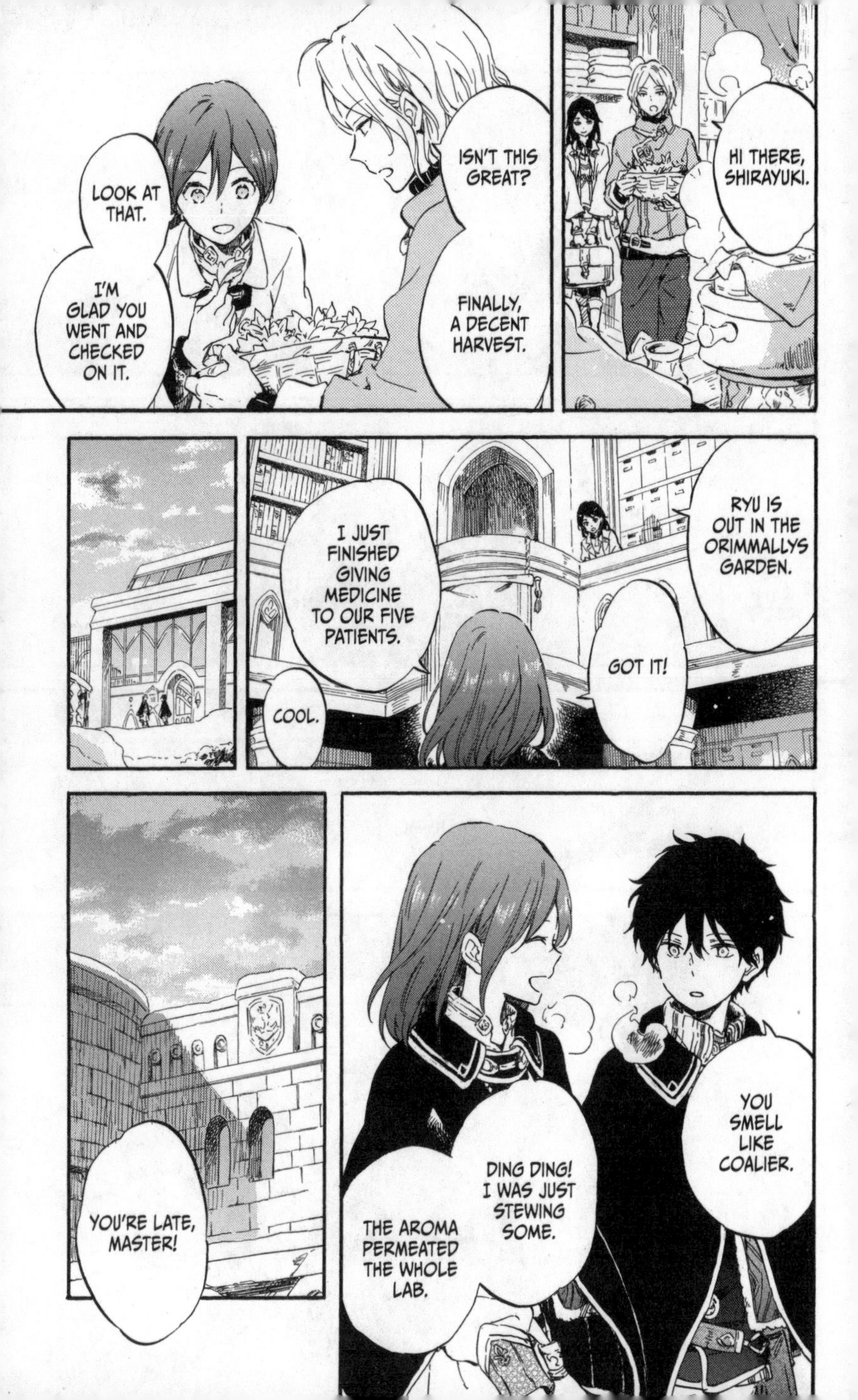
HI THERE, SHIRAYUKI.
ISN'T THIS GREAT?
FINALLY, A DECENT HARVEST.
LOOK AT THAT.
I'M GLAD YOU WENT AND CHECKED ON IT.
RYU IS OUT IN THE ORIMMALLYS GARDEN.
I JUST FINISHED GIVING MEDICINE TO OUR FIVE PATIENTS.
GOT IT!
COOL.
YOU SMELL LIKE COALIER.
DING DING! I WAS JUST STEWING SOME.
THE AROMA PERMEATED THE WHOLE LAB.
YOU'RE LATE, MASTER!

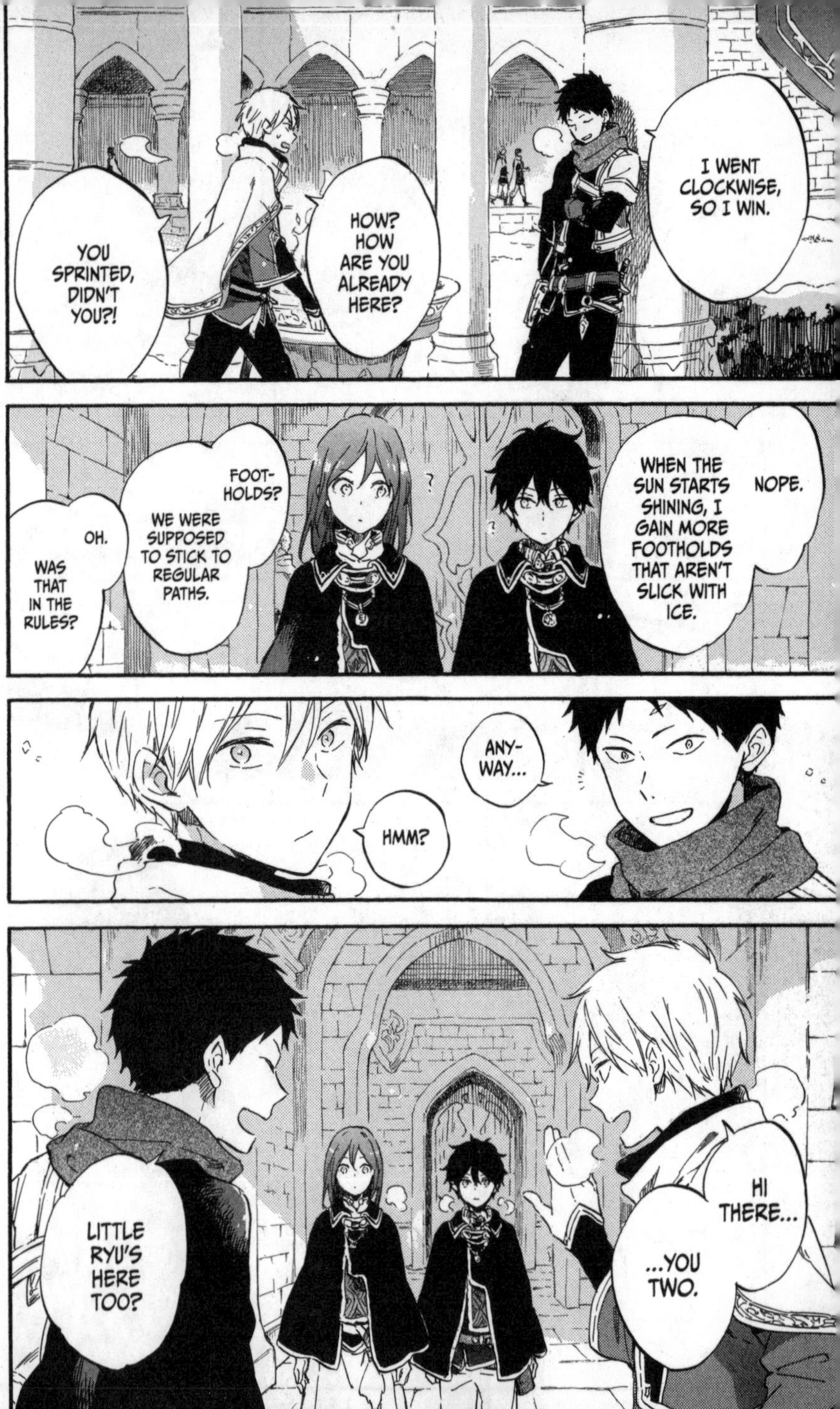
I WENT CLOCKWISE, SO I WIN.
HOW? HOW ARE YOU ALREADY HERE?
YOU SPRINTED, DIDN'T YOU?!
NOPE.
WHEN THE SUN STARTS SHINING, I GAIN MORE FOOTHOLDS THAT AREN'T SLICK WITH ICE.
FOOT-HOLDS?
WE WERE SUPPOSED TO STICK TO REGULAR PATHS.
OH.
WAS THAT IN THE RULES?
ANY-WAY...
HMM?
HI THERE...
...YOU TWO.
LITTLE RYU'S HERE TOO?

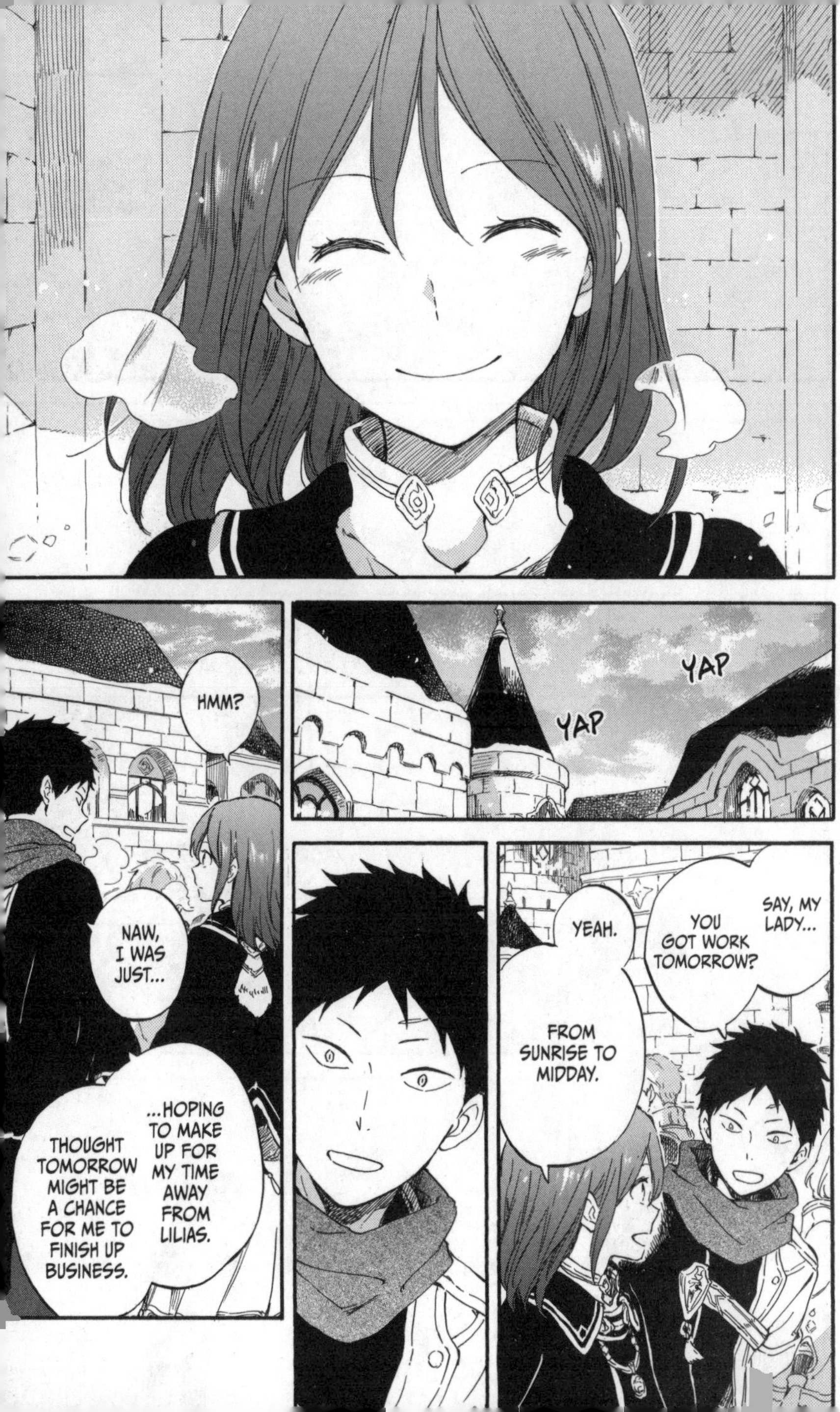
YAP
YAP
SAY, MY LADY...
YOU GOT WORK TOMORROW?
YEAH.
FROM SUNRISE TO MIDDAY.
HMM?
NAW, I WAS JUST...
...HOPING TO MAKE UP FOR MY TIME AWAY FROM LILIAS.
THOUGHT TOMORROW MIGHT BE A CHANCE FOR ME TO FINISH UP BUSINESS.

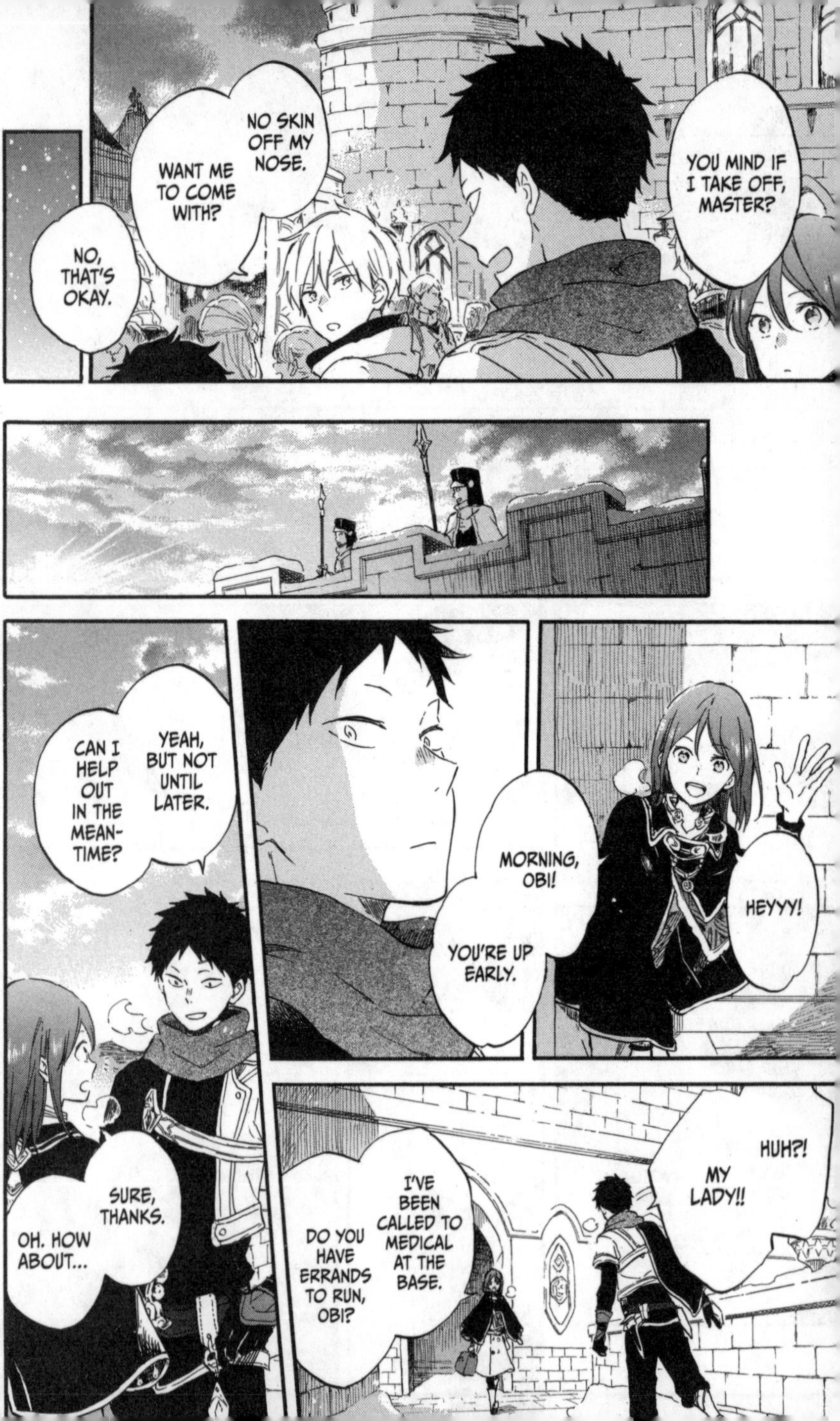
YOU MIND IF I TAKE OFF, MASTER?
NO SKIN OFF MY NOSE.
WANT ME TO COME WITH?
NO, THAT'S OKAY.
HEYYY!
MORNING, OBI!
YOU'RE UP EARLY.
HUH?!
MY LADY!!
I'VE BEEN CALLED TO MEDICAL AT THE BASE.
DO YOU HAVE ERRANDS TO RUN, OBI?
YEAH, BUT NOT UNTIL LATER.
CAN I HELP OUT IN THE MEAN-TIME?
SURE, THANKS.
OH. HOW ABOUT...

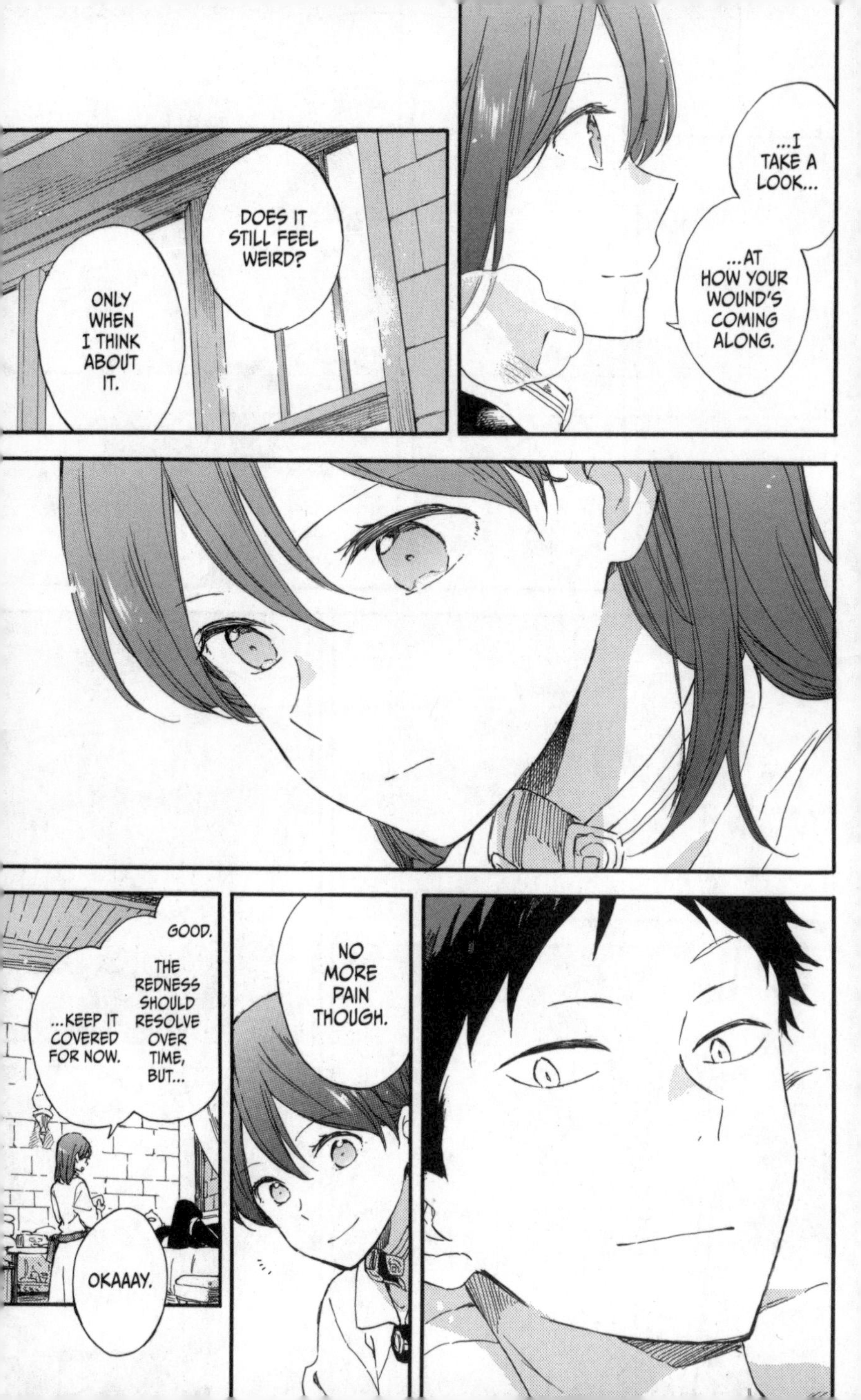
...I TAKE A LOOK...
...AT HOW YOUR WOUND'S COMING ALONG.
DOES IT STILL FEEL WEIRD?
ONLY WHEN I THINK ABOUT IT.
NO MORE PAIN THOUGH.
GOOD.
THE REDNESS SHOULD RESOLVE OVER TIME, BUT...
...KEEP IT COVERED FOR NOW.
OKAAAY.

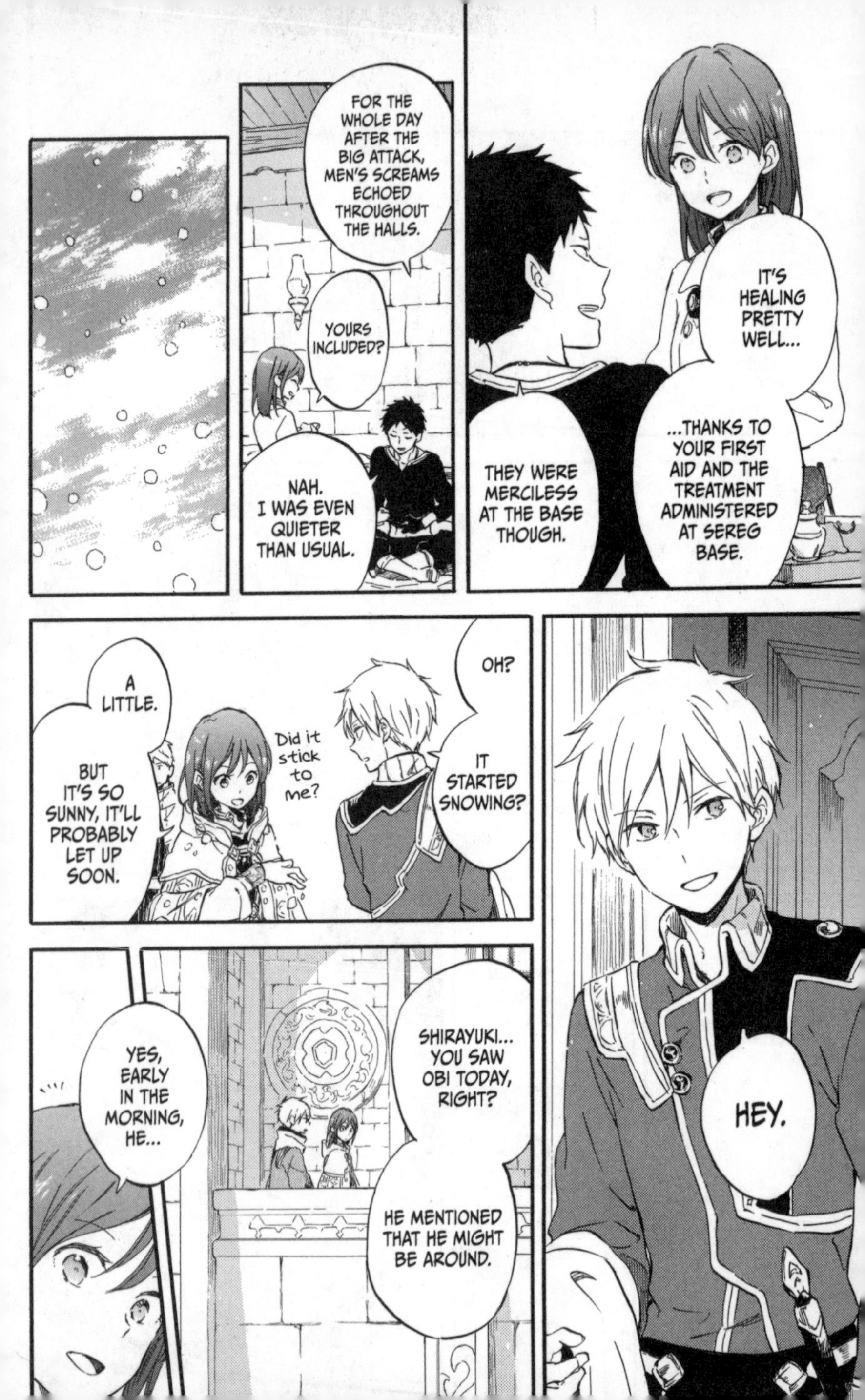
IT'S HEALING PRETTY WELL...
...THANKS TO YOUR FIRST AID AND THE TREATMENT ADMINISTERED AT SEREG BASE.
THEY WERE MERCILESS AT THE BASE THOUGH.
FOR THE WHOLE DAY AFTER THE BIG ATTACK, MEN'S SCREAMS ECHOED THROUGHOUT THE HALLS.
YOURS INCLUDED?
NAH. I WAS EVEN QUIETER THAN USUAL.
HEY.
OH?
IT STARTED SNOWING?
Did it stick to me?
A LITTLE.
BUT IT'S SO SUNNY, IT'LL PROBABLY LET UP SOON.
SHIRAYUKI... YOU SAW OBI TODAY, RIGHT?
HE MENTIONED THAT HE MIGHT BE AROUND.
YES, EARLY IN THE MORNING, HE...

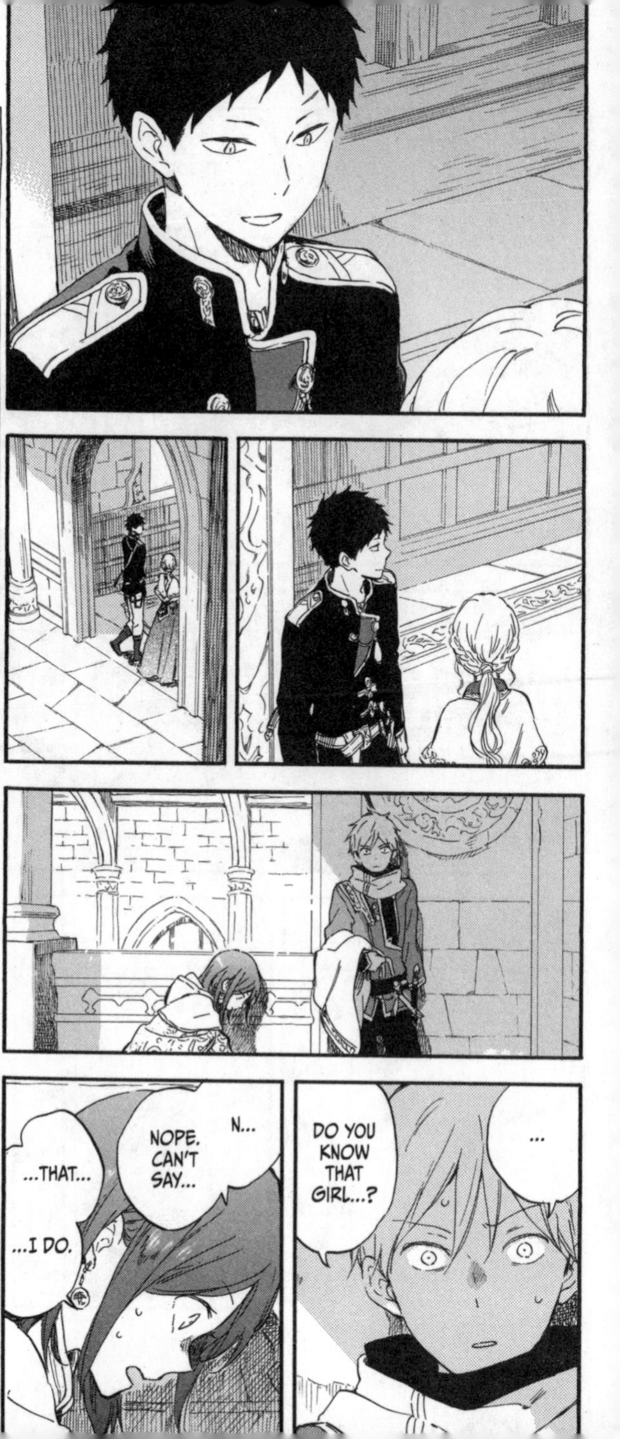
...
DO YOU KNOW THAT GIRL...?
N...
NOPE. CAN'T SAY...
...THAT...
...I DO.

GREETINGS

Hello, everyone! Thanks for picking up volume 20 of Snow White with the Red Hair. One hundred whole chapters! We've made it through 100 chapters with Shirayuki and the gang. How moving.

Thank you so, so much to all you readers and everyone who sends those kind, delightful letters of support.

I'm going to take my time to make every single chapter the best it can be.

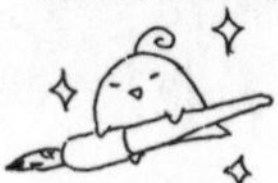

I draw with a NIKKO G Pen.

Anyhow! After a long absence, I'm back with another edition of my travel diary.

My destination? The Republic of Malta! It was a seven-day trip, and same as always, Hachi and Toki Yajima were the ones who invited me along.

Bon voyage!

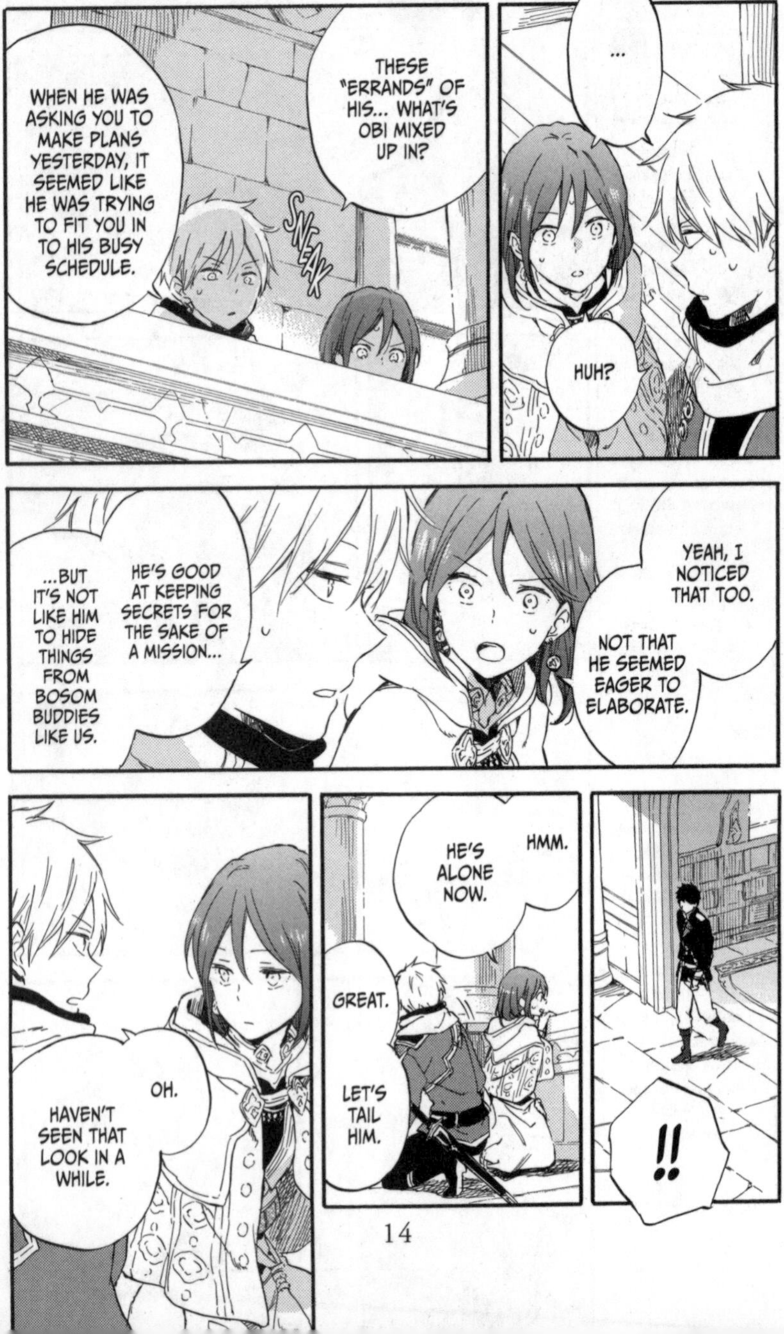
...
HUH?
THESE "ERRANDS" OF HIS... WHAT'S OBI MIXED UP IN?
WHEN HE WAS ASKING YOU TO MAKE PLANS YESTERDAY, IT SEEMED LIKE HE WAS TRYING TO FIT YOU IN TO HIS BUSY SCHEDULE.
SNEAK
YEAH, I NOTICED THAT TOO.
NOT THAT HE SEEMED EAGER TO ELABORATE.
HE'S GOOD AT KEEPING SECRETS FOR THE SAKE OF A MISSION...
...BUT IT'S NOT LIKE HIM TO HIDE THINGS FROM BOSOM BUDDIES LIKE US.
!!
HMM.
HE'S ALONE NOW.
GREAT.
LET'S TAIL HIM.
OH.
HAVEN'T SEEN THAT LOOK IN A WHILE.

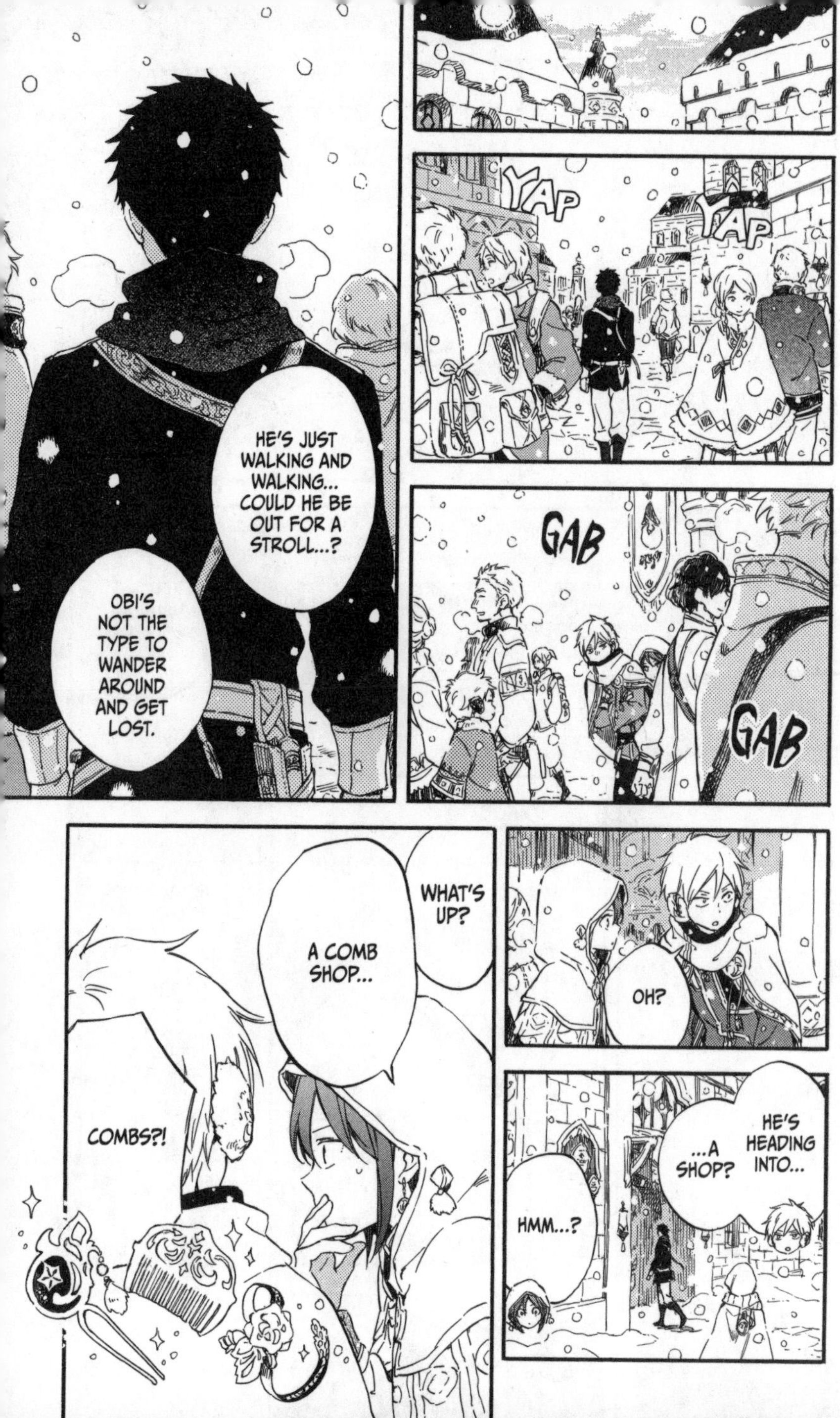
YAP
YAP
GAB
GAB
HE'S JUST WALKING AND WALKING... COULD HE BE OUT FOR A STROLL...?
OBI'S NOT THE TYPE TO WANDER AROUND AND GET LOST.
OH?
HE'S HEADING INTO...
...A SHOP?
HMM...?
WHAT'S UP?
A COMB SHOP...
COMBS?!

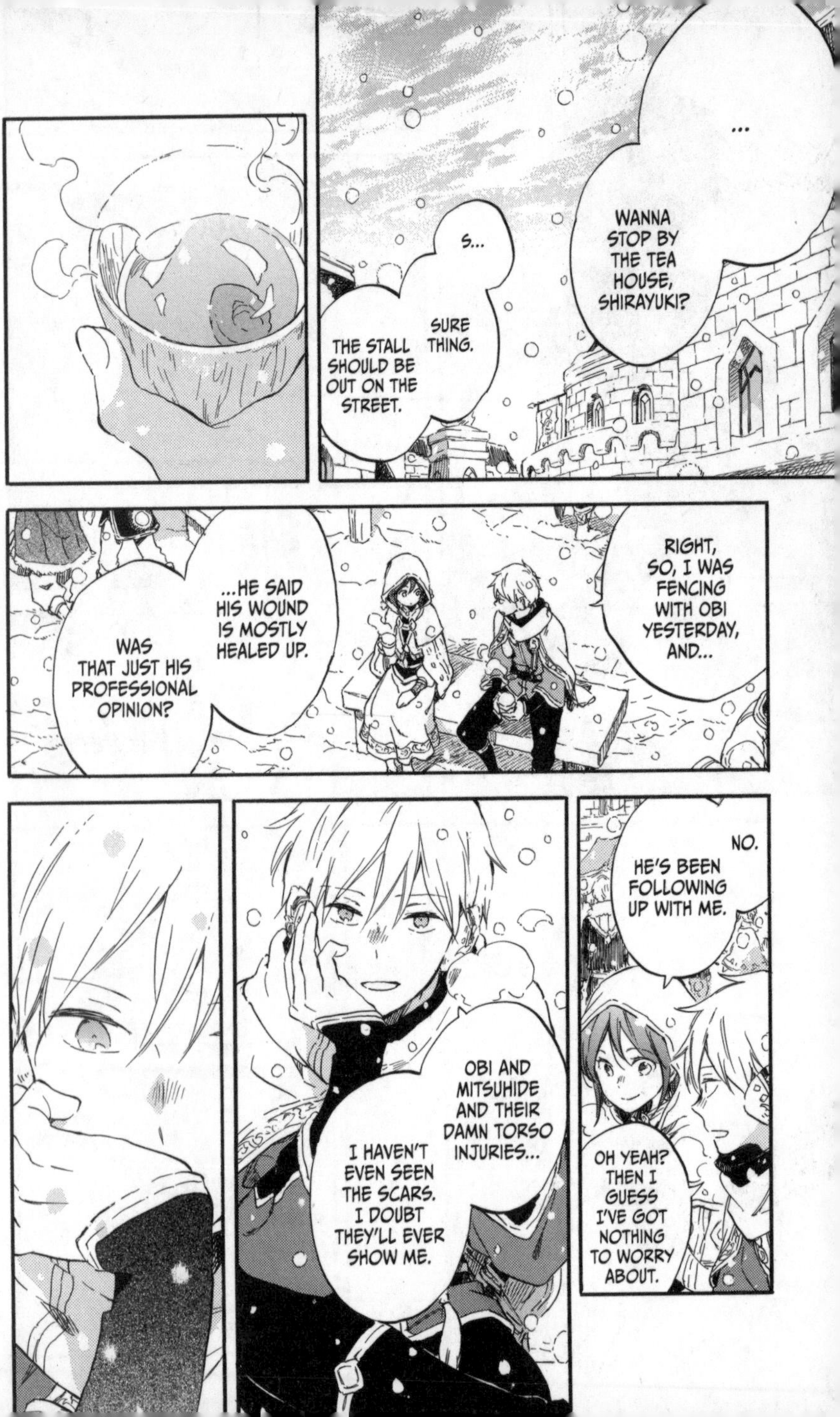
...
WANNA STOP BY THE TEA HOUSE, SHIRAYUKI?
S...
SURE THING.
THE STALL SHOULD BE OUT ON THE STREET.
RIGHT, SO, I WAS FENCING WITH OBI YESTERDAY, AND...
...HE SAID HIS WOUND IS MOSTLY HEALED UP.
WAS THAT JUST HIS PROFESSIONAL OPINION?
NO.
HE'S BEEN FOLLOWING UP WITH ME.
OH YEAH? THEN I GUESS I'VE GOT NOTHING TO WORRY ABOUT.
OBI AND MITSUHIDE AND THEIR DAMN TORSO INJURIES...
I HAVEN'T EVEN SEEN THE SCARS. I DOUBT THEY'LL EVER SHOW ME.

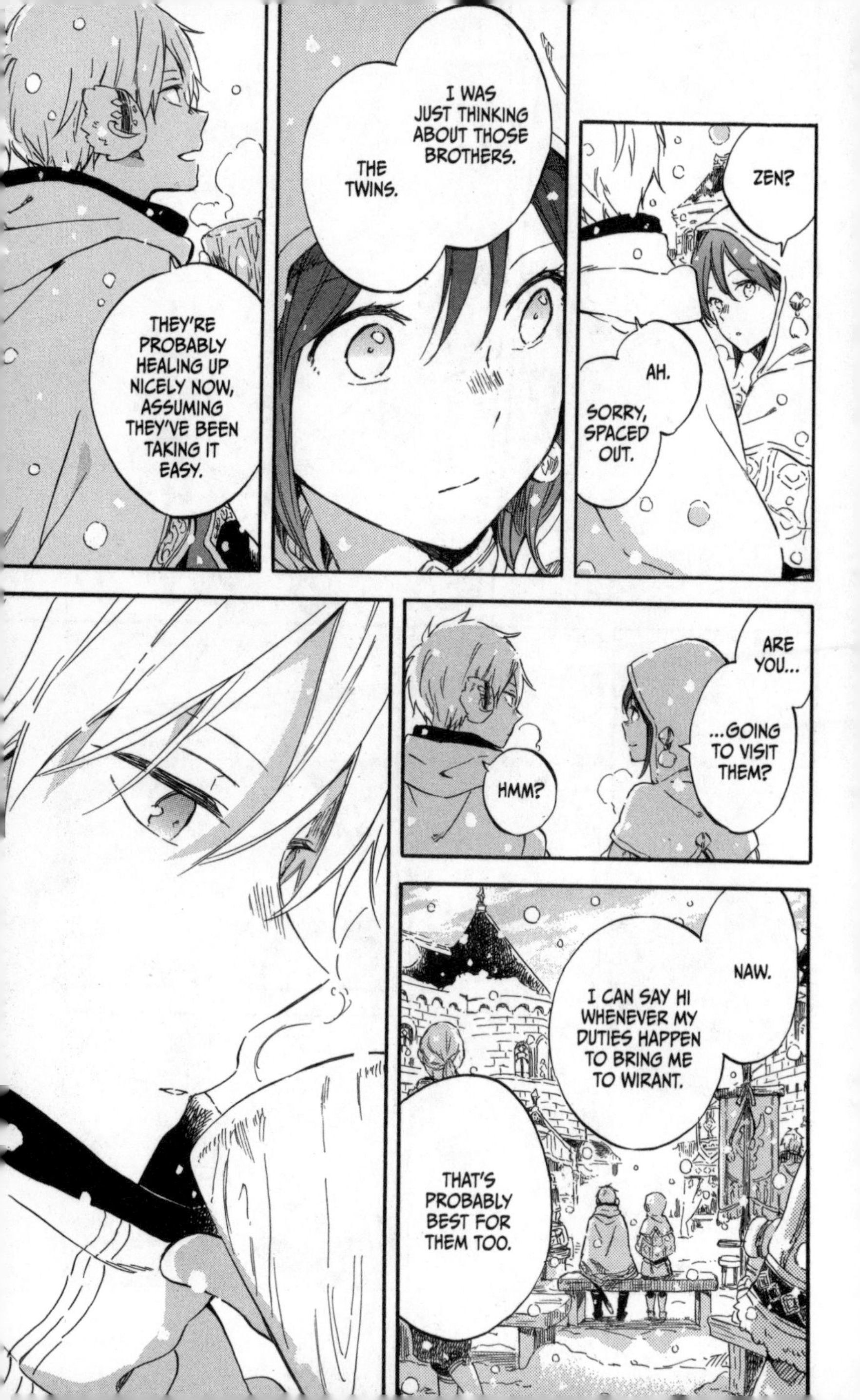
ZEN?
AH.
SORRY, SPACED OUT.
I WAS JUST THINKING ABOUT THOSE BROTHERS.
THE TWINS.
THEY'RE PROBABLY HEALING UP NICELY NOW, ASSUMING THEY'VE BEEN TAKING IT EASY.
ARE YOU...
...GOING TO VISIT THEM?
HMM?
NAW.
I CAN SAY HI WHENEVER MY DUTIES HAPPEN TO BRING ME TO WIRANT.
THAT'S PROBABLY BEST FOR THEM TOO.

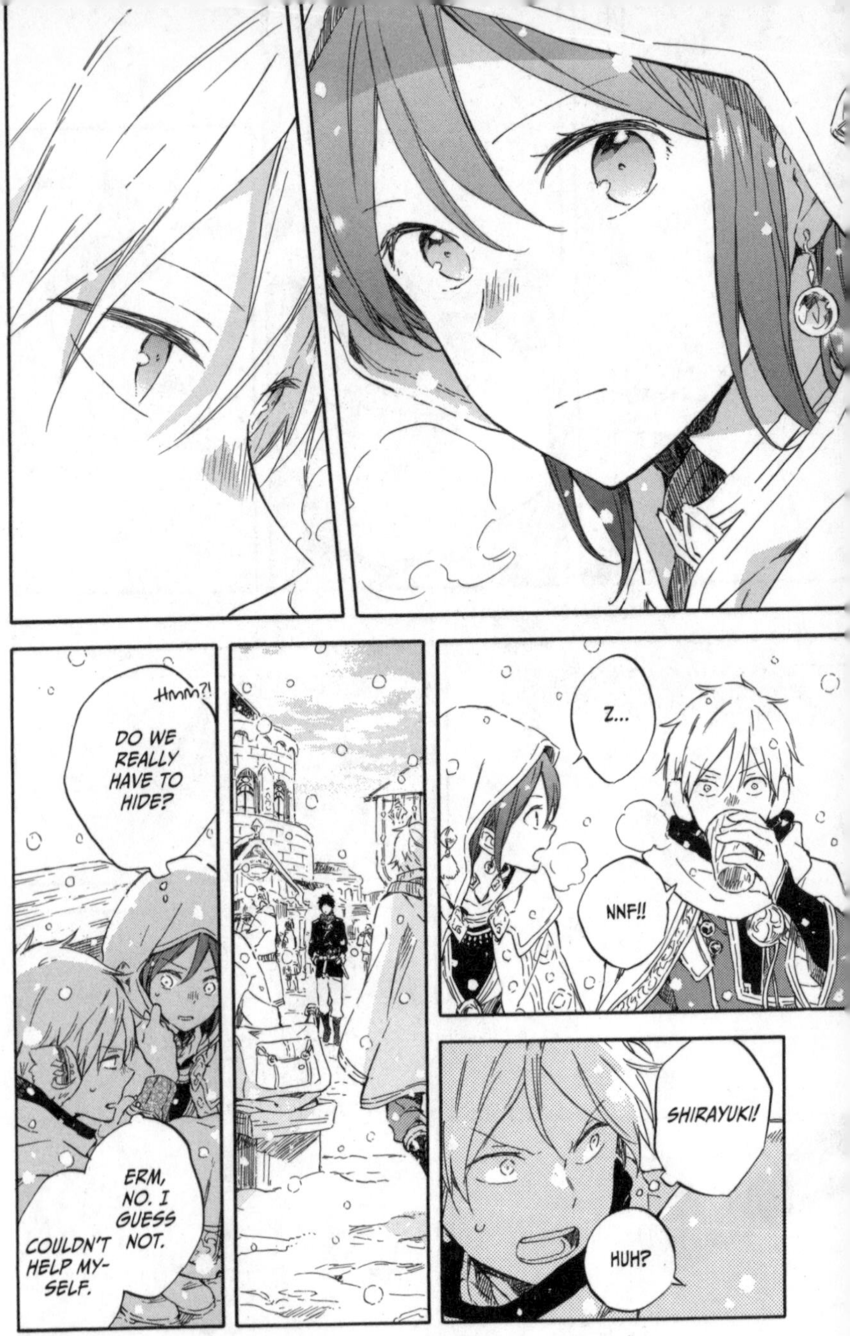
Z...
NNF!!
SHIRAYUKI!
HUH?
Hmm?!
DO WE REALLY HAVE TO HIDE?
ERM, NO. I GUESS NOT.
COULDN'T HELP MY-SELF.

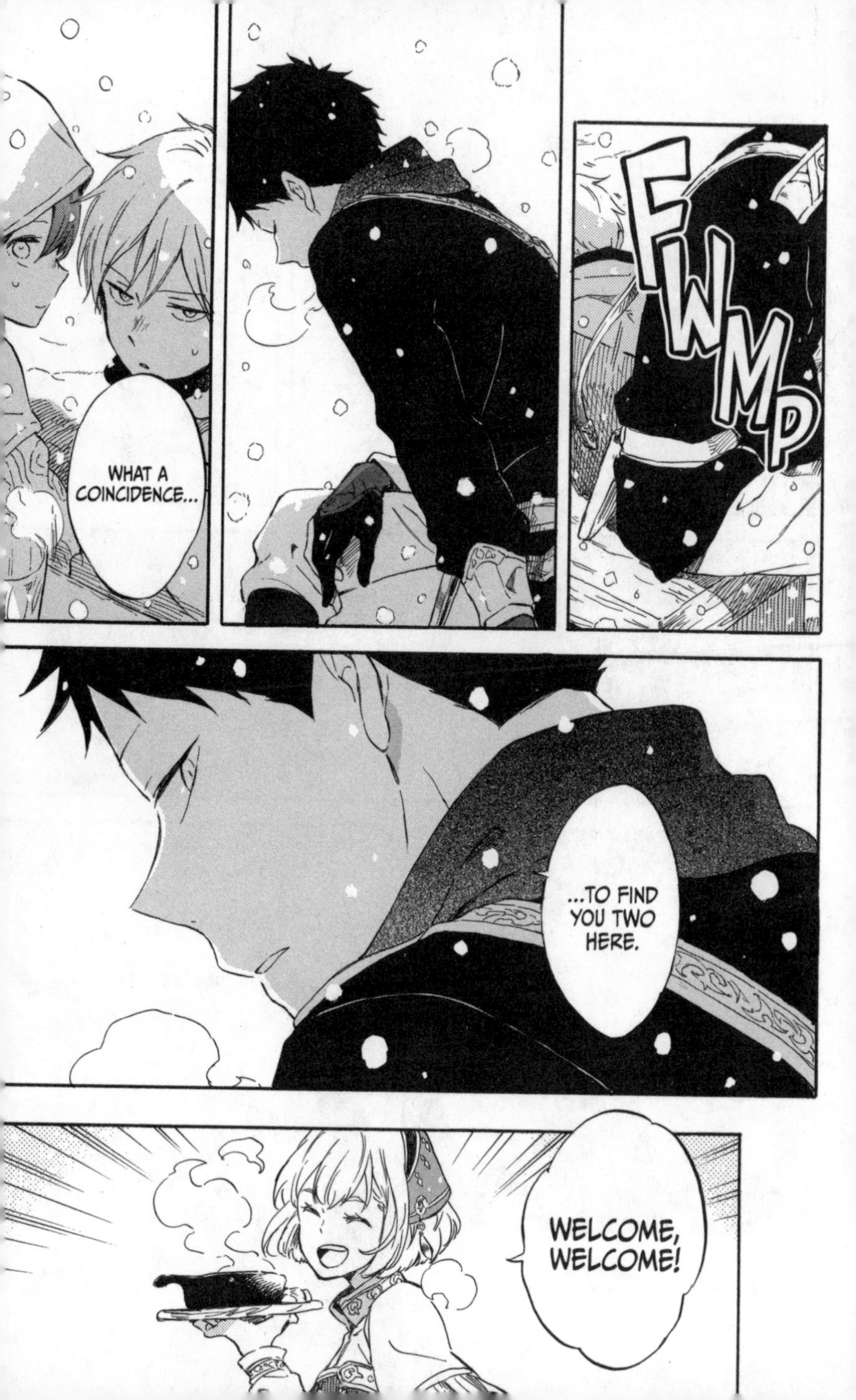
FWMP
WHAT A COINCIDENCE...
...TO FIND YOU TWO HERE.
WELCOME, WELCOME!

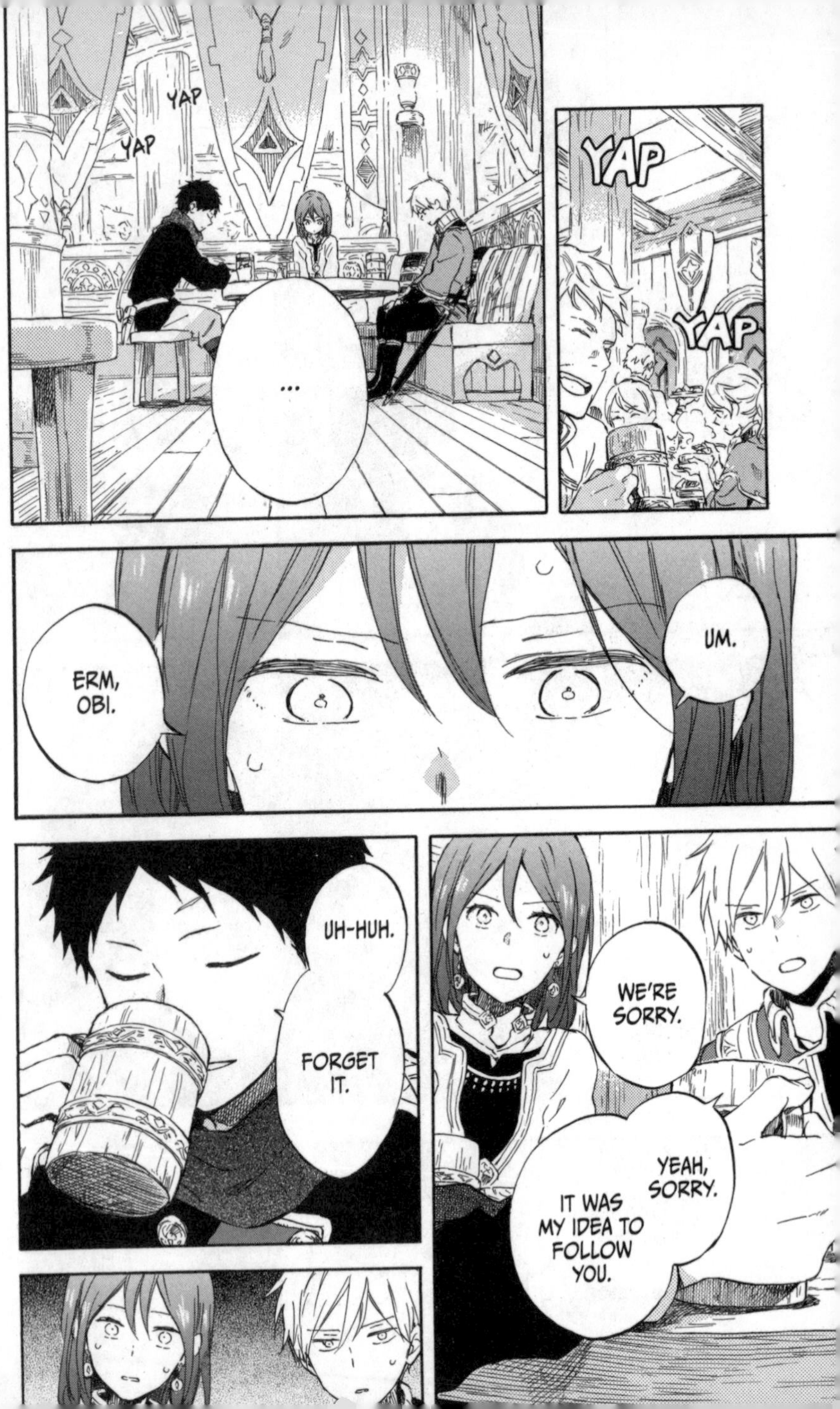
YAP
YAP
YAP
YAP
...
UM.
ERM, OBI.
WE'RE SORRY.
YEAH, SORRY.
IT WAS MY IDEA TO FOLLOW YOU.
UH-HUH.
FORGET IT.

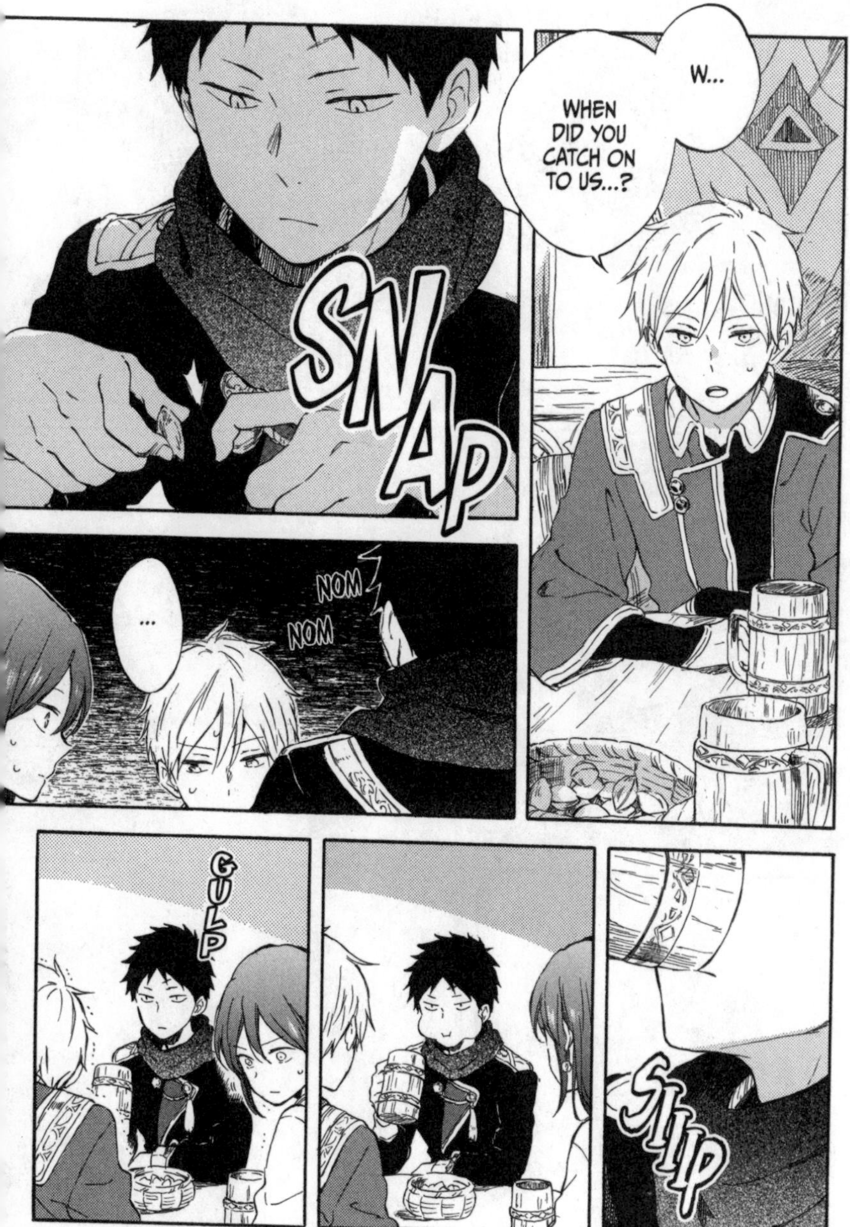
W...
WHEN DID YOU CATCH ON TO US...?
SNAP
...
NOM NOM
SIIIP
GULP

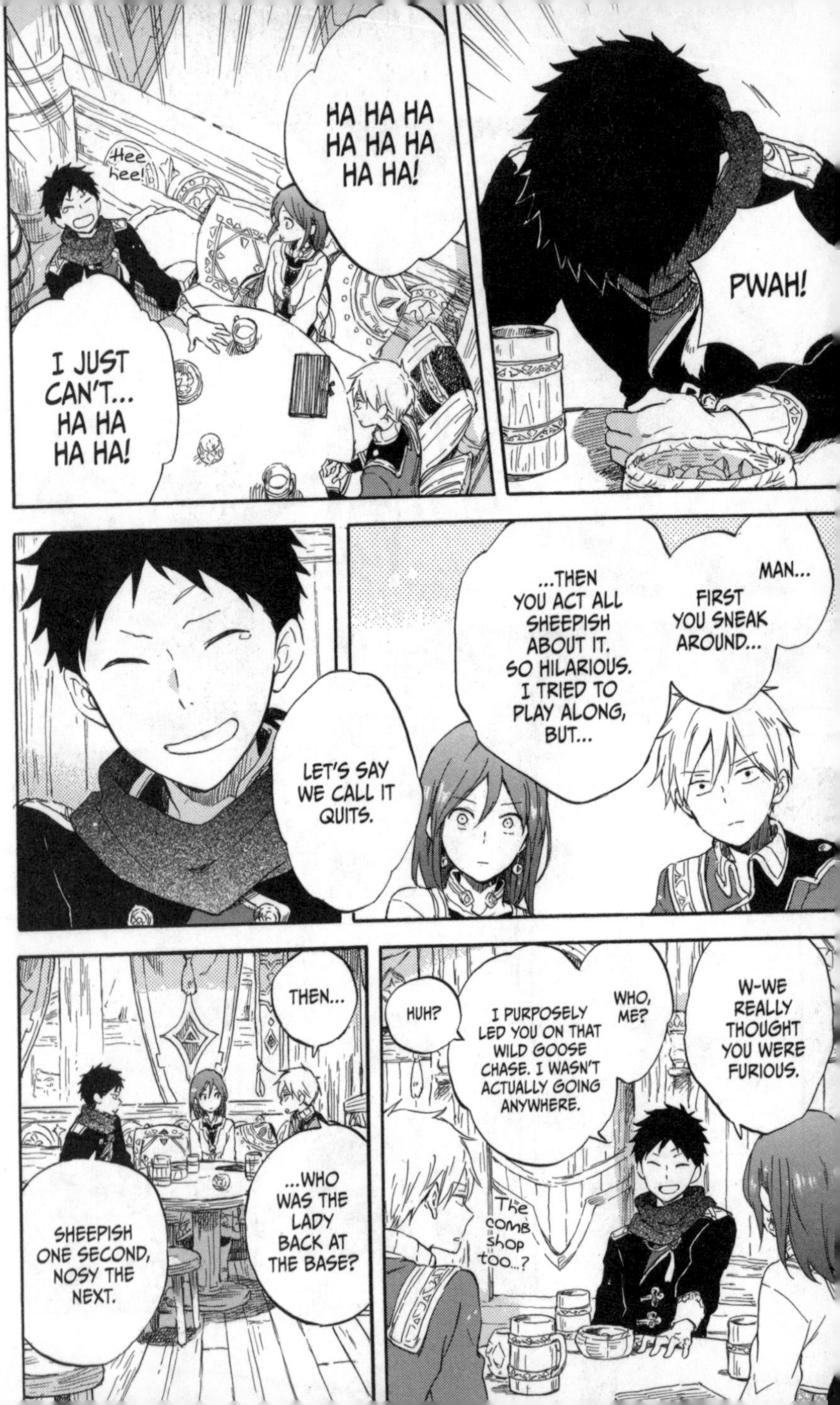
PWAH!
HA HA HA HA HA HA HA HA!
Hee hee!
I JUST CAN'T... HA HA HA HA!
MAN...
FIRST YOU SNEAK AROUND...
...THEN YOU ACT ALL SHEEPISH ABOUT IT. SO HILARIOUS. I TRIED TO PLAY ALONG, BUT...
LET'S SAY WE CALL IT QUITS.
W-WE REALLY THOUGHT YOU WERE FURIOUS.
WHO, ME?
I PURPOSELY LED YOU ON THAT WILD GOOSE CHASE. I WASN'T ACTUALLY GOING ANYWHERE.
HUH?
The comb shop too...?
THEN...
...WHO WAS THE LADY BACK AT THE BASE?
SHEEPISH ONE SECOND, NOSY THE NEXT.

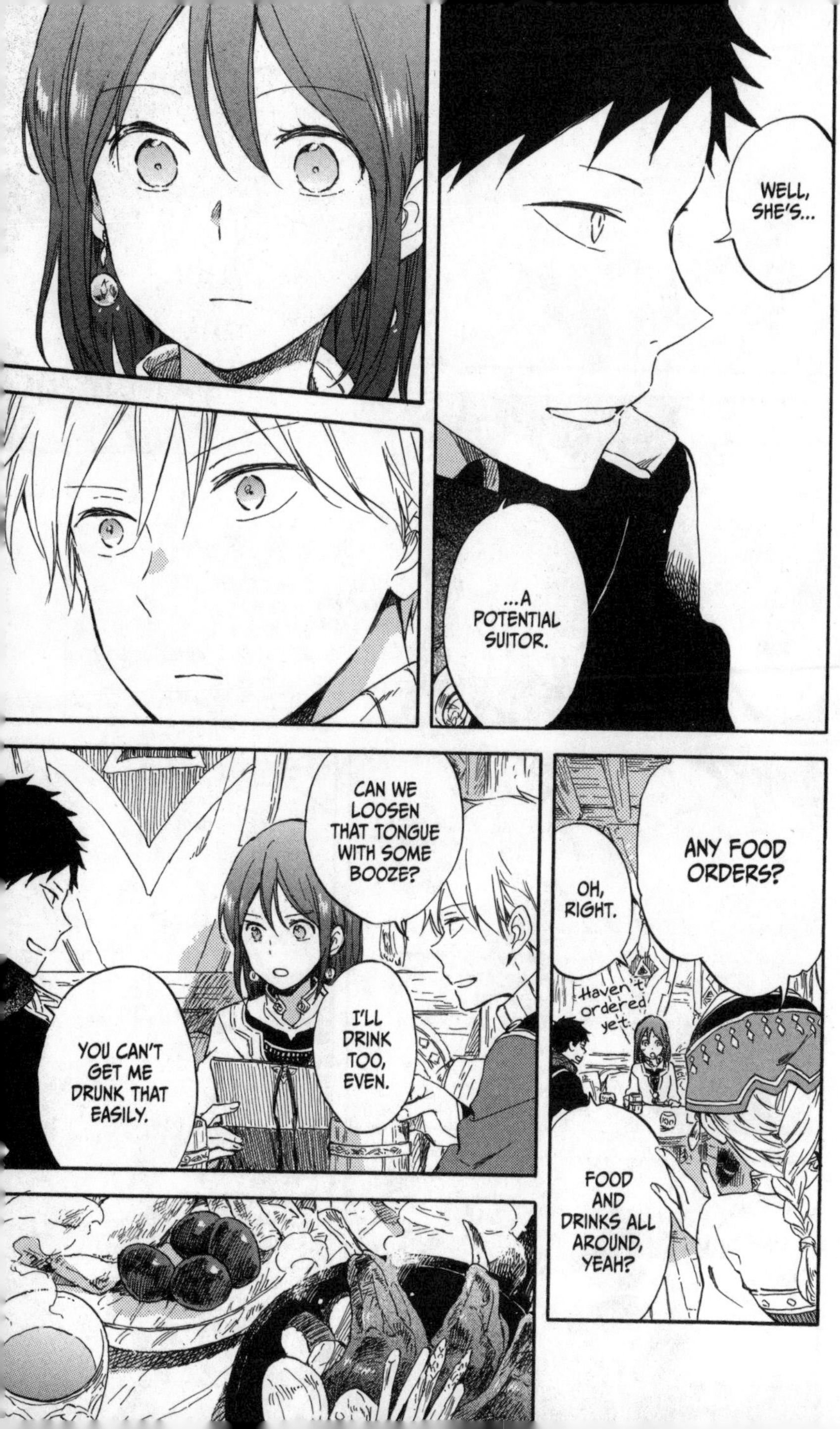
WELL, SHE'S...
...A POTENTIAL SUITOR.
ANY FOOD ORDERS?
OH, RIGHT.
Haven't ordered yet.
FOOD AND DRINKS ALL AROUND, YEAH?
CAN WE LOOSEN THAT TONGUE WITH SOME BOOZE?
I'LL DRINK TOO, EVEN.
YOU CAN'T GET ME DRUNK THAT EASILY.

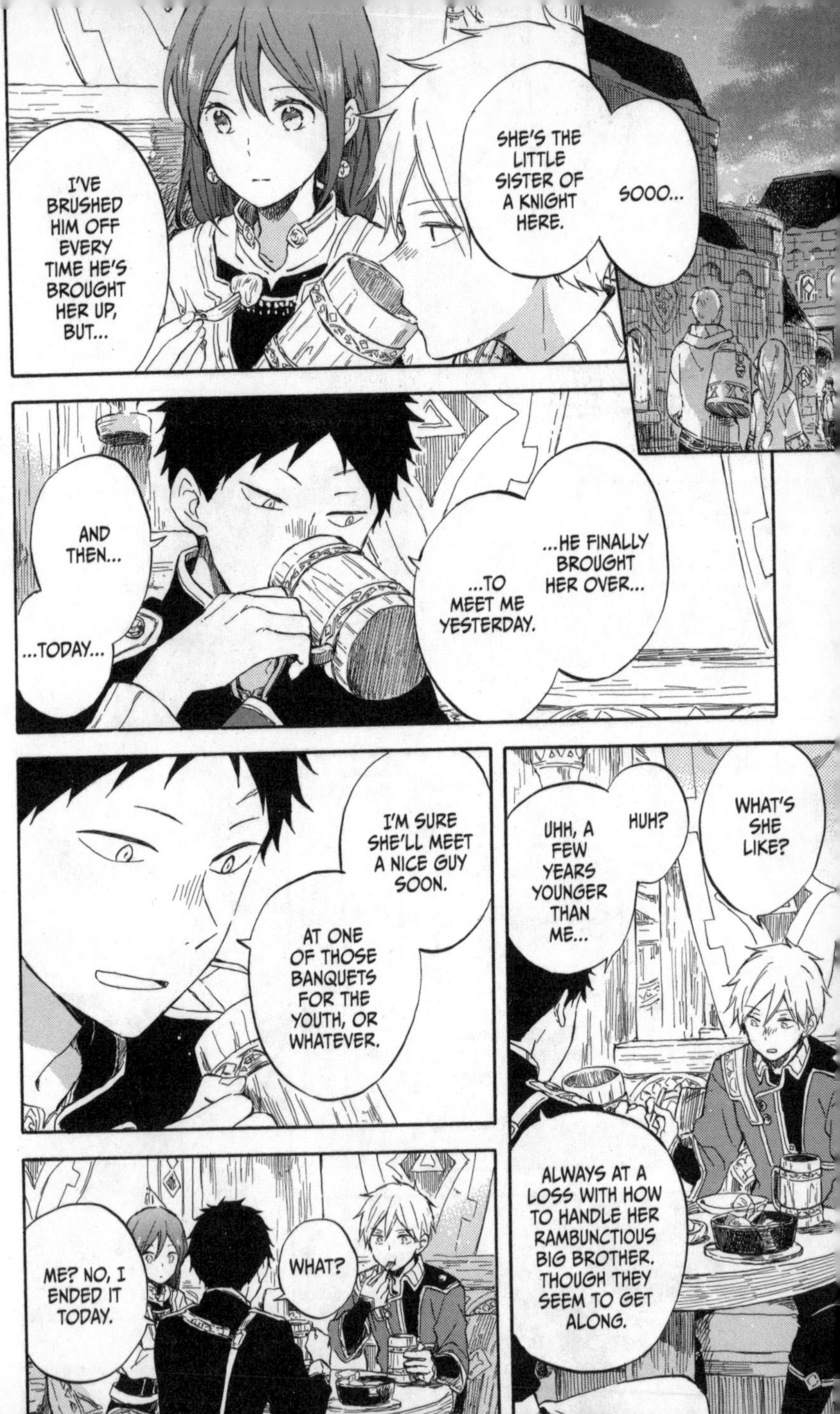
SOOO...
SHE'S THE LITTLE SISTER OF A KNIGHT HERE.
I'VE BRUSHED HIM OFF EVERY TIME HE'S BROUGHT HER UP, BUT...
...HE FINALLY BROUGHT HER OVER...
...TO MEET ME YESTERDAY.
AND THEN...
...TODAY...
WHAT'S SHE LIKE?
HUH?
UHH, A FEW YEARS YOUNGER THAN ME...
ALWAYS AT A LOSS WITH HOW TO HANDLE HER RAMBUNCTIOUS BIG BROTHER. THOUGH THEY SEEM TO GET ALONG.
I'M SURE SHE'LL MEET A NICE GUY SOON.
AT ONE OF THOSE BANQUETS FOR THE YOUTH, OR WHATEVER.
WHAT?
ME? NO, I ENDED IT TODAY.

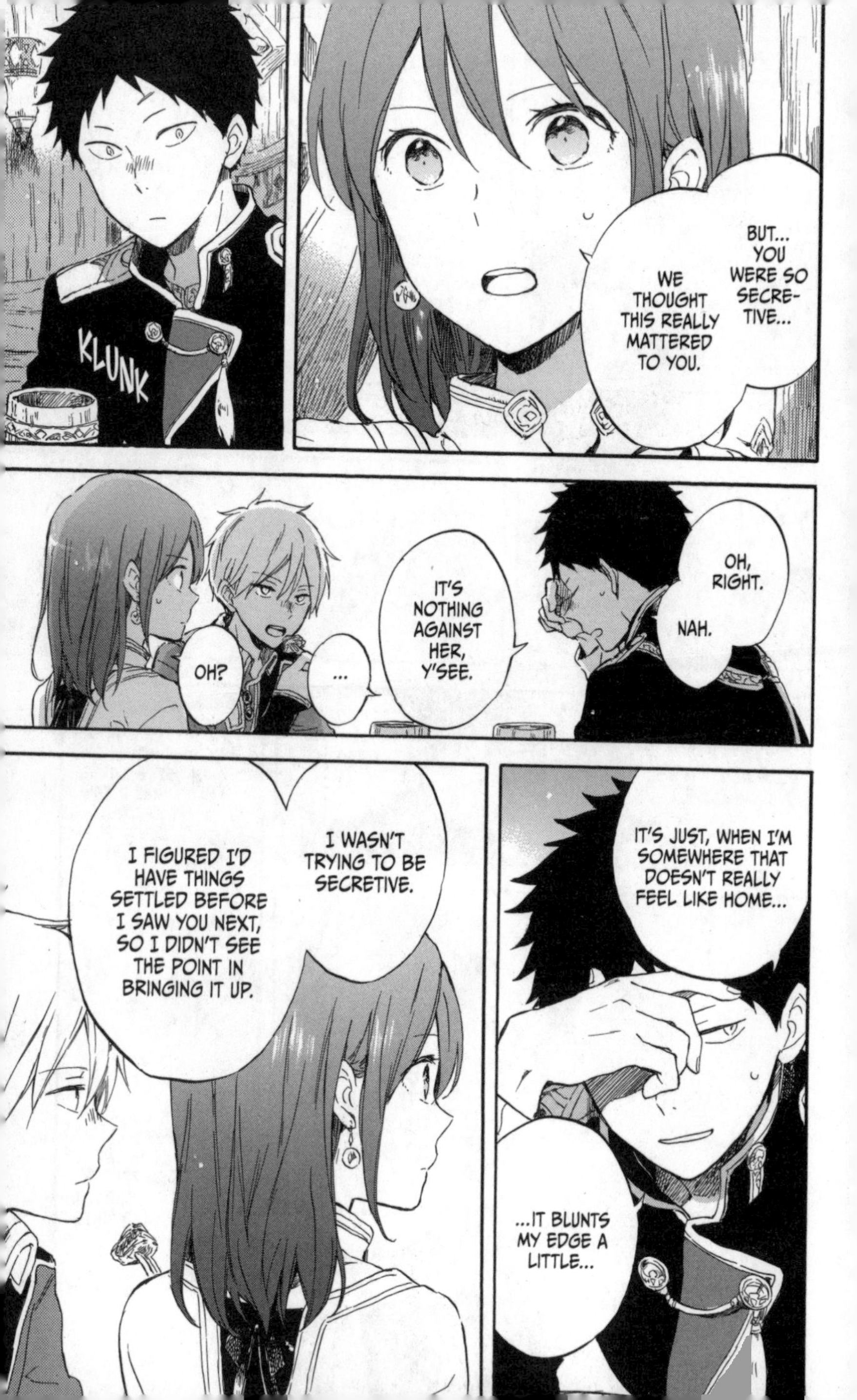
BUT... YOU WERE SO SECRETIVE...
WE THOUGHT THIS REALLY MATTERED TO YOU.
KLUNK
OH, RIGHT.
NAH.
IT'S NOTHING AGAINST HER, Y'SEE.
...
OH?
IT'S JUST, WHEN I'M SOMEWHERE THAT DOESN'T REALLY FEEL LIKE HOME...
...IT BLUNTS MY EDGE A LITTLE...
I WASN'T TRYING TO BE SECRETIVE.
I FIGURED I'D HAVE THINGS SETTLED BEFORE I SAW YOU NEXT, SO I DIDN'T SEE THE POINT IN BRINGING IT UP.

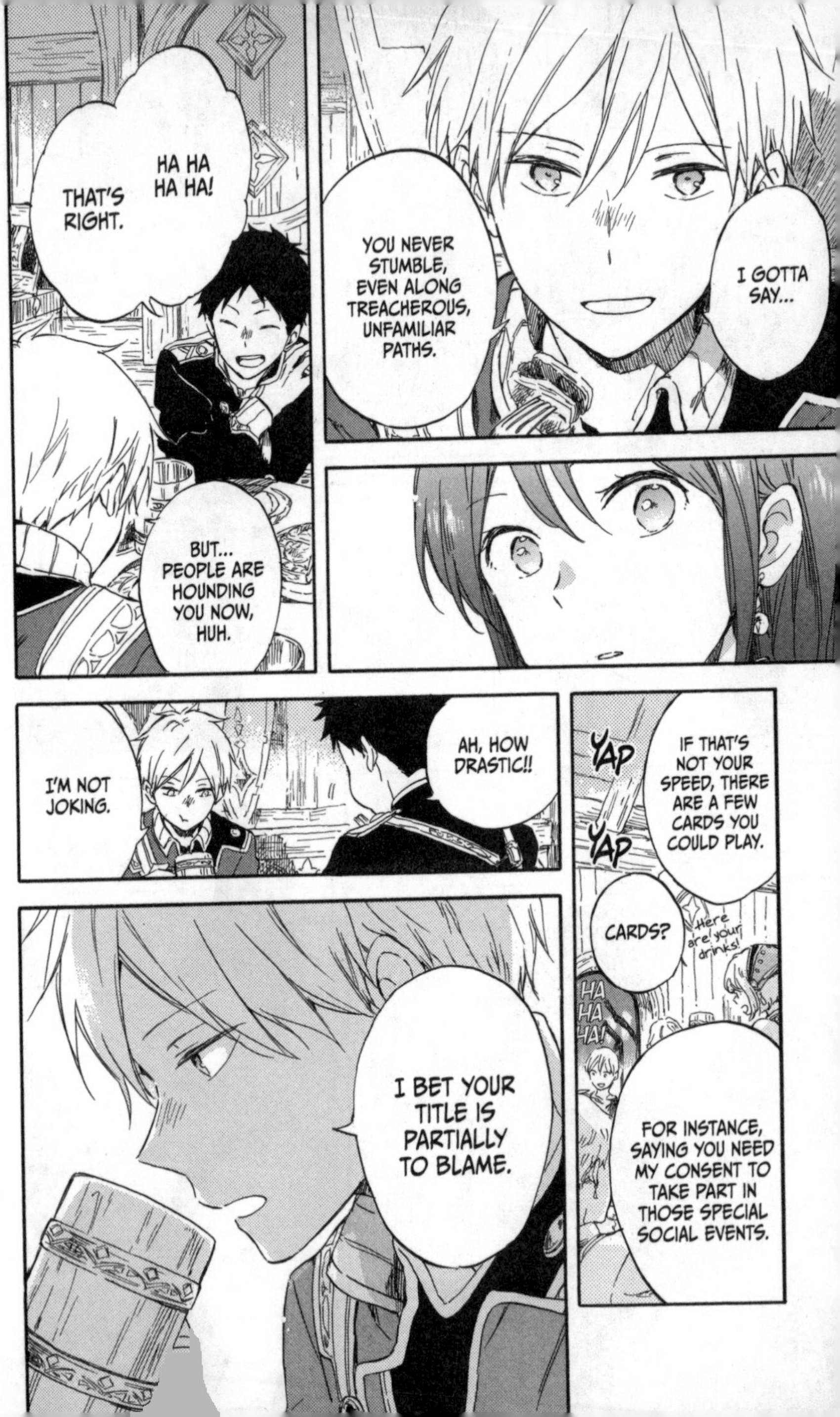
I GOTTA SAY...
YOU NEVER STUMBLE, EVEN ALONG TREACHEROUS, UNFAMILIAR PATHS.
HA HA HA HA!
THAT'S RIGHT.
BUT... PEOPLE ARE HOUNDING YOU NOW, HUH.
AH, HOW DRASTIC!!
I'M NOT JOKING.
I BET YOUR TITLE IS PARTIALLY TO BLAME.
YAP
YAP
IF THAT'S NOT YOUR SPEED, THERE ARE A FEW CARDS YOU COULD PLAY.
CARDS?
Here are your drinks!
HA HA HA!
FOR INSTANCE, SAYING YOU NEED MY CONSENT TO TAKE PART IN THOSE SPECIAL SOCIAL EVENTS.

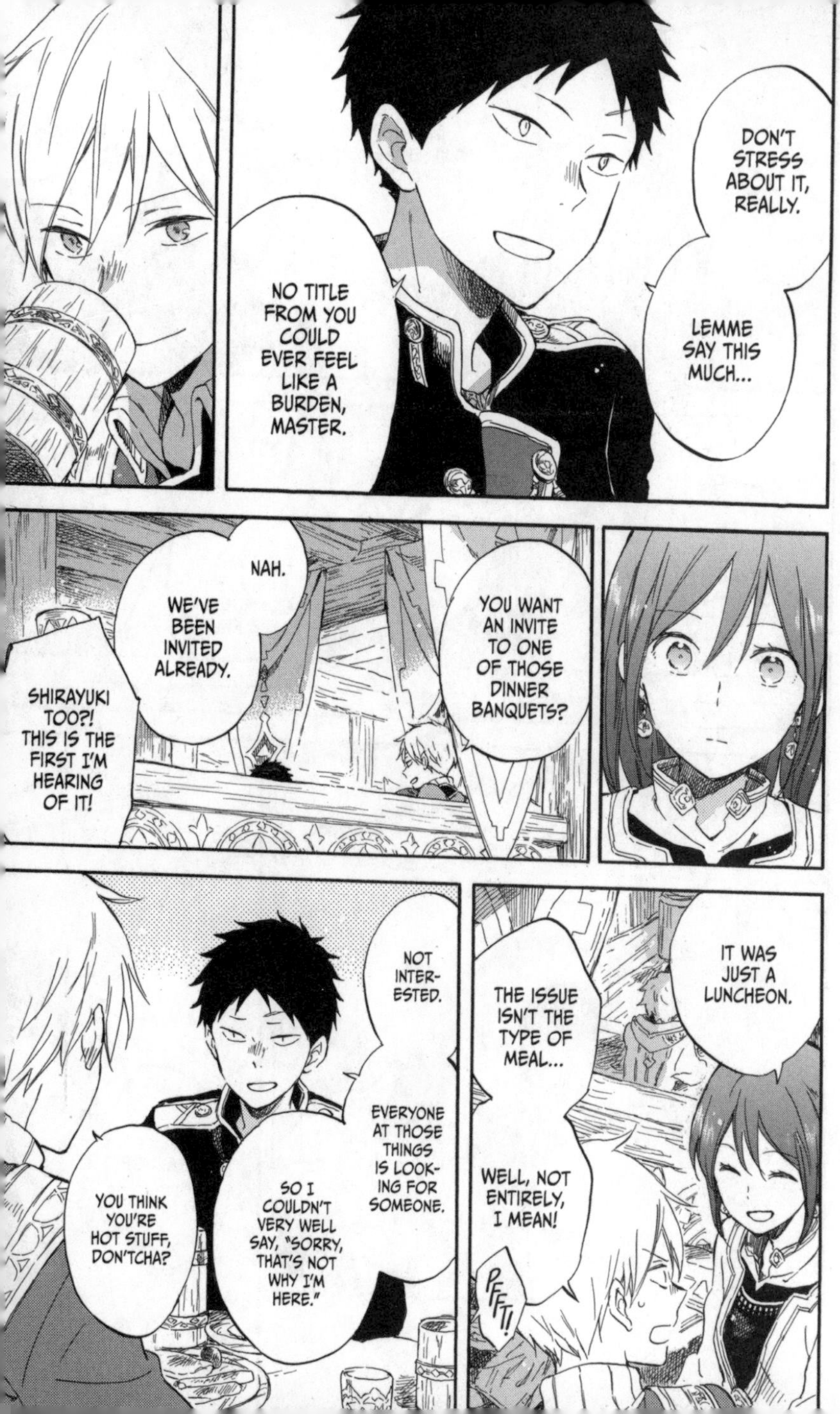
DON'T STRESS ABOUT IT, REALLY.
LEMME SAY THIS MUCH...
NO TITLE FROM YOU COULD EVER FEEL LIKE A BURDEN, MASTER.
YOU WANT AN INVITE TO ONE OF THOSE DINNER BANQUETS?
NAH.
WE'VE BEEN INVITED ALREADY.
SHIRAYUKI TOO?! THIS IS THE FIRST I'M HEARING OF IT!
IT WAS JUST A LUNCHEON.
THE ISSUE ISN'T THE TYPE OF MEAL...
WELL, NOT ENTIRELY, I MEAN!
PFFT!
NOT INTER-ESTED.
EVERYONE AT THOSE THINGS IS LOOK-ING FOR SOMEONE.
SO I COULDN'T VERY WELL SAY, "SORRY, THAT'S NOT WHY I'M HERE."
YOU THINK YOU'RE HOT STUFF, DON'TCHA?

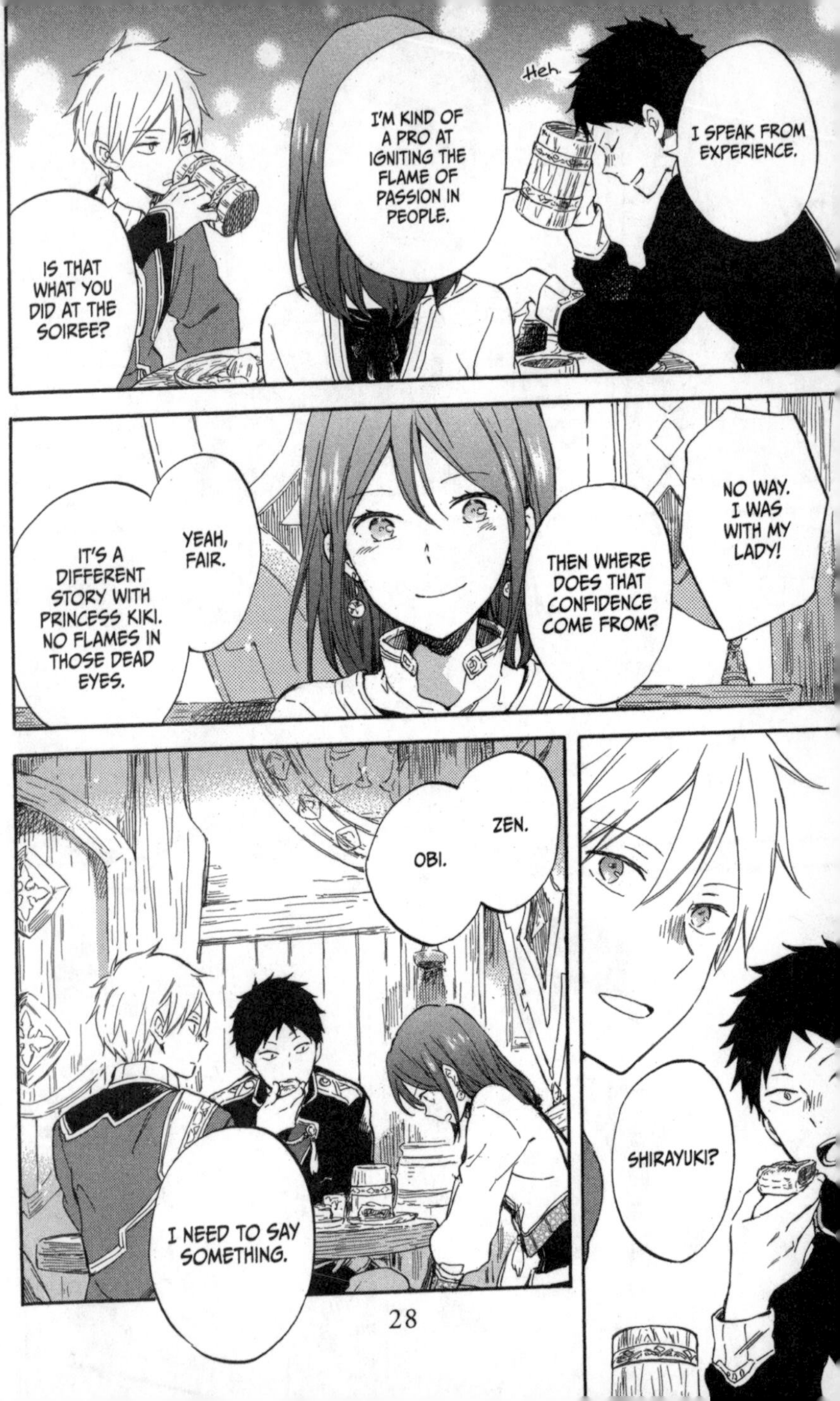

Heh.
I SPEAK FROM EXPERIENCE.
I'M KIND OF A PRO AT IGNITING THE FLAME OF PASSION IN PEOPLE.
IS THAT WHAT YOU DID AT THE SOIREE?
NO WAY. I WAS WITH MY LADY!
THEN WHERE DOES THAT CONFIDENCE COME FROM?
YEAH, FAIR.
IT'S A DIFFERENT STORY WITH PRINCESS KIKI. NO FLAMES IN THOSE DEAD EYES.
SHIRAYUKI?
ZEN.
OBI.
I NEED TO SAY SOMETHING.

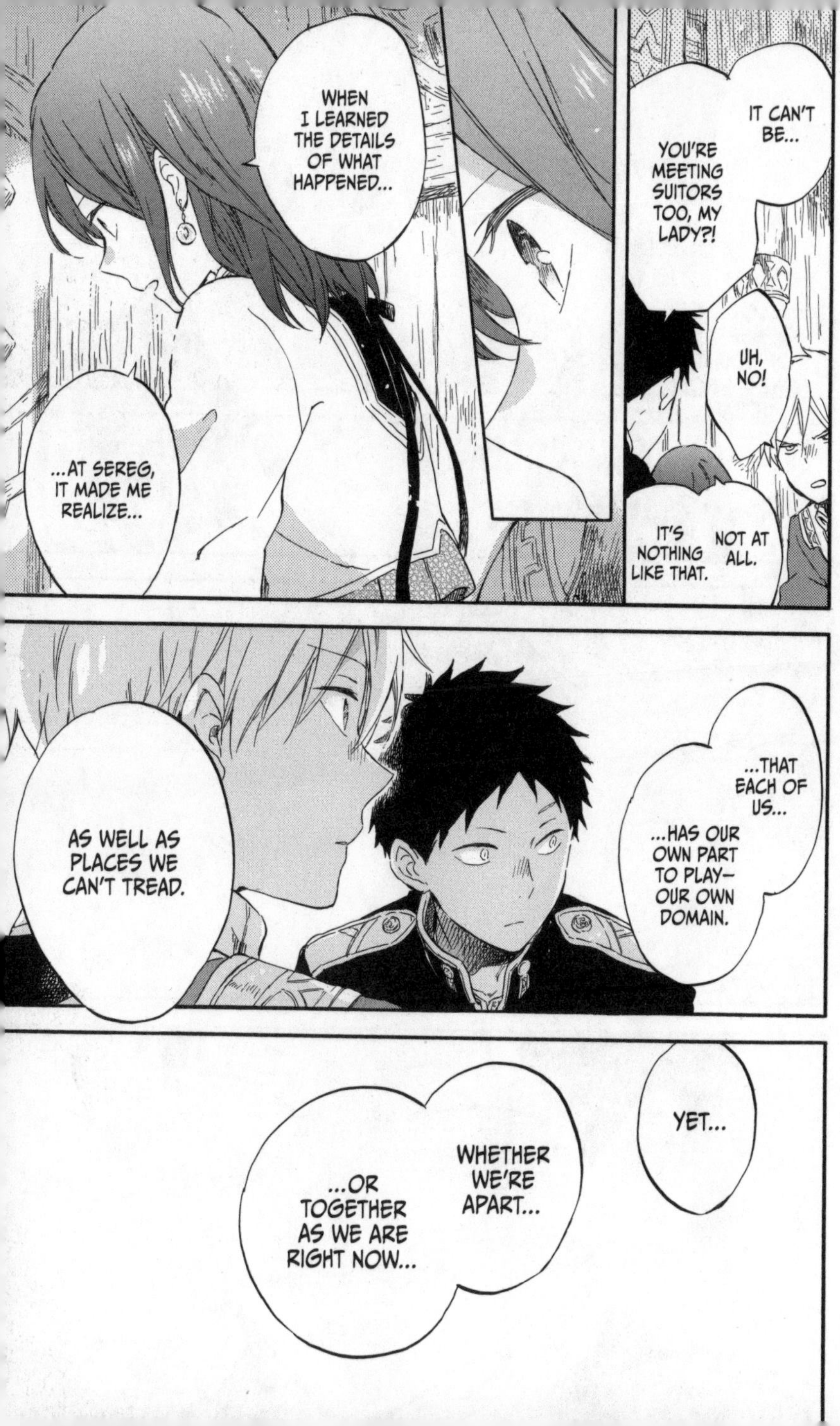
IT CAN'T BE...
YOU'RE MEETING SUITORS TOO, MY LADY?!
UH, NO!
NOT AT ALL.
IT'S NOTHING LIKE THAT.
WHEN I LEARNED THE DETAILS OF WHAT HAPPENED...
...AT SEREG, IT MADE ME REALIZE...
...THAT EACH OF US...
...HAS OUR OWN PART TO PLAY—OUR OWN DOMAIN.
AS WELL AS PLACES WE CAN'T TREAD.
YET...
WHETHER WE'RE APART...
...OR TOGETHER AS WE ARE RIGHT NOW...

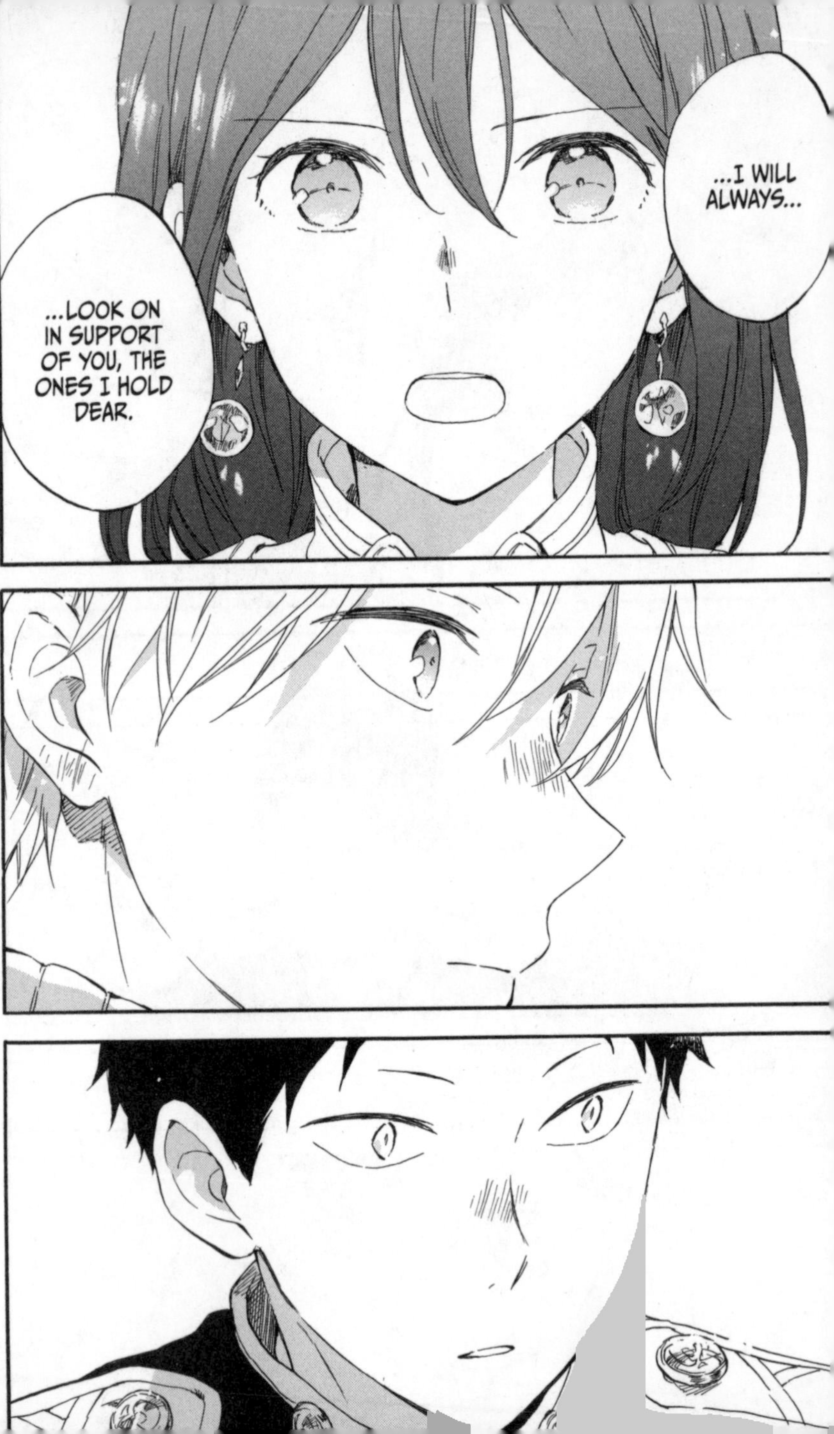
...I WILL ALWAYS...
...LOOK ON IN SUPPORT OF YOU, THE ONES I HOLD DEAR.

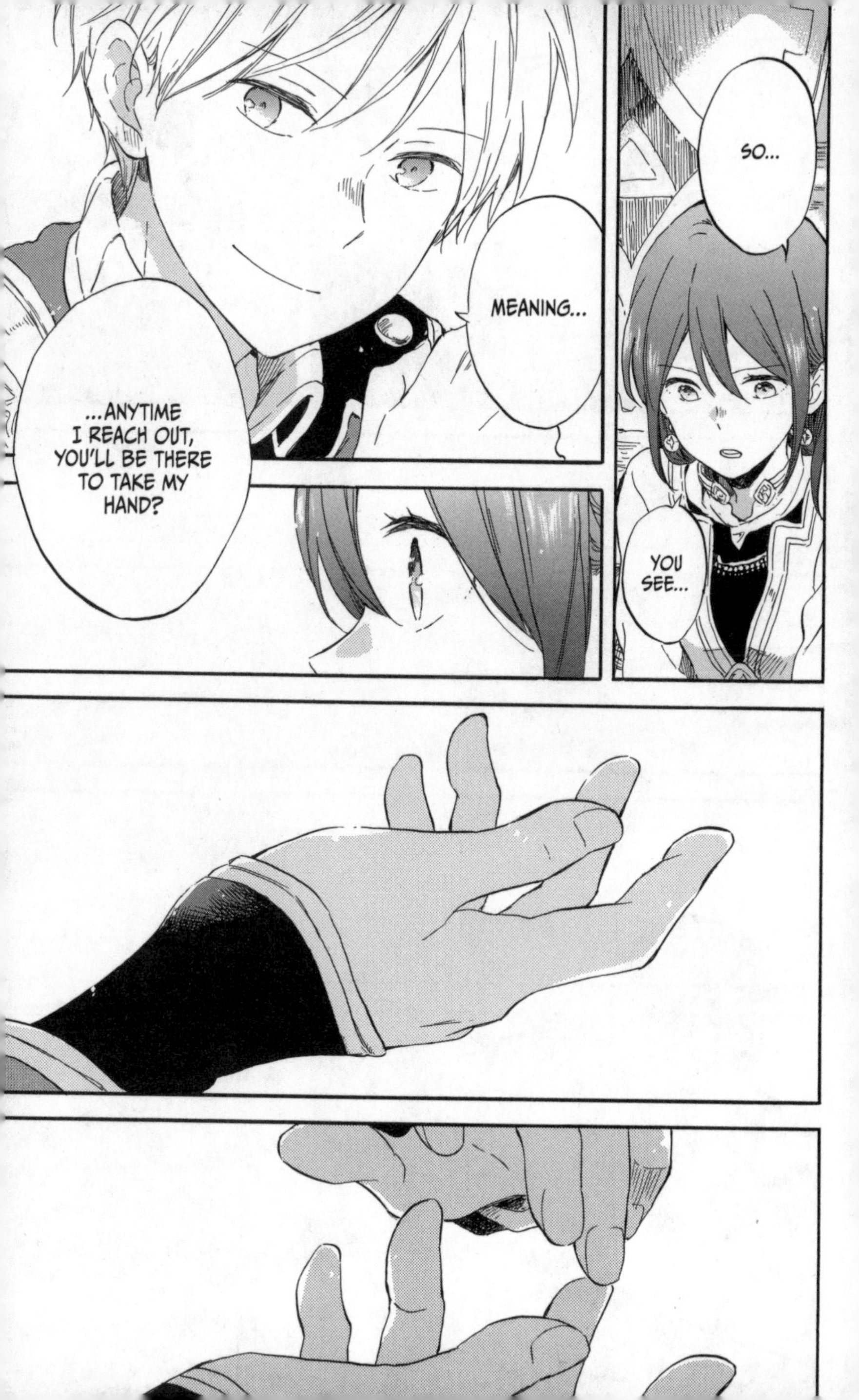
SO...
YOU SEE...
MEANING...
...ANYTIME I REACH OUT, YOU'LL BE THERE TO TAKE MY HAND?

THAT'S MY WAY OF SAYING, "WHAT SHE SAID."

AHEM.

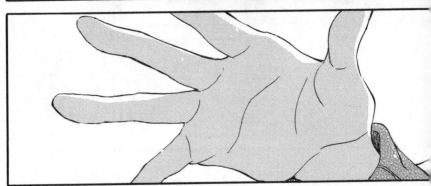

MM-HM.

GRP

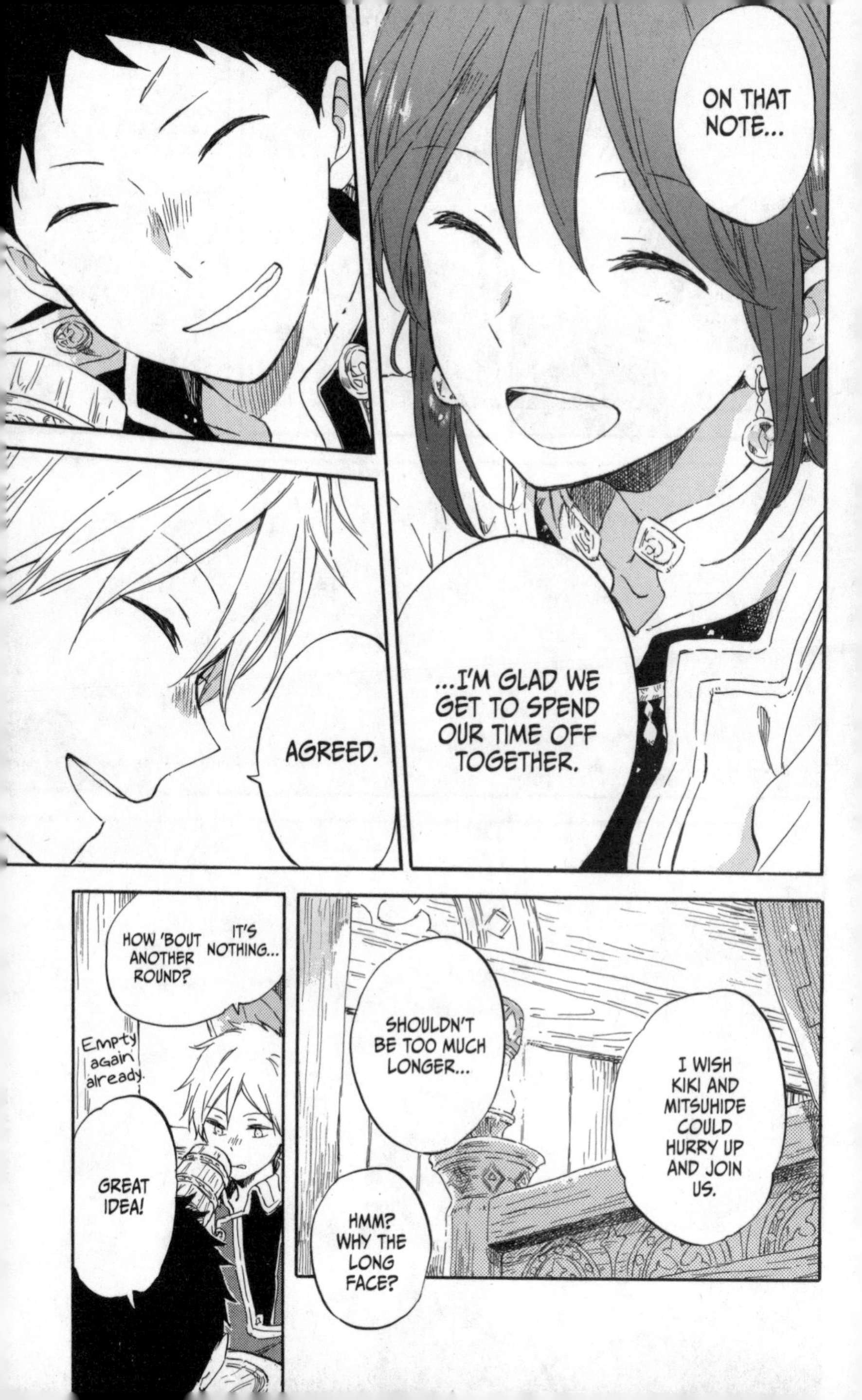
ON THAT NOTE...
...I'M GLAD WE GET TO SPEND OUR TIME OFF TOGETHER.
AGREED.
I WISH KIKI AND MITSUHIDE COULD HURRY UP AND JOIN US.
SHOULDN'T BE TOO MUCH LONGER...
HMM? WHY THE LONG FACE?
IT'S NOTHING...
HOW 'BOUT ANOTHER ROUND?
Empty again already.
GREAT IDEA!

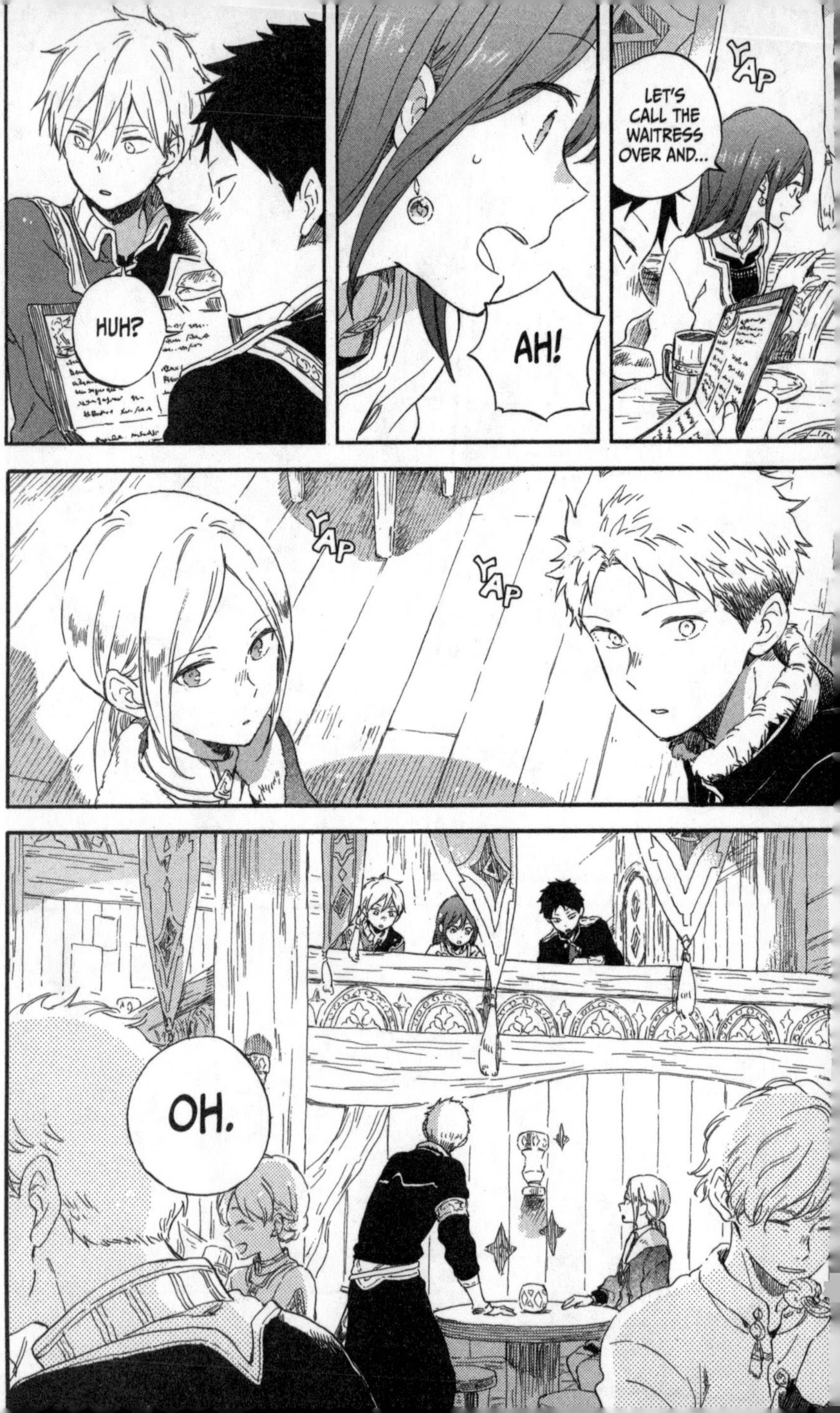
YAP
LET'S CALL THE WAITRESS OVER AND...
AH!
HUH?
YAP
YAP
OH.

Snow White with the Red Hair

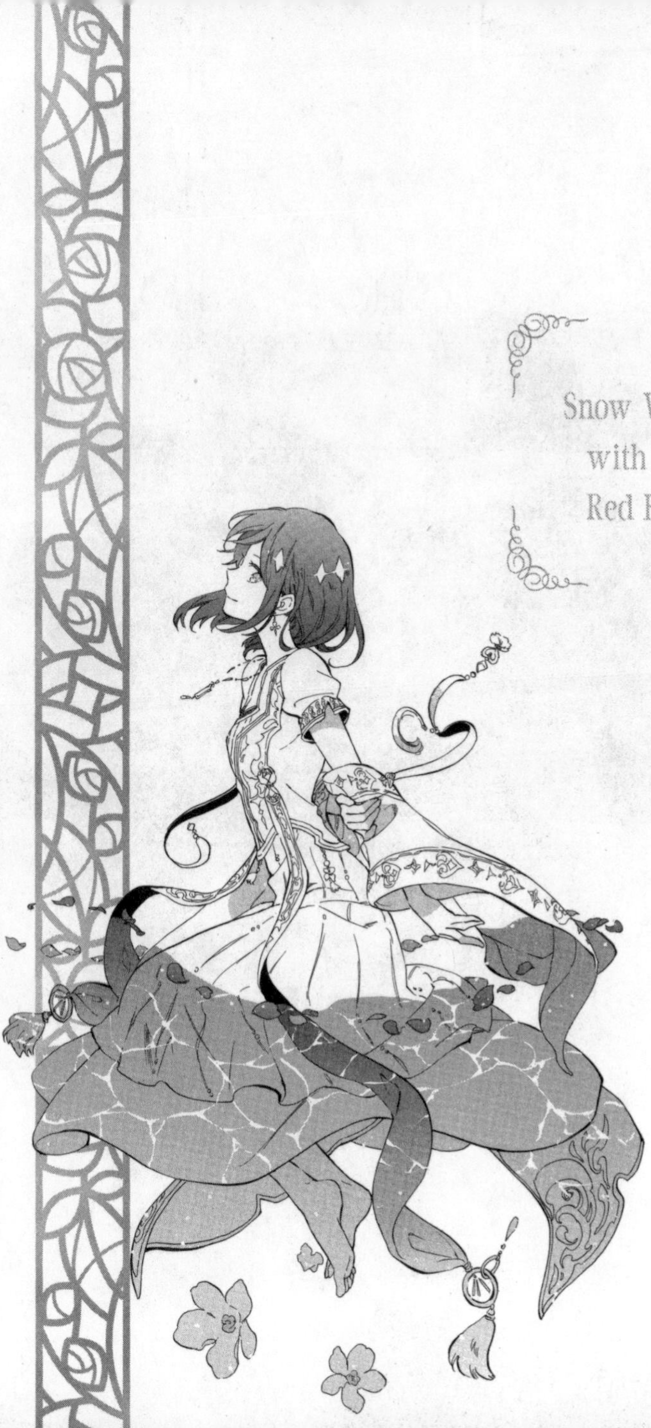

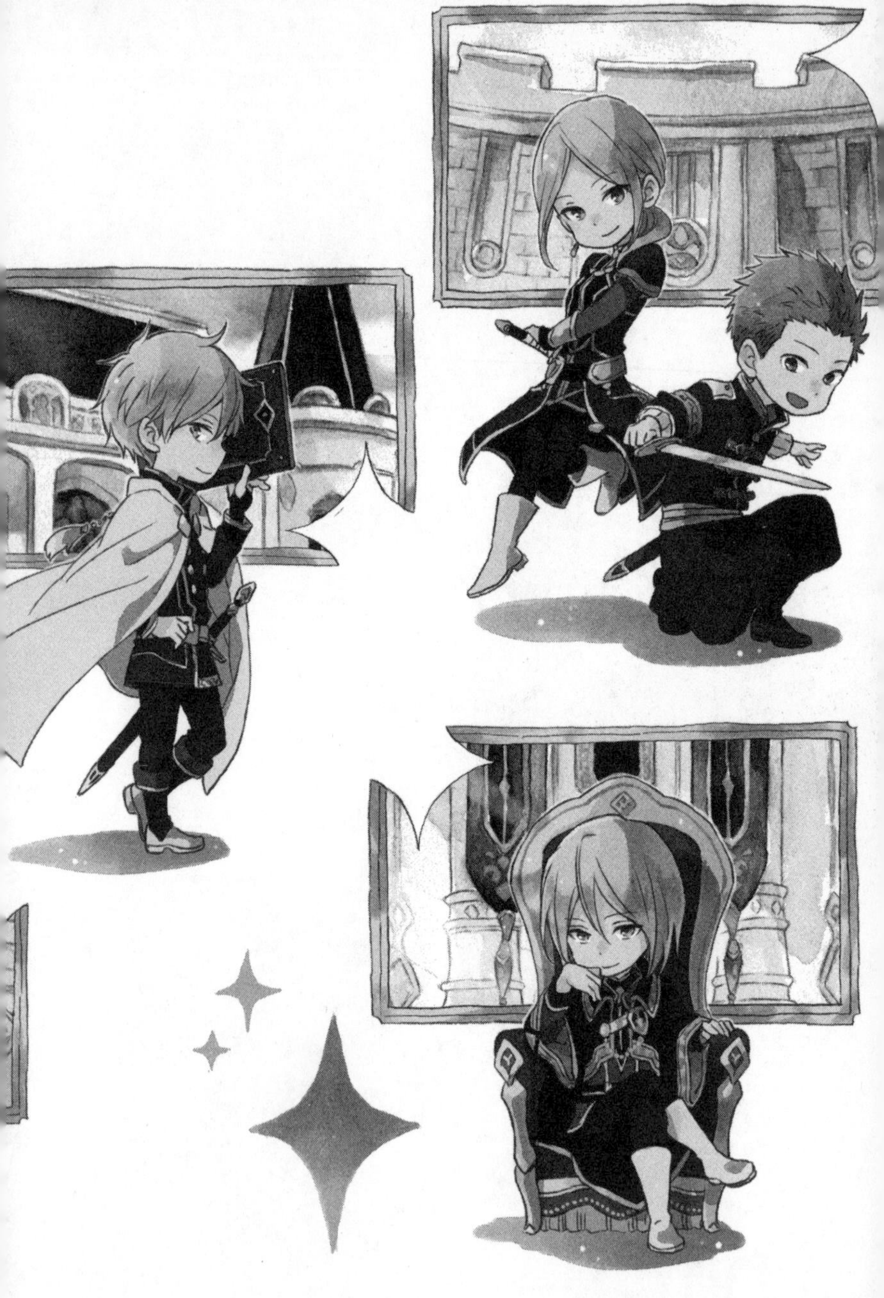

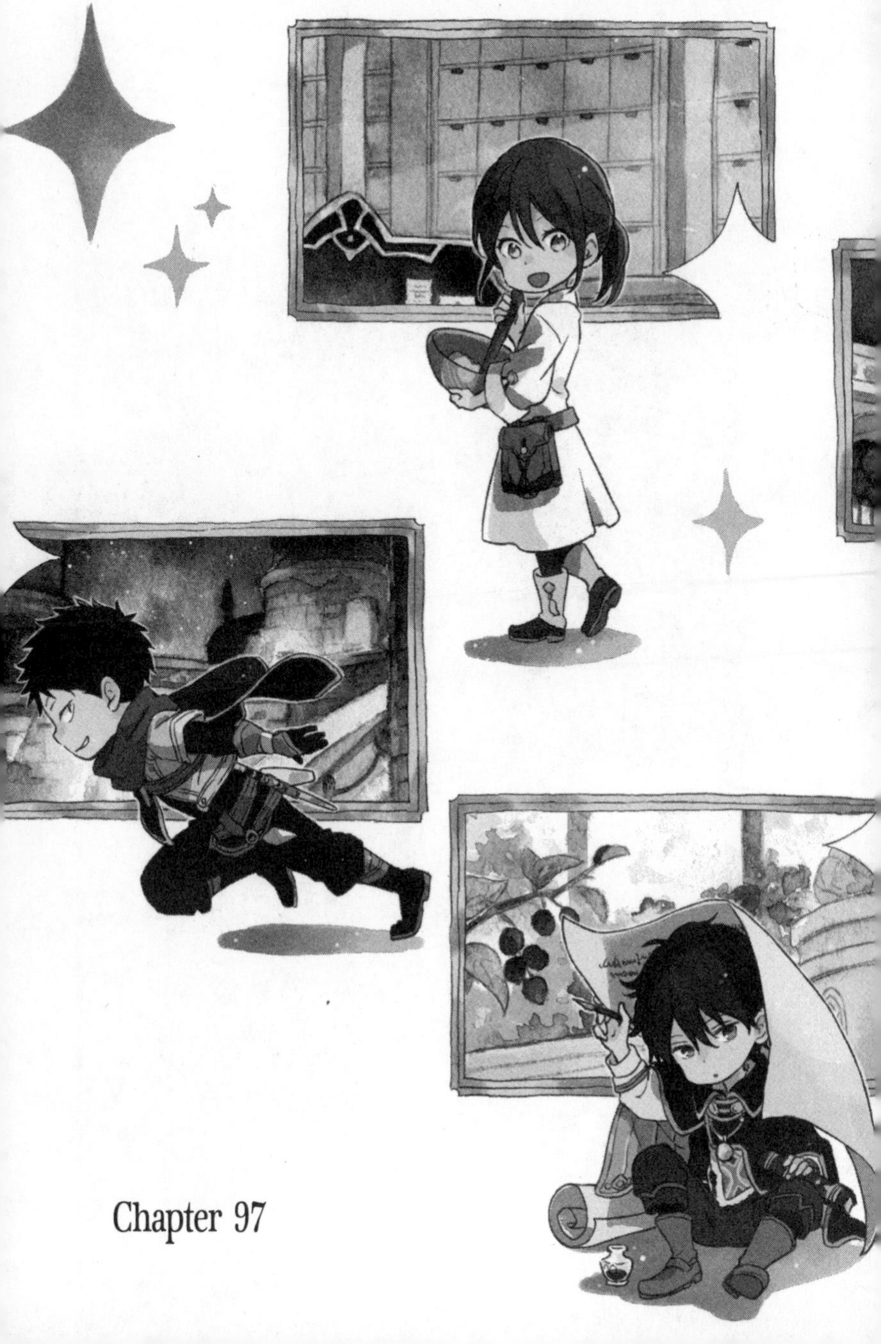

Chapter 97

Snow White
with the
Red Hair

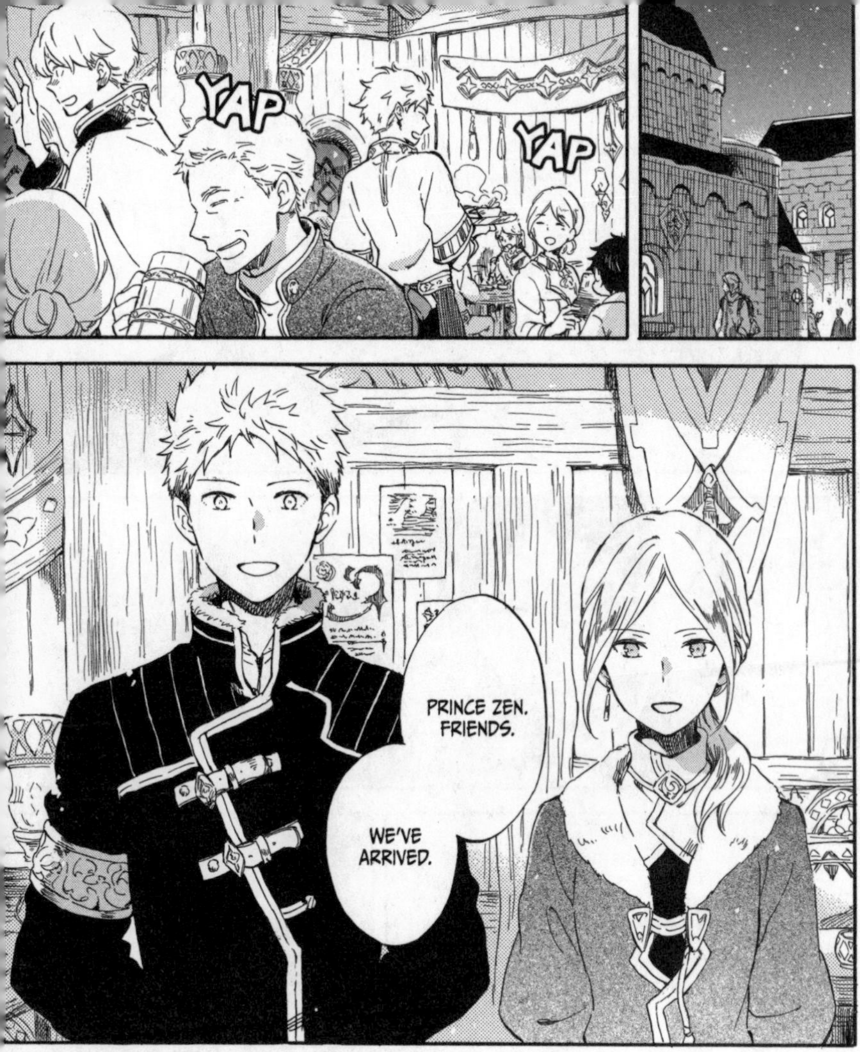
YAP
YAP
PRINCE ZEN. FRIENDS.
WE'VE ARRIVED.

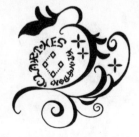

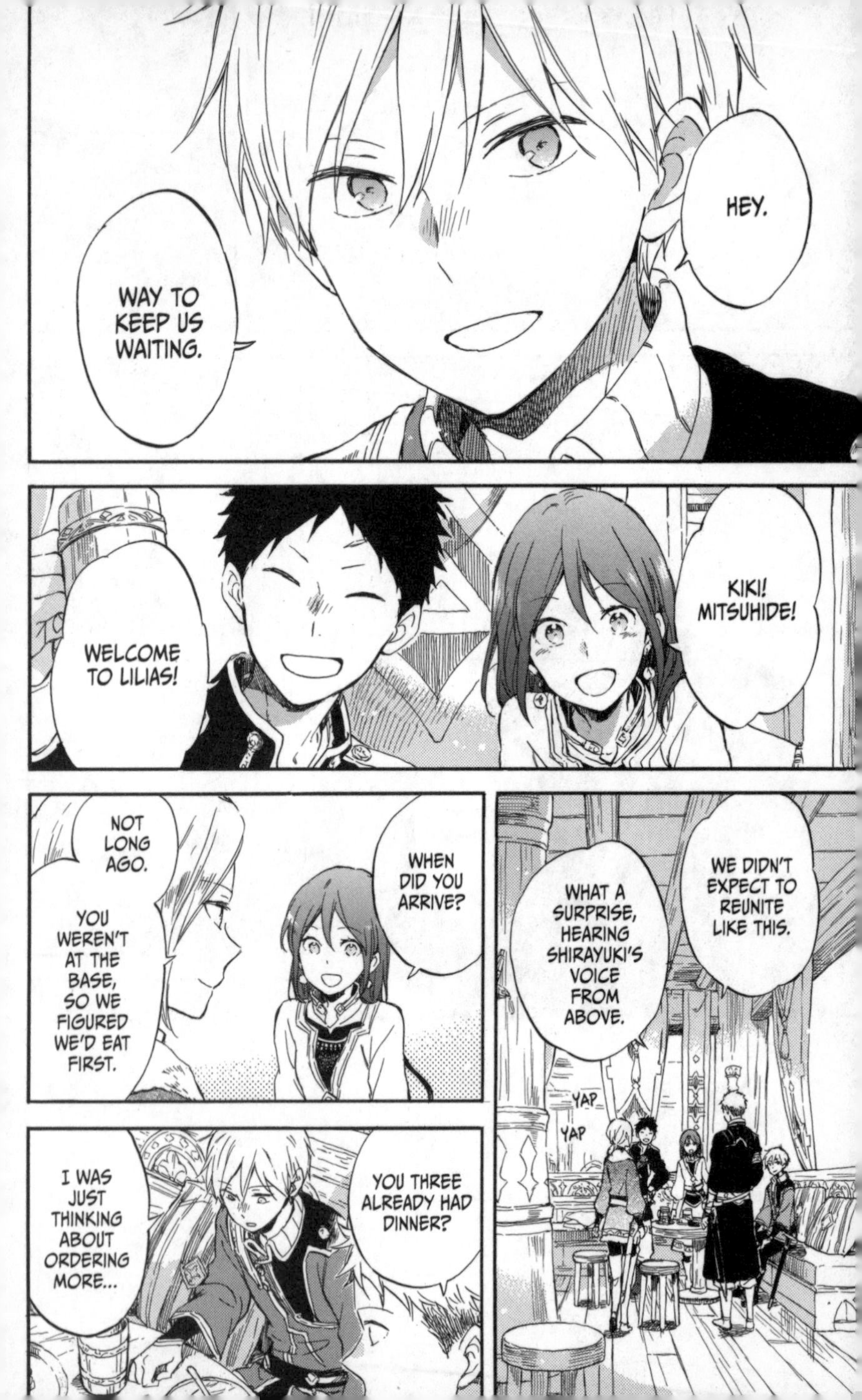
HEY.
WAY TO KEEP US WAITING.
KIKI! MITSUHIDE!
WELCOME TO LILIAS!
WE DIDN'T EXPECT TO REUNITE LIKE THIS.
WHAT A SURPRISE, HEARING SHIRAYUKI'S VOICE FROM ABOVE.
YAP
YAP
WHEN DID YOU ARRIVE?
NOT LONG AGO.
YOU WEREN'T AT THE BASE, SO WE FIGURED WE'D EAT FIRST.
YOU THREE ALREADY HAD DINNER?
I WAS JUST THINKING ABOUT ORDERING MORE...

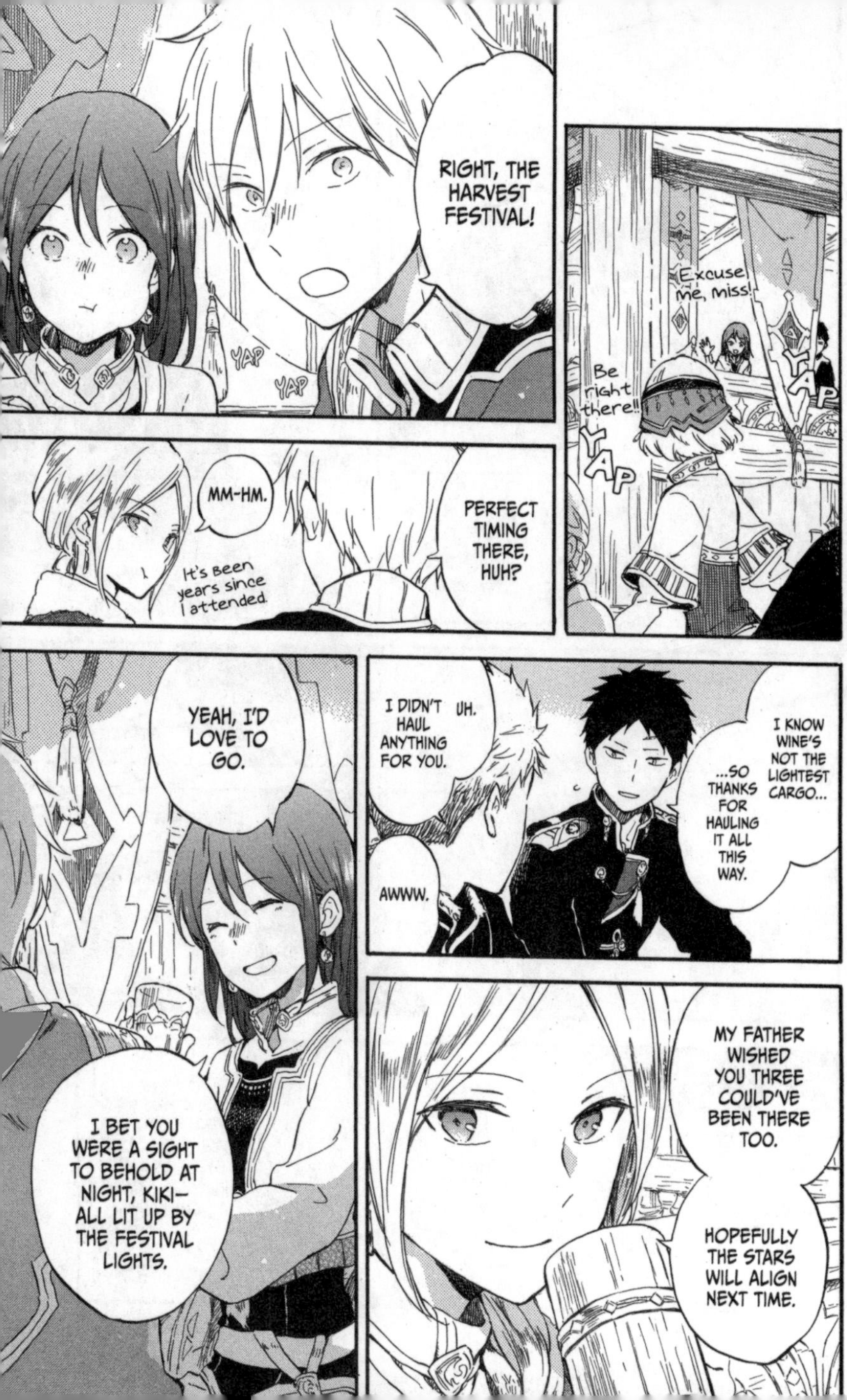
Excuse me, miss!
Be right there!!
YAP
YAP
RIGHT, THE HARVEST FESTIVAL!
YAP
YAP
PERFECT TIMING THERE, HUH?
MM-HM.
It's been years since I attended.
I KNOW WINE'S NOT THE LIGHTEST CARGO...
...SO THANKS FOR HAULING IT ALL THIS WAY.
UH.
I DIDN'T HAUL ANYTHING FOR YOU.
AWWW.
MY FATHER WISHED YOU THREE COULD'VE BEEN THERE TOO.
HOPEFULLY THE STARS WILL ALIGN NEXT TIME.
YEAH, I'D LOVE TO GO.
I BET YOU WERE A SIGHT TO BEHOLD AT NIGHT, KIKI—ALL LIT UP BY THE FESTIVAL LIGHTS.

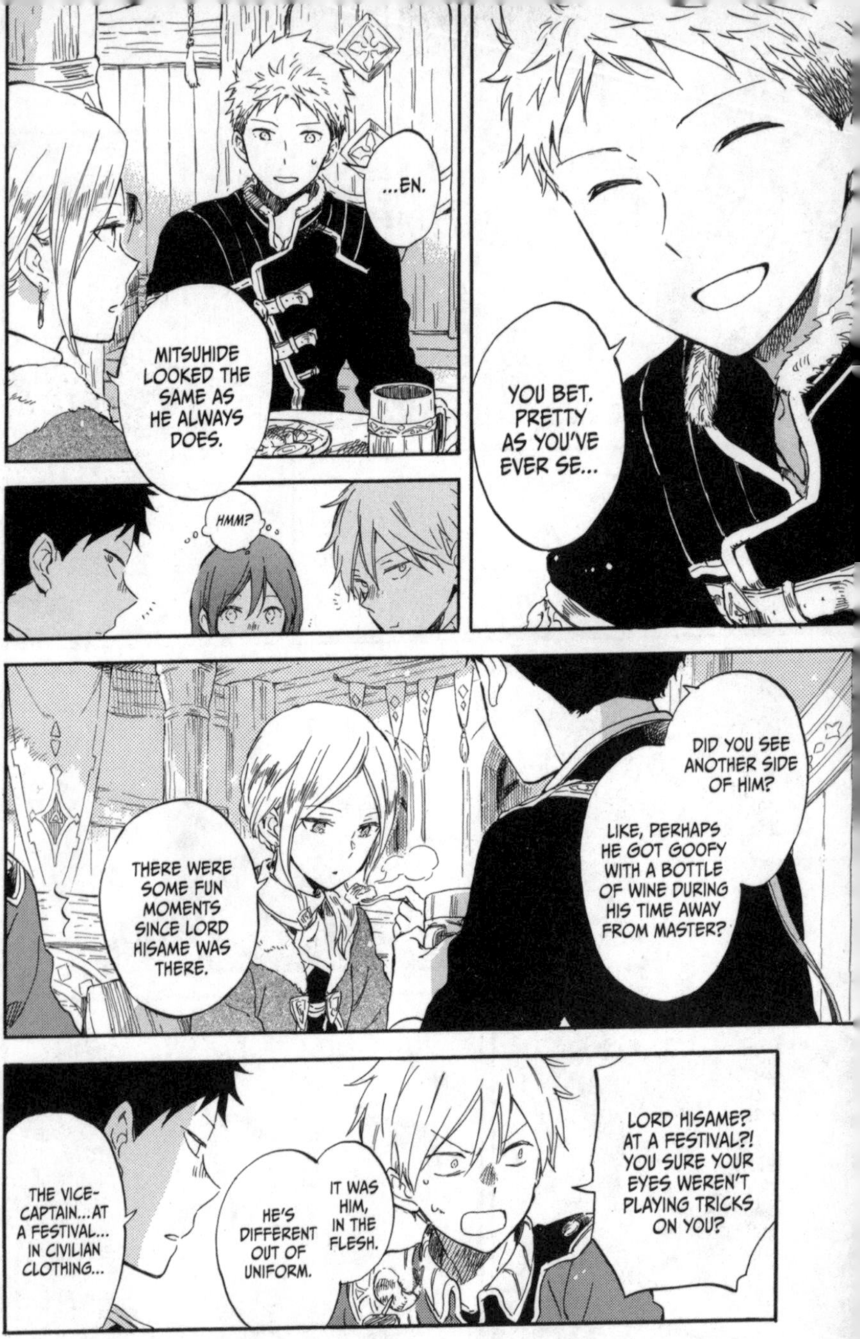
YOU BET. PRETTY AS YOU'VE EVER SE...
...EN.
MITSUHIDE LOOKED THE SAME AS HE ALWAYS DOES.
HMM?
DID YOU SEE ANOTHER SIDE OF HIM?
LIKE, PERHAPS HE GOT GOOFY WITH A BOTTLE OF WINE DURING HIS TIME AWAY FROM MASTER?
THERE WERE SOME FUN MOMENTS SINCE LORD HISAME WAS THERE.
LORD HISAME? AT A FESTIVAL?! YOU SURE YOUR EYES WEREN'T PLAYING TRICKS ON YOU?
IT WAS HIM, IN THE FLESH.
HE'S DIFFERENT OUT OF UNIFORM.
THE VICE-CAPTAIN...AT A FESTIVAL... IN CIVILIAN CLOTHING...

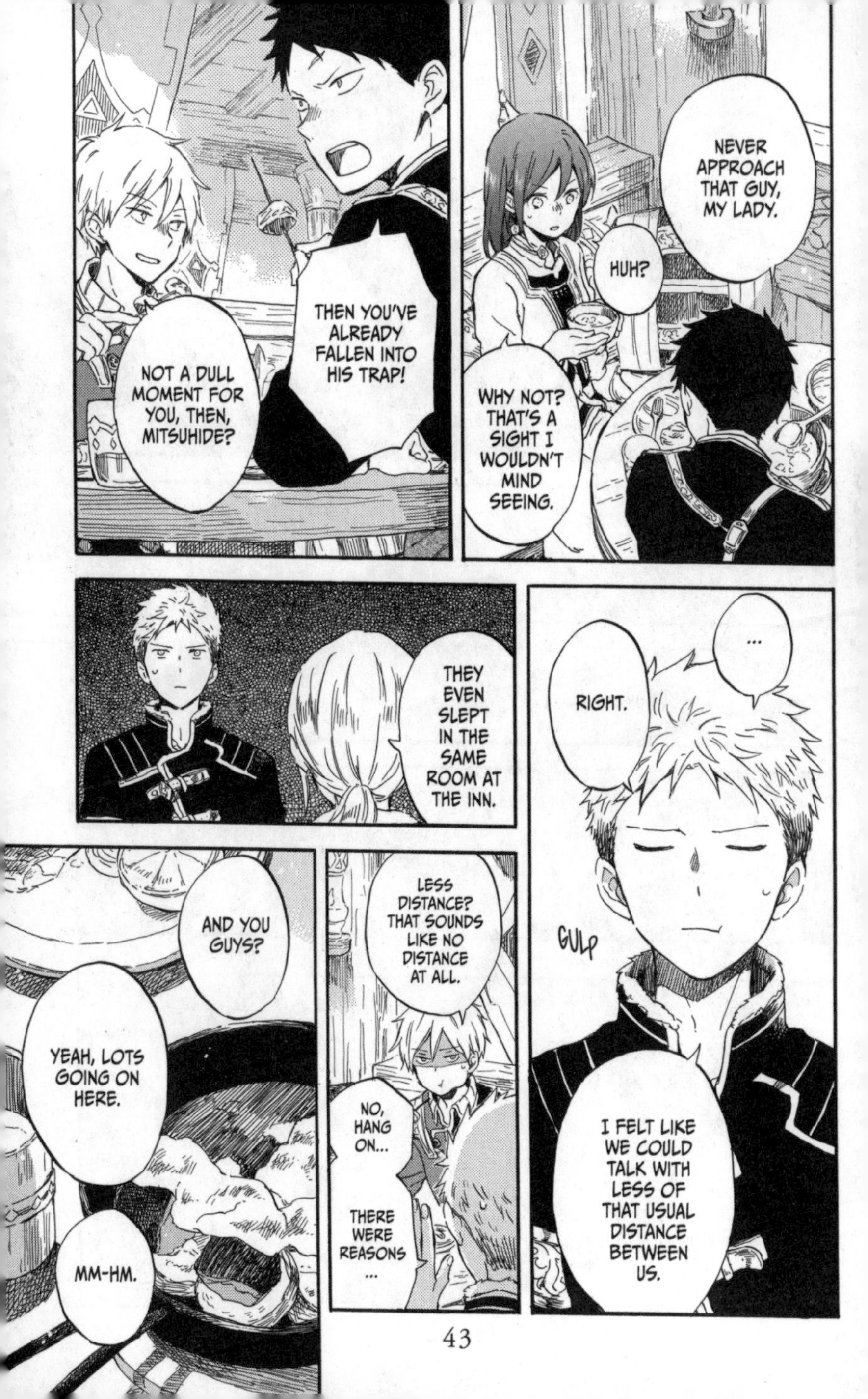
NEVER APPROACH THAT GUY, MY LADY.
HUH?
WHY NOT? THAT'S A SIGHT I WOULDN'T MIND SEEING.
THEN YOU'VE ALREADY FALLEN INTO HIS TRAP!
NOT A DULL MOMENT FOR YOU, THEN, MITSUHIDE?
...
RIGHT.
GULP
I FELT LIKE WE COULD TALK WITH LESS OF THAT USUAL DISTANCE BETWEEN US.
THEY EVEN SLEPT IN THE SAME ROOM AT THE INN.
LESS DISTANCE? THAT SOUNDS LIKE NO DISTANCE AT ALL.
NO, HANG ON...
THERE WERE REASONS ...
AND YOU GUYS?
YEAH, LOTS GOING ON HERE.
MM-HM.

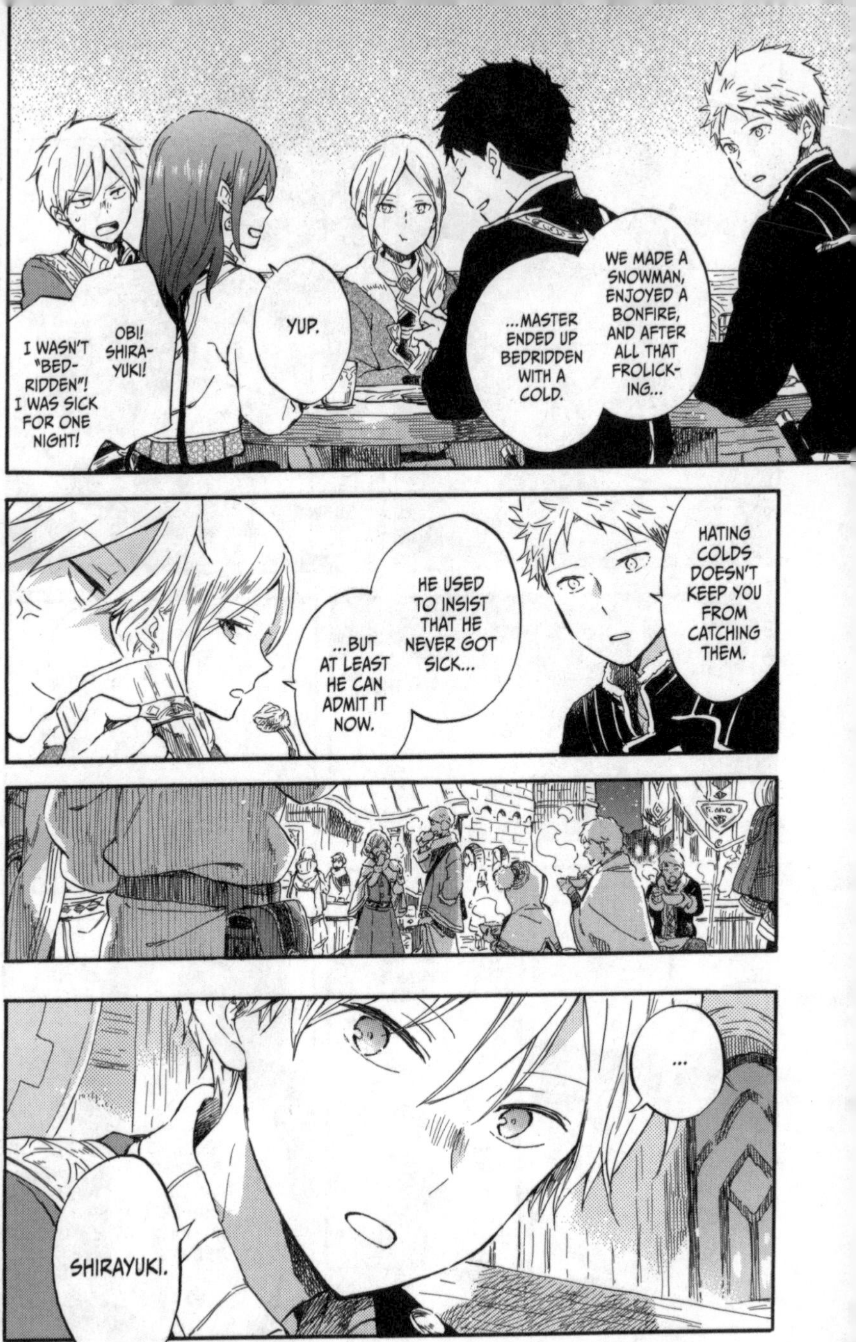
WE MADE A SNOWMAN, ENJOYED A BONFIRE, AND AFTER ALL THAT FROLICKING...
...MASTER ENDED UP BEDRIDDEN WITH A COLD.
YUP.
OBI! SHIRAYUKI!
I WASN'T "BEDRIDDEN"! I WAS SICK FOR ONE NIGHT!
HATING COLDS DOESN'T KEEP YOU FROM CATCHING THEM.
HE USED TO INSIST THAT HE NEVER GOT SICK...
...BUT AT LEAST HE CAN ADMIT IT NOW.
...
SHIRAYUKI.

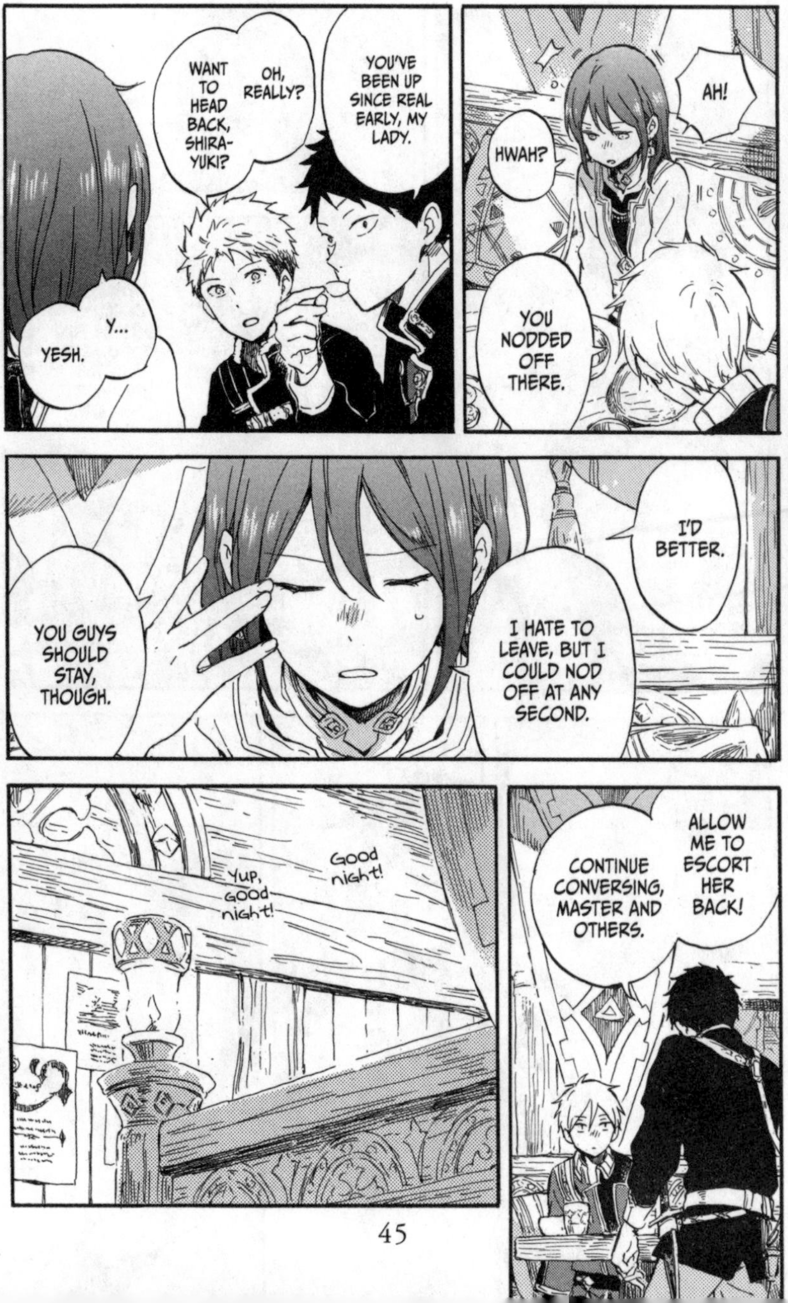
AH!
HWAH?
YOU NODDED OFF THERE.
YOU'VE BEEN UP SINCE REAL EARLY, MY LADY.
OH, REALLY?
WANT TO HEAD BACK, SHIRAYUKI?
Y... YESH.
I'D BETTER.
I HATE TO LEAVE, BUT I COULD NOD OFF AT ANY SECOND.
YOU GUYS SHOULD STAY, THOUGH.
ALLOW ME TO ESCORT HER BACK!
CONTINUE CONVERSING, MASTER AND OTHERS.
Good night!
Yup, good night!

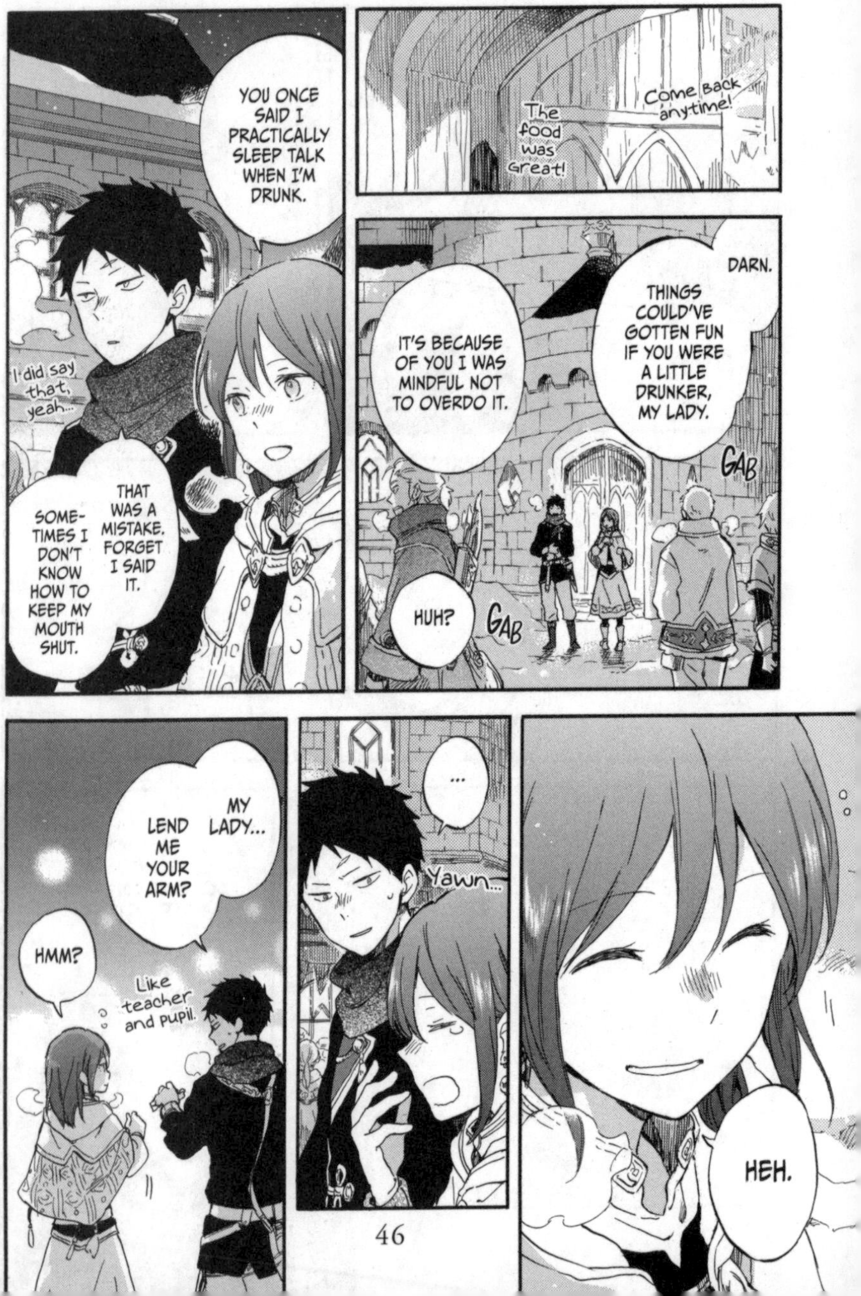

Come back anytime!
The food was great!
DARN.
THINGS COULD'VE GOTTEN FUN IF YOU WERE A LITTLE DRUNKER, MY LADY.
GAB
IT'S BECAUSE OF YOU I WAS MINDFUL NOT TO OVERDO IT.
HUH?
GAB
YOU ONCE SAID I PRACTICALLY SLEEP TALK WHEN I'M DRUNK.
I did say that, yeah...
THAT WAS A MISTAKE. FORGET I SAID IT.
SOME-TIMES I DON'T KNOW HOW TO KEEP MY MOUTH SHUT.
HEH.
...
Yawn...
MY LADY...
LEND ME YOUR ARM?
HMM?
Like teacher and pupil.

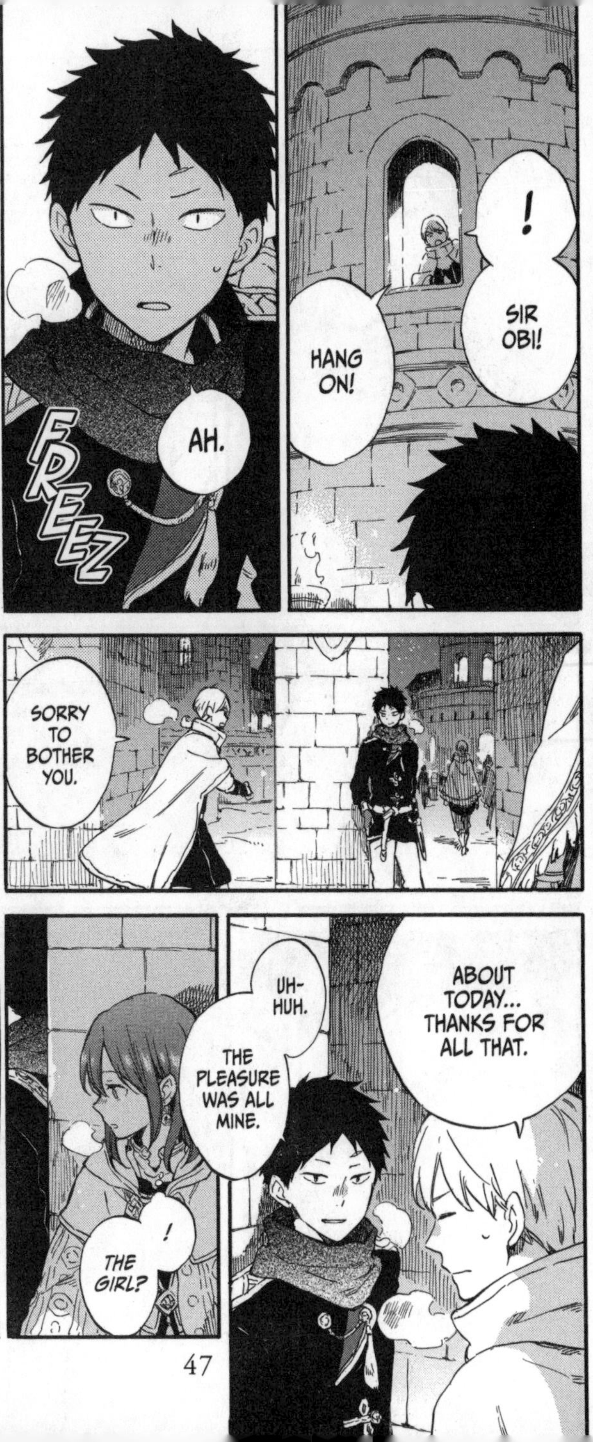
!
SIR OBI!
HANG ON!
AH.
FREEZ
SORRY TO BOTHER YOU.
ABOUT TODAY... THANKS FOR ALL THAT.
UH-HUH.
THE PLEASURE WAS ALL MINE.
!
THE GIRL?

2

TRIP DIARY, PART 1

I called it a seven-day trip, but the first two days were mostly spent traveling. L-long trip!! The flight felt like it went on forever since we were crammed in our seats the whole time. The in-flight meals came one after the other, so we were always full. "I-I'm full." That's the English phrase I picked up on the flight.

We had a transfer in Dubai. We couldn't leave the airport, but we walked around and checked out the souvenirs on offer, including some really slick pajamas. And every shop had dates! Dates here, dates there! Dates every which way! Must be a popular snack.

A date

Finally, we arrived on the isle of Malta! That's right—it's an island! Then we took a bus to a very lovely hotel. I couldn't see the beach from my room, but I could see...a cliff? And a parking lot? Our first stop: a supermarket in walking distance!

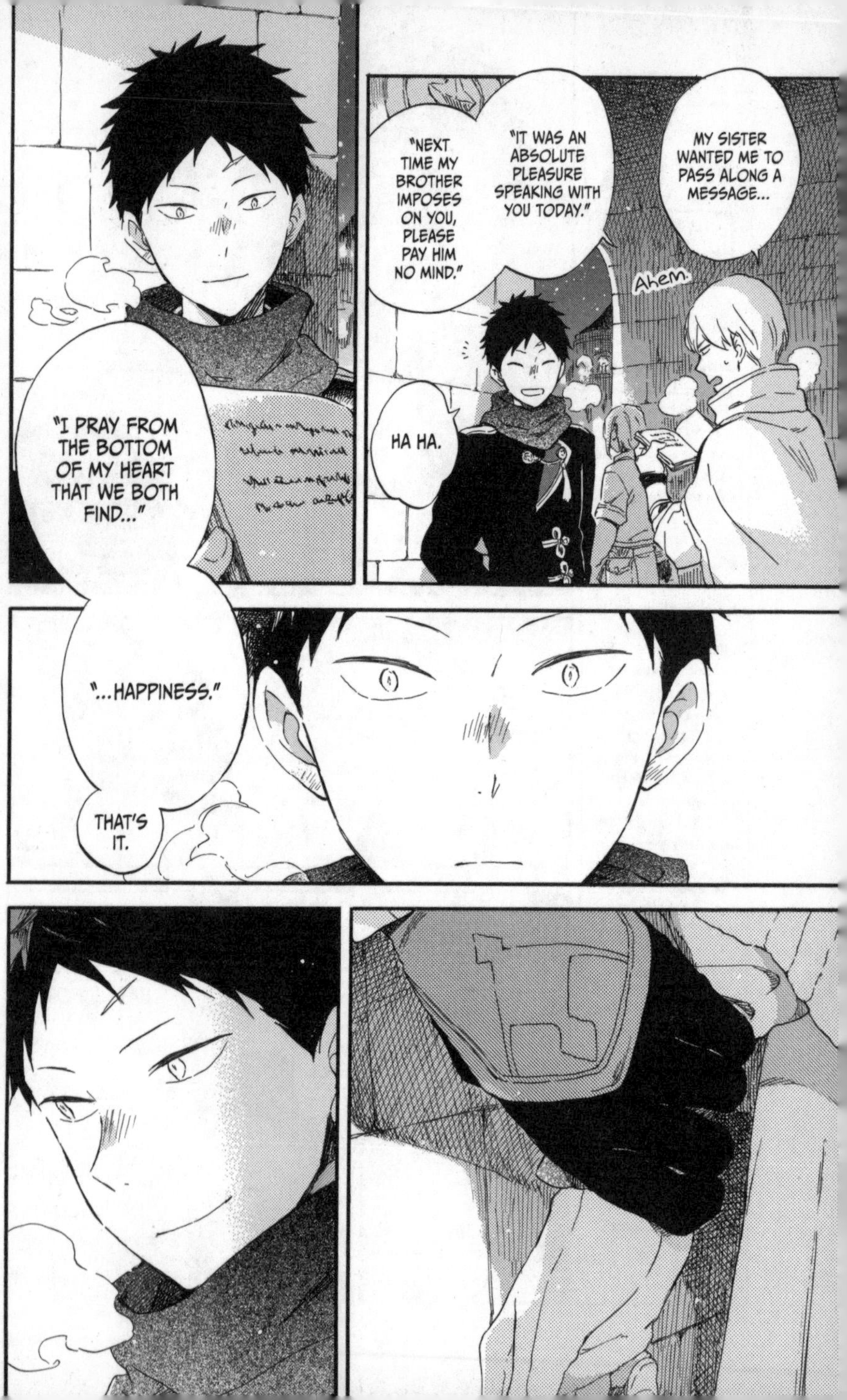
MY SISTER WANTED ME TO PASS ALONG A MESSAGE...
Ahem.
"IT WAS AN ABSOLUTE PLEASURE SPEAKING WITH YOU TODAY."
"NEXT TIME MY BROTHER IMPOSES ON YOU, PLEASE PAY HIM NO MIND."
HA HA.
"I PRAY FROM THE BOTTOM OF MY HEART THAT WE BOTH FIND..."
"...HAPPINESS."
THAT'S IT.

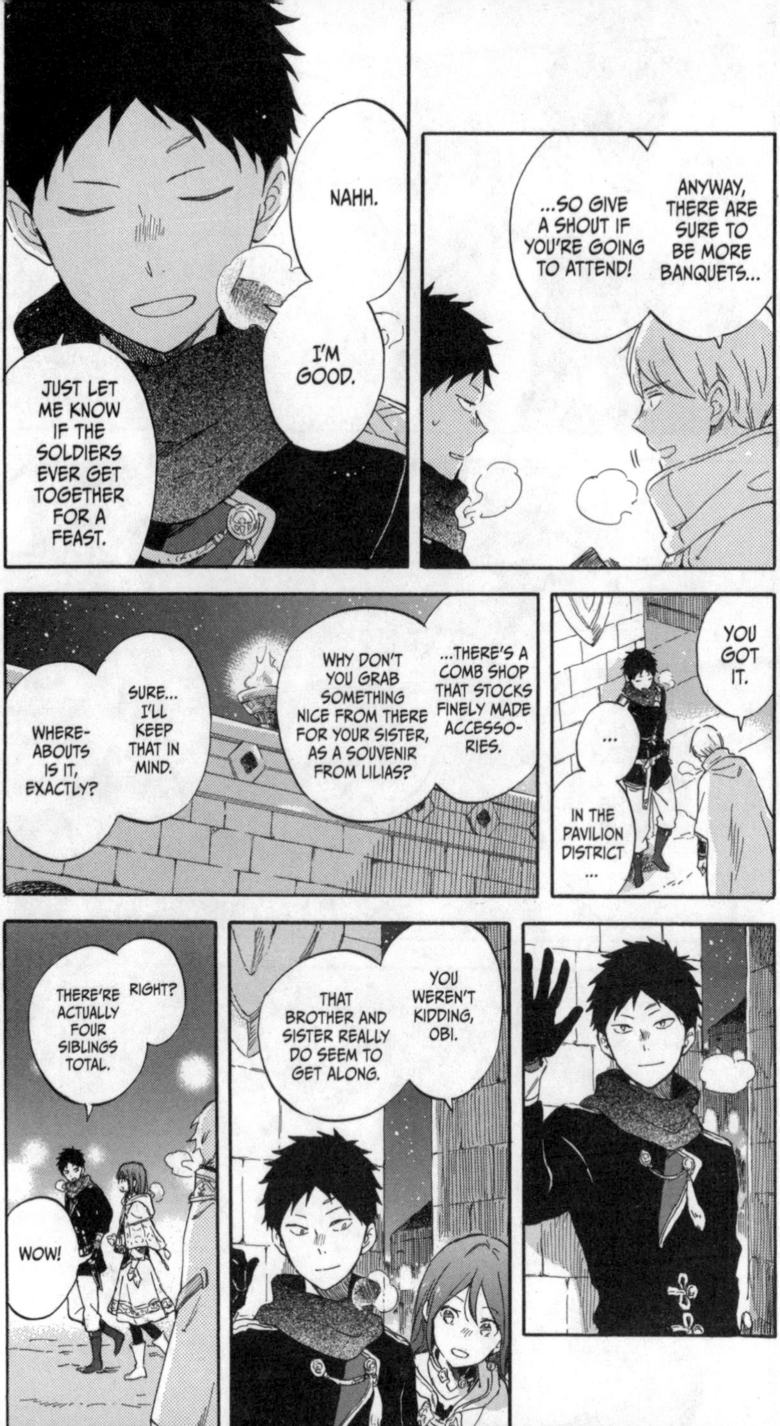
ANYWAY, THERE ARE SURE TO BE MORE BANQUETS...
...SO GIVE A SHOUT IF YOU'RE GOING TO ATTEND!
NAHH.
I'M GOOD.
JUST LET ME KNOW IF THE SOLDIERS EVER GET TOGETHER FOR A FEAST.
YOU GOT IT.
...
IN THE PAVILION DISTRICT...
...THERE'S A COMB SHOP THAT STOCKS FINELY MADE ACCESSORIES.
WHY DON'T YOU GRAB SOMETHING NICE FROM THERE FOR YOUR SISTER, AS A SOUVENIR FROM LILIAS?
SURE... I'LL KEEP THAT IN MIND.
WHERE-ABOUTS IS IT, EXACTLY?
YOU WEREN'T KIDDING, OBI.
THAT BROTHER AND SISTER REALLY DO SEEM TO GET ALONG.
RIGHT?
THERE'RE ACTUALLY FOUR SIBLINGS TOTAL.
WOW!

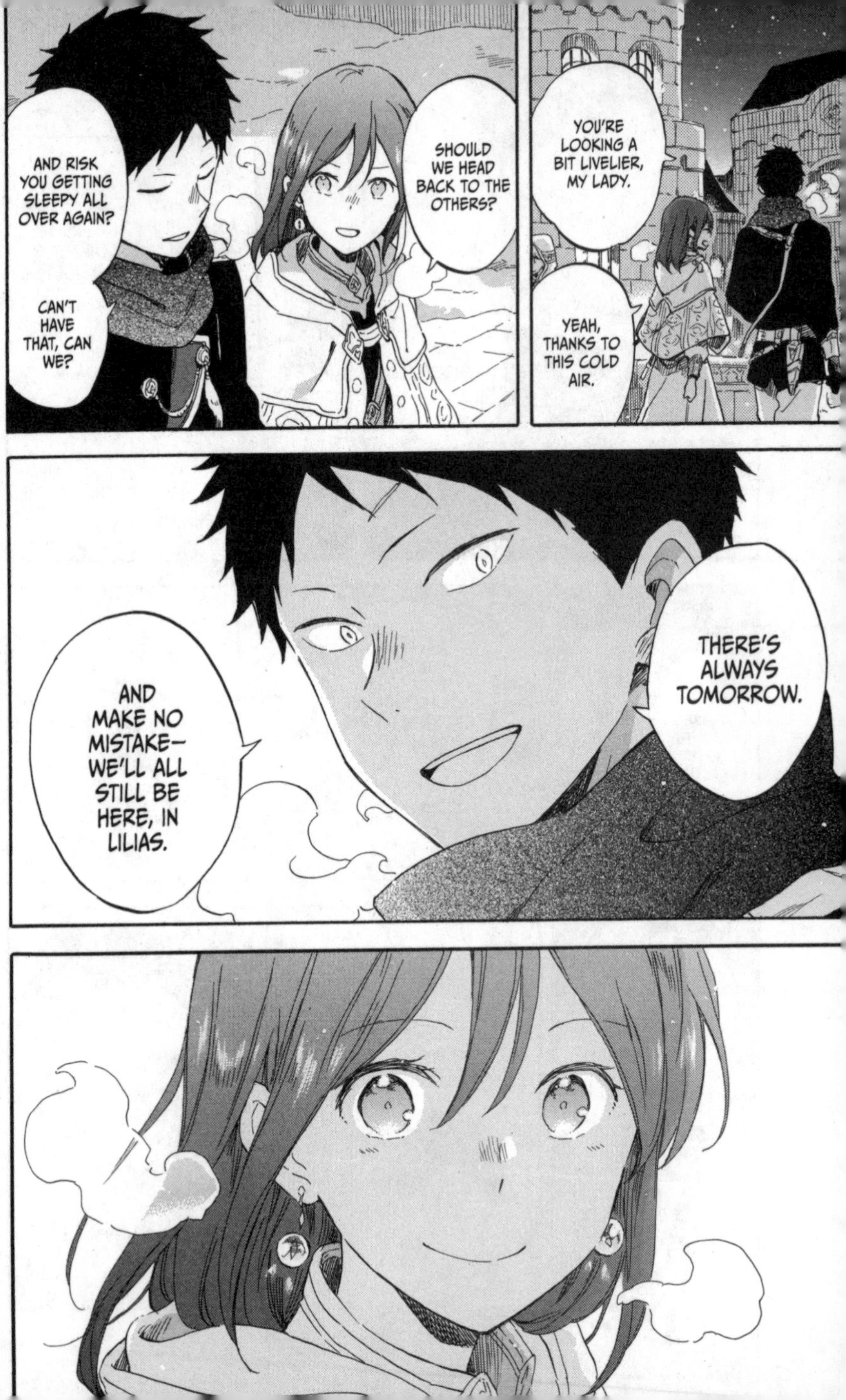
YOU'RE LOOKING A BIT LIVELIER, MY LADY.
YEAH, THANKS TO THIS COLD AIR.
SHOULD WE HEAD BACK TO THE OTHERS?
AND RISK YOU GETTING SLEEPY ALL OVER AGAIN?
CAN'T HAVE THAT, CAN WE?
THERE'S ALWAYS TOMORROW.
AND MAKE NO MISTAKE— WE'LL ALL STILL BE HERE, IN LILIAS.

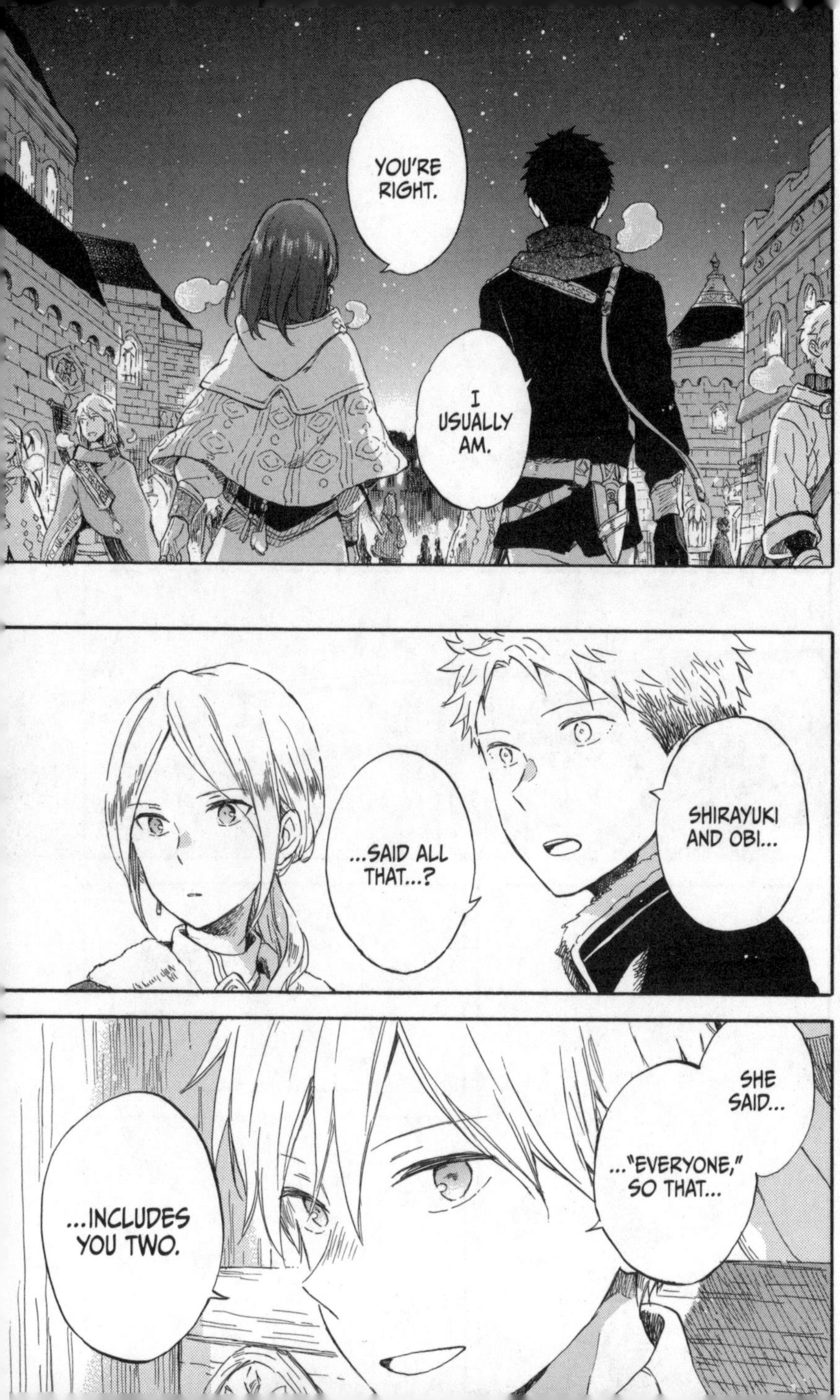
YOU'RE RIGHT.
I USUALLY AM.
SHIRAYUKI AND OBI...
...SAID ALL THAT...?
SHE SAID...
..."EVERYONE," SO THAT...
...INCLUDES YOU TWO.

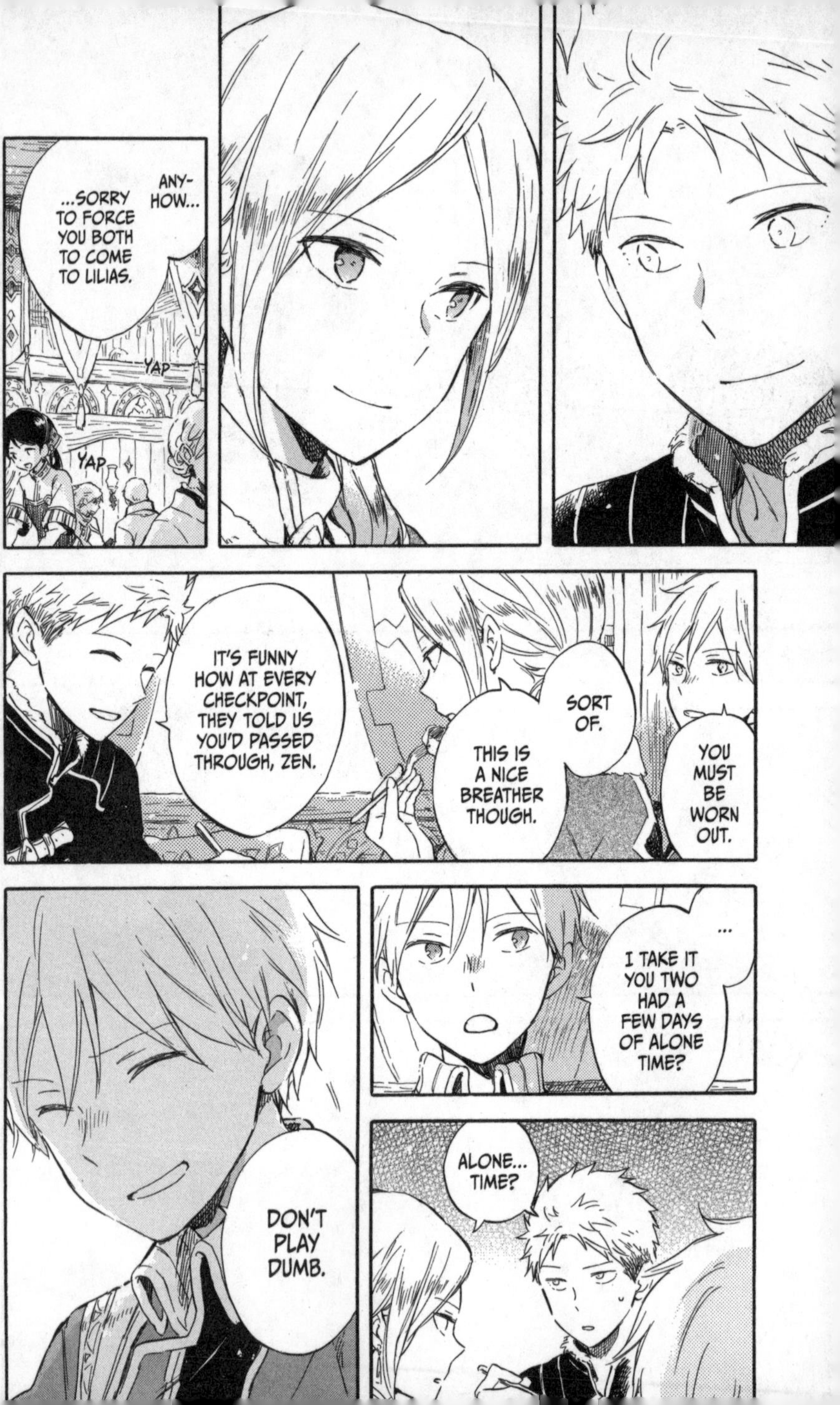
ANY-HOW...
...SORRY TO FORCE YOU BOTH TO COME TO LILIAS.
YAP
YAP
YOU MUST BE WORN OUT.
SORT OF.
THIS IS A NICE BREATHER THOUGH.
IT'S FUNNY HOW AT EVERY CHECKPOINT, THEY TOLD US YOU'D PASSED THROUGH, ZEN.
...
I TAKE IT YOU TWO HAD A FEW DAYS OF ALONE TIME?
ALONE... TIME?
DON'T PLAY DUMB.

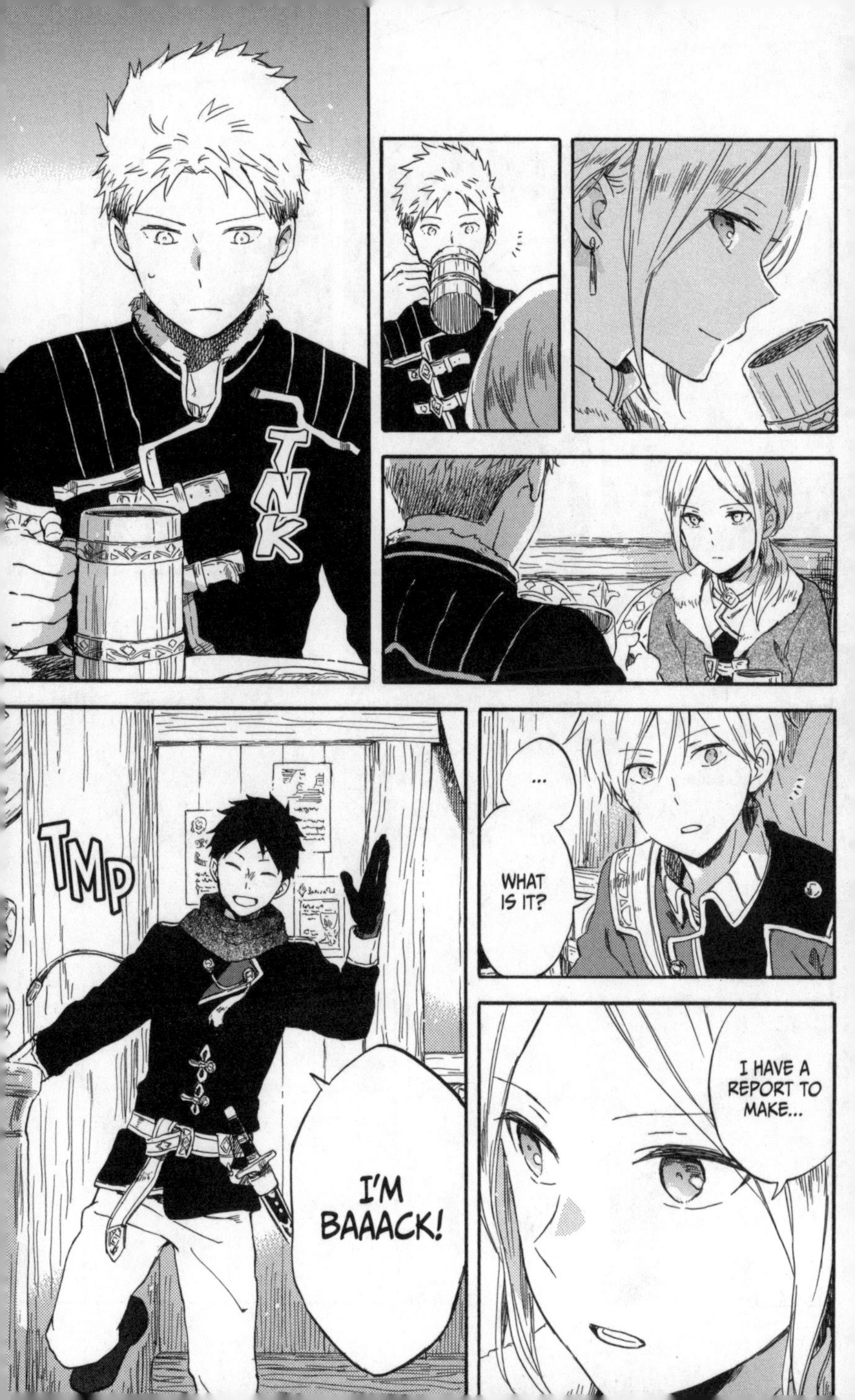
TNK
...
WHAT IS IT?
I HAVE A REPORT TO MAKE...
TMP
I'M BAAACK!

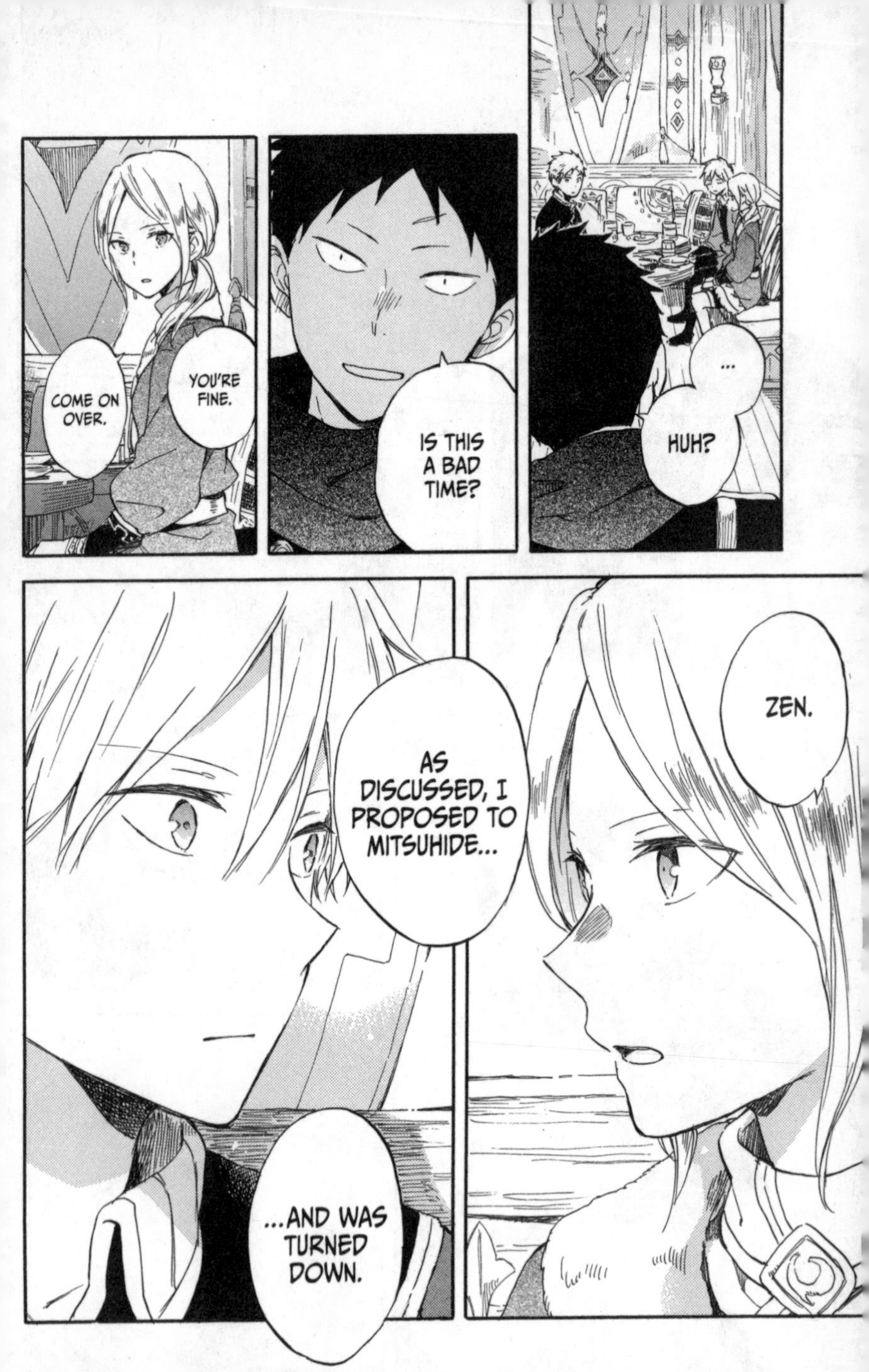
...
HUH?
IS THIS A BAD TIME?
YOU'RE FINE.
COME ON OVER.
ZEN.
AS DISCUSSED, I PROPOSED TO MITSUHIDE...
...AND WAS TURNED DOWN.

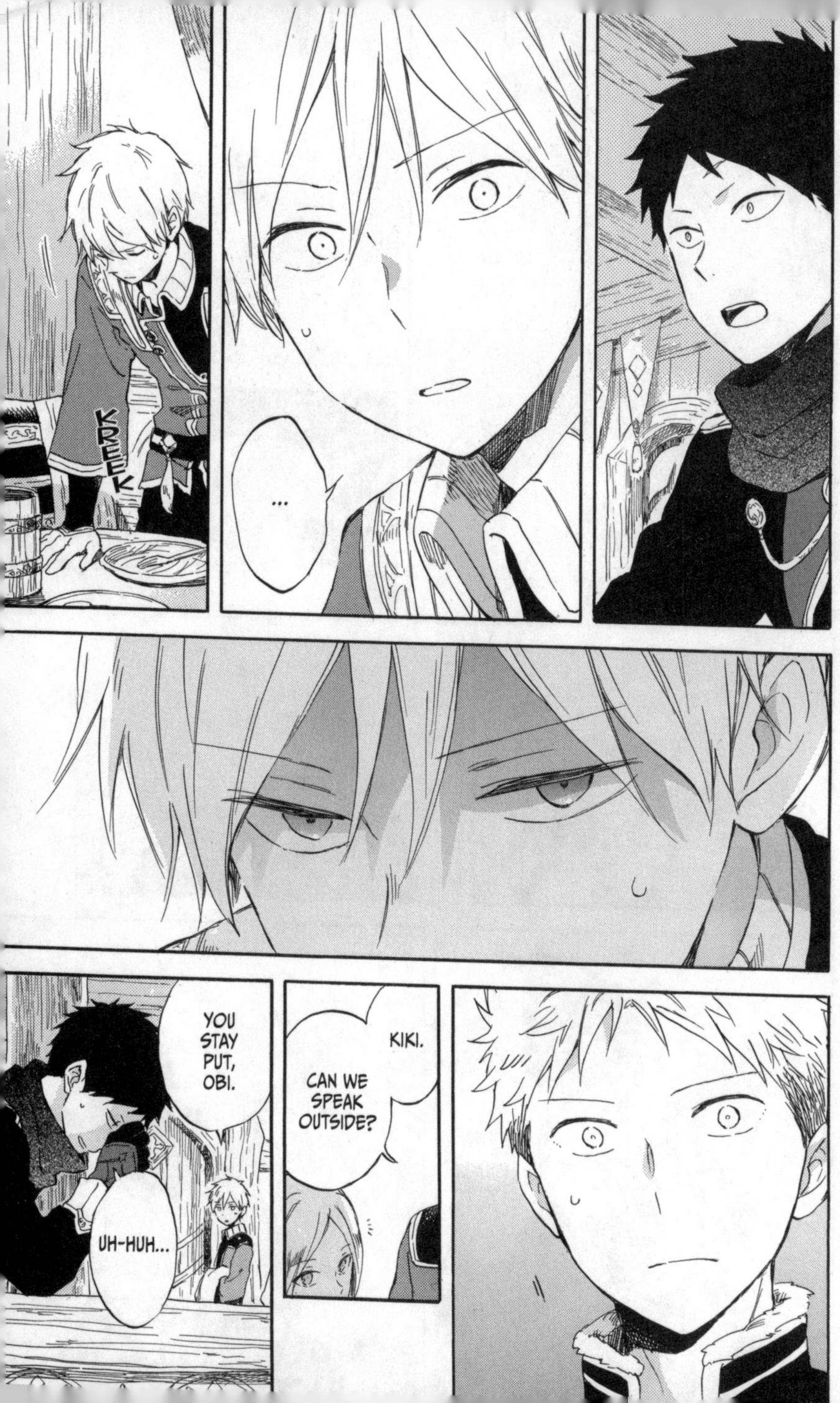
...
KREEK
KIKI.
CAN WE SPEAK OUTSIDE?
YOU STAY PUT, OBI.
UH-HUH...

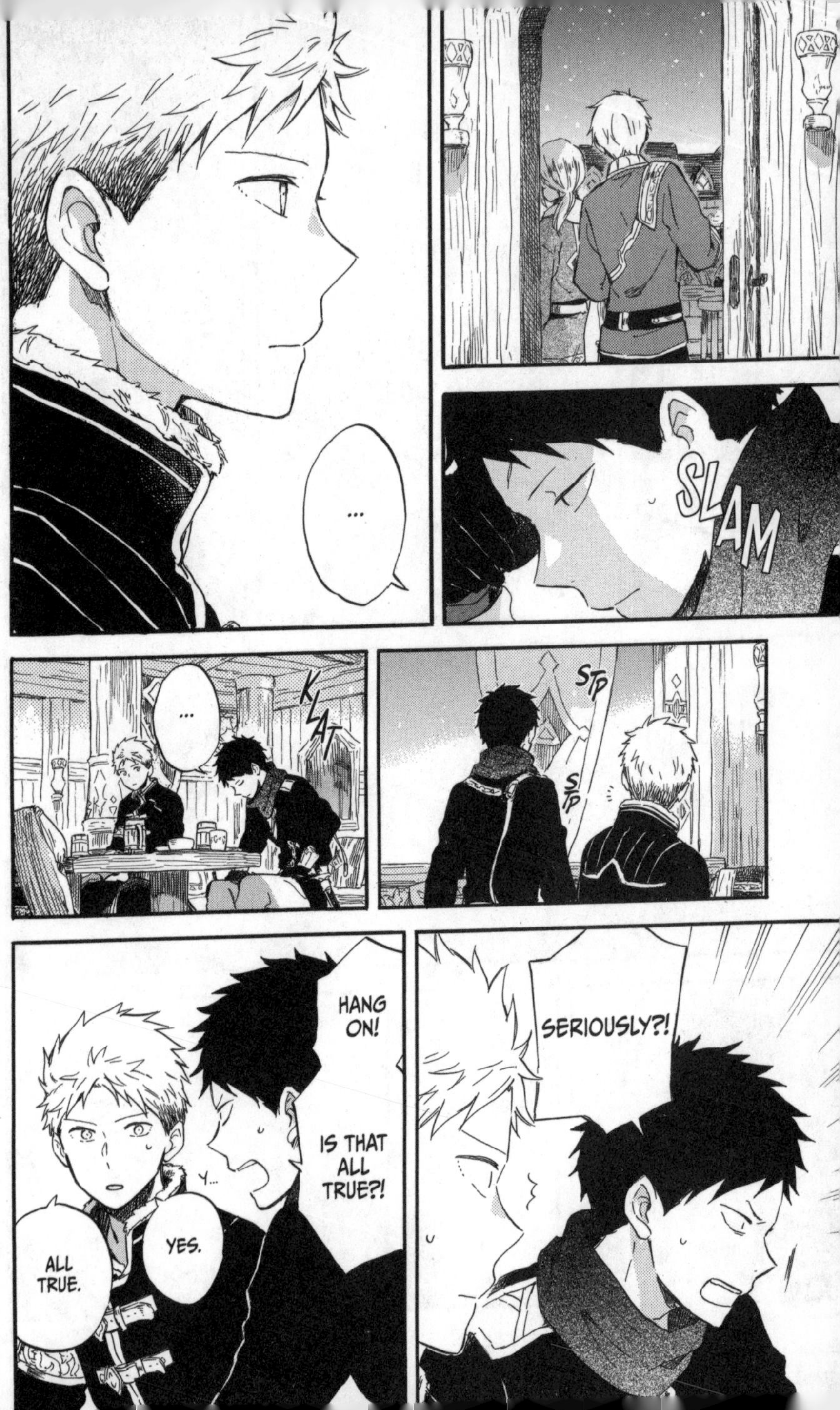
SLAM
...
STP
STP
...
KLAT
SERIOUSLY?!
HANG ON!
IS THAT ALL TRUE?!
Y...
YES.
ALL TRUE.

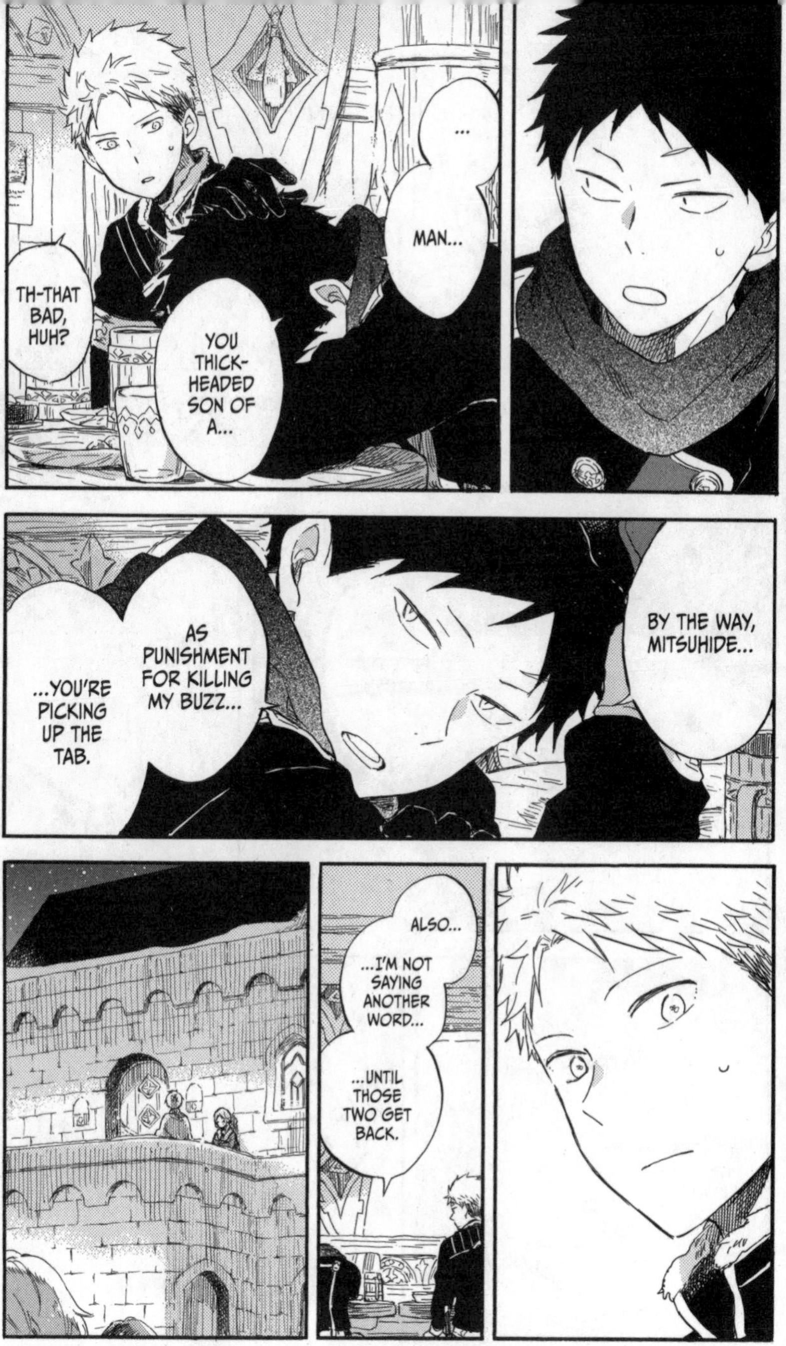
...
MAN...
YOU THICK-HEADED SON OF A...
TH-THAT BAD, HUH?
BY THE WAY, MITSUHIDE...
AS PUNISHMENT FOR KILLING MY BUZZ...
...YOU'RE PICKING UP THE TAB.
ALSO...
...I'M NOT SAYING ANOTHER WORD...
...UNTIL THOSE TWO GET BACK.

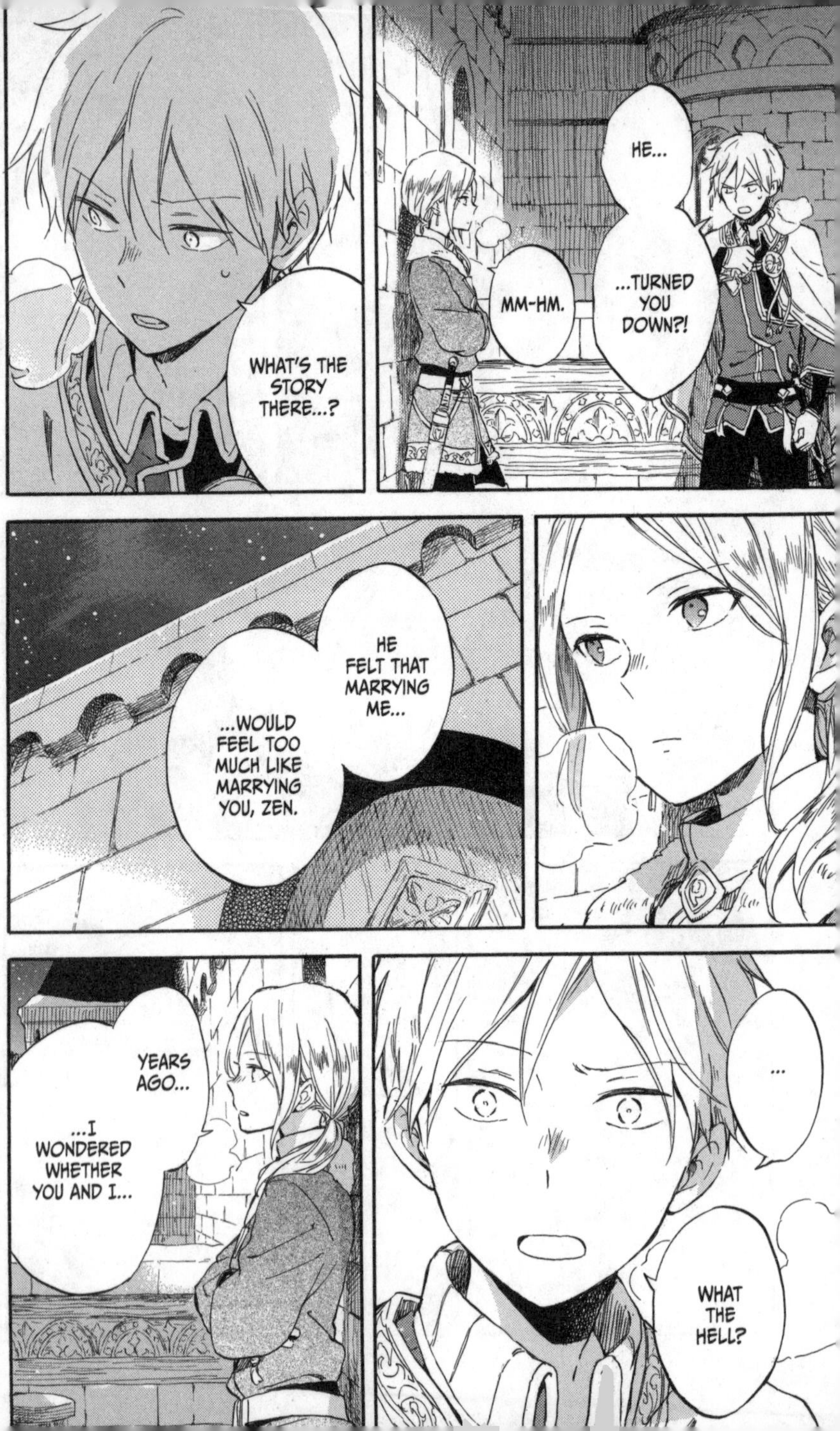
HE...
...TURNED YOU DOWN?!
MM-HM.
WHAT'S THE STORY THERE...?
HE FELT THAT MARRYING ME...
...WOULD FEEL TOO MUCH LIKE MARRYING YOU, ZEN.
...
WHAT THE HELL?
YEARS AGO...
...I WONDERED WHETHER YOU AND I...

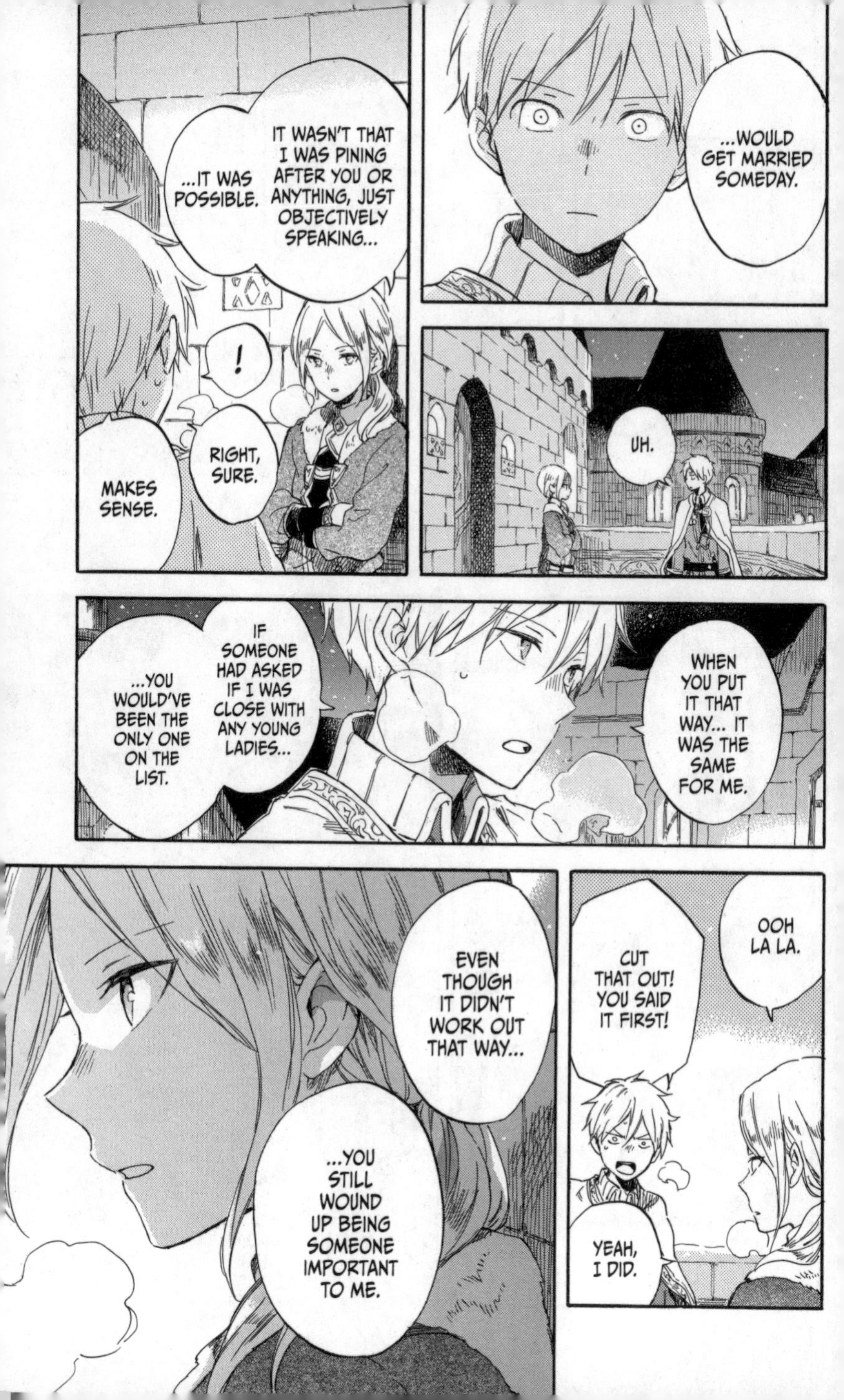
...WOULD GET MARRIED SOMEDAY.
UH.
IT WASN'T THAT I WAS PINING AFTER YOU OR ANYTHING, JUST OBJECTIVELY SPEAKING...
...IT WAS POSSIBLE.
!
RIGHT, SURE.
MAKES SENSE.
WHEN YOU PUT IT THAT WAY... IT WAS THE SAME FOR ME.
IF SOMEONE HAD ASKED IF I WAS CLOSE WITH ANY YOUNG LADIES...
...YOU WOULD'VE BEEN THE ONLY ONE ON THE LIST.
OOH LA LA.
CUT THAT OUT! YOU SAID IT FIRST!
YEAH, I DID.
EVEN THOUGH IT DIDN'T WORK OUT THAT WAY...
...YOU STILL WOUND UP BEING SOMEONE IMPORTANT TO ME.

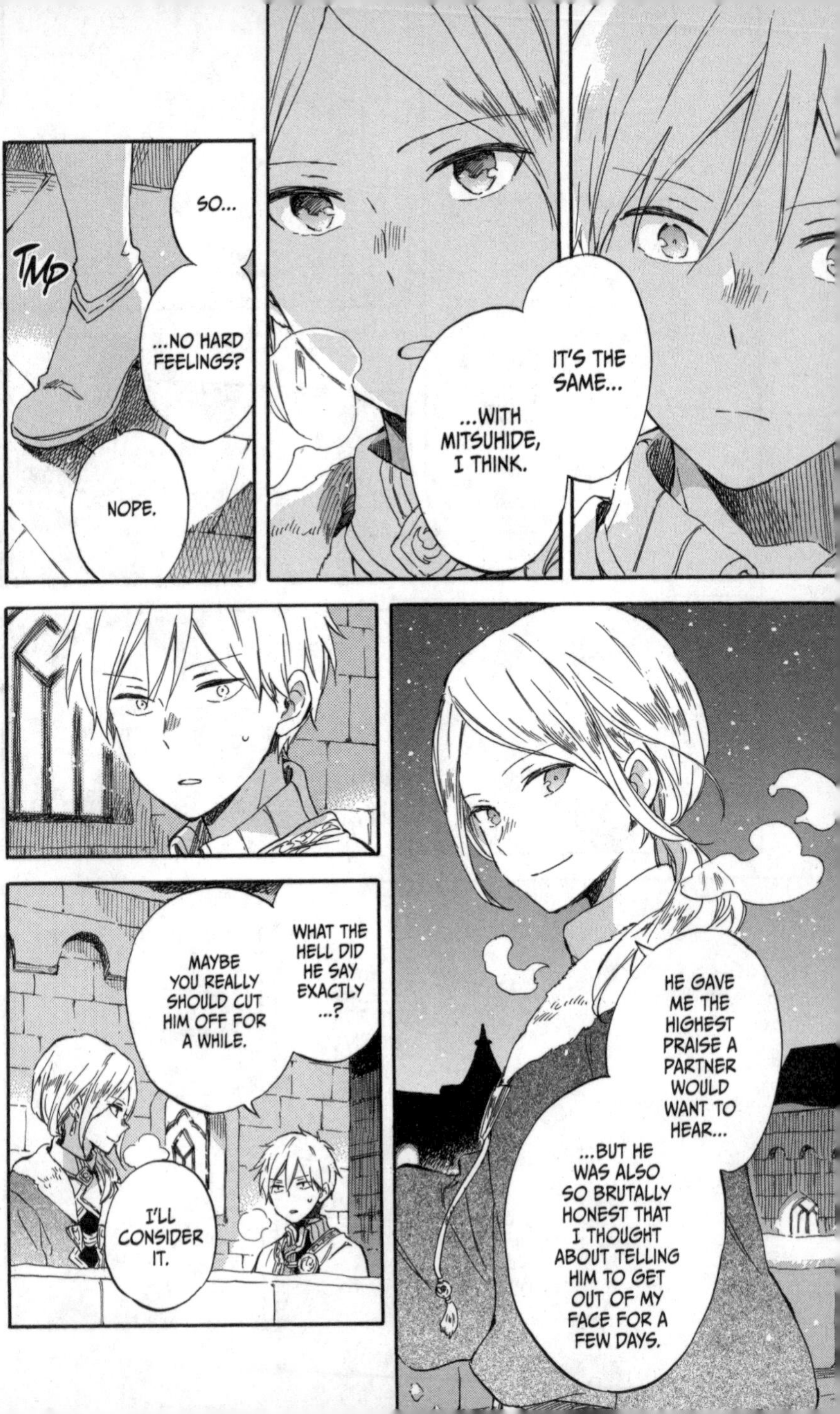
IT'S THE SAME...
...WITH MITSUHIDE, I THINK.
SO...
TMP
...NO HARD FEELINGS?
NOPE.
HE GAVE ME THE HIGHEST PRAISE A PARTNER WOULD WANT TO HEAR...
...BUT HE WAS ALSO SO BRUTALLY HONEST THAT I THOUGHT ABOUT TELLING HIM TO GET OUT OF MY FACE FOR A FEW DAYS.
WHAT THE HELL DID HE SAY EXACTLY ...?
MAYBE YOU REALLY SHOULD CUT HIM OFF FOR A WHILE.
I'LL CONSIDER IT.

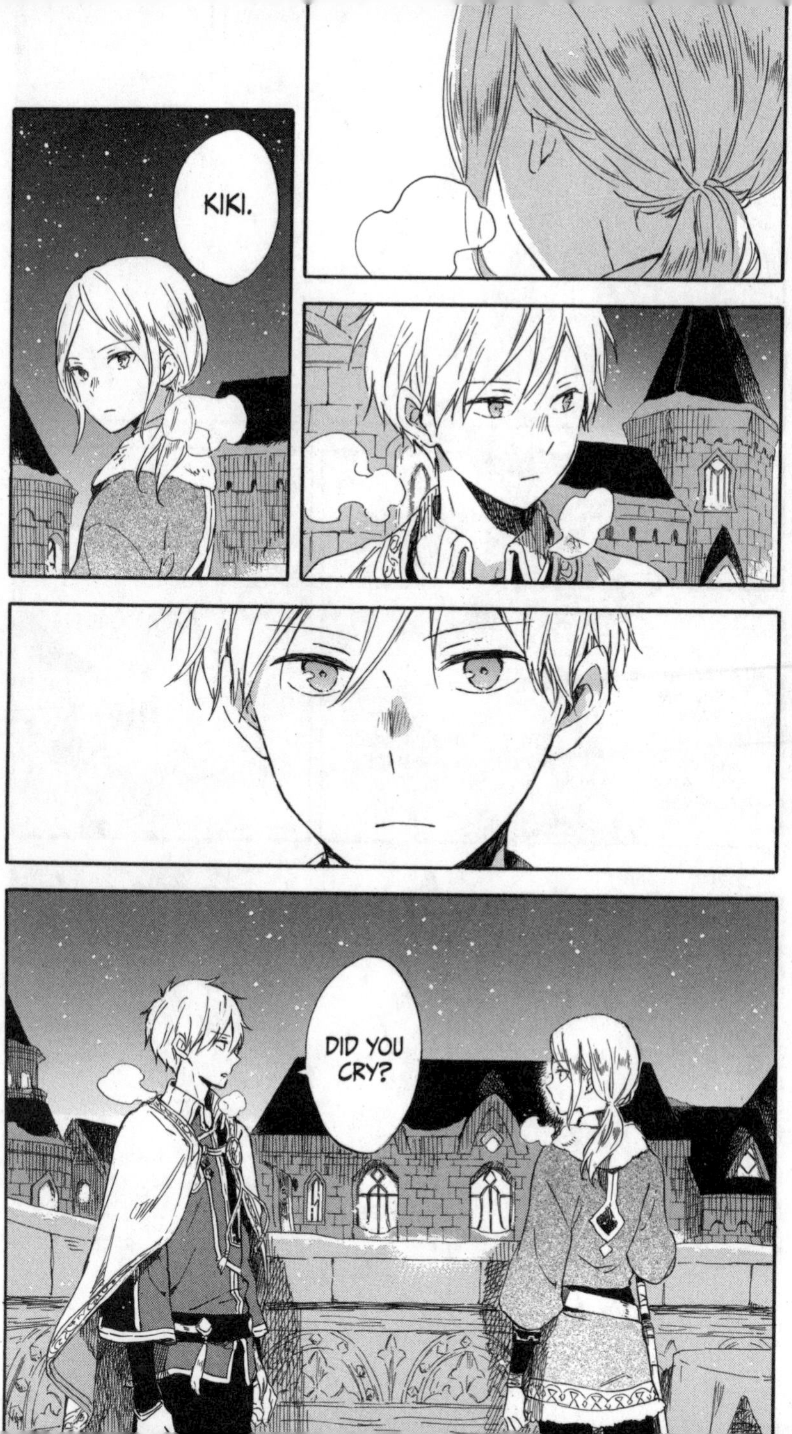
KIKI.
DID YOU CRY?

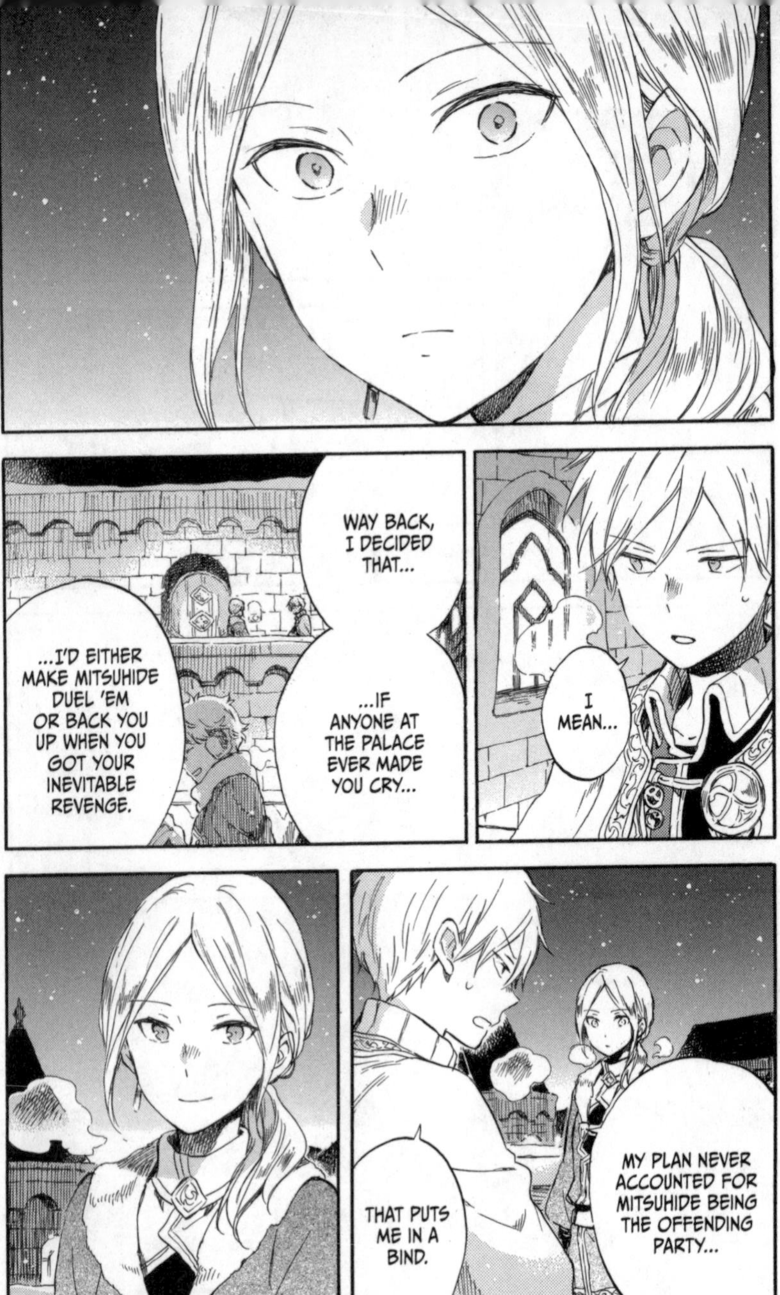
I MEAN...
WAY BACK, I DECIDED THAT...
...IF ANYONE AT THE PALACE EVER MADE YOU CRY...
...I'D EITHER MAKE MITSUHIDE DUEL 'EM OR BACK YOU UP WHEN YOU GOT YOUR INEVITABLE REVENGE.
MY PLAN NEVER ACCOUNTED FOR MITSUHIDE BEING THE OFFENDING PARTY...
THAT PUTS ME IN A BIND.

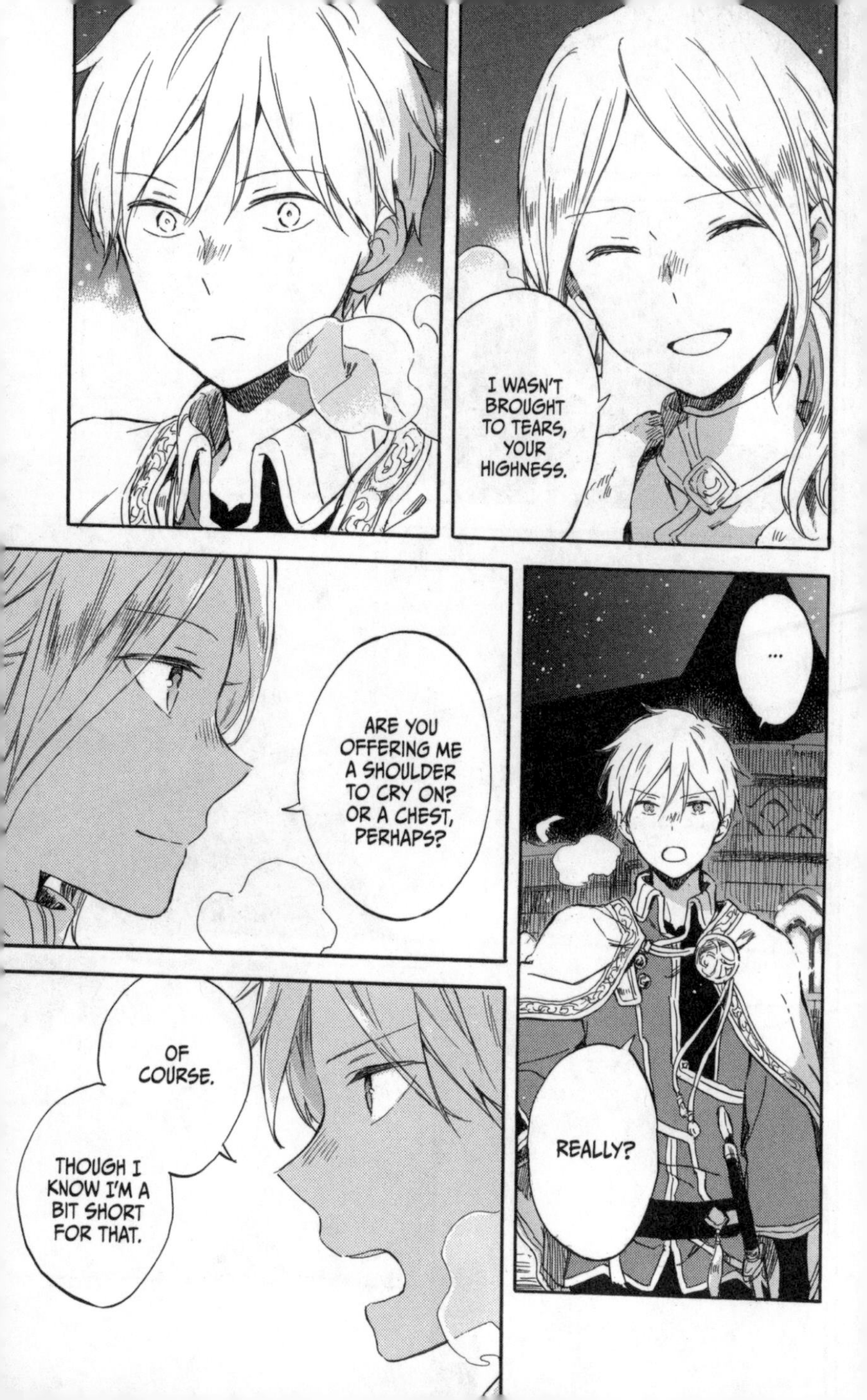
I WASN'T BROUGHT TO TEARS, YOUR HIGHNESS.
...
REALLY?
ARE YOU OFFERING ME A SHOULDER TO CRY ON? OR A CHEST, PERHAPS?
OF COURSE.
THOUGH I KNOW I'M A BIT SHORT FOR THAT.

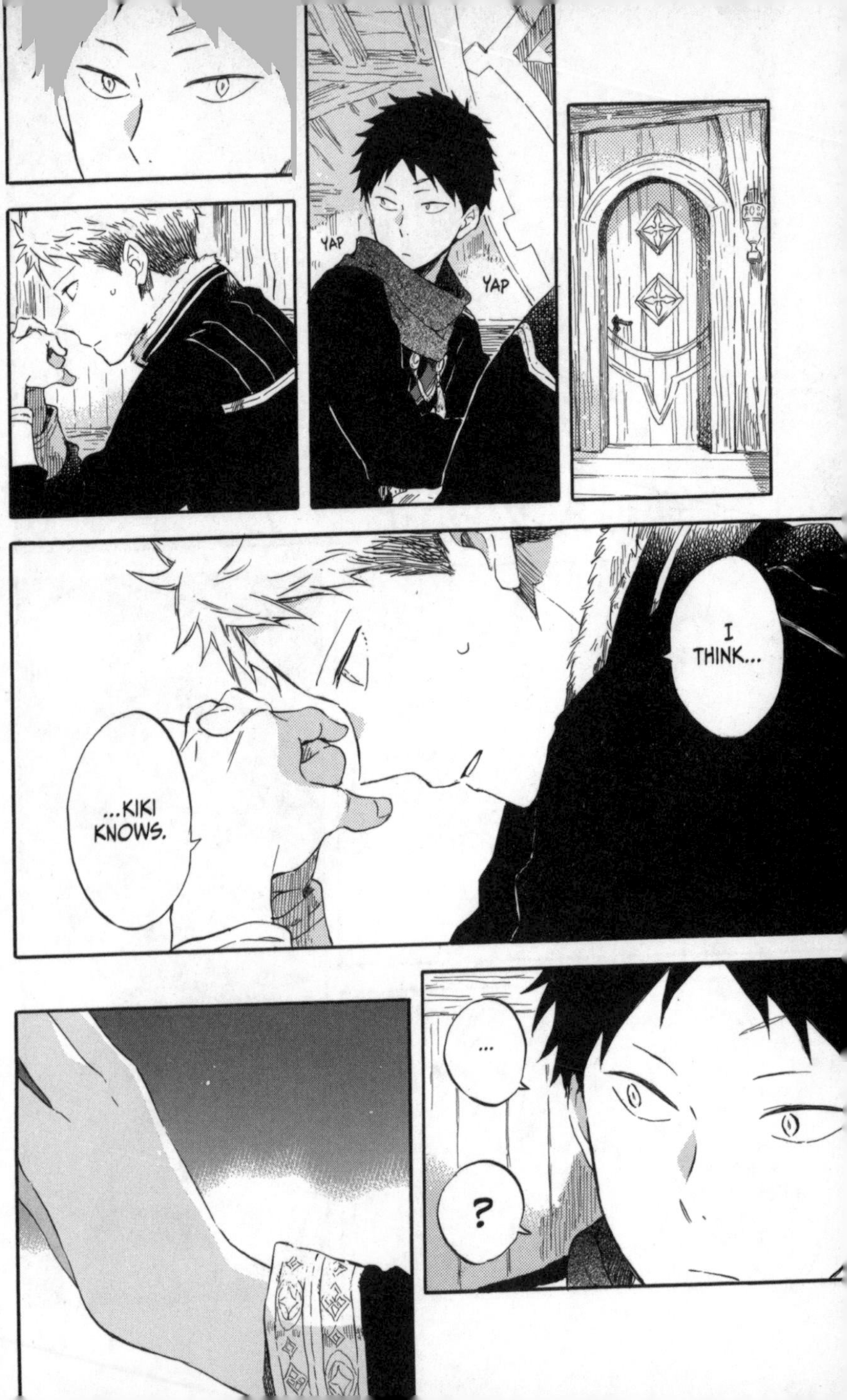
YAP
YAP
I THINK...
...KIKI KNOWS.
...
?

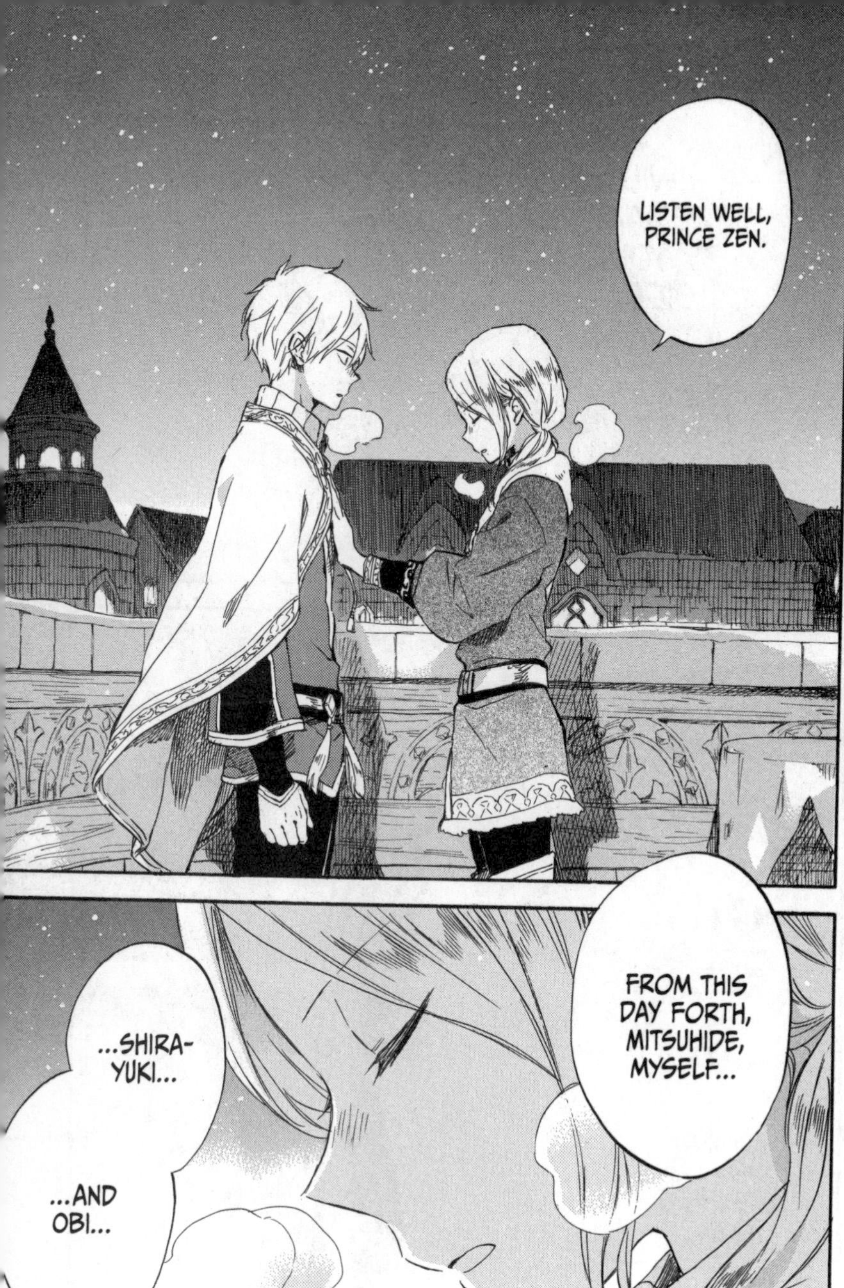
LISTEN WELL, PRINCE ZEN.
FROM THIS DAY FORTH, MITSUHIDE, MYSELF...
...SHIRA-YUKI...
...AND OBI...

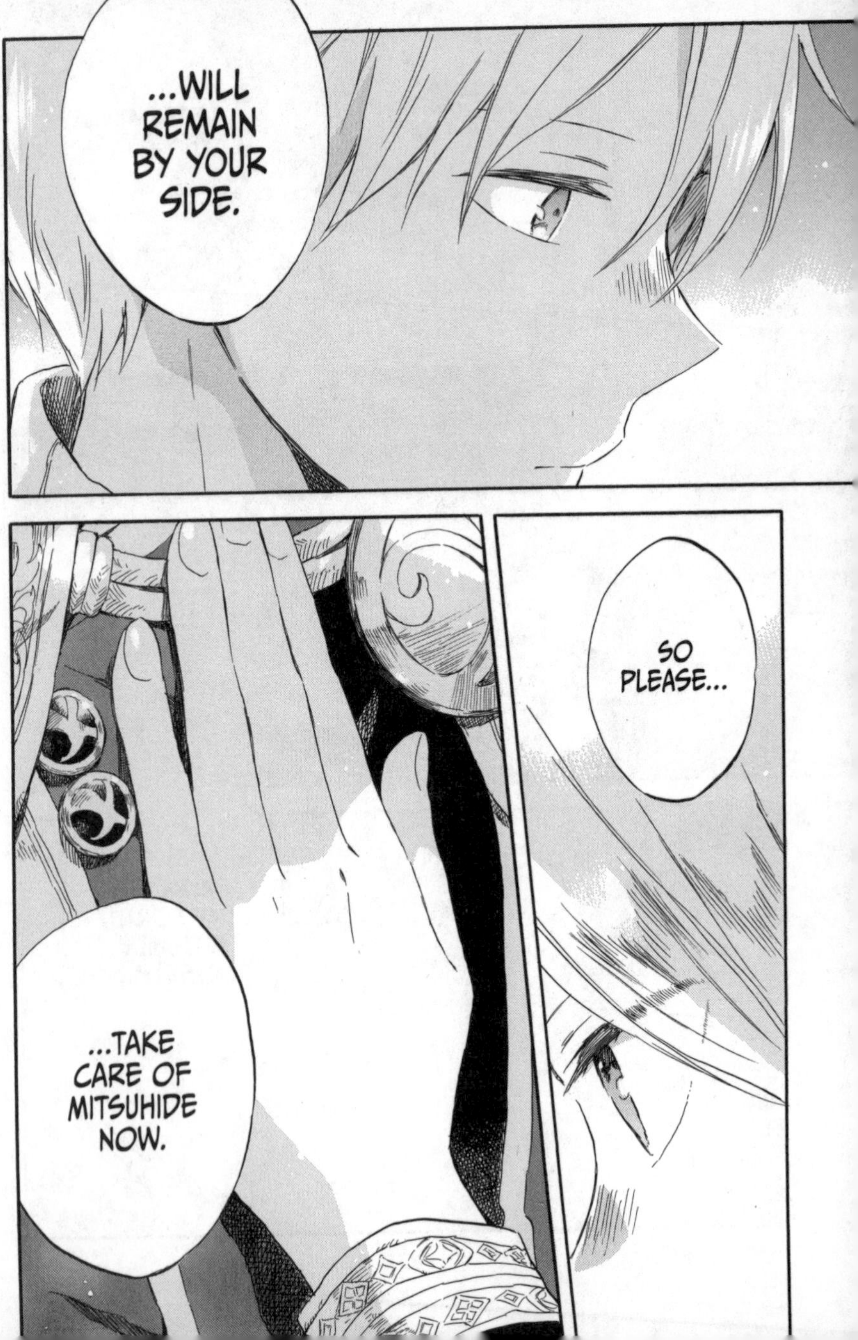
...WILL REMAIN BY YOUR SIDE.
SO PLEASE...
...TAKE CARE OF MITSUHIDE NOW.

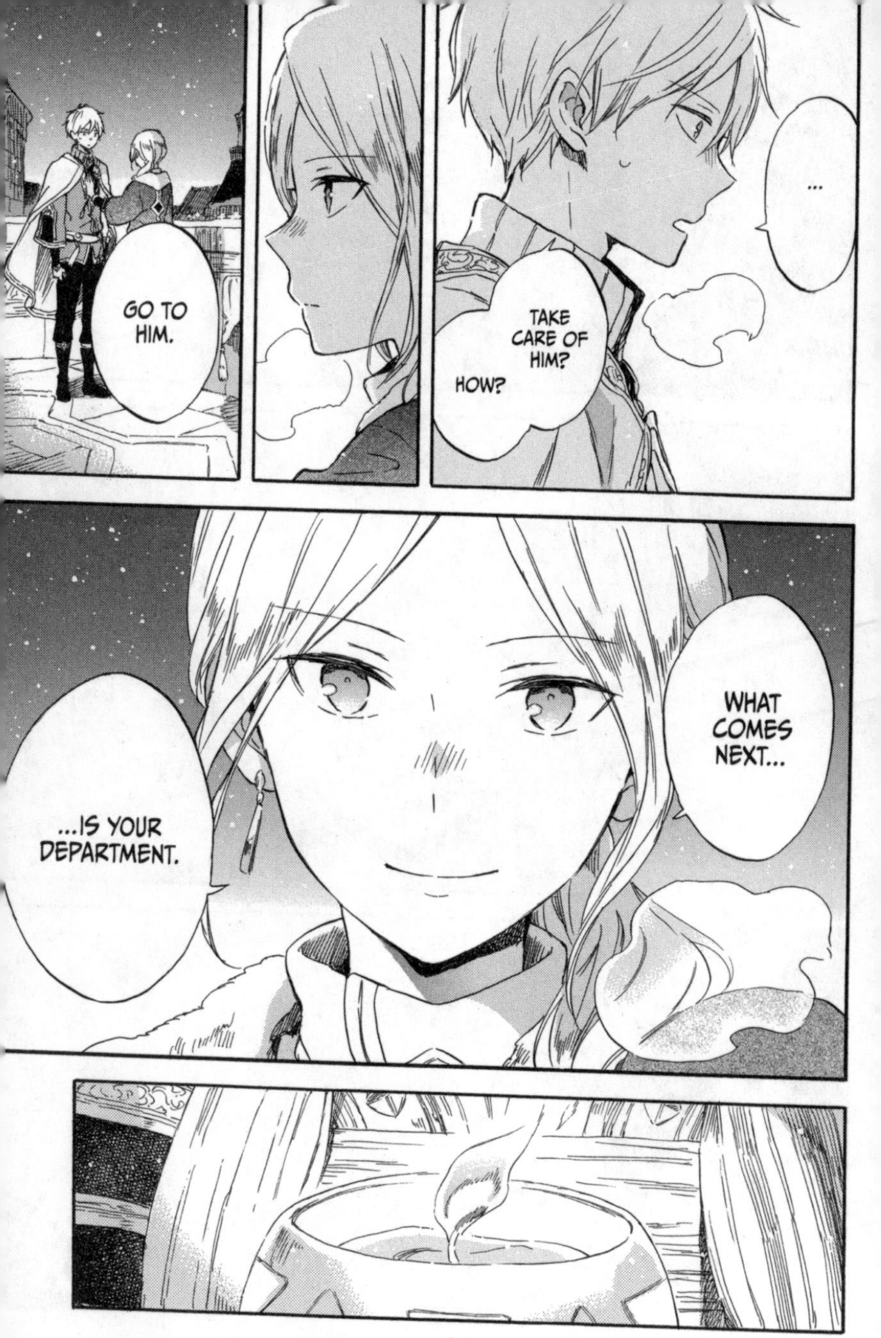
...
TAKE CARE OF HIM?
HOW?
GO TO HIM.
WHAT COMES NEXT...
...IS YOUR DEPARTMENT.

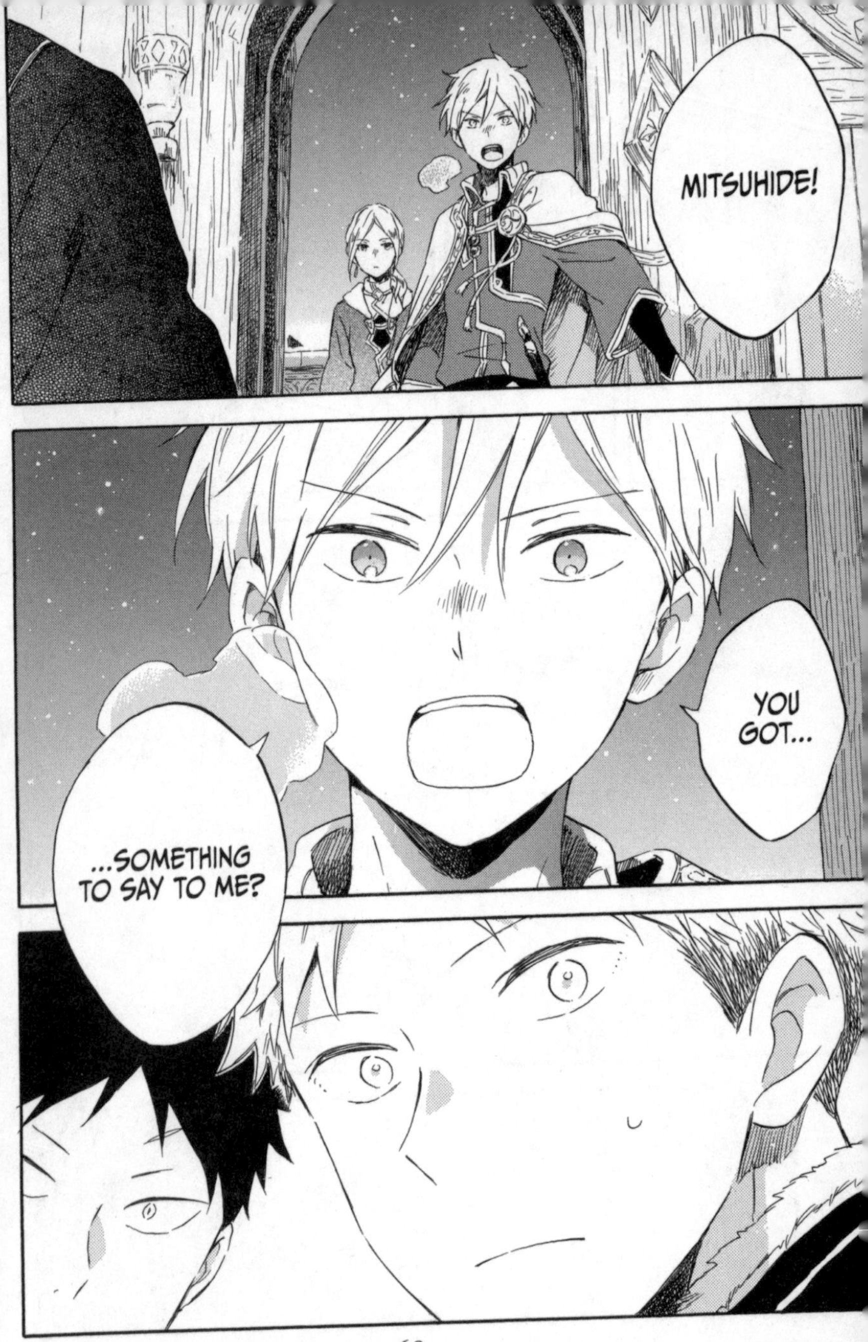
MITSUHIDE!
YOU GOT...
...SOMETHING TO SAY TO ME?

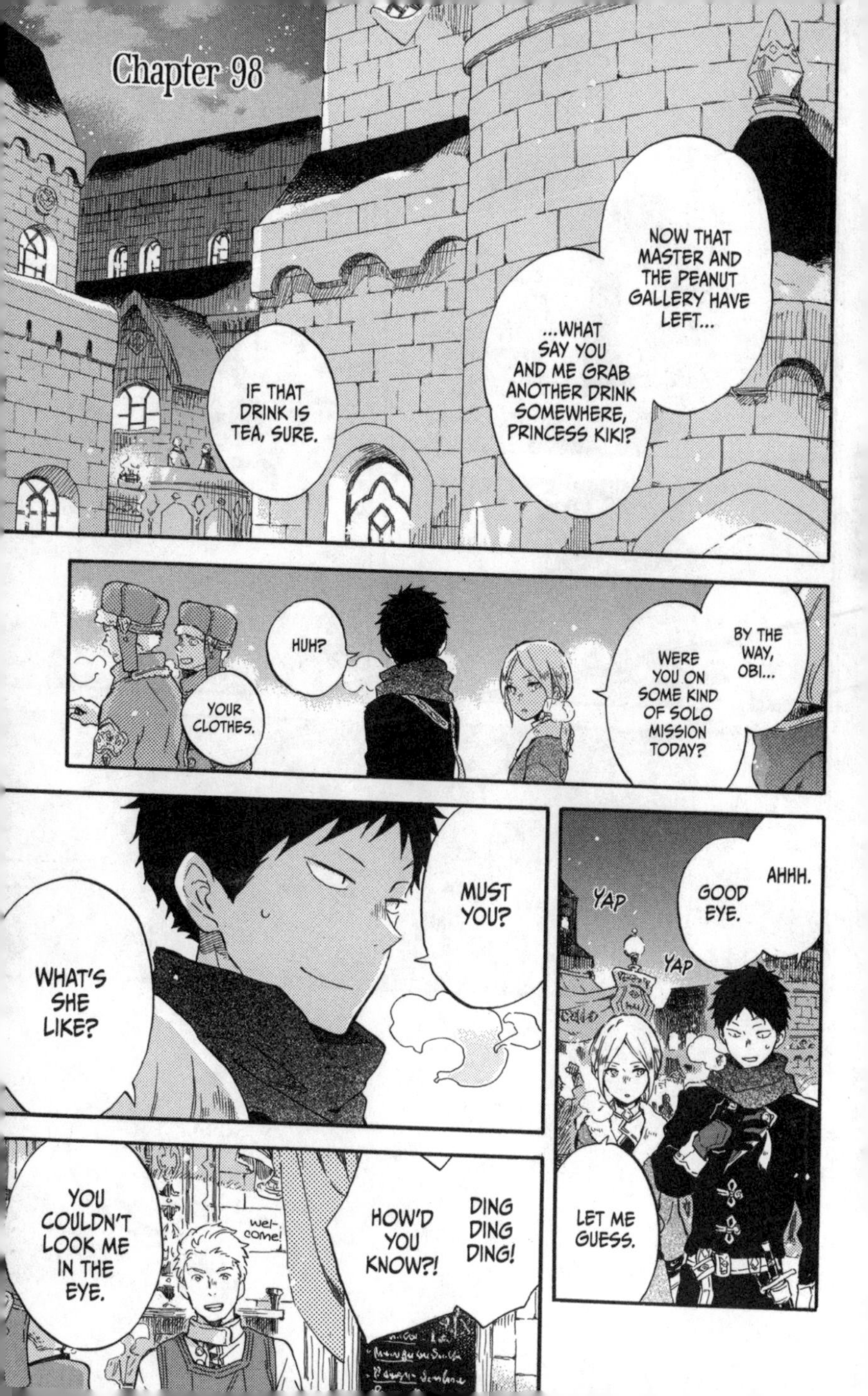
Chapter 98
NOW THAT MASTER AND THE PEANUT GALLERY HAVE LEFT...
...WHAT SAY YOU AND ME GRAB ANOTHER DRINK SOMEWHERE, PRINCESS KIKI?
IF THAT DRINK IS TEA, SURE.
BY THE WAY, OBI...
WERE YOU ON SOME KIND OF SOLO MISSION TODAY?
HUH?
YOUR CLOTHES.
AHHH.
GOOD EYE.
YAP
YAP
LET ME GUESS.
MUST YOU?
WHAT'S SHE LIKE?
DING DING DING!
HOW'D YOU KNOW?!
wel-come!
YOU COULDN'T LOOK ME IN THE EYE.

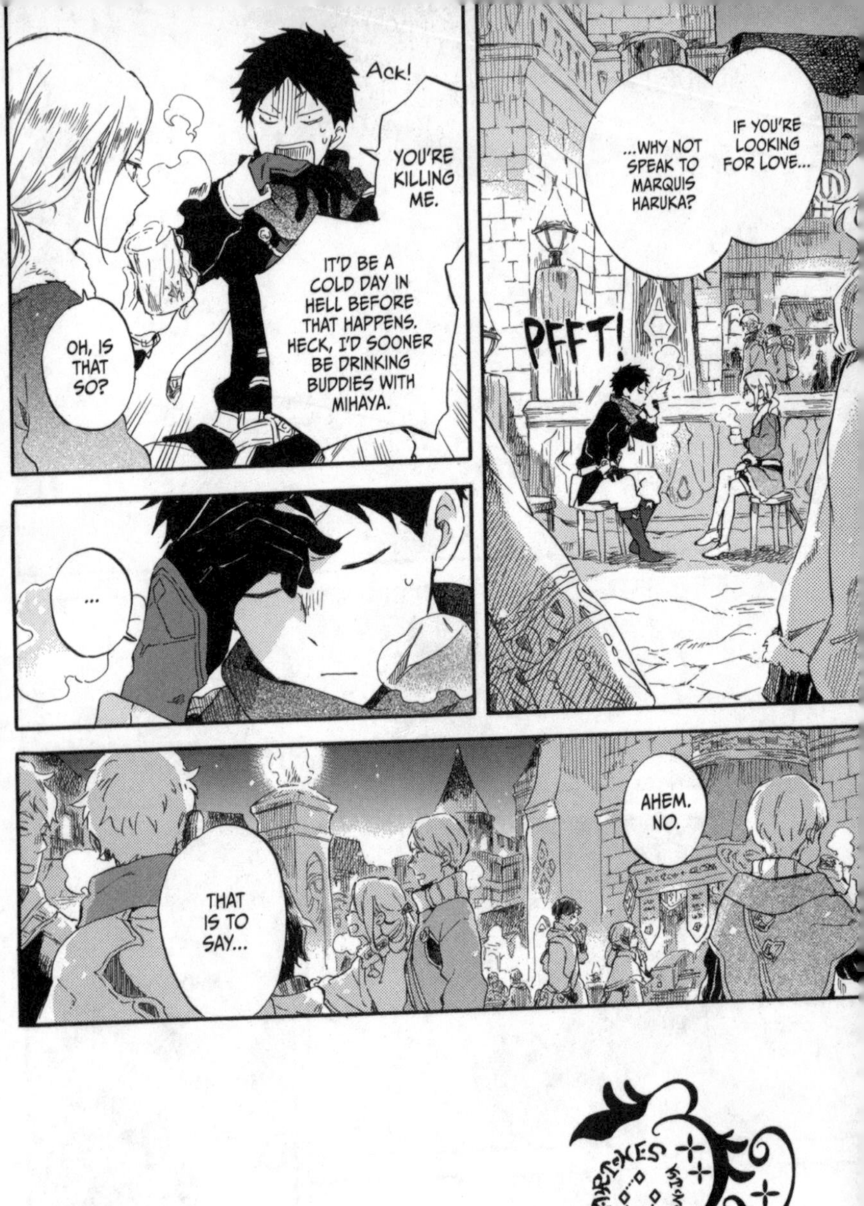
IF YOU'RE LOOKING FOR LOVE...
...WHY NOT SPEAK TO MARQUIS HARUKA?
PFFT!
Ack!
YOU'RE KILLING ME.
IT'D BE A COLD DAY IN HELL BEFORE THAT HAPPENS. HECK, I'D SOONER BE DRINKING BUDDIES WITH MIHAYA.
OH, IS THAT SO?
...
AHEM. NO.
THAT IS TO SAY...

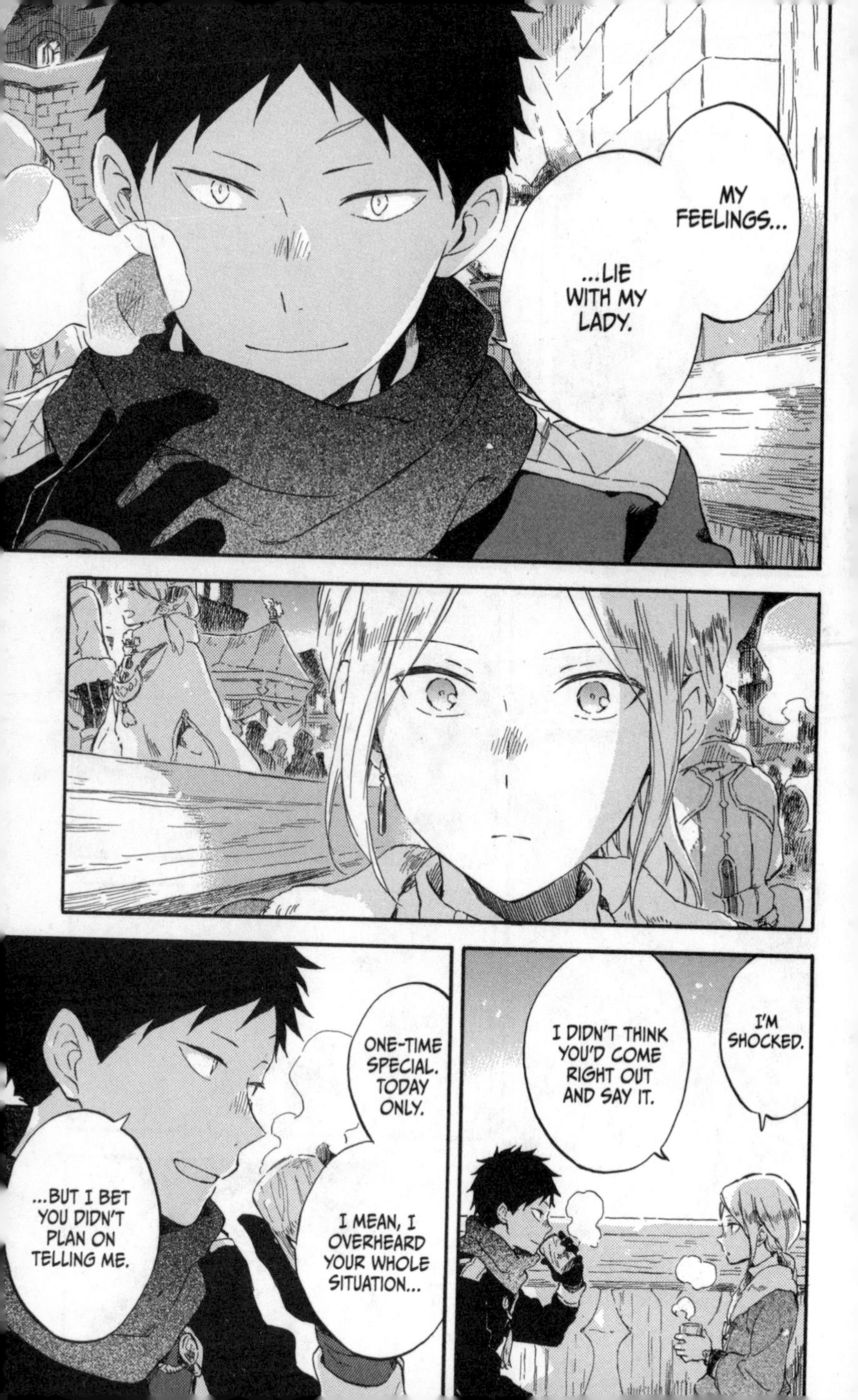
MY FEELINGS...
...LIE WITH MY LADY.
I'M SHOCKED.
I DIDN'T THINK YOU'D COME RIGHT OUT AND SAY IT.
ONE-TIME SPECIAL. TODAY ONLY.
I MEAN, I OVERHEARD YOUR WHOLE SITUATION...
...BUT I BET YOU DIDN'T PLAN ON TELLING ME.

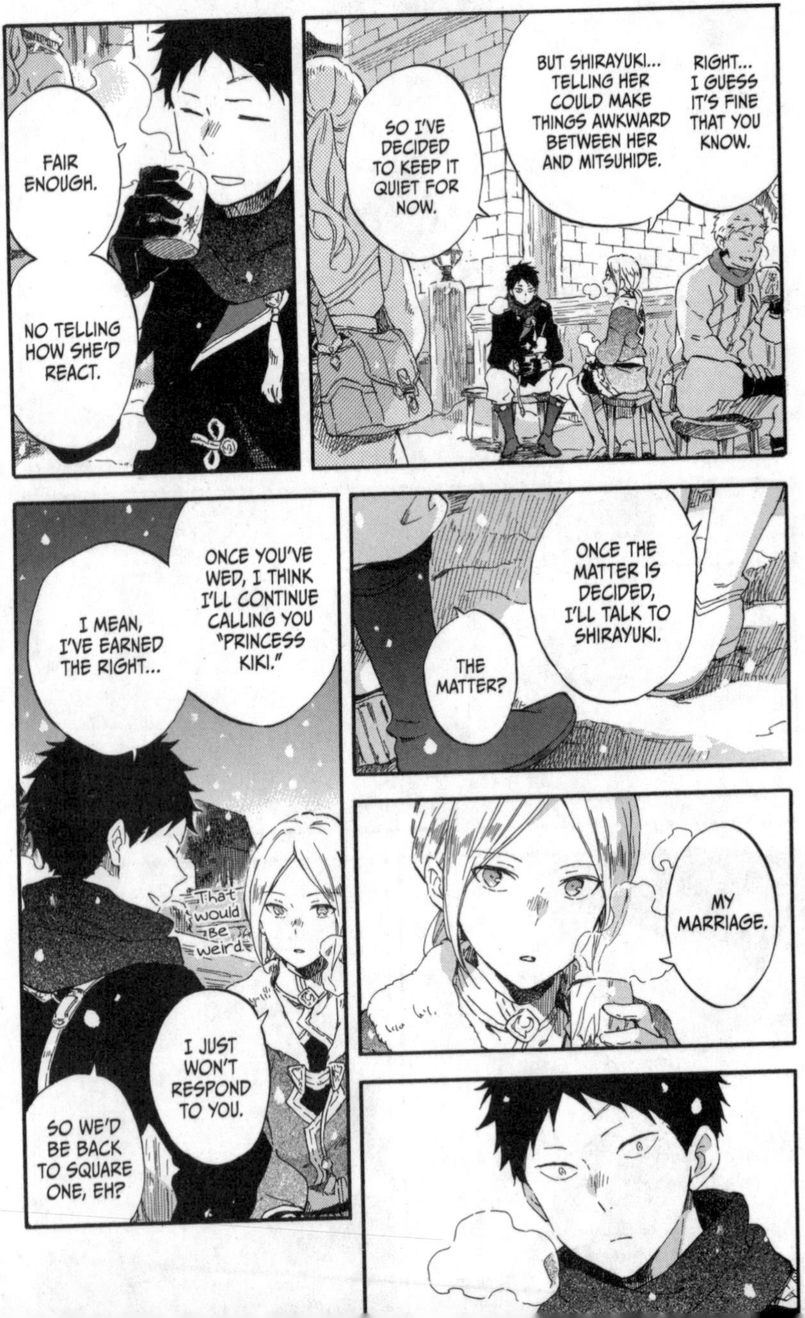
RIGHT... I GUESS IT'S FINE THAT YOU KNOW.
BUT SHIRAYUKI... TELLING HER COULD MAKE THINGS AWKWARD BETWEEN HER AND MITSUHIDE.
SO I'VE DECIDED TO KEEP IT QUIET FOR NOW.
FAIR ENOUGH.
NO TELLING HOW SHE'D REACT.
ONCE THE MATTER IS DECIDED, I'LL TALK TO SHIRAYUKI.
THE MATTER?
MY MARRIAGE.
ONCE YOU'VE WED, I THINK I'LL CONTINUE CALLING YOU "PRINCESS KIKI."
I MEAN, I'VE EARNED THE RIGHT...
That would be weird.
I JUST WON'T RESPOND TO YOU.
SO WE'D BE BACK TO SQUARE ONE, EH?

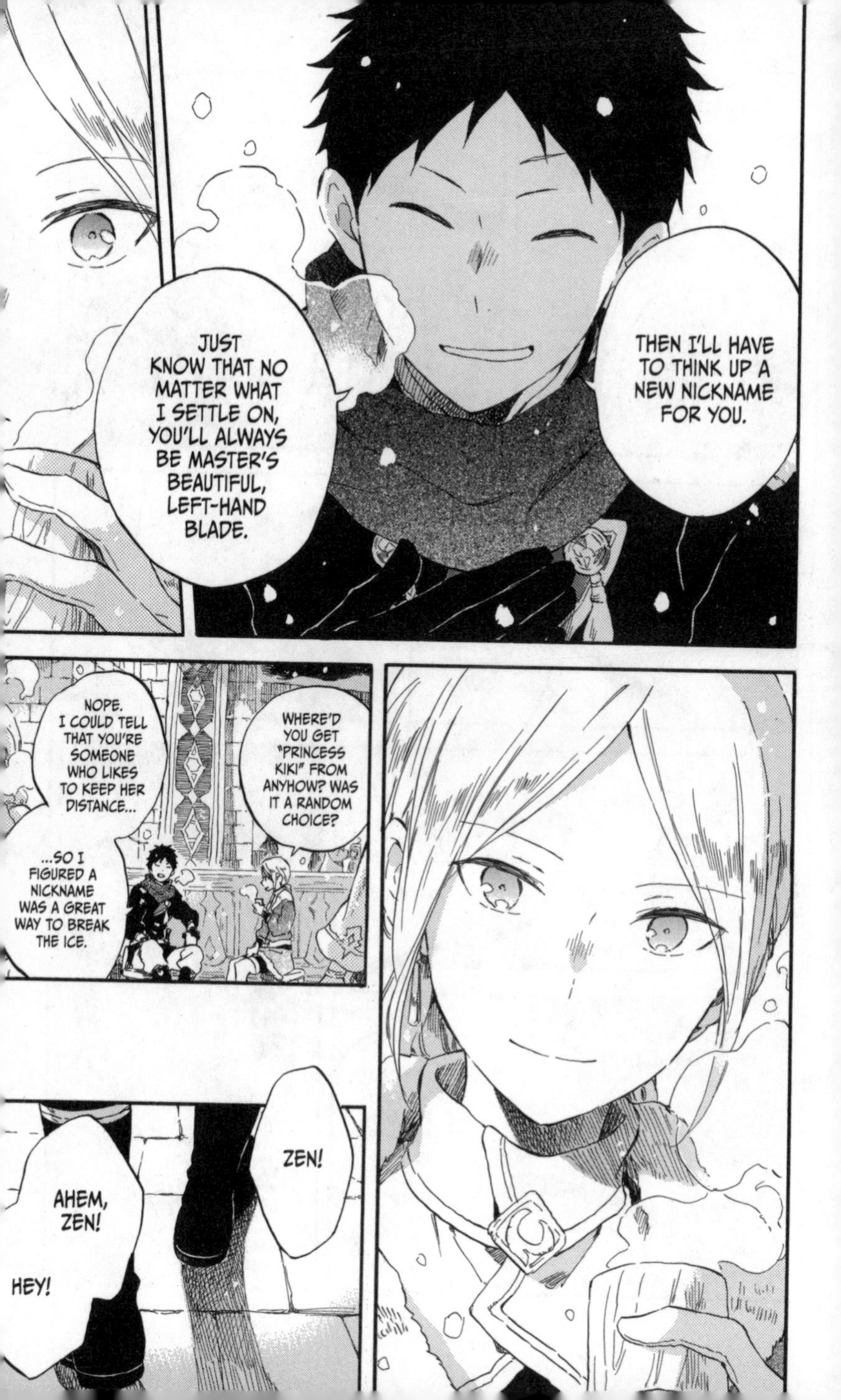
THEN I'LL HAVE TO THINK UP A NEW NICKNAME FOR YOU.
JUST KNOW THAT NO MATTER WHAT I SETTLE ON, YOU'LL ALWAYS BE MASTER'S BEAUTIFUL, LEFT-HAND BLADE.
WHERE'D YOU GET "PRINCESS KIKI" FROM ANYHOW? WAS IT A RANDOM CHOICE?
NOPE. I COULD TELL THAT YOU'RE SOMEONE WHO LIKES TO KEEP HER DISTANCE...
...SO I FIGURED A NICKNAME WAS A GREAT WAY TO BREAK THE ICE.
ZEN!
AHEM, ZEN!
HEY!

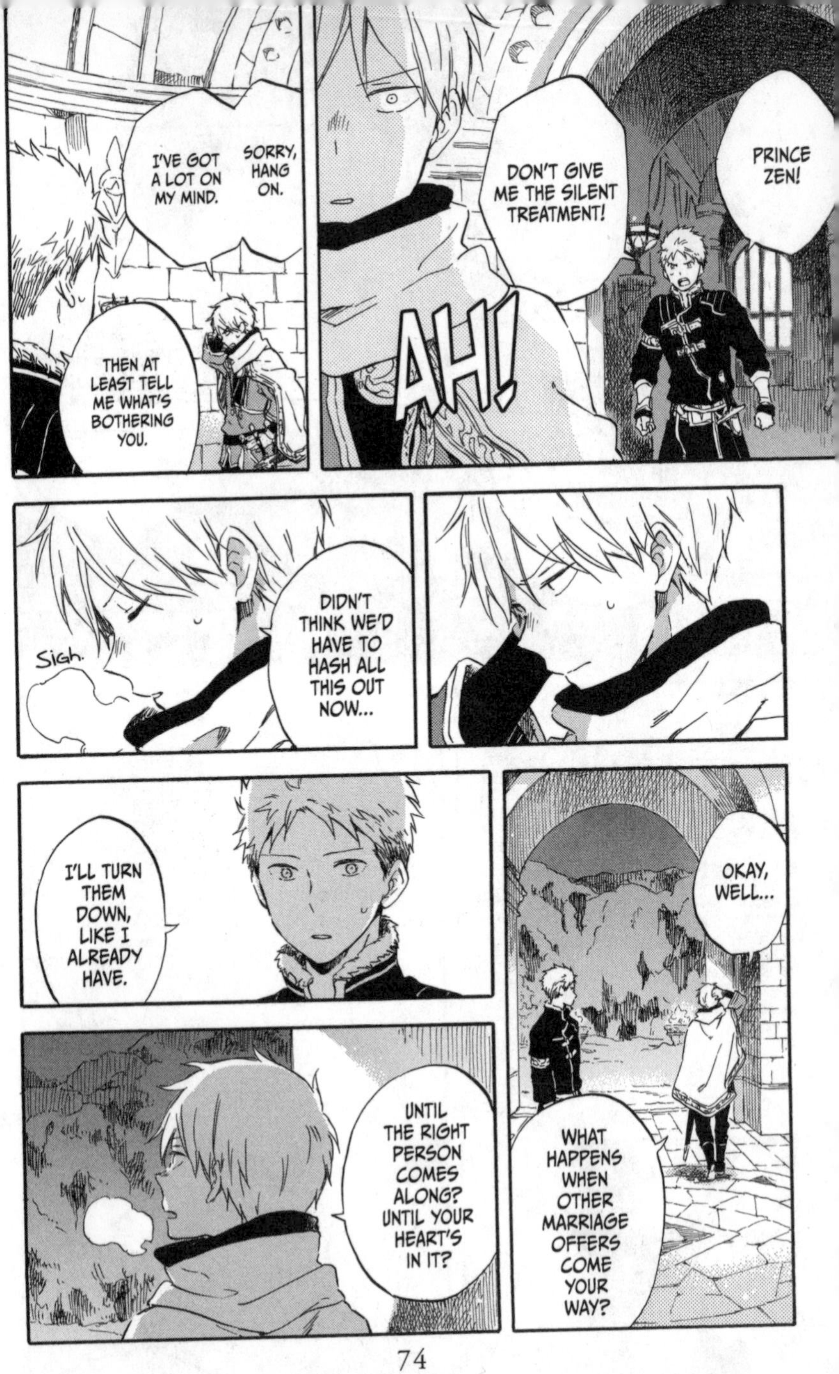
PRINCE ZEN!
DON'T GIVE ME THE SILENT TREATMENT!
AH!
SORRY, HANG ON.
I'VE GOT A LOT ON MY MIND.
THEN AT LEAST TELL ME WHAT'S BOTHERING YOU.
DIDN'T THINK WE'D HAVE TO HASH ALL THIS OUT NOW...
Sigh.
OKAY, WELL...
WHAT HAPPENS WHEN OTHER MARRIAGE OFFERS COME YOUR WAY?
I'LL TURN THEM DOWN, LIKE I ALREADY HAVE.
UNTIL THE RIGHT PERSON COMES ALONG? UNTIL YOUR HEART'S IN IT?

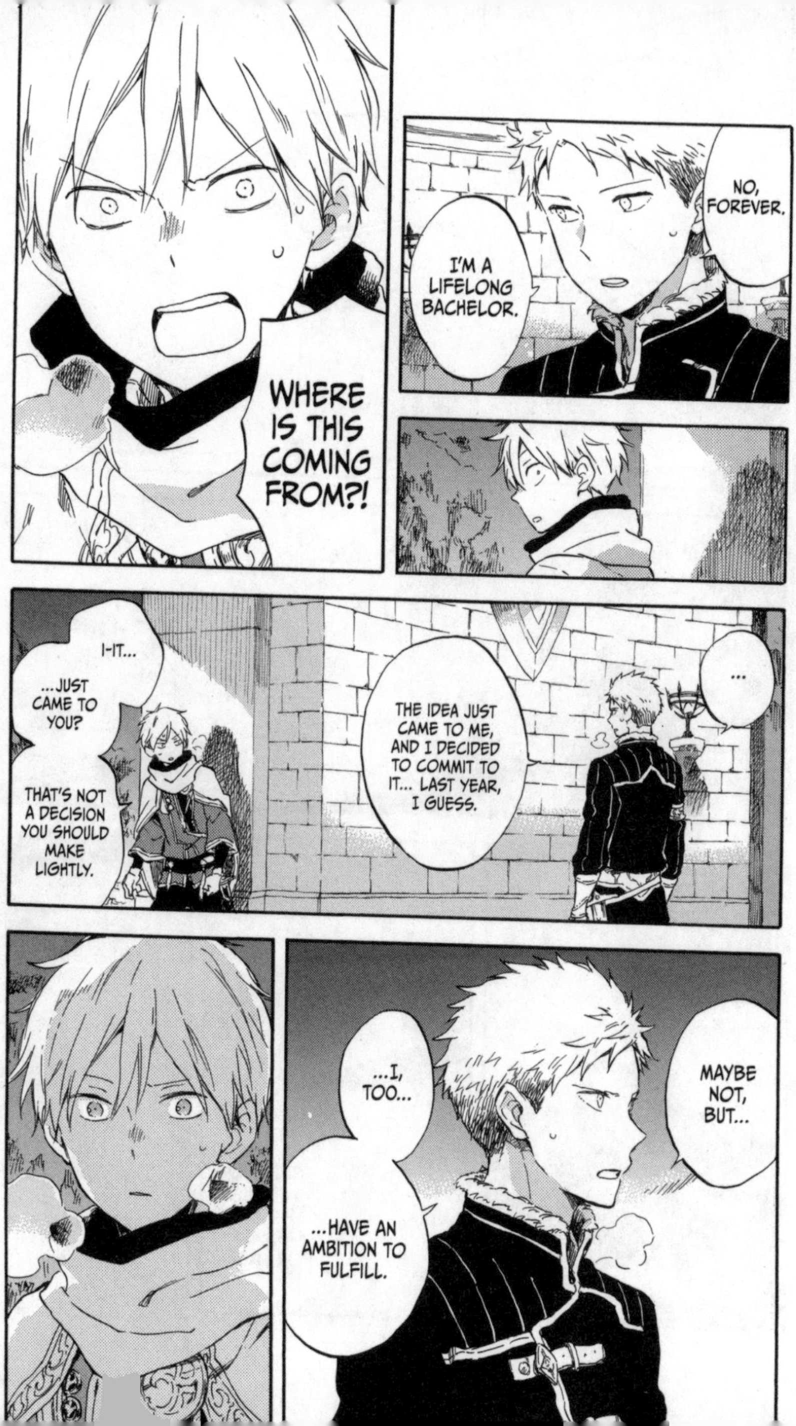
NO, FOREVER.
I'M A LIFELONG BACHELOR.
WHERE IS THIS COMING FROM?!
...
THE IDEA JUST CAME TO ME, AND I DECIDED TO COMMIT TO IT... LAST YEAR, I GUESS.
I-IT...
...JUST CAME TO YOU?
THAT'S NOT A DECISION YOU SHOULD MAKE LIGHTLY.
MAYBE NOT, BUT...
...I, TOO...
...HAVE AN AMBITION TO FULFILL.

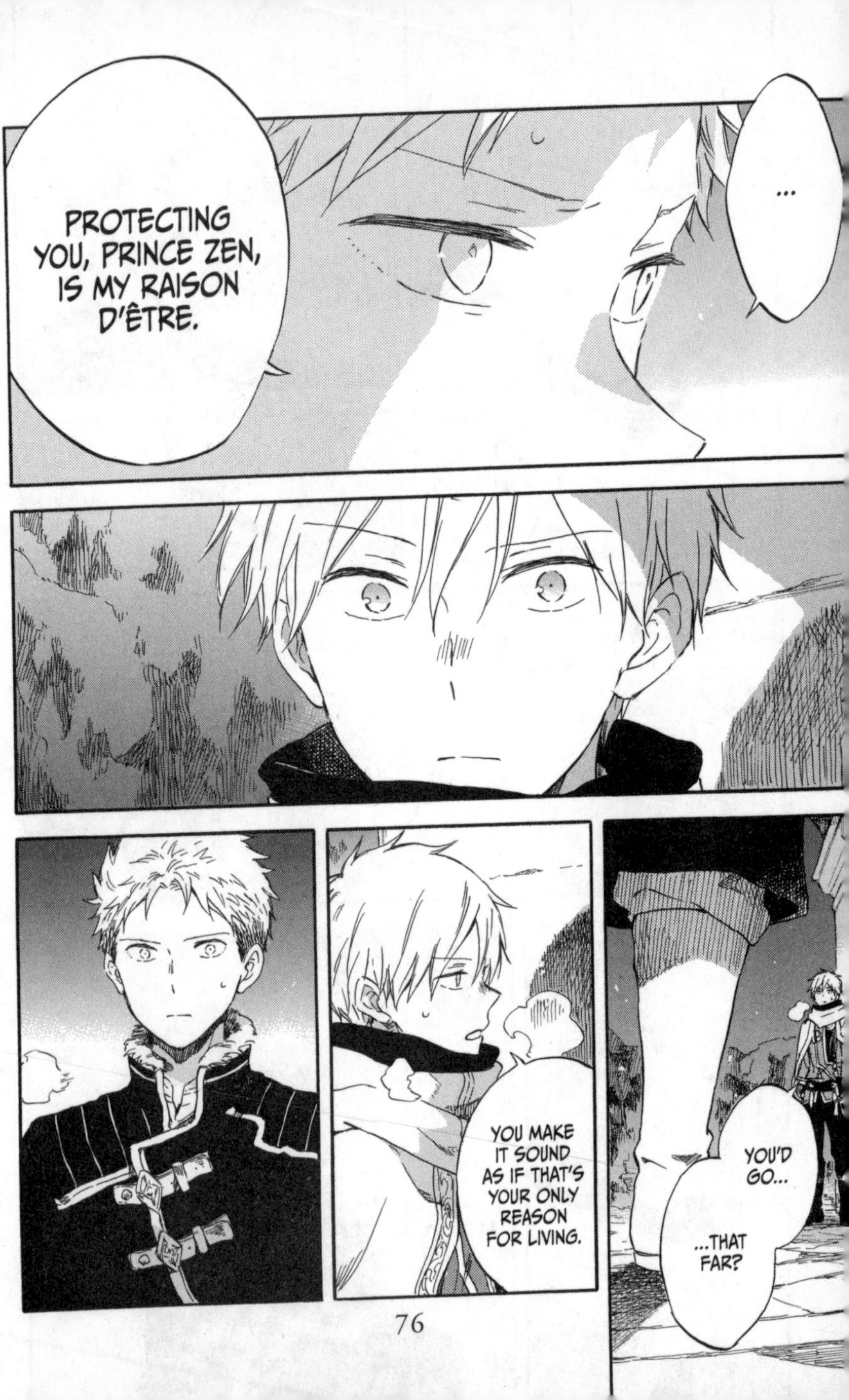
...
PROTECTING YOU, PRINCE ZEN, IS MY RAISON D'ÊTRE.
YOU'D GO...
...THAT FAR?
YOU MAKE IT SOUND AS IF THAT'S YOUR ONLY REASON FOR LIVING.

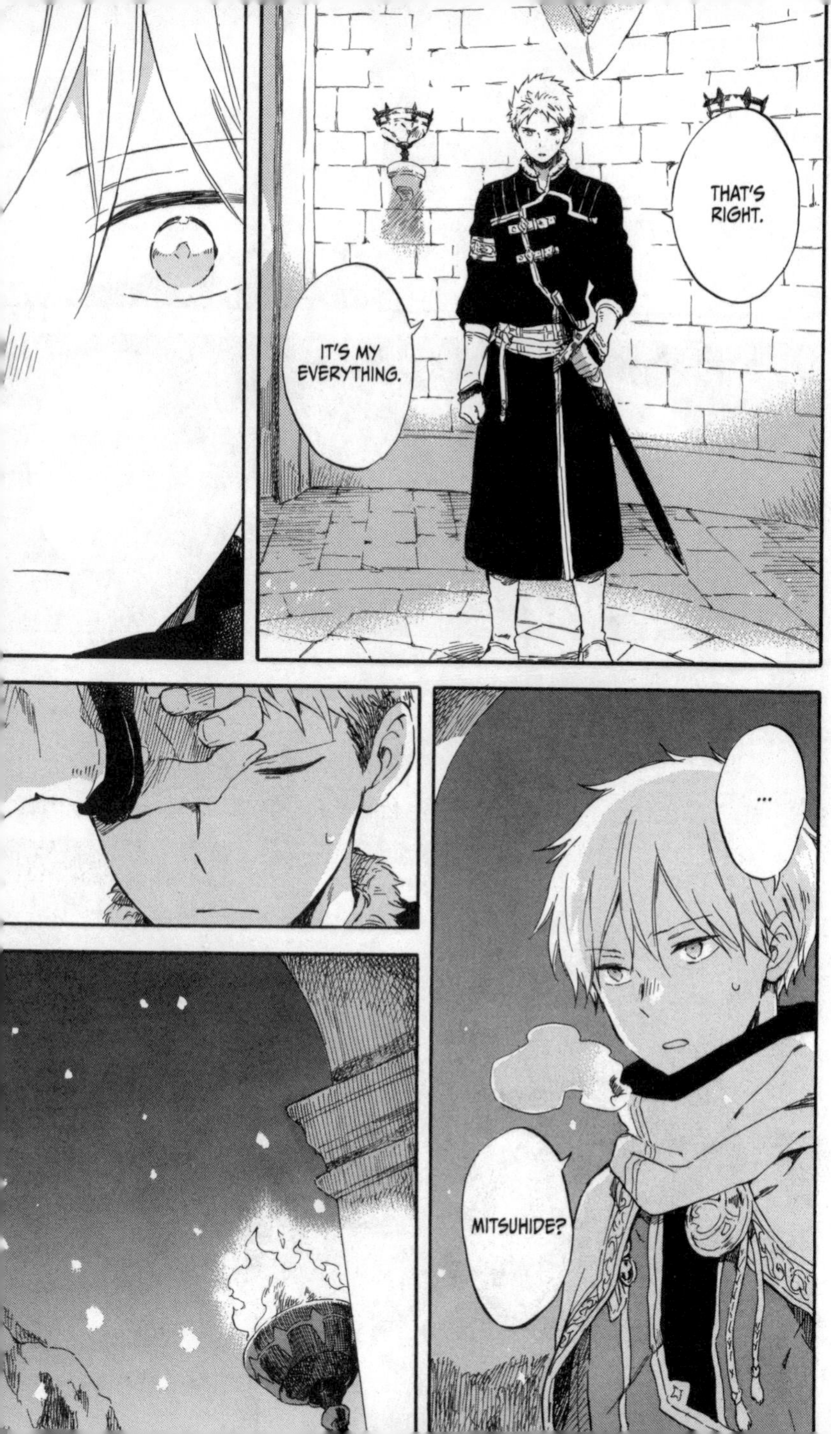
THAT'S RIGHT.
IT'S MY EVERYTHING.
...
MITSUHIDE?

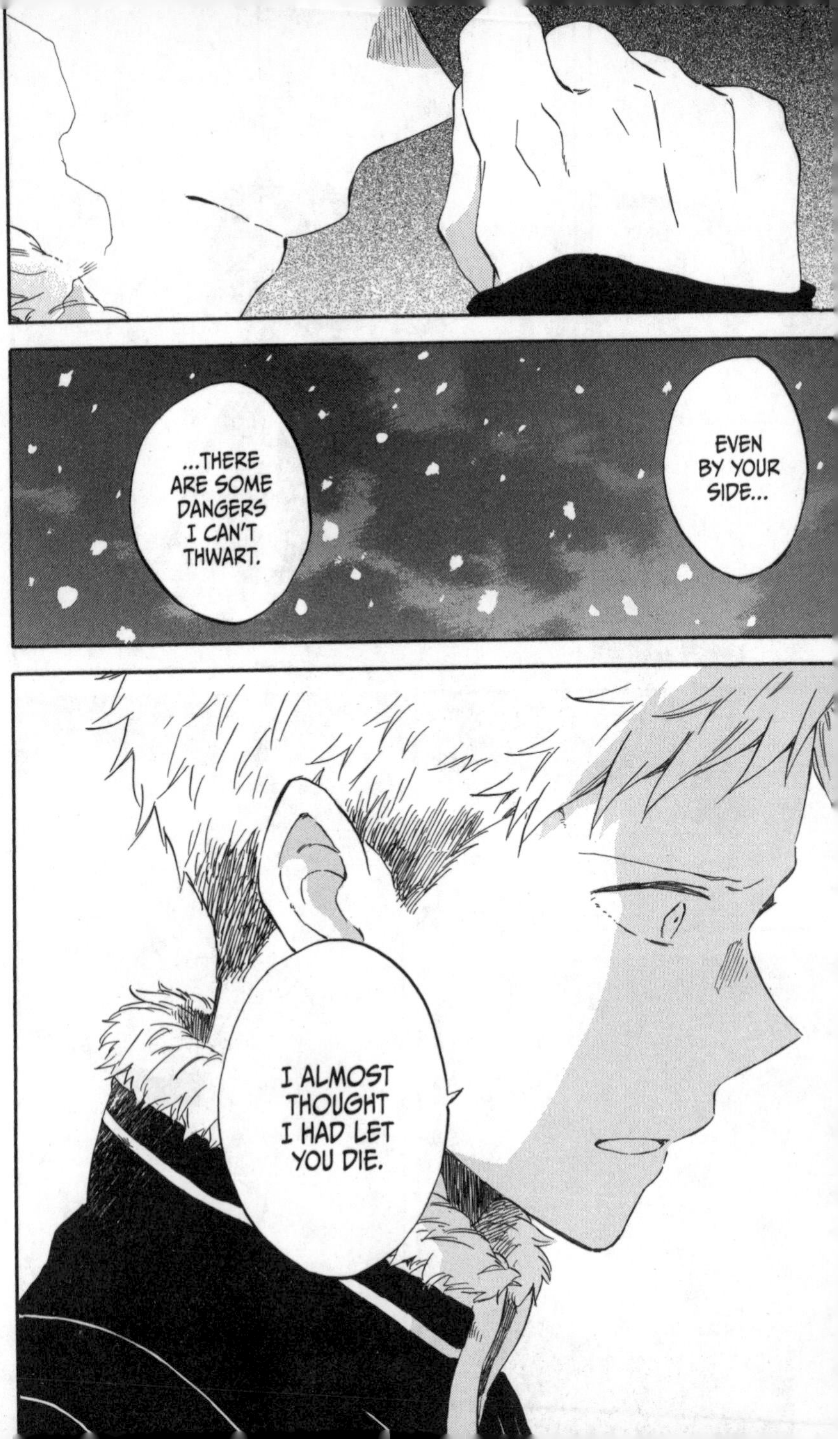
EVEN BY YOUR SIDE...
...THERE ARE SOME DANGERS I CAN'T THWART.
I ALMOST THOUGHT I HAD LET YOU DIE.

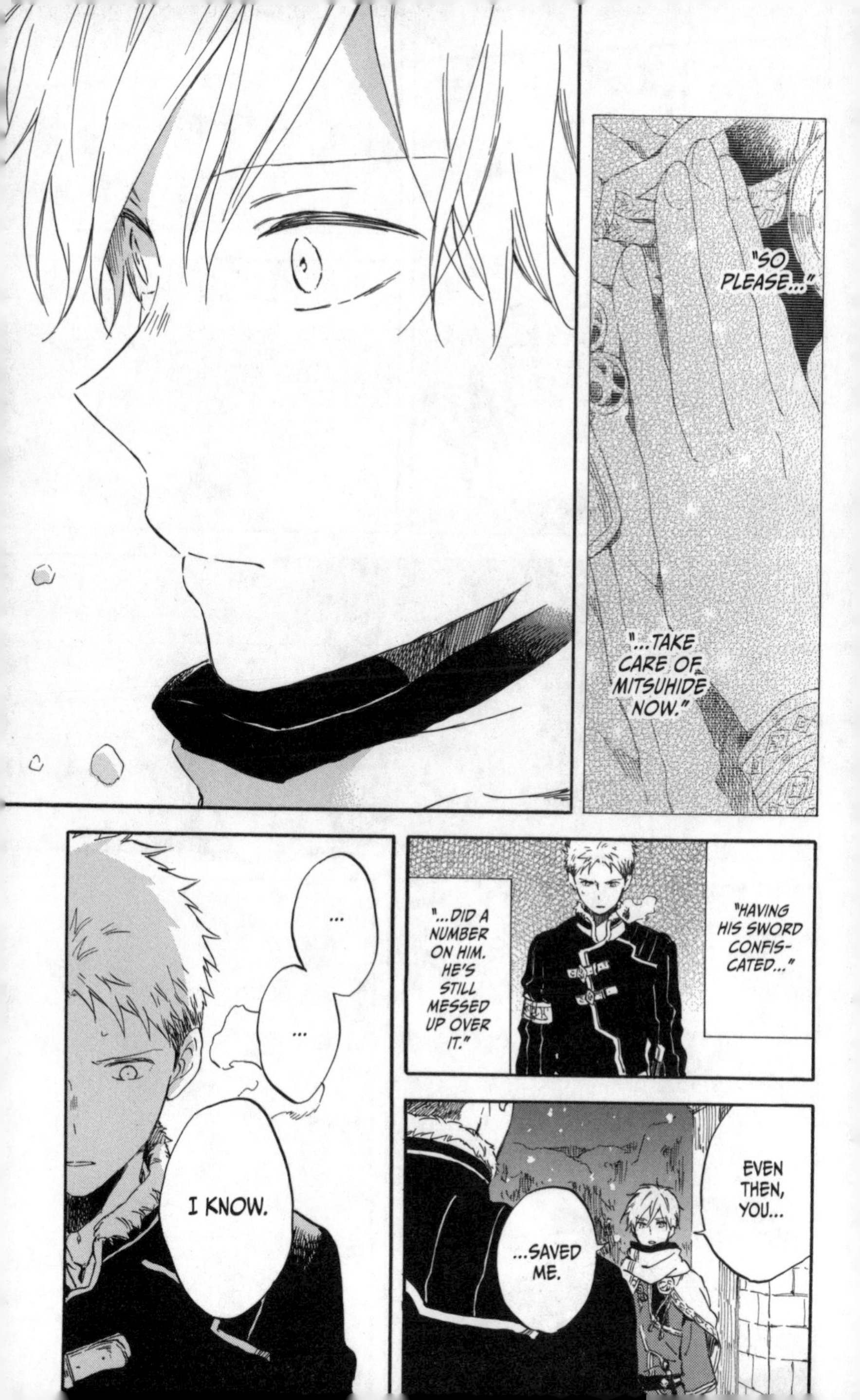
"SO PLEASE..."
"...TAKE CARE OF MITSUHIDE NOW."
"HAVING HIS SWORD CONFISCATED..."
"...DID A NUMBER ON HIM. HE'S STILL MESSED UP OVER IT."
EVEN THEN, YOU...
...SAVED ME.
...
...
I KNOW.

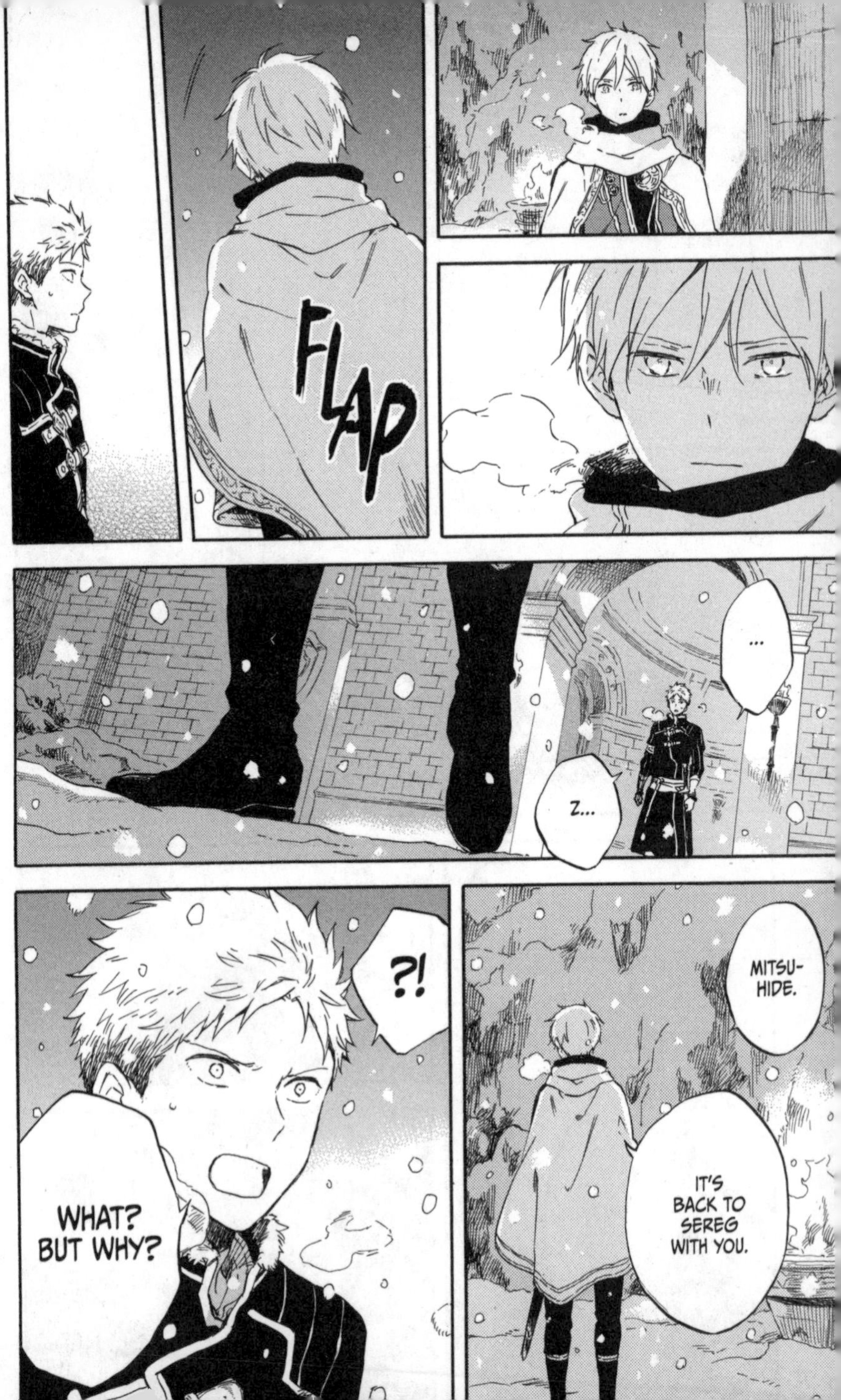
FLAP
...
Z...
MITSU-HIDE.
IT'S BACK TO SEREG WITH YOU.
?!
WHAT? BUT WHY?

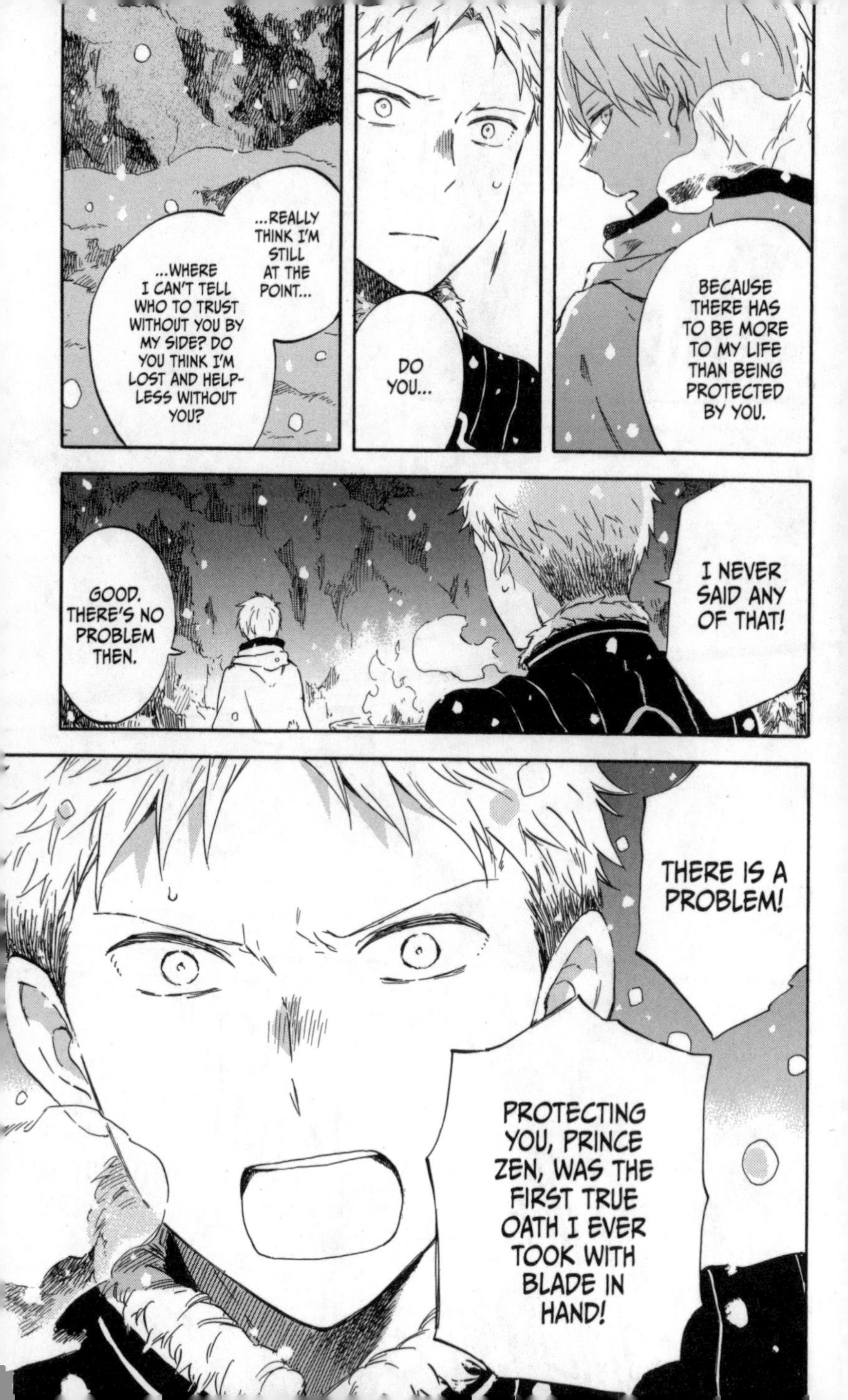
BECAUSE THERE HAS TO BE MORE TO MY LIFE THAN BEING PROTECTED BY YOU.
DO YOU...
...REALLY THINK I'M STILL AT THE POINT...
...WHERE I CAN'T TELL WHO TO TRUST WITHOUT YOU BY MY SIDE? DO YOU THINK I'M LOST AND HELP-LESS WITHOUT YOU?
I NEVER SAID ANY OF THAT!
GOOD. THERE'S NO PROBLEM THEN.
THERE IS A PROBLEM!
PROTECTING YOU, PRINCE ZEN, WAS THE FIRST TRUE OATH I EVER TOOK WITH BLADE IN HAND!

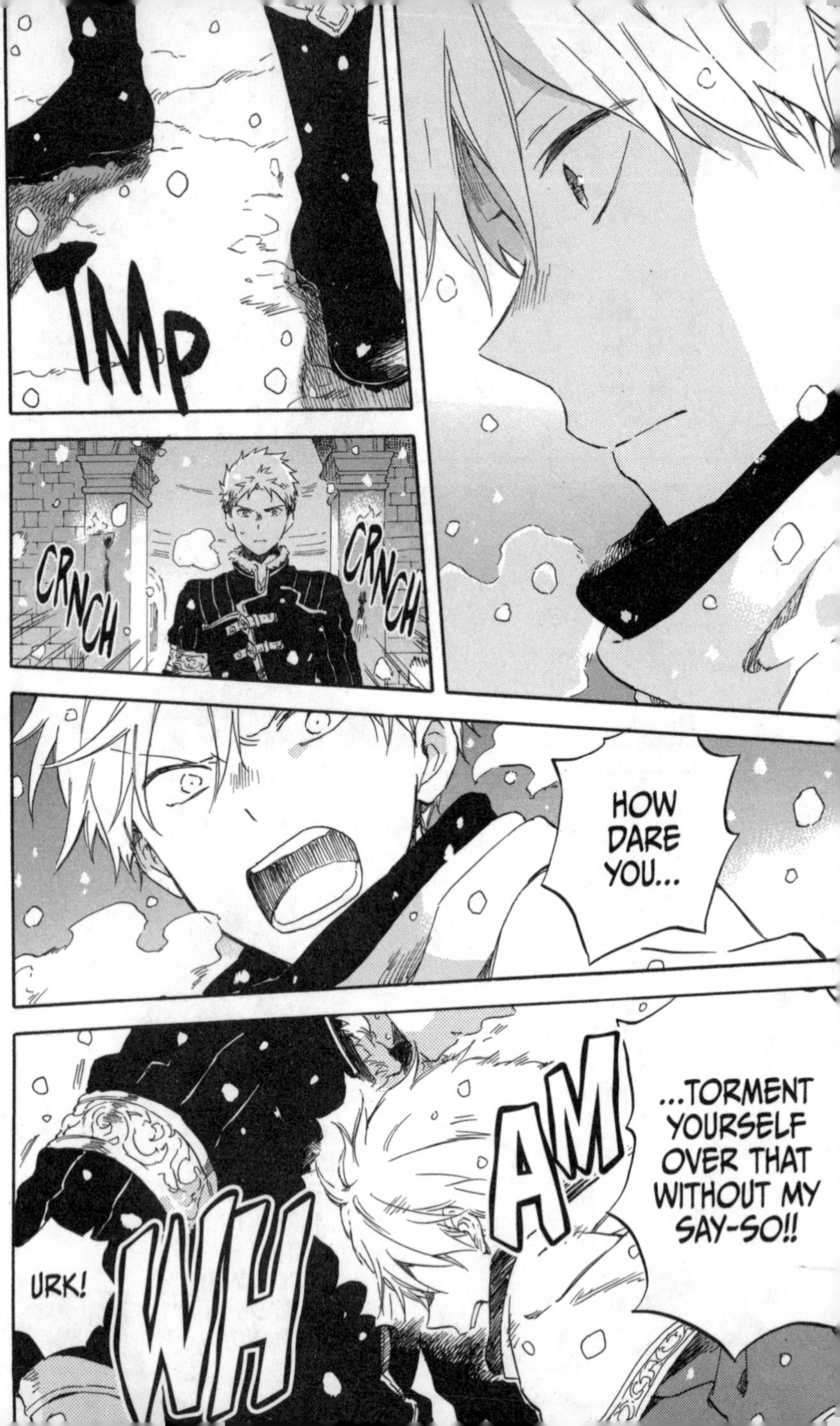
TMP
CRNCH
CRNCH
HOW DARE YOU...
...TORMENT YOURSELF OVER THAT WITHOUT MY SAY-SO!!
AM
WH
URK!

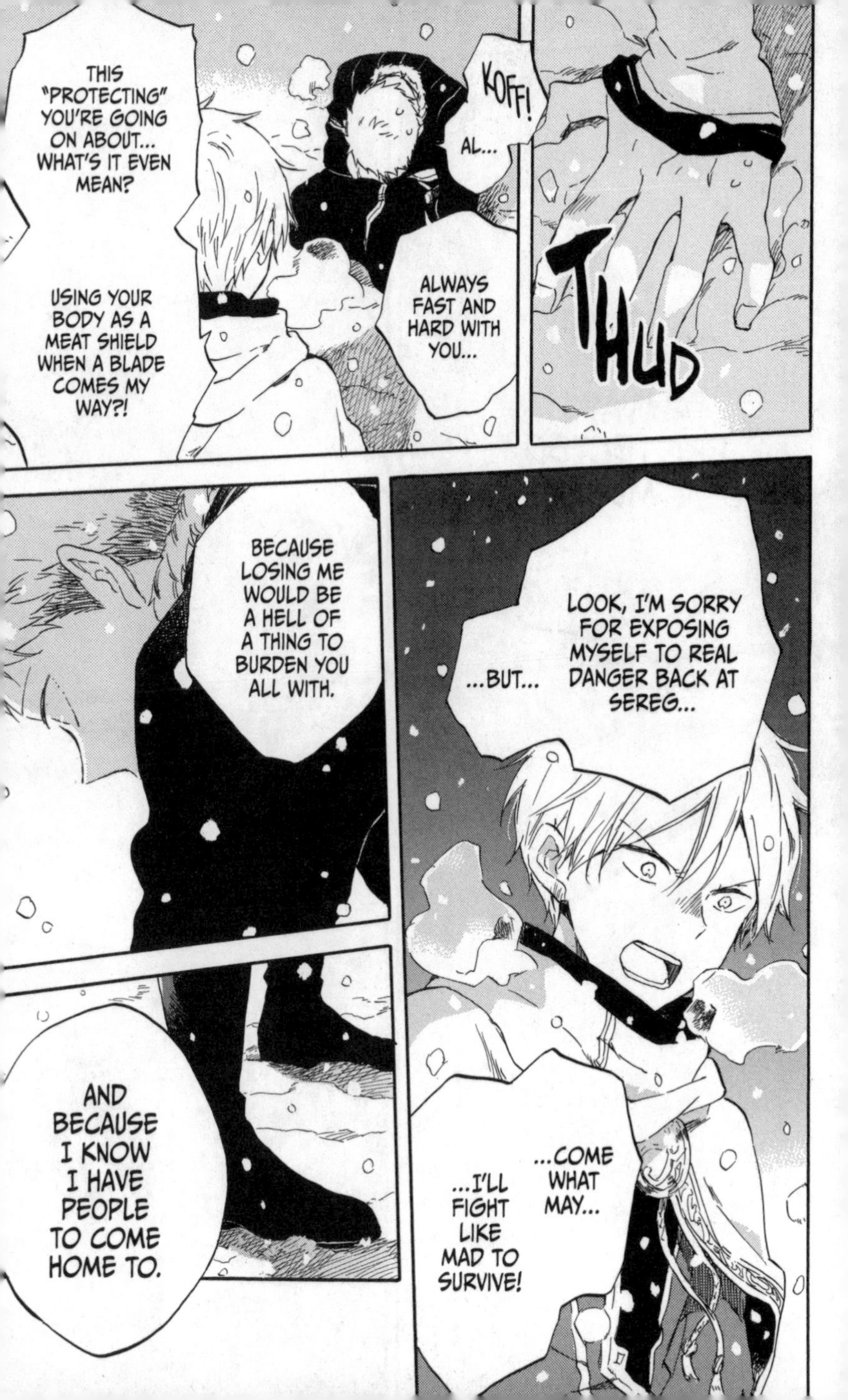
THUD
KOFF!
AL...
ALWAYS FAST AND HARD WITH YOU...
THIS "PROTECTING" YOU'RE GOING ON ABOUT... WHAT'S IT EVEN MEAN?
USING YOUR BODY AS A MEAT SHIELD WHEN A BLADE COMES MY WAY?!
LOOK, I'M SORRY FOR EXPOSING MYSELF TO REAL DANGER BACK AT SEREG...
...BUT...
...COME WHAT MAY...
...I'LL FIGHT LIKE MAD TO SURVIVE!
BECAUSE LOSING ME WOULD BE A HELL OF A THING TO BURDEN YOU ALL WITH.
AND BECAUSE I KNOW I HAVE PEOPLE TO COME HOME TO.

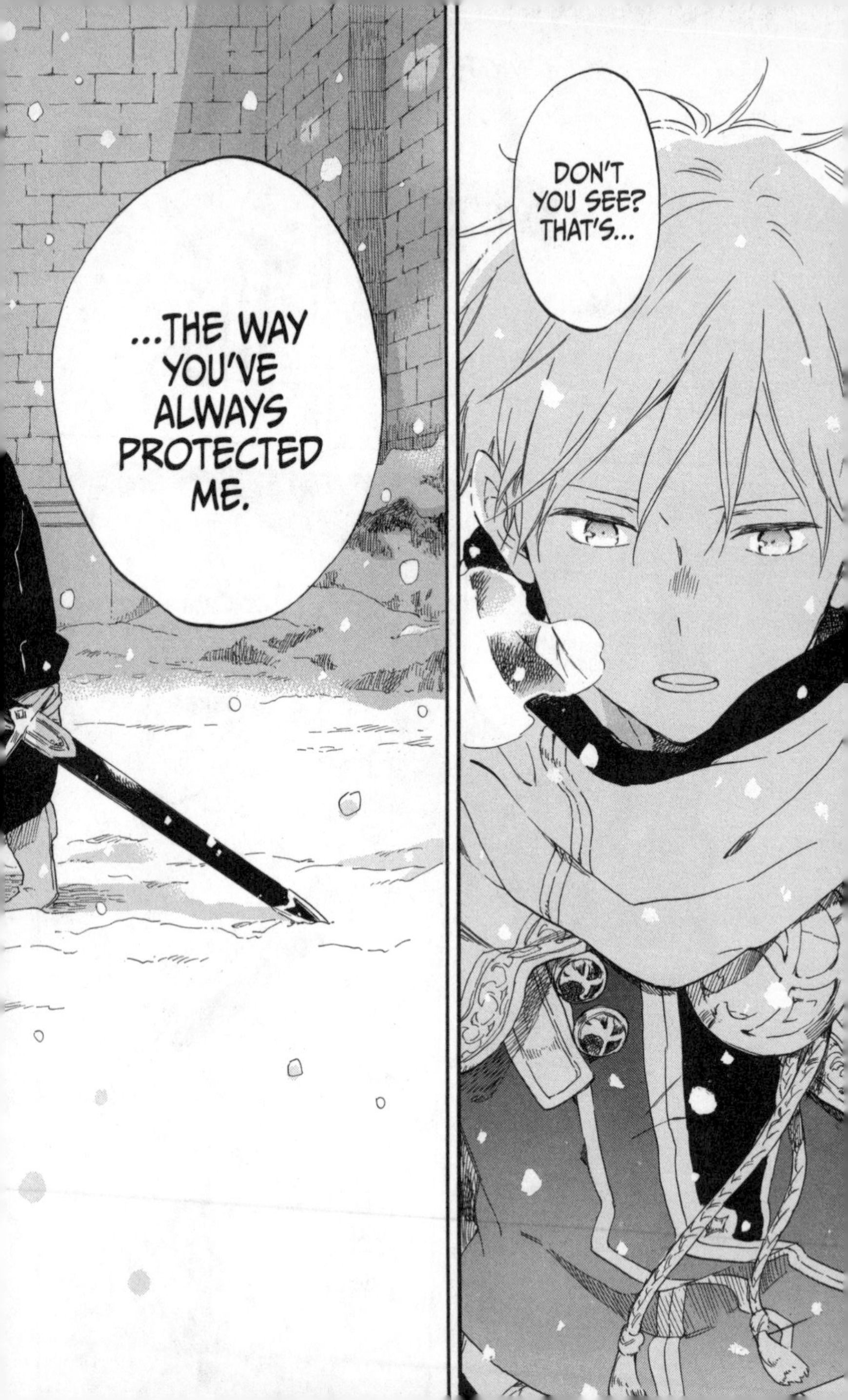
DON'T YOU SEE? THAT'S...
...THE WAY YOU'VE ALWAYS PROTECTED ME.

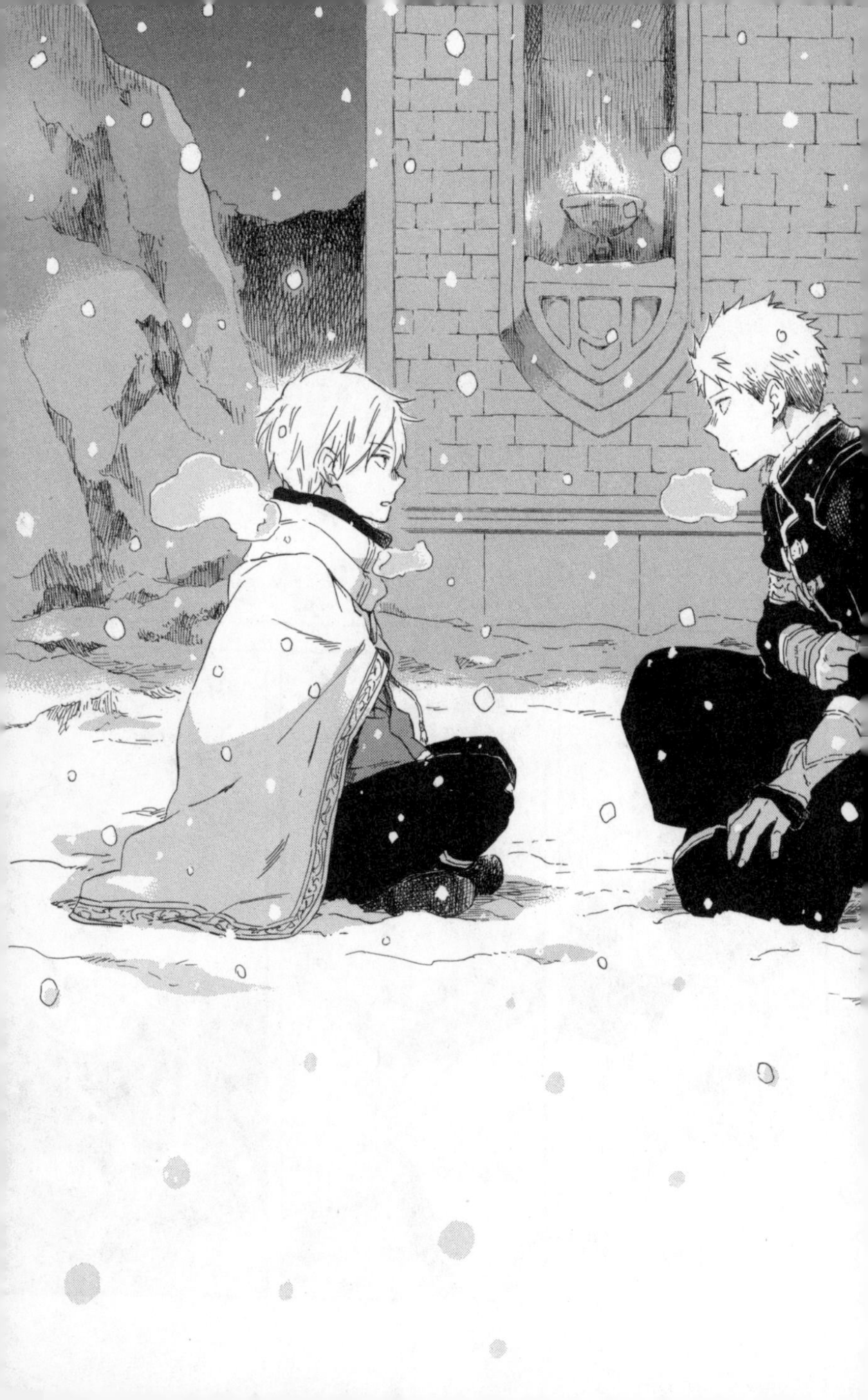

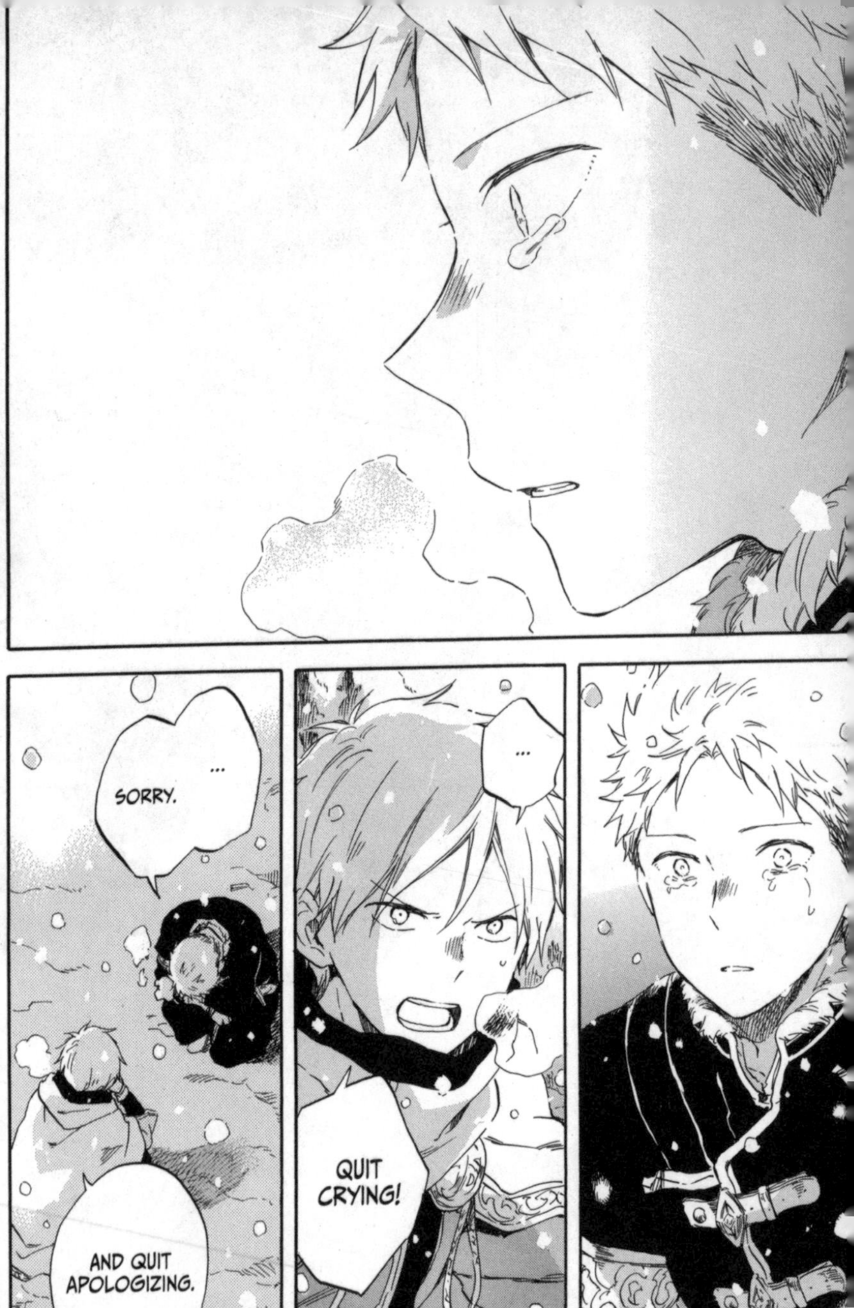
...
QUIT CRYING!
...
SORRY.
AND QUIT APOLOGIZING.

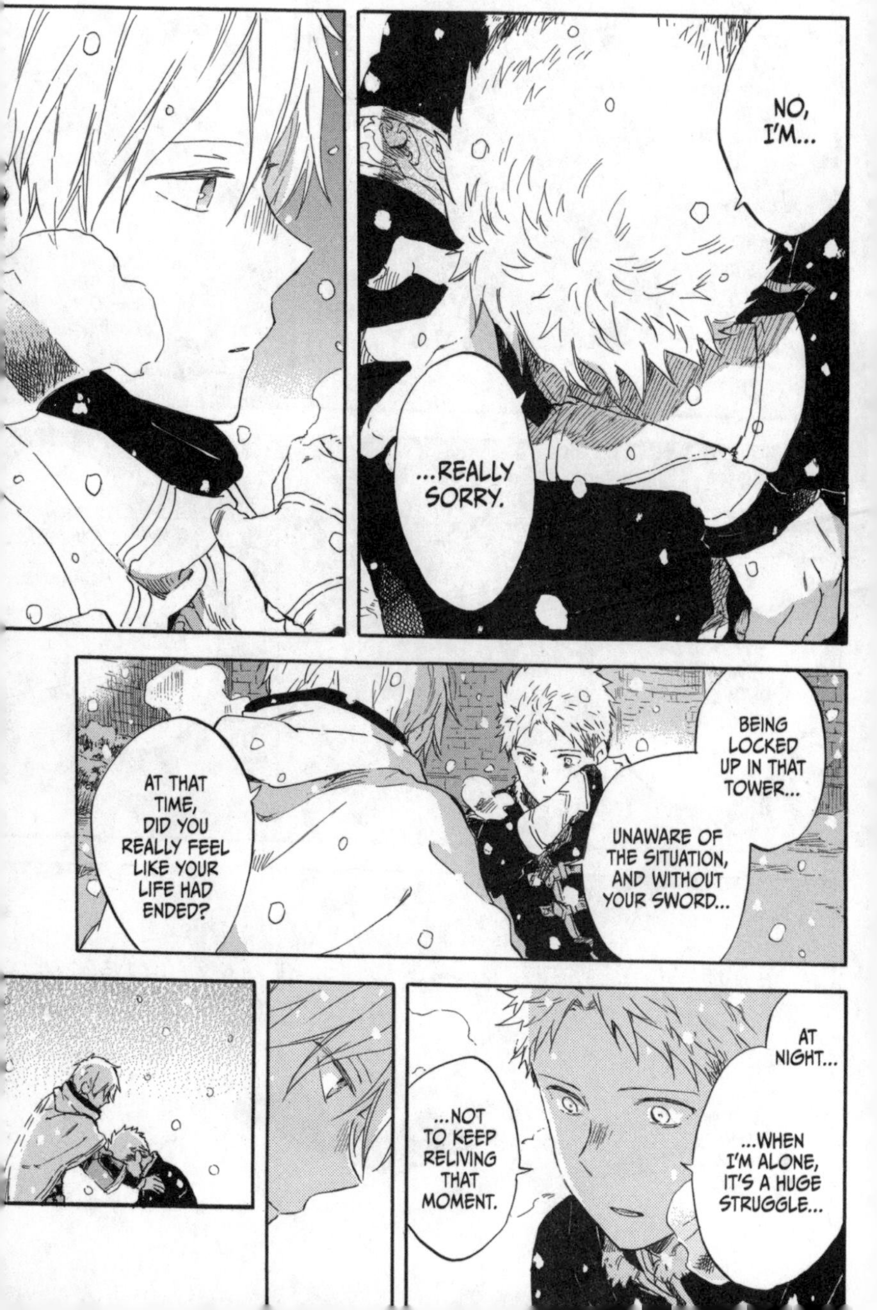
NO, I'M...
...REALLY SORRY.
BEING LOCKED UP IN THAT TOWER...
UNAWARE OF THE SITUATION, AND WITHOUT YOUR SWORD...
AT THAT TIME, DID YOU REALLY FEEL LIKE YOUR LIFE HAD ENDED?
AT NIGHT...
...WHEN I'M ALONE, IT'S A HUGE STRUGGLE...
...NOT TO KEEP RELIVING THAT MOMENT.

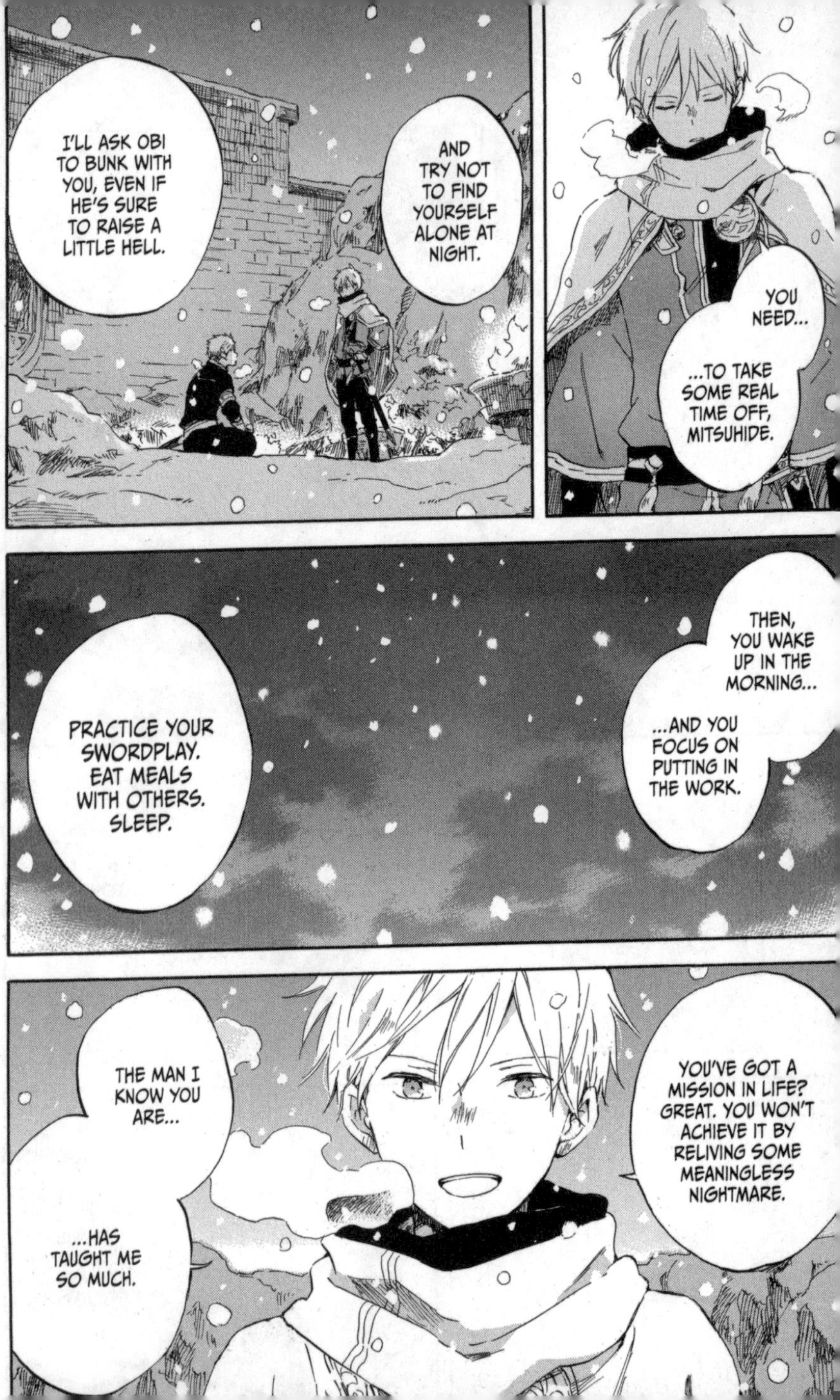
YOU NEED...
...TO TAKE SOME REAL TIME OFF, MITSUHIDE.
AND TRY NOT TO FIND YOURSELF ALONE AT NIGHT.
I'LL ASK OBI TO BUNK WITH YOU, EVEN IF HE'S SURE TO RAISE A LITTLE HELL.
THEN, YOU WAKE UP IN THE MORNING...
...AND YOU FOCUS ON PUTTING IN THE WORK.
PRACTICE YOUR SWORDPLAY. EAT MEALS WITH OTHERS. SLEEP.
YOU'VE GOT A MISSION IN LIFE? GREAT. YOU WON'T ACHIEVE IT BY RELIVING SOME MEANINGLESS NIGHTMARE.
THE MAN I KNOW YOU ARE...
...HAS TAUGHT ME SO MUCH.

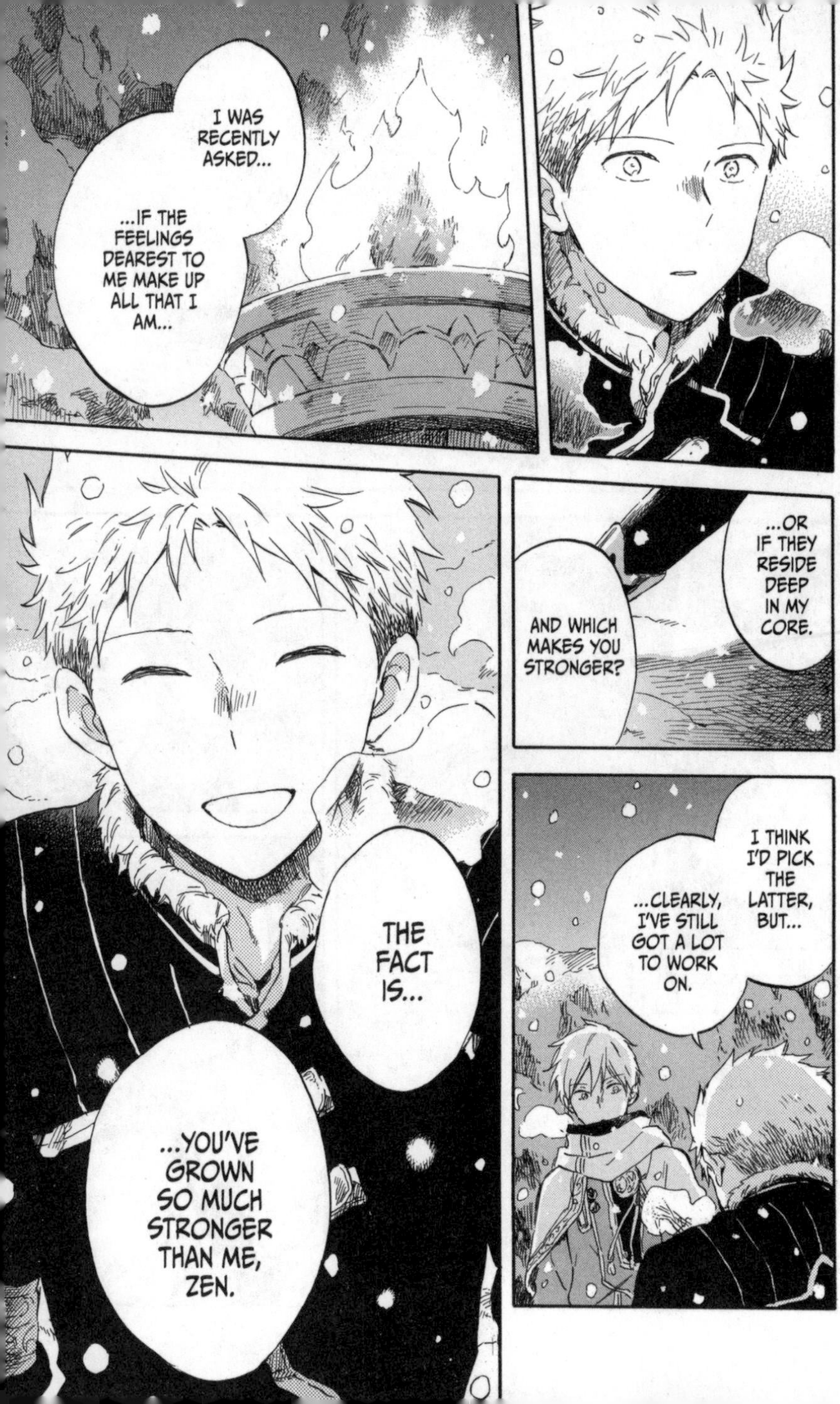
I WAS RECENTLY ASKED...
...IF THE FEELINGS DEAREST TO ME MAKE UP ALL THAT I AM...
...OR IF THEY RESIDE DEEP IN MY CORE.
AND WHICH MAKES YOU STRONGER?
I THINK I'D PICK THE LATTER, BUT...
...CLEARLY, I'VE STILL GOT A LOT TO WORK ON.
THE FACT IS...
...YOU'VE GROWN SO MUCH STRONGER THAN ME, ZEN.

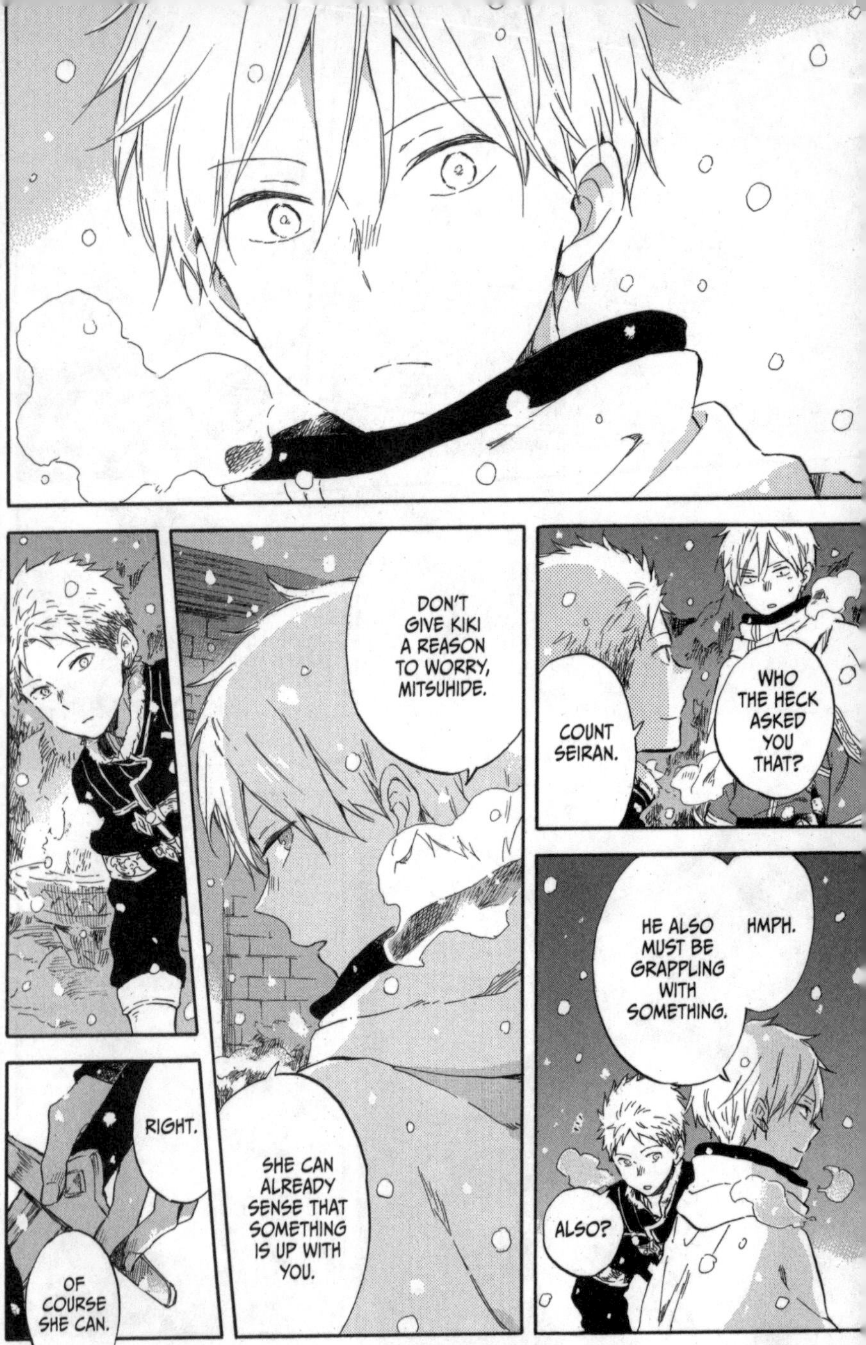
WHO THE HECK ASKED YOU THAT?
COUNT SEIRAN.
HMPH.
HE ALSO MUST BE GRAPPLING WITH SOMETHING.
ALSO?
DON'T GIVE KIKI A REASON TO WORRY, MITSUHIDE.
SHE CAN ALREADY SENSE THAT SOMETHING IS UP WITH YOU.
RIGHT.
OF COURSE SHE CAN.

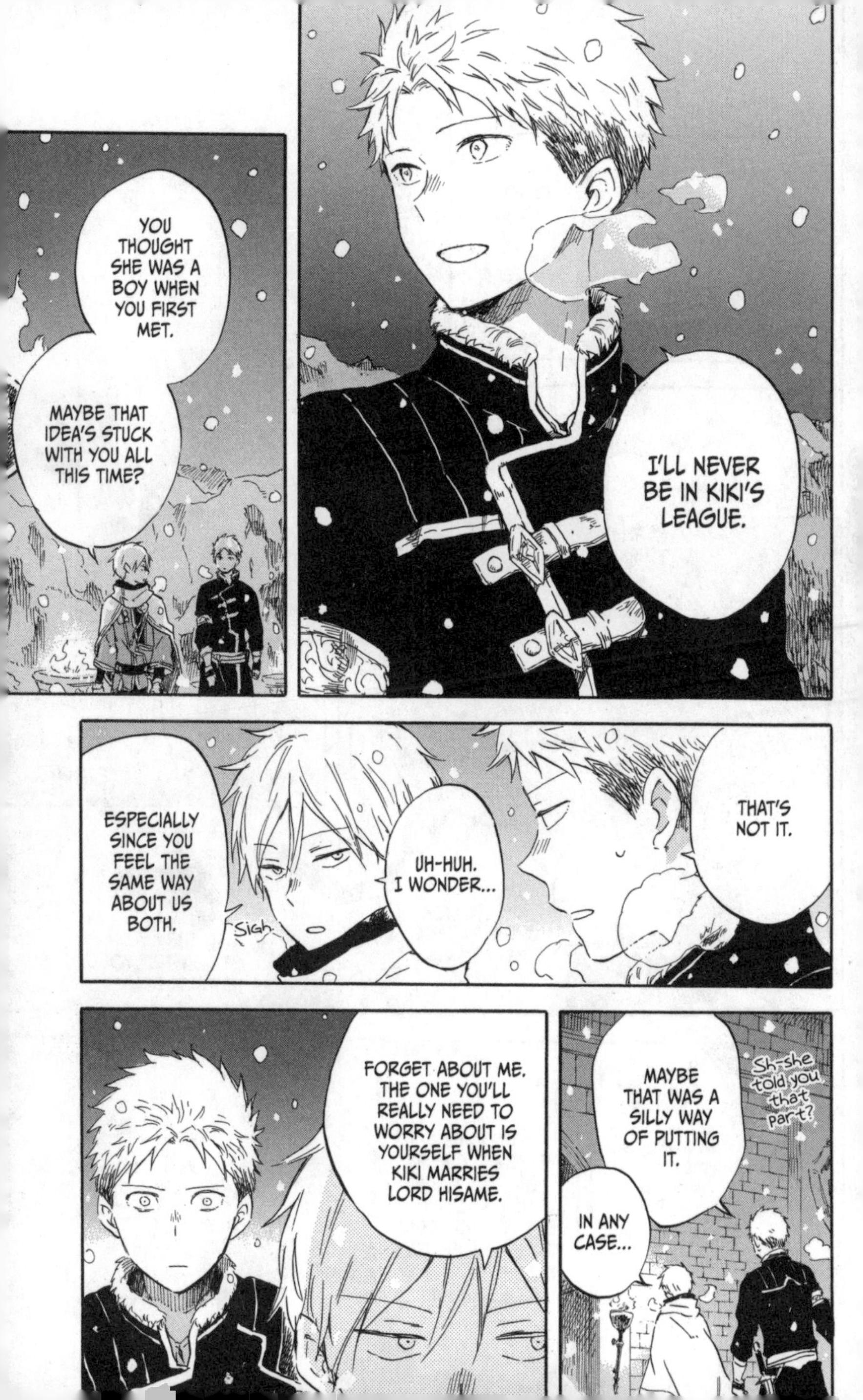
I'LL NEVER BE IN KIKI'S LEAGUE.
YOU THOUGHT SHE WAS A BOY WHEN YOU FIRST MET.
MAYBE THAT IDEA'S STUCK WITH YOU ALL THIS TIME?
THAT'S NOT IT.
UH-HUH. I WONDER...
Sigh
ESPECIALLY SINCE YOU FEEL THE SAME WAY ABOUT US BOTH.
Sh-she told you that part?
MAYBE THAT WAS A SILLY WAY OF PUTTING IT.
IN ANY CASE...
FORGET ABOUT ME. THE ONE YOU'LL REALLY NEED TO WORRY ABOUT IS YOURSELF WHEN KIKI MARRIES LORD HISAME.

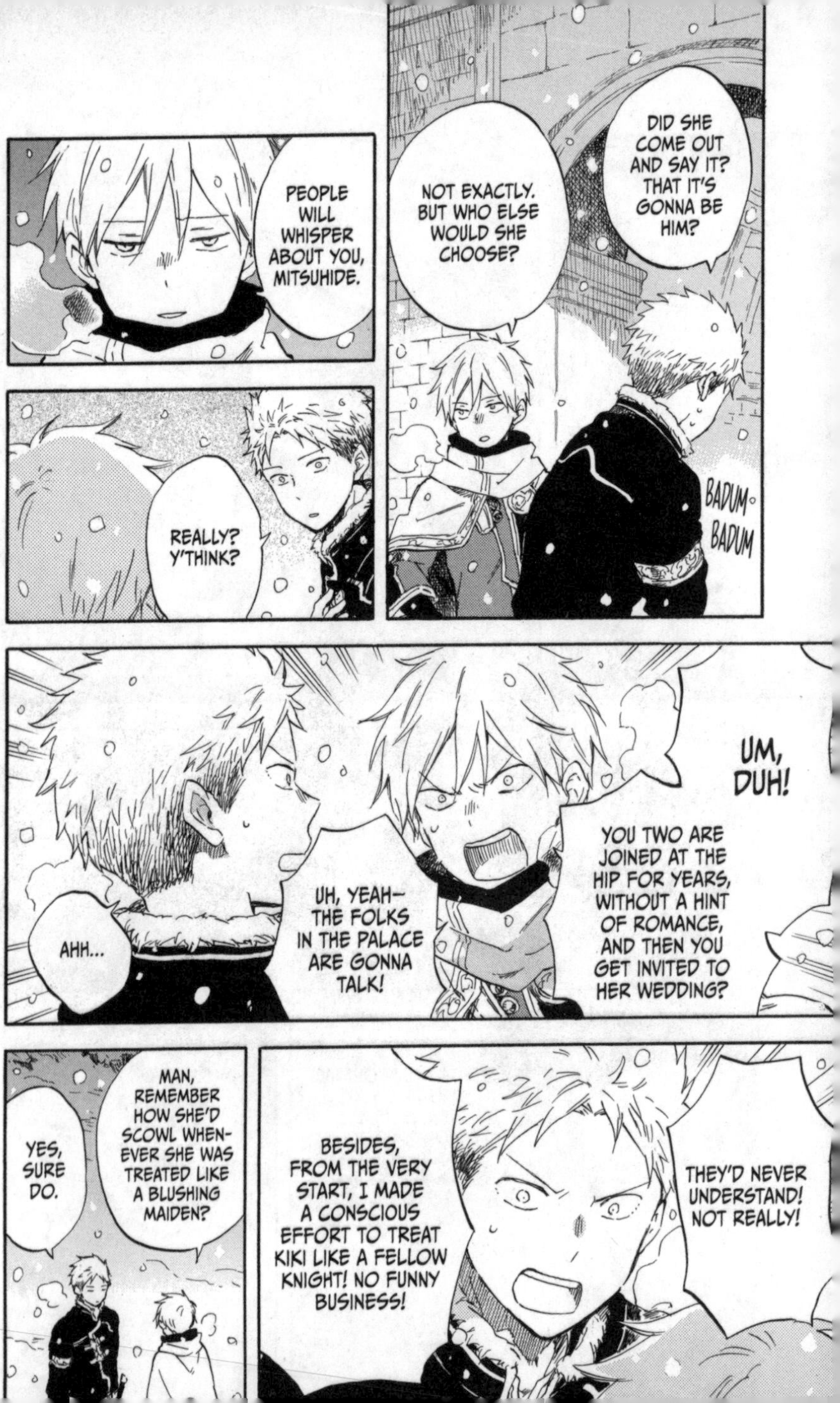

DID SHE COME OUT AND SAY IT? THAT IT'S GONNA BE HIM?
NOT EXACTLY. BUT WHO ELSE WOULD SHE CHOOSE?
BADUM BADUM
PEOPLE WILL WHISPER ABOUT YOU, MITSUHIDE.
REALLY? Y'THINK?
UM, DUH!
YOU TWO ARE JOINED AT THE HIP FOR YEARS, WITHOUT A HINT OF ROMANCE, AND THEN YOU GET INVITED TO HER WEDDING?
UH, YEAH— THE FOLKS IN THE PALACE ARE GONNA TALK!
AHH...
THEY'D NEVER UNDERSTAND! NOT REALLY!
BESIDES, FROM THE VERY START, I MADE A CONSCIOUS EFFORT TO TREAT KIKI LIKE A FELLOW KNIGHT! NO FUNNY BUSINESS!
MAN, REMEMBER HOW SHE'D SCOWL WHEN-EVER SHE WAS TREATED LIKE A BLUSHING MAIDEN?
YES, SURE DO.

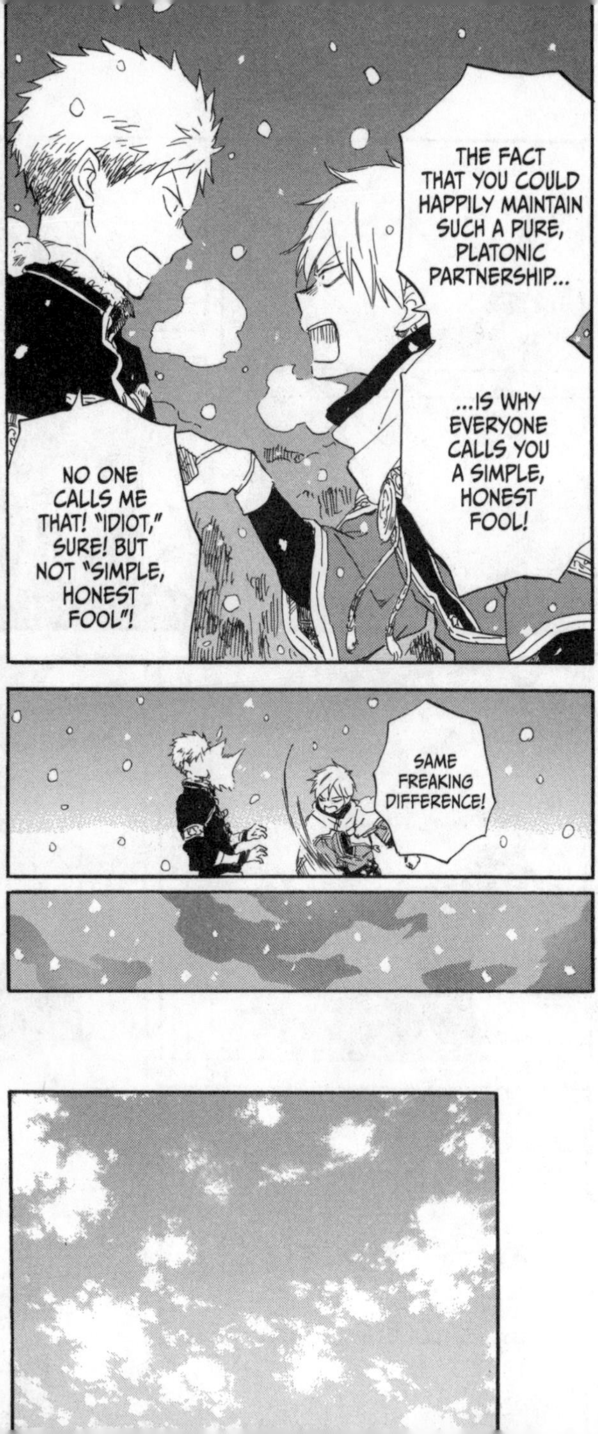
THE FACT THAT YOU COULD HAPPILY MAINTAIN SUCH A PURE, PLATONIC PARTNERSHIP...
...IS WHY EVERYONE CALLS YOU A SIMPLE, HONEST FOOL!
NO ONE CALLS ME THAT! "IDIOT," SURE! BUT NOT "SIMPLE, HONEST FOOL"!
SAME FREAKING DIFFERENCE!

3

TRIP DIARY, PART 2

Lost

We got lost on the way to the supermarket, which gave us an unexpected chance to see some of the city. That's when we came to realize that there's an unspoken rule that cars have to stop when a pedestrian clearly wants to cross the street. Imagine that! Or you could wait for the crossing signal. There was one lady on a motorcycle who even did her own countdown when a pedestrian wanted to cross.

"Go, go, go! Five, four, three, two, one!" Some people waved and flashed smiles as a way of saying thank you. What a lively city!

We slept like logs that night.

~Day 3~

Breakfast at the hotel... was yummy! The grilled tomatoes... Delish!

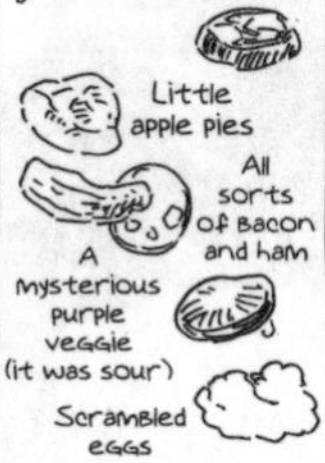
Little apple pies
All sorts of bacon and ham
A mysterious purple veggie (it was sour)
Scrambled eggs

There was an egg station where the on-duty chef would make your eggs however you liked, but given my lack of English-speaking ability, I...never worked up the courage to order from there.

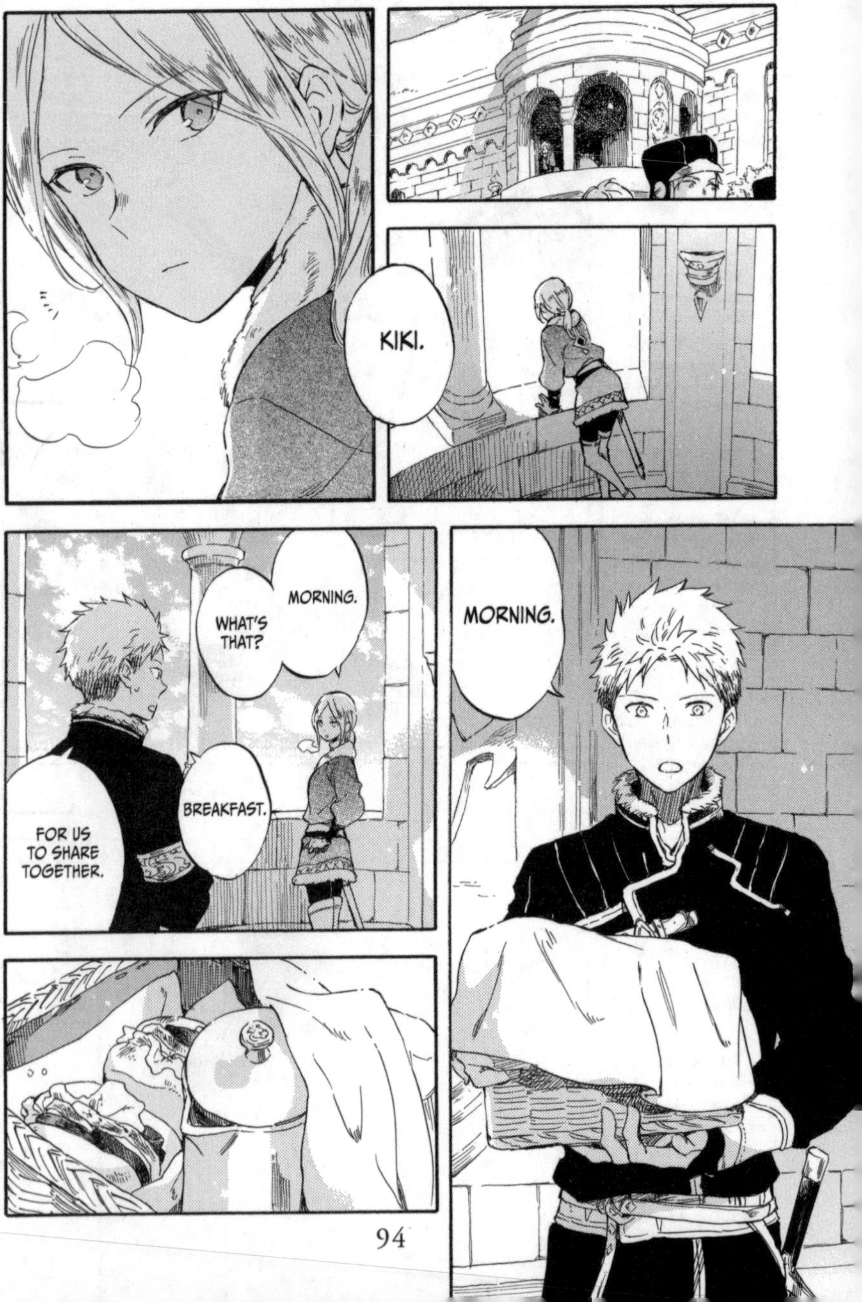
KIKI.
MORNING.
MORNING.
WHAT'S THAT?
BREAKFAST.
FOR US TO SHARE TOGETHER.

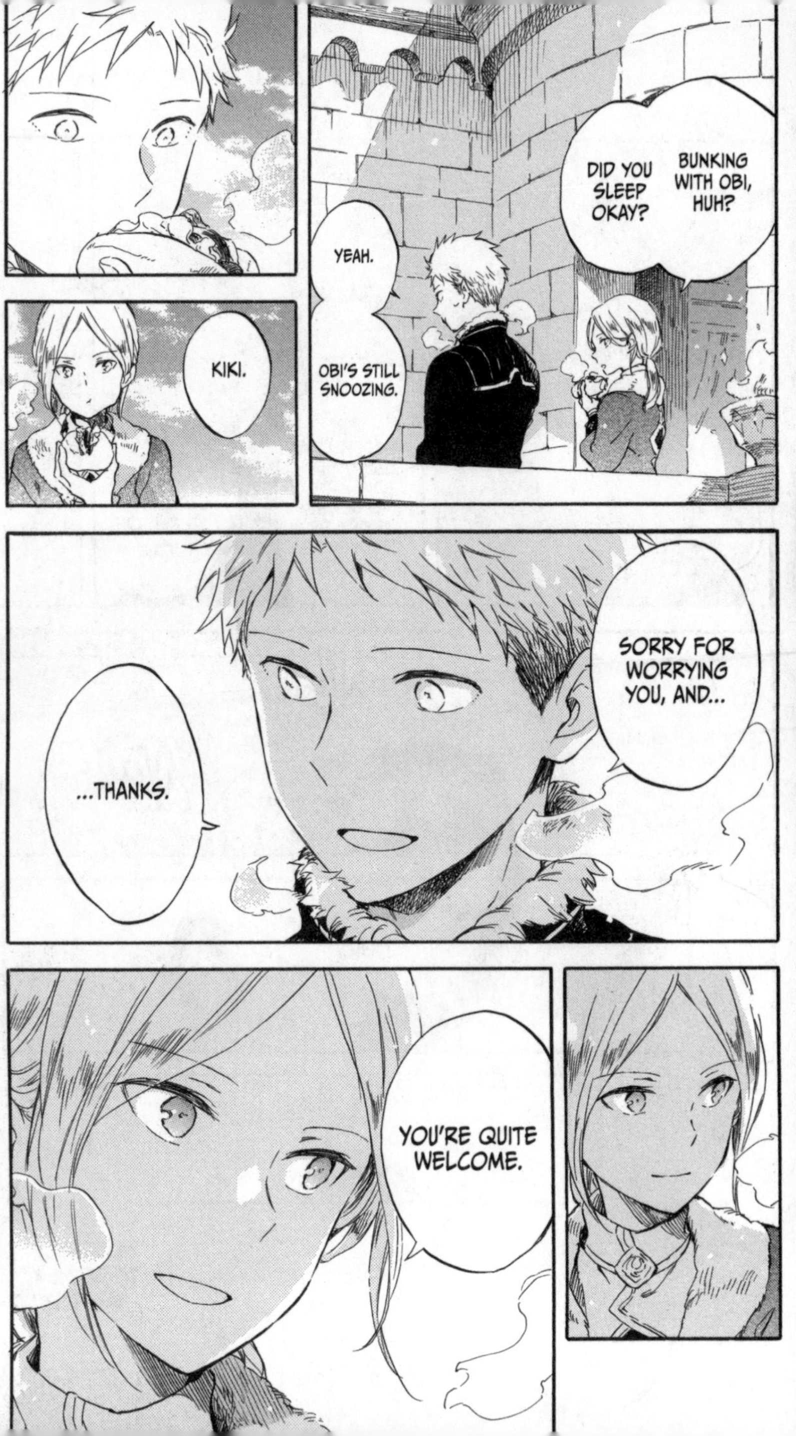
BUNKING WITH OBI, HUH?
DID YOU SLEEP OKAY?
YEAH.
OBI'S STILL SNOOZING.
KIKI.
SORRY FOR WORRYING YOU, AND...
...THANKS.
YOU'RE QUITE WELCOME.

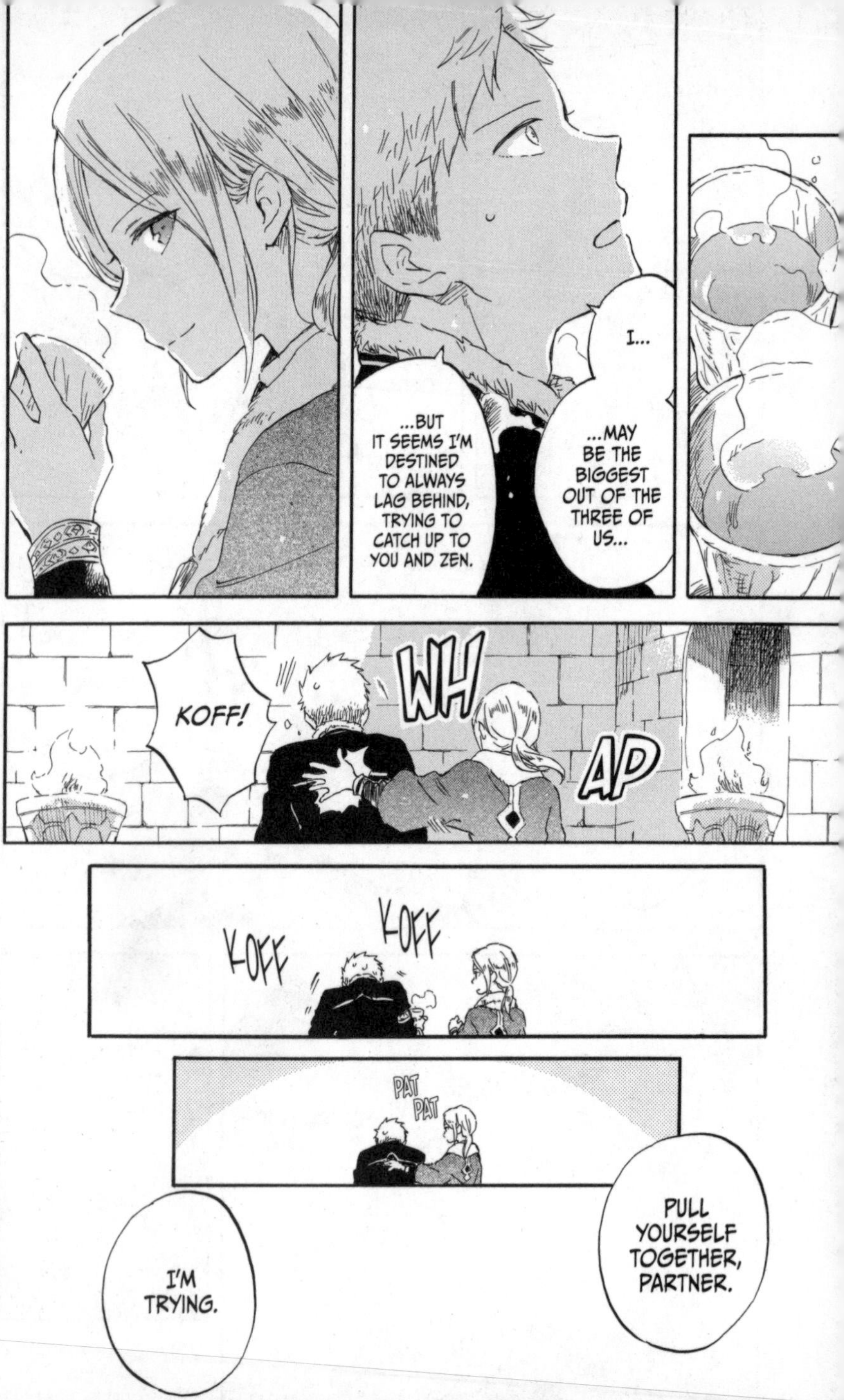
I...
...MAY BE THE BIGGEST OUT OF THE THREE OF US...
...BUT IT SEEMS I'M DESTINED TO ALWAYS LAG BEHIND, TRYING TO CATCH UP TO YOU AND ZEN.
WH
AP
KOFF!
KOFF
KOFF
PAT
PAT
PULL YOURSELF TOGETHER, PARTNER.
I'M TRYING.

Chapter 99

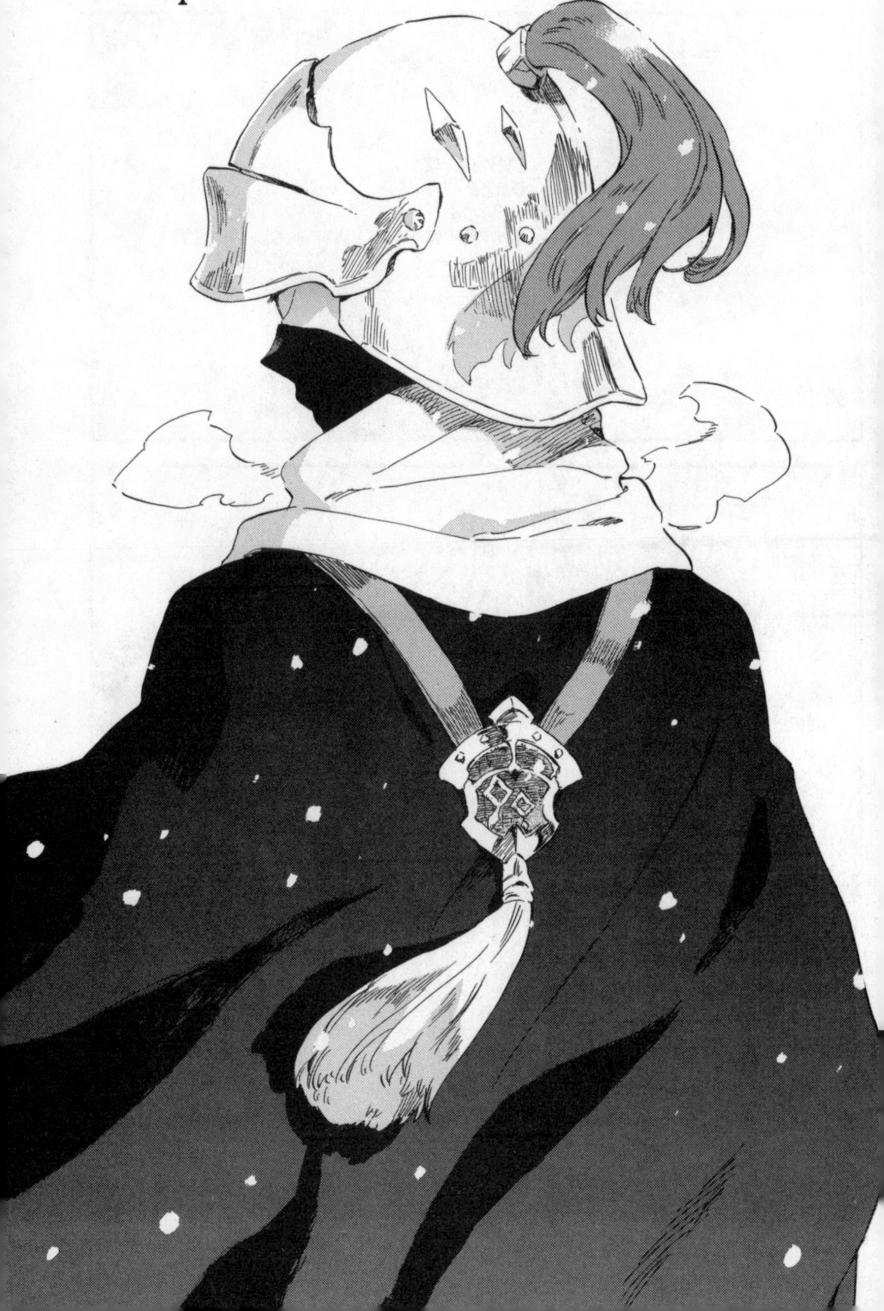

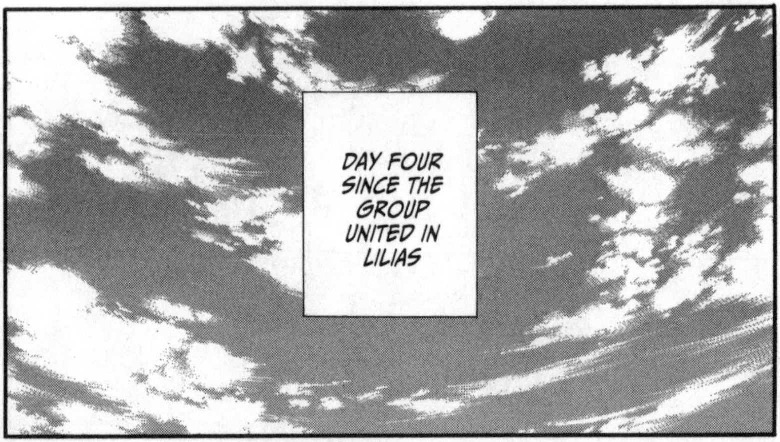
DAY FOUR SINCE THE GROUP UNITED IN LILIAS

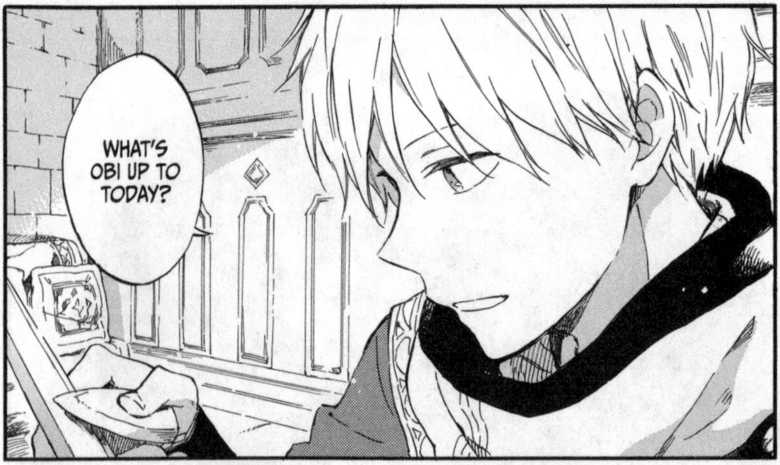
WHAT'S OBI UP TO TODAY?

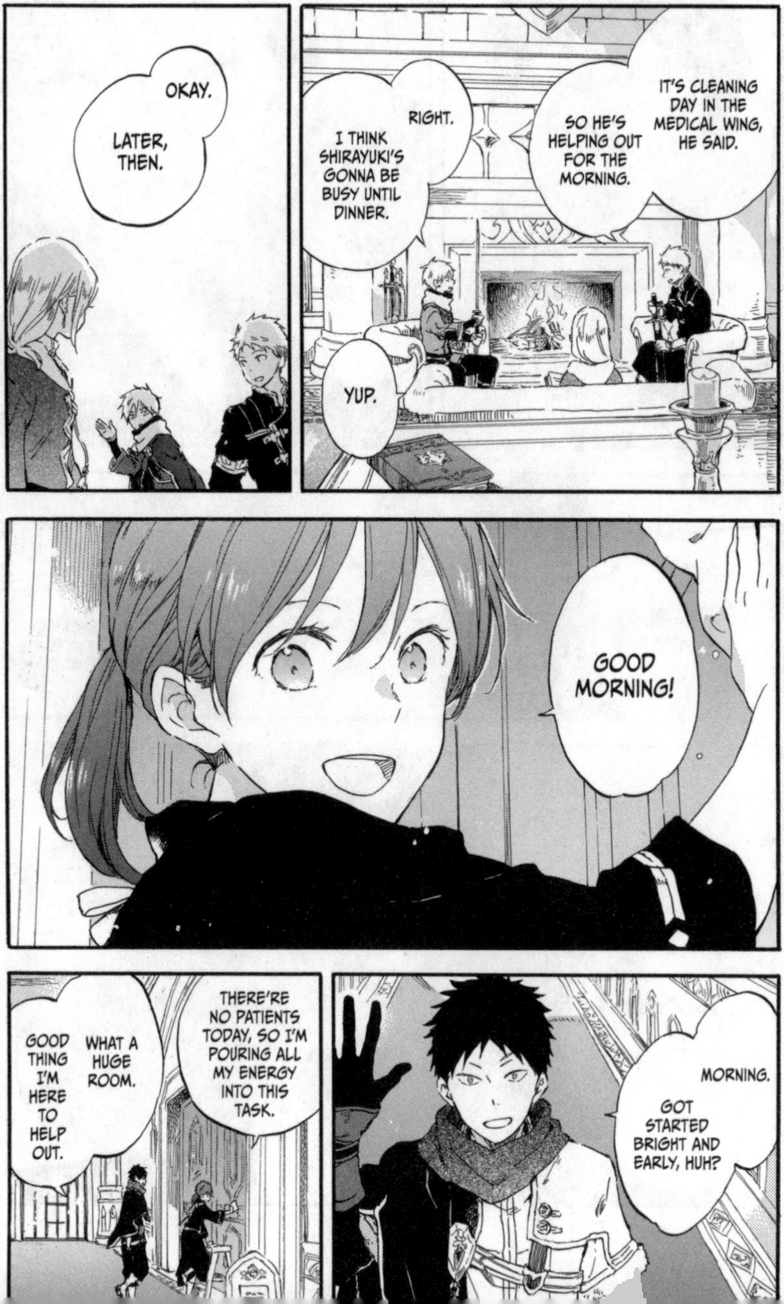
IT'S CLEANING DAY IN THE MEDICAL WING, HE SAID.
SO HE'S HELPING OUT FOR THE MORNING.
RIGHT.
I THINK SHIRAYUKI'S GONNA BE BUSY UNTIL DINNER.
YUP.
OKAY.
LATER, THEN.
GOOD MORNING!
MORNING.
GOT STARTED BRIGHT AND EARLY, HUH?
THERE'RE NO PATIENTS TODAY, SO I'M POURING ALL MY ENERGY INTO THIS TASK.
WHAT A HUGE ROOM.
GOOD THING I'M HERE TO HELP OUT.

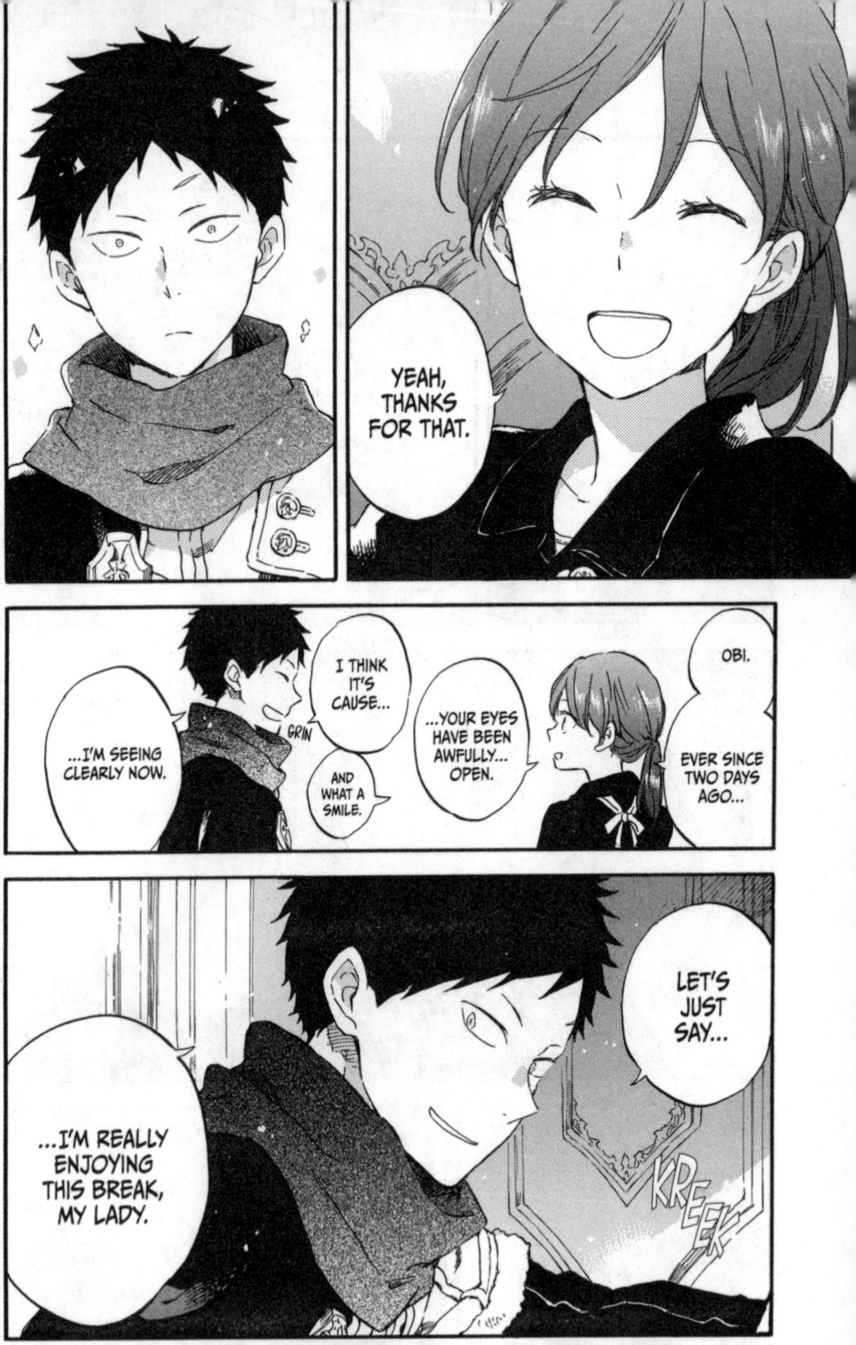
YEAH, THANKS FOR THAT.
OBI.
EVER SINCE TWO DAYS AGO...
...YOUR EYES HAVE BEEN AWFULLY... OPEN.
AND WHAT A SMILE.
I THINK IT'S CAUSE...
GRIN
...I'M SEEING CLEARLY NOW.
LET'S JUST SAY...
KREEK
...I'M REALLY ENJOYING THIS BREAK, MY LADY.

SUZU

HMM?

YOU'RE ON LEAVE, OBI?

THEN THIS HAS YOUR NAME ON IT.

FWUFF

YOU COME PREPARED.

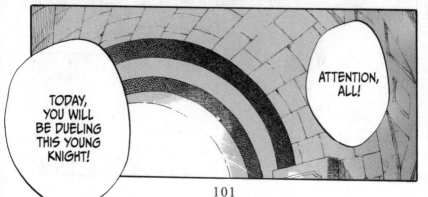

ATTENTION, ALL!

TODAY, YOU WILL BE DUELING THIS YOUNG KNIGHT!

101

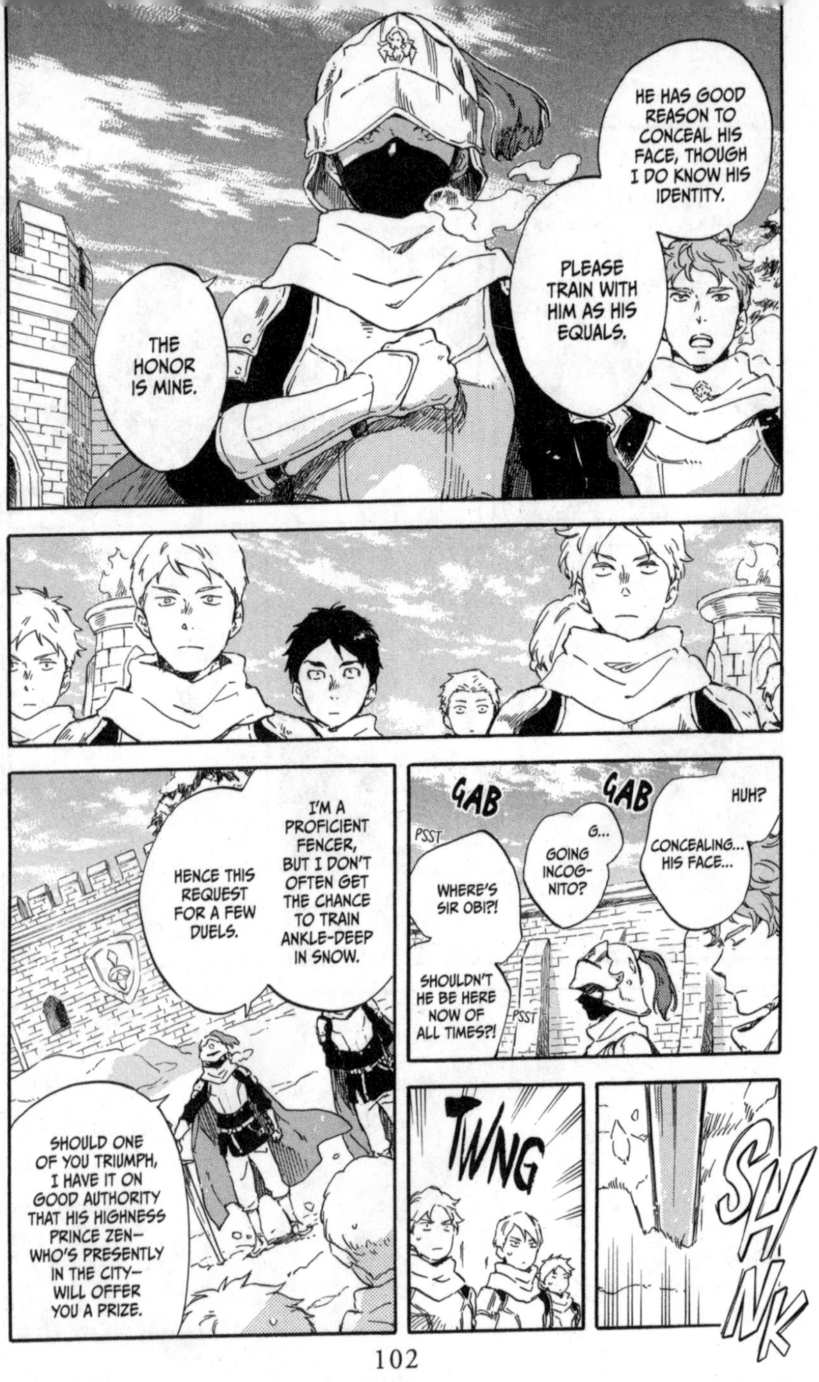
HE HAS GOOD REASON TO CONCEAL HIS FACE, THOUGH I DO KNOW HIS IDENTITY.
PLEASE TRAIN WITH HIM AS HIS EQUALS.
THE HONOR IS MINE.
HUH?
CONCEALING... HIS FACE...
GAB
GAB
G... GOING INCOGNITO?
PSST
WHERE'S SIR OBI?!
SHOULDN'T HE BE HERE NOW OF ALL TIMES?!
PSST
I'M A PROFICIENT FENCER, BUT I DON'T OFTEN GET THE CHANCE TO TRAIN ANKLE-DEEP IN SNOW.
HENCE THIS REQUEST FOR A FEW DUELS.
SHOULD ONE OF YOU TRIUMPH, I HAVE IT ON GOOD AUTHORITY THAT HIS HIGHNESS PRINCE ZEN—WHO'S PRESENTLY IN THE CITY—WILL OFFER YOU A PRIZE.
SHNK
TWNG

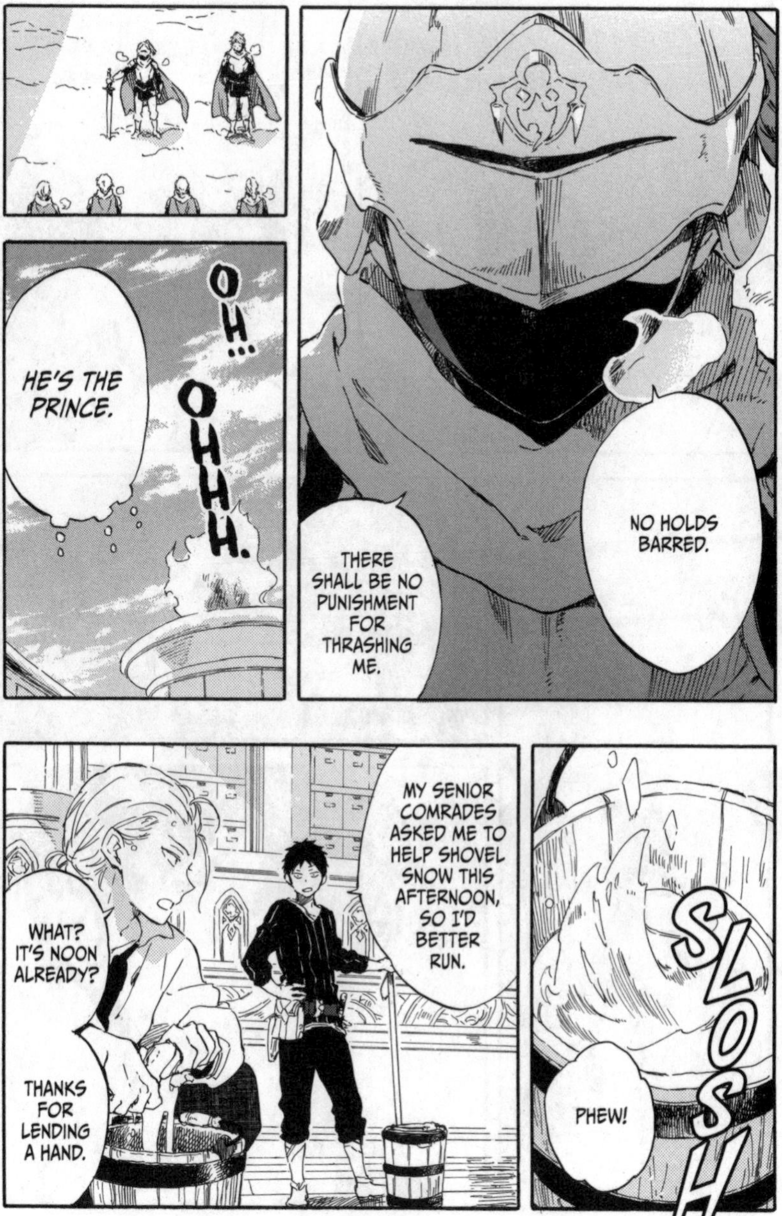
NO HOLDS BARRED.
THERE SHALL BE NO PUNISHMENT FOR THRASHING ME.
OH... OHHHH.
HE'S THE PRINCE.
SLOSH
PHEW!
MY SENIOR COMRADES ASKED ME TO HELP SHOVEL SNOW THIS AFTERNOON, SO I'D BETTER RUN.
WHAT? IT'S NOON ALREADY?
THANKS FOR LENDING A HAND.

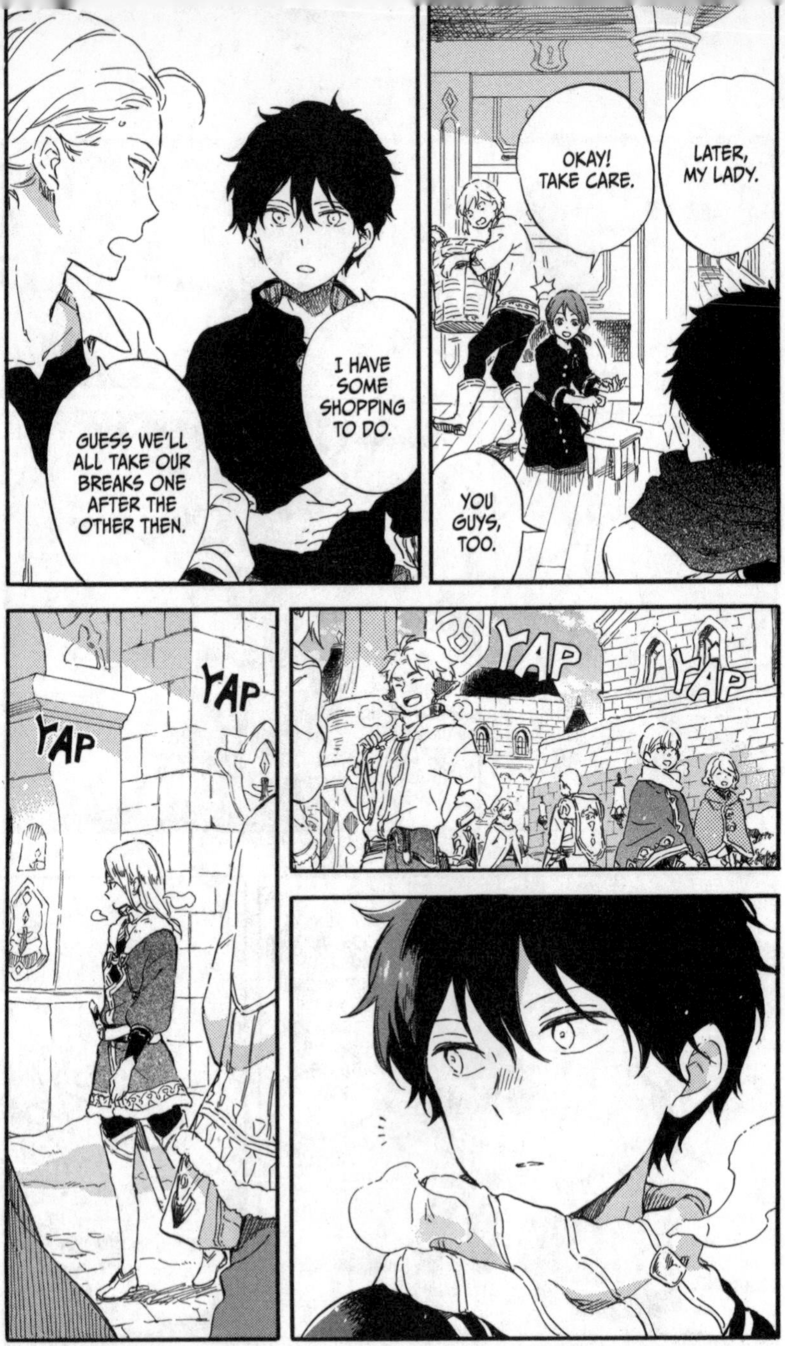
LATER, MY LADY.
OKAY! TAKE CARE.
YOU GUYS, TOO.
I HAVE SOME SHOPPING TO DO.
GUESS WE'LL ALL TAKE OUR BREAKS ONE AFTER THE OTHER THEN.
YAP
YAP
YAP
YAP

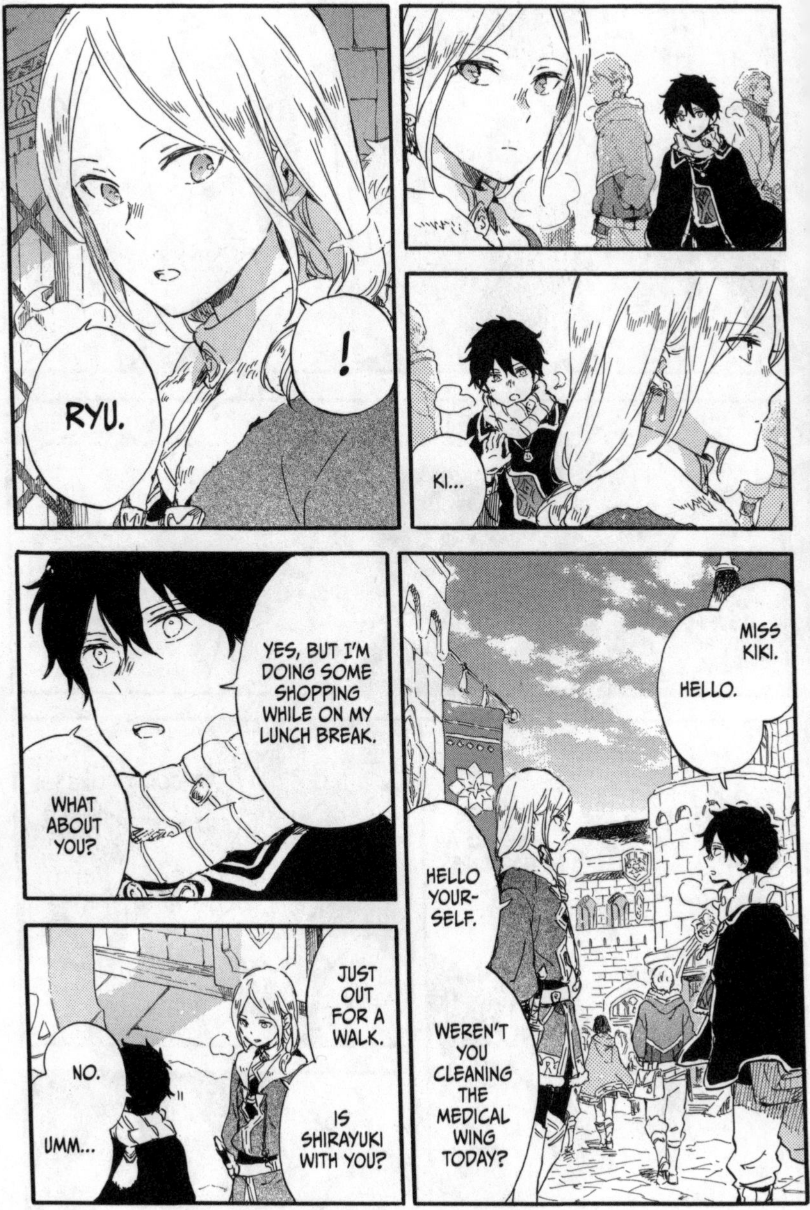
KI...
!
RYU.
MISS KIKI.
HELLO.
HELLO YOURSELF.
WEREN'T YOU CLEANING THE MEDICAL WING TODAY?
YES, BUT I'M DOING SOME SHOPPING WHILE ON MY LUNCH BREAK.
WHAT ABOUT YOU?
JUST OUT FOR A WALK.
IS SHIRAYUKI WITH YOU?
NO.
UMM...

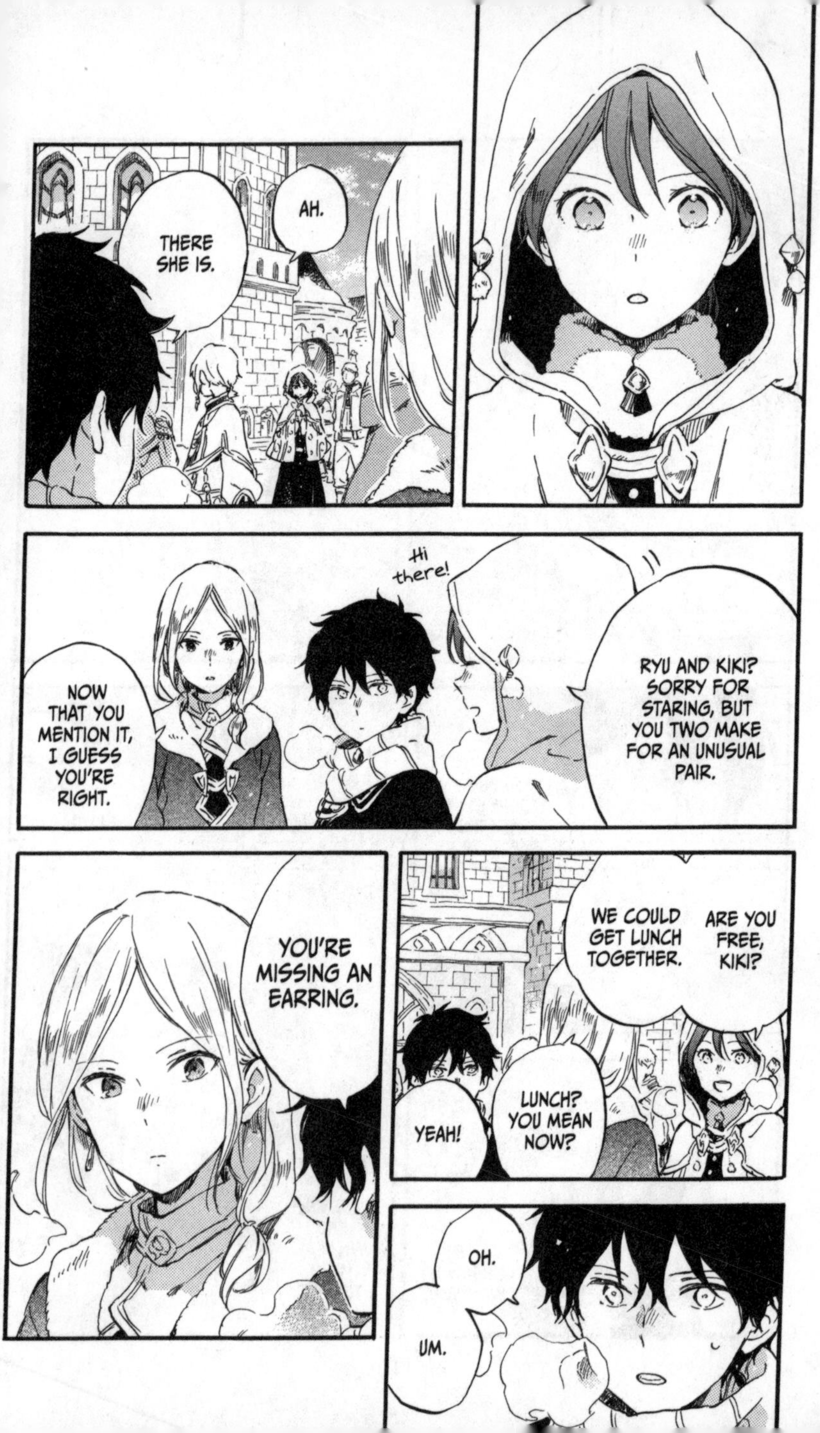
AH.
THERE SHE IS.
Hi there!
RYU AND KIKI? SORRY FOR STARING, BUT YOU TWO MAKE FOR AN UNUSUAL PAIR.
NOW THAT YOU MENTION IT, I GUESS YOU'RE RIGHT.
ARE YOU FREE, KIKI?
WE COULD GET LUNCH TOGETHER.
LUNCH? YOU MEAN NOW?
YEAH!
OH.
UM.
YOU'RE MISSING AN EARRING.

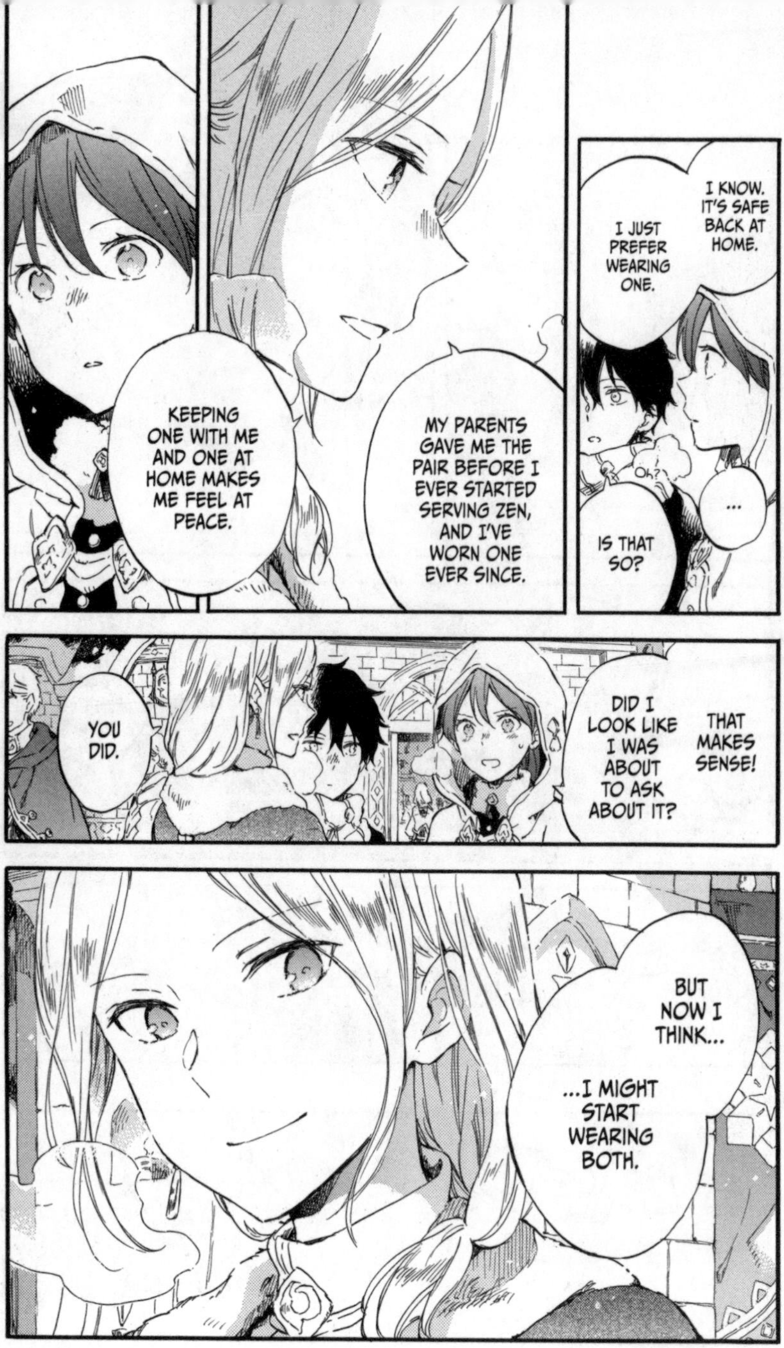
I KNOW. IT'S SAFE BACK AT HOME.
I JUST PREFER WEARING ONE.
Oh?
...
IS THAT SO?
MY PARENTS GAVE ME THE PAIR BEFORE I EVER STARTED SERVING ZEN, AND I'VE WORN ONE EVER SINCE.
KEEPING ONE WITH ME AND ONE AT HOME MAKES ME FEEL AT PEACE.
THAT MAKES SENSE!
DID I LOOK LIKE I WAS ABOUT TO ASK ABOUT IT?
YOU DID.
BUT NOW I THINK...
...I MIGHT START WEARING BOTH.

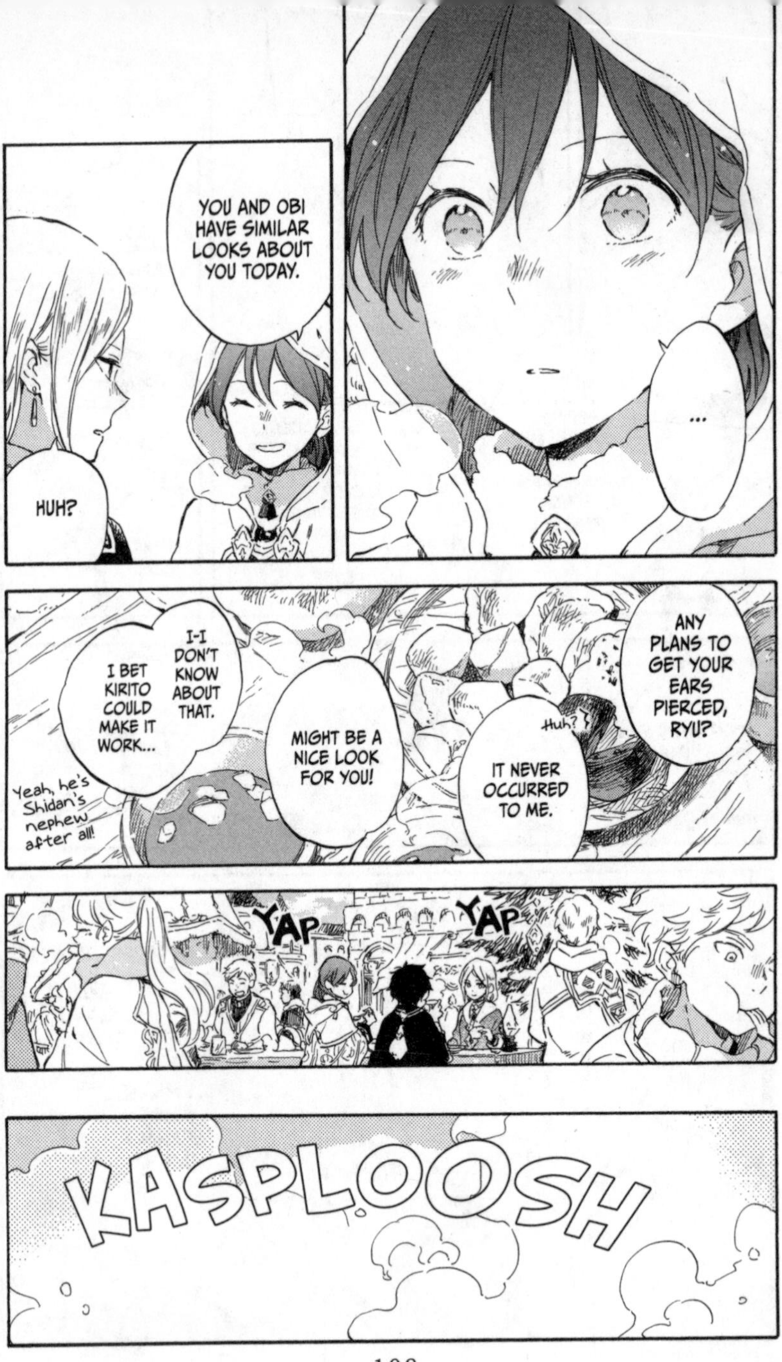
...
YOU AND OBI HAVE SIMILAR LOOKS ABOUT YOU TODAY.
HUH?
ANY PLANS TO GET YOUR EARS PIERCED, RYU?
Huh?
IT NEVER OCCURRED TO ME.
MIGHT BE A NICE LOOK FOR YOU!
I-I DON'T KNOW ABOUT THAT.
I BET KIRITO COULD MAKE IT WORK...
Yeah, he's Shidan's nephew after all!
YAP
YAP
KASPLOOSH

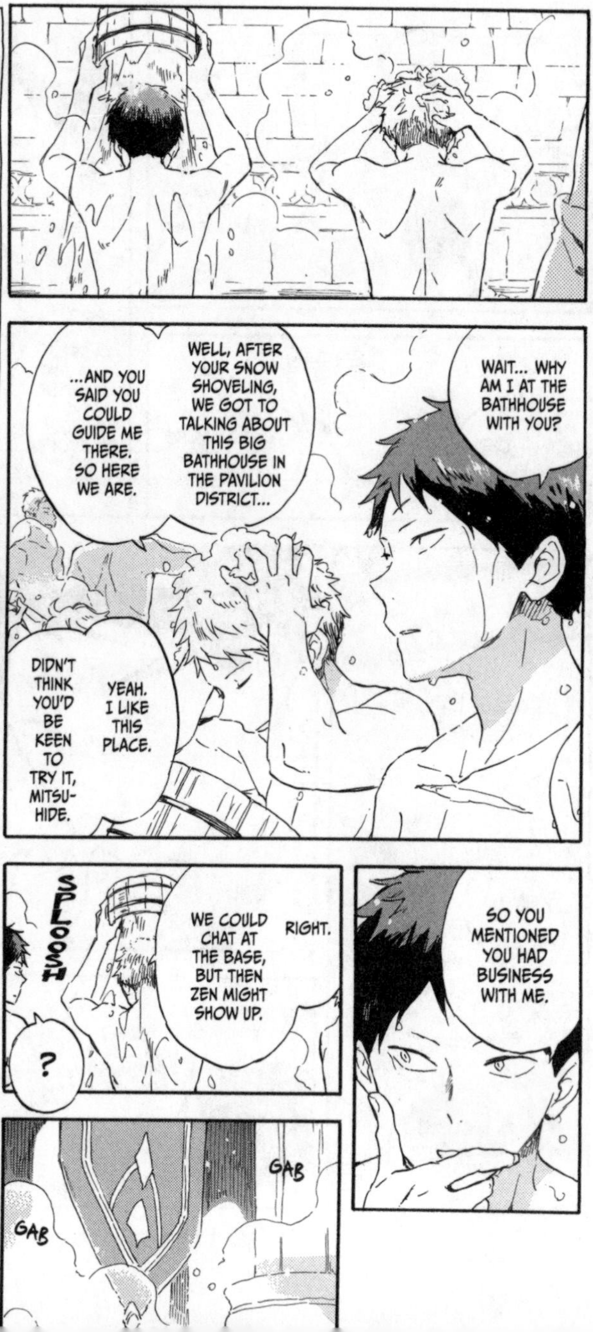
WAIT... WHY AM I AT THE BATHHOUSE WITH YOU?
WELL, AFTER YOUR SNOW SHOVELING, WE GOT TO TALKING ABOUT THIS BIG BATHHOUSE IN THE PAVILION DISTRICT...
...AND YOU SAID YOU COULD GUIDE ME THERE. SO HERE WE ARE.
YEAH. I LIKE THIS PLACE.
DIDN'T THINK YOU'D BE KEEN TO TRY IT, MITSU-HIDE.
SO YOU MENTIONED YOU HAD BUSINESS WITH ME.
RIGHT.
WE COULD CHAT AT THE BASE, BUT THEN ZEN MIGHT SHOW UP.
SPLOOSH
?
GAB
GAB

4

TRIP DIARY, PART 3

Some of our sightseeing was called off due to bad weather, but we still managed to have lots of fun.

We saw a 3D movie at a museum, but all I can remember are the live lizards. Mind you, this was not a lizard museum.

Temples, museums, a knight captain's palace! Malta has a long history with orders of knights, so definitely check that out if you're interested.

The palace was in the fortified city, but since we had a restaurant reservation, we didn't have much time to sightsee. So instead of taking my sweet time to explore...I took a million photos (for research)!! My camera got a real workout. I was especially grateful that photos were allowed inside the rooms. The floors were decorated with lots of crests and symbols, and I managed to capture them all.

The guidebook later informed me that the floors were made of marble. Pretty sweet, no? So shiny and sparkly! *snap snap*

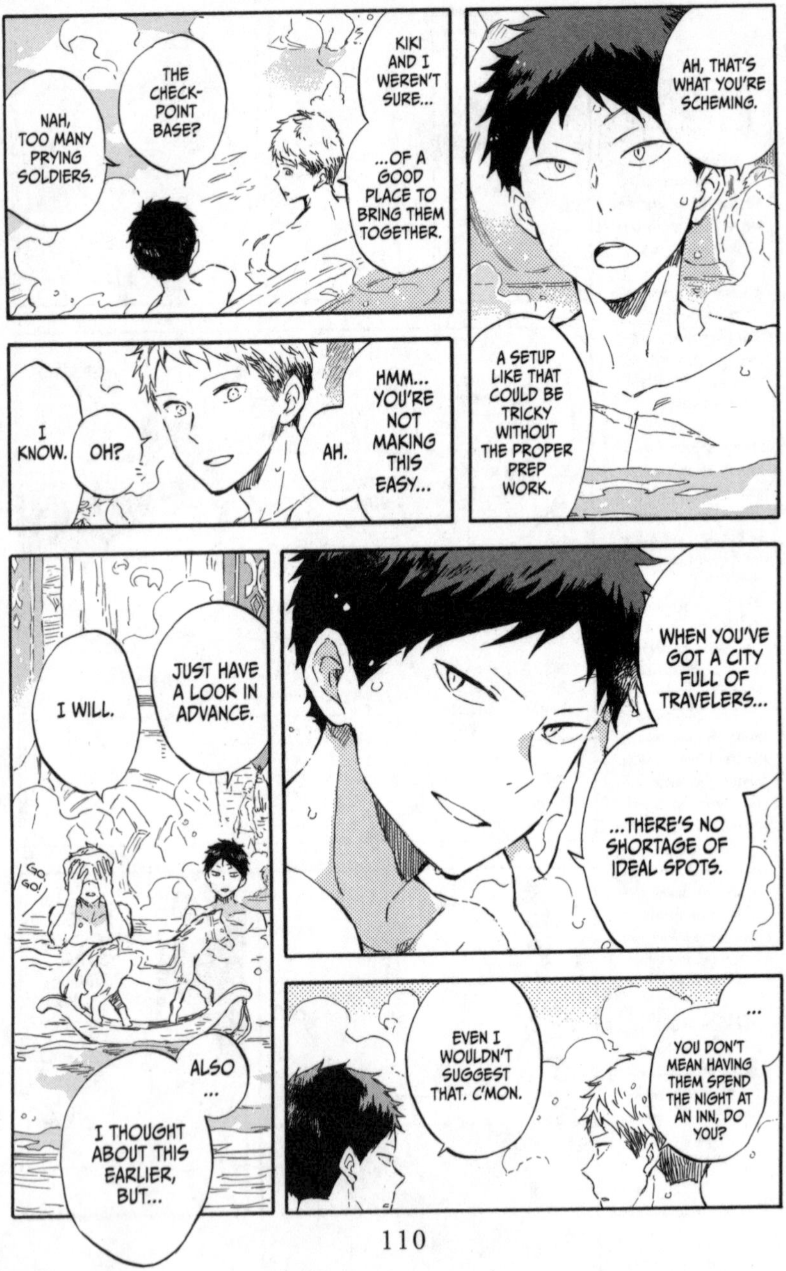
AH, THAT'S WHAT YOU'RE SCHEMING.
A SETUP LIKE THAT COULD BE TRICKY WITHOUT THE PROPER PREP WORK.
KIKI AND I WEREN'T SURE...
...OF A GOOD PLACE TO BRING THEM TOGETHER.
THE CHECK-POINT BASE?
NAH, TOO MANY PRYING SOLDIERS.
HMM... YOU'RE NOT MAKING THIS EASY...
AH.
OH?
I KNOW.
WHEN YOU'VE GOT A CITY FULL OF TRAVELERS...
...THERE'S NO SHORTAGE OF IDEAL SPOTS.
...
YOU DON'T MEAN HAVING THEM SPEND THE NIGHT AT AN INN, DO YOU?
EVEN I WOULDN'T SUGGEST THAT. C'MON.
JUST HAVE A LOOK IN ADVANCE.
I WILL.
GO, GO!
ALSO...
I THOUGHT ABOUT THIS EARLIER, BUT...

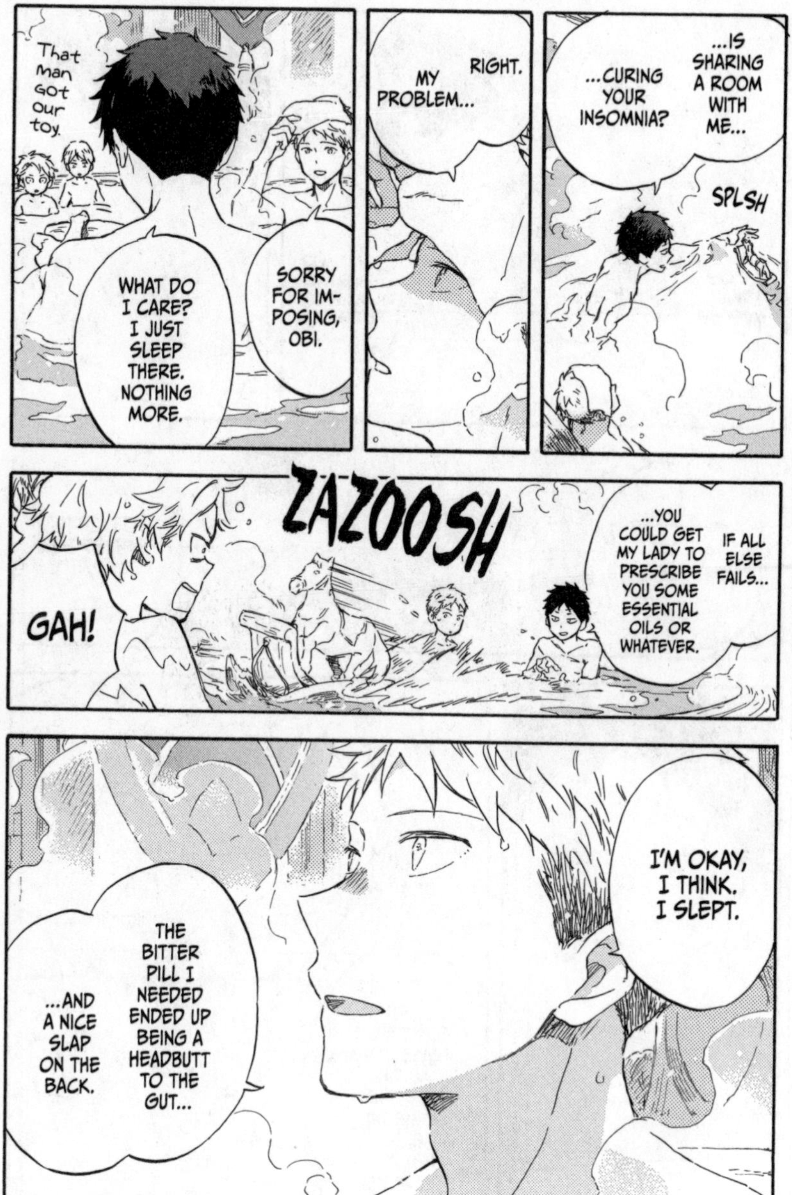
...IS SHARING A ROOM WITH ME...
...CURING YOUR INSOMNIA?
SPLSH
RIGHT.
MY PROBLEM...
SORRY FOR IMPOSING, OBI.
WHAT DO I CARE? I JUST SLEEP THERE. NOTHING MORE.
That man got our toy.
IF ALL ELSE FAILS...
...YOU COULD GET MY LADY TO PRESCRIBE YOU SOME ESSENTIAL OILS OR WHATEVER.
ZAZOOSH
GAH!
I'M OKAY, I THINK. I SLEPT.
THE BITTER PILL I NEEDED ENDED UP BEING A HEADBUTT TO THE GUT...
...AND A NICE SLAP ON THE BACK.

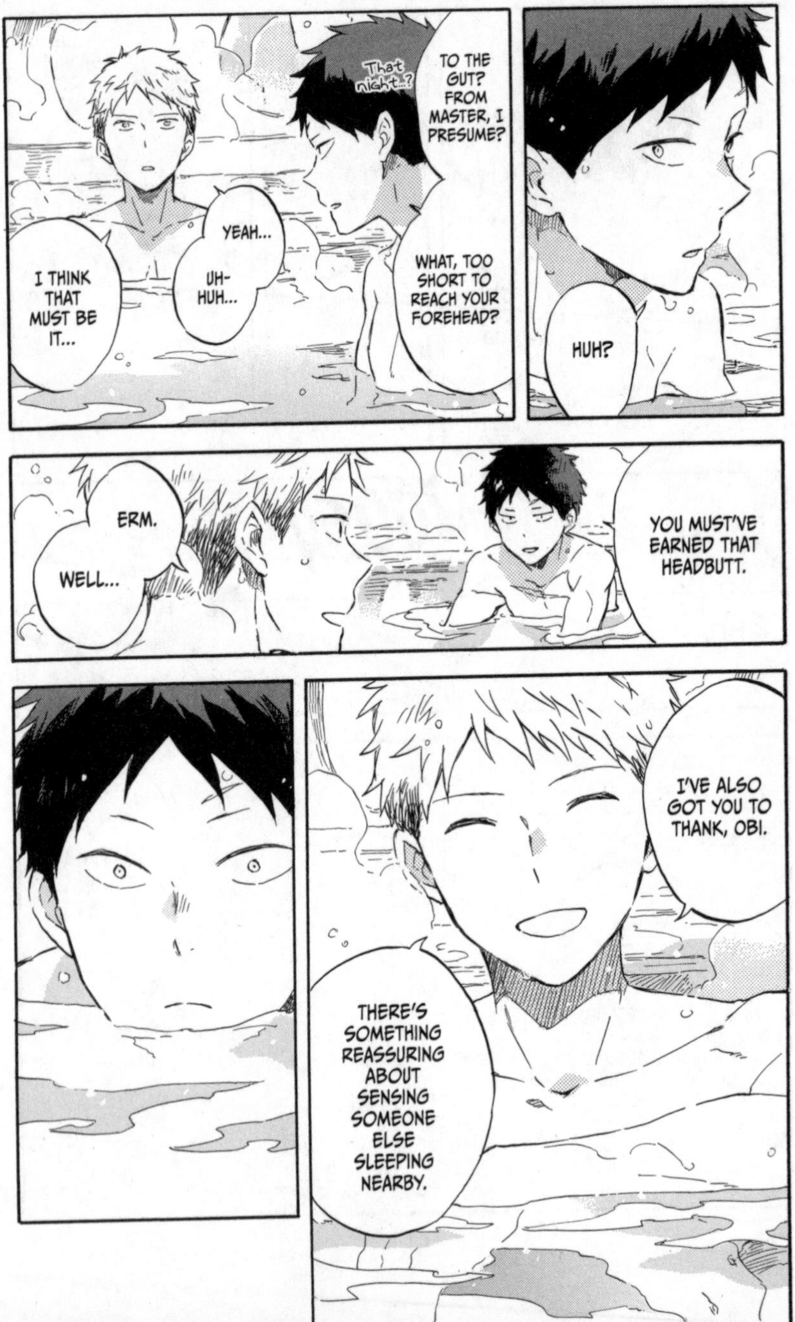
HUH?
That night...?
TO THE GUT? FROM MASTER, I PRESUME?
WHAT, TOO SHORT TO REACH YOUR FOREHEAD?
YEAH...
UH-HUH...
I THINK THAT MUST BE IT...
YOU MUST'VE EARNED THAT HEADBUTT.
ERM.
WELL...
I'VE ALSO GOT YOU TO THANK, OBI.
THERE'S SOMETHING REASSURING ABOUT SENSING SOMEONE ELSE SLEEPING NEARBY.

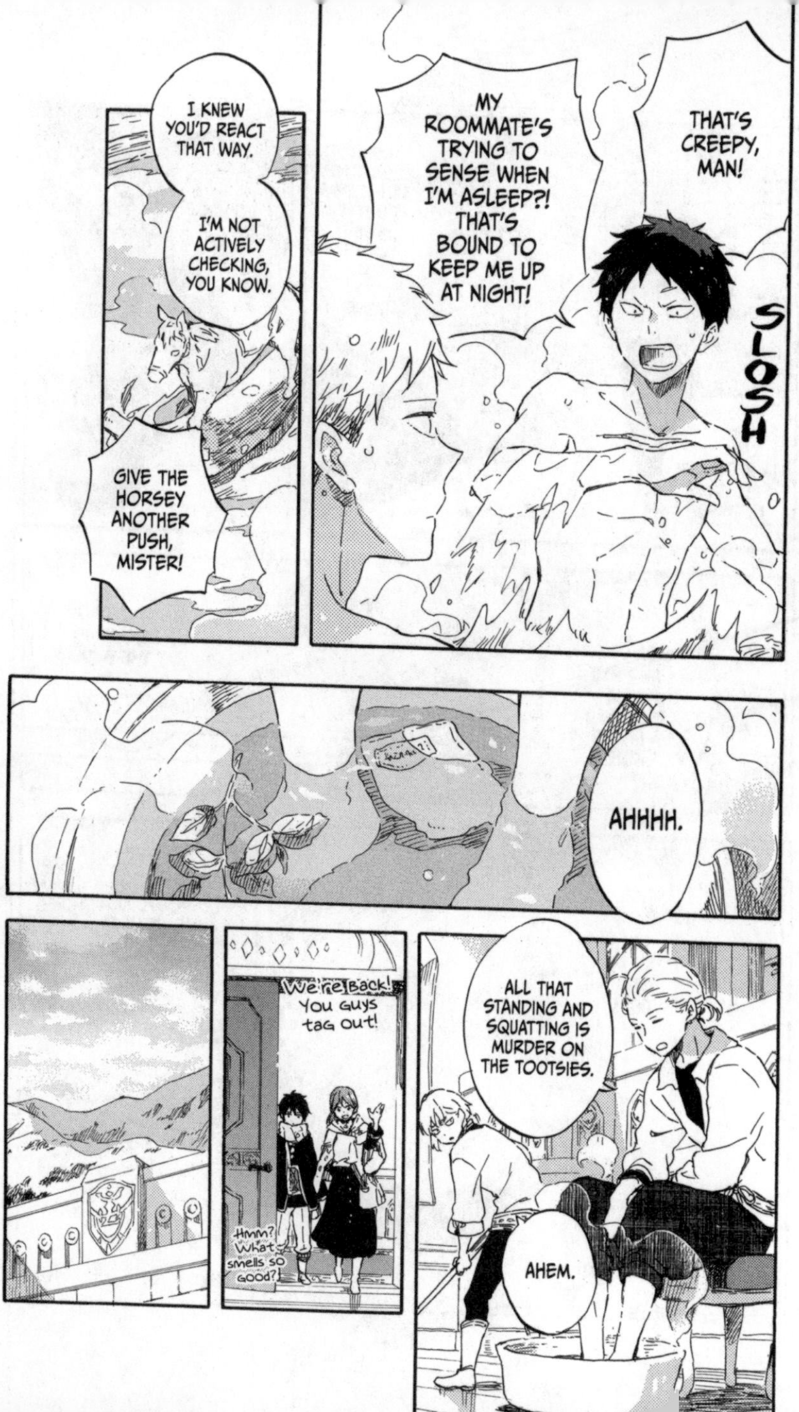
THAT'S CREEPY, MAN!
MY ROOMMATE'S TRYING TO SENSE WHEN I'M ASLEEP?! THAT'S BOUND TO KEEP ME UP AT NIGHT!
SLOSH
I KNEW YOU'D REACT THAT WAY.
I'M NOT ACTIVELY CHECKING, YOU KNOW.
GIVE THE HORSEY ANOTHER PUSH, MISTER!
AHHHH.
ALL THAT STANDING AND SQUATTING IS MURDER ON THE TOOTSIES.
AHEM.
We're Back! You guys tag out!
Hmm? What smells so good?

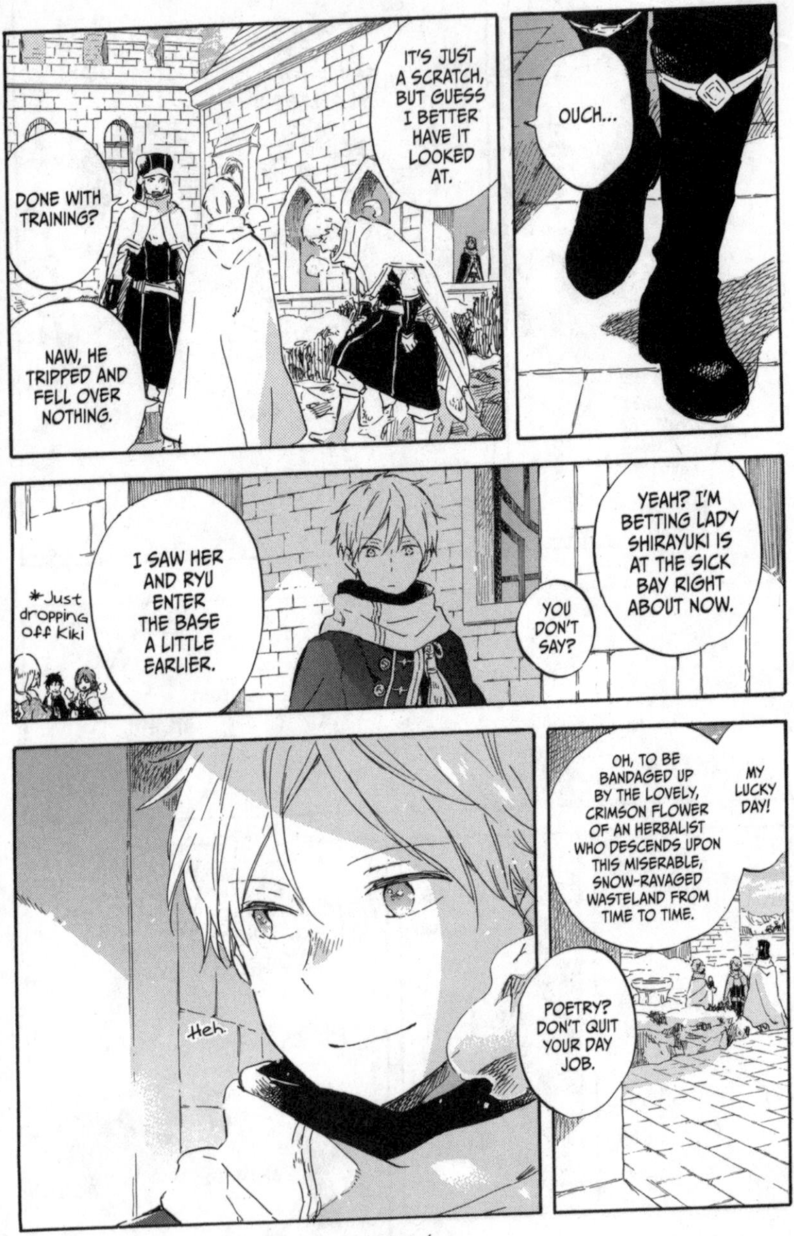
OUCH...
IT'S JUST A SCRATCH, BUT GUESS I BETTER HAVE IT LOOKED AT.
DONE WITH TRAINING?
NAW, HE TRIPPED AND FELL OVER NOTHING.
YEAH? I'M BETTING LADY SHIRAYUKI IS AT THE SICK BAY RIGHT ABOUT NOW.
YOU DON'T SAY?
I SAW HER AND RYU ENTER THE BASE A LITTLE EARLIER.
*Just dropping off Kiki
MY LUCKY DAY!
OH, TO BE BANDAGED UP BY THE LOVELY, CRIMSON FLOWER OF AN HERBALIST WHO DESCENDS UPON THIS MISERABLE, SNOW-RAVAGED WASTELAND FROM TIME TO TIME.
POETRY? DON'T QUIT YOUR DAY JOB.
Heh.

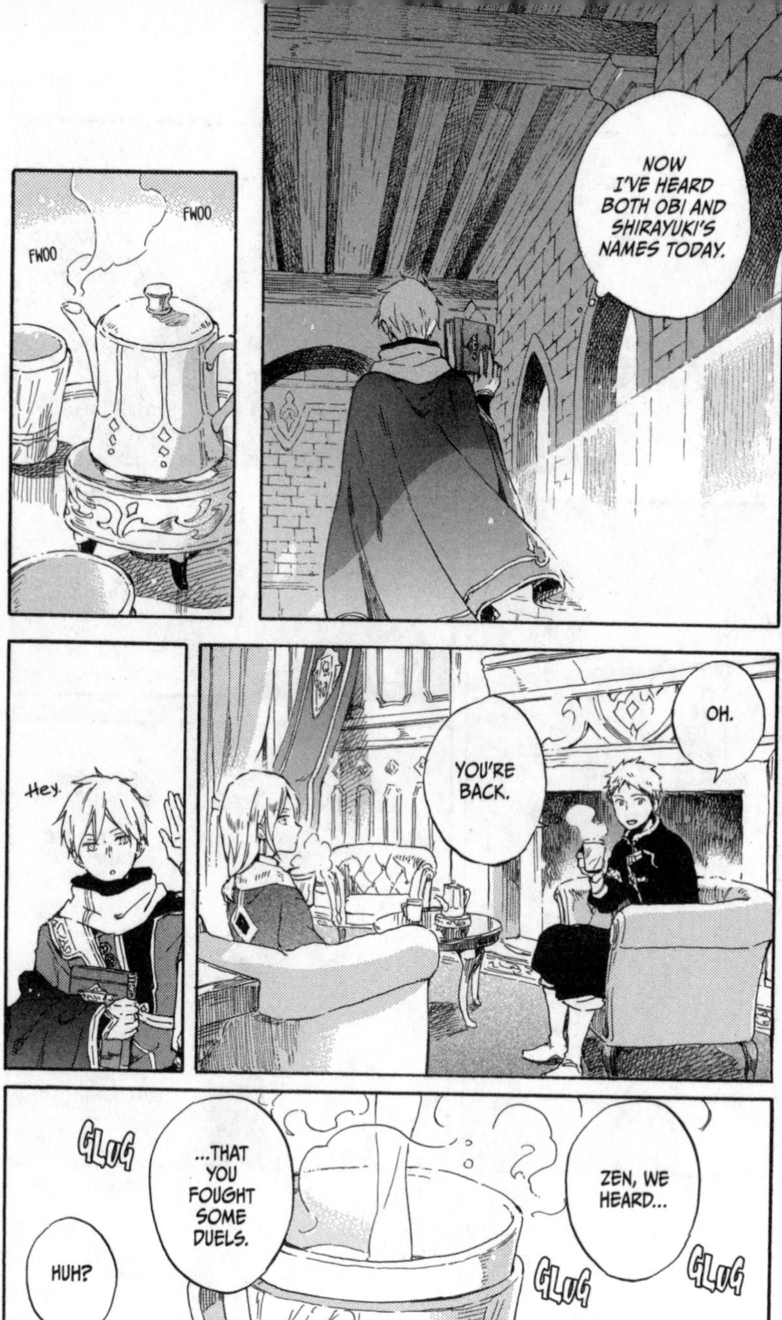
NOW I'VE HEARD BOTH OBI AND SHIRAYUKI'S NAMES TODAY.
FWOO
FWOO
OH.
YOU'RE BACK.
Hey.
GLUG
ZEN, WE HEARD...
GLUG
...THAT YOU FOUGHT SOME DUELS.
GLUG
HUH?

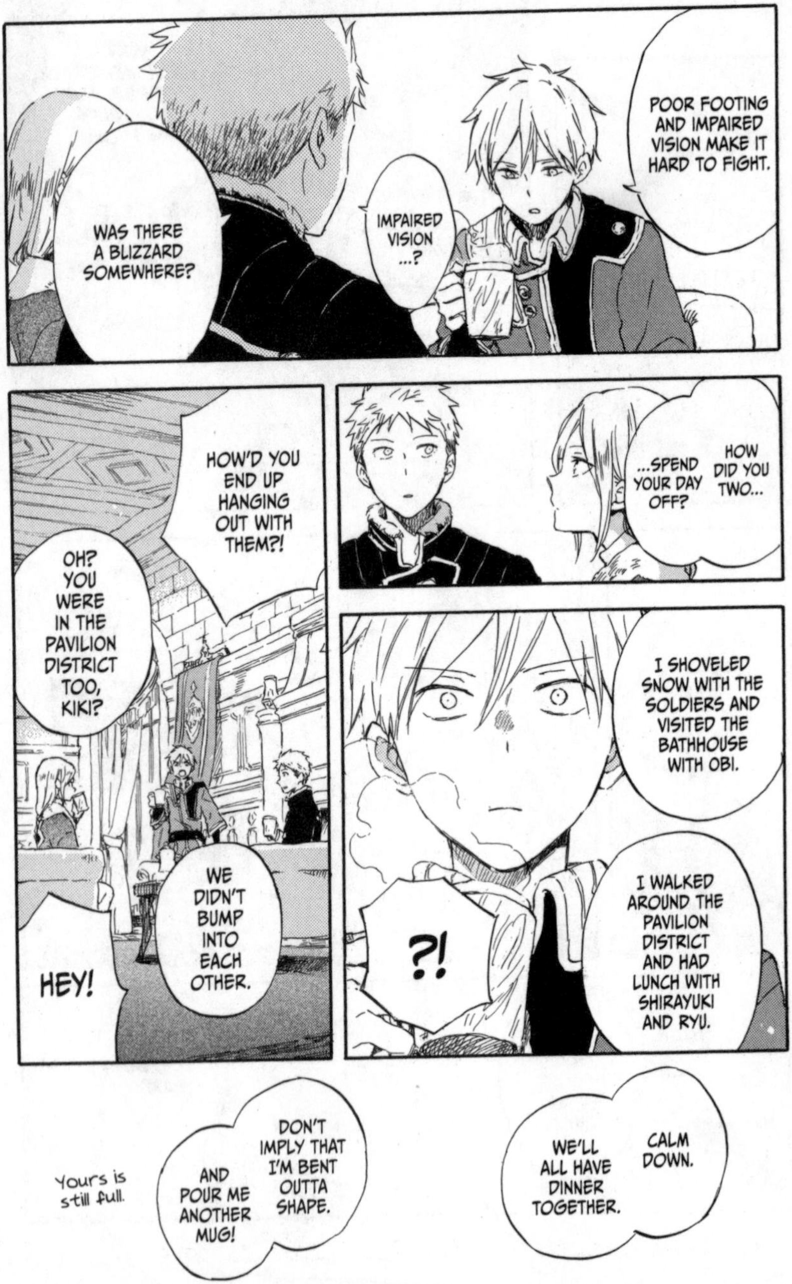
POOR FOOTING AND IMPAIRED VISION MAKE IT HARD TO FIGHT.
IMPAIRED VISION ...?
WAS THERE A BLIZZARD SOMEWHERE?
HOW DID YOU TWO...
...SPEND YOUR DAY OFF?
I SHOVELED SNOW WITH THE SOLDIERS AND VISITED THE BATHHOUSE WITH OBI.
I WALKED AROUND THE PAVILION DISTRICT AND HAD LUNCH WITH SHIRAYUKI AND RYU.
?!
HOW'D YOU END UP HANGING OUT WITH THEM?!
OH? YOU WERE IN THE PAVILION DISTRICT TOO, KIKI?
WE DIDN'T BUMP INTO EACH OTHER.
HEY!
CALM DOWN.
WE'LL ALL HAVE DINNER TOGETHER.
DON'T IMPLY THAT I'M BENT OUTTA SHAPE.
AND POUR ME ANOTHER MUG!
Yours is still full.

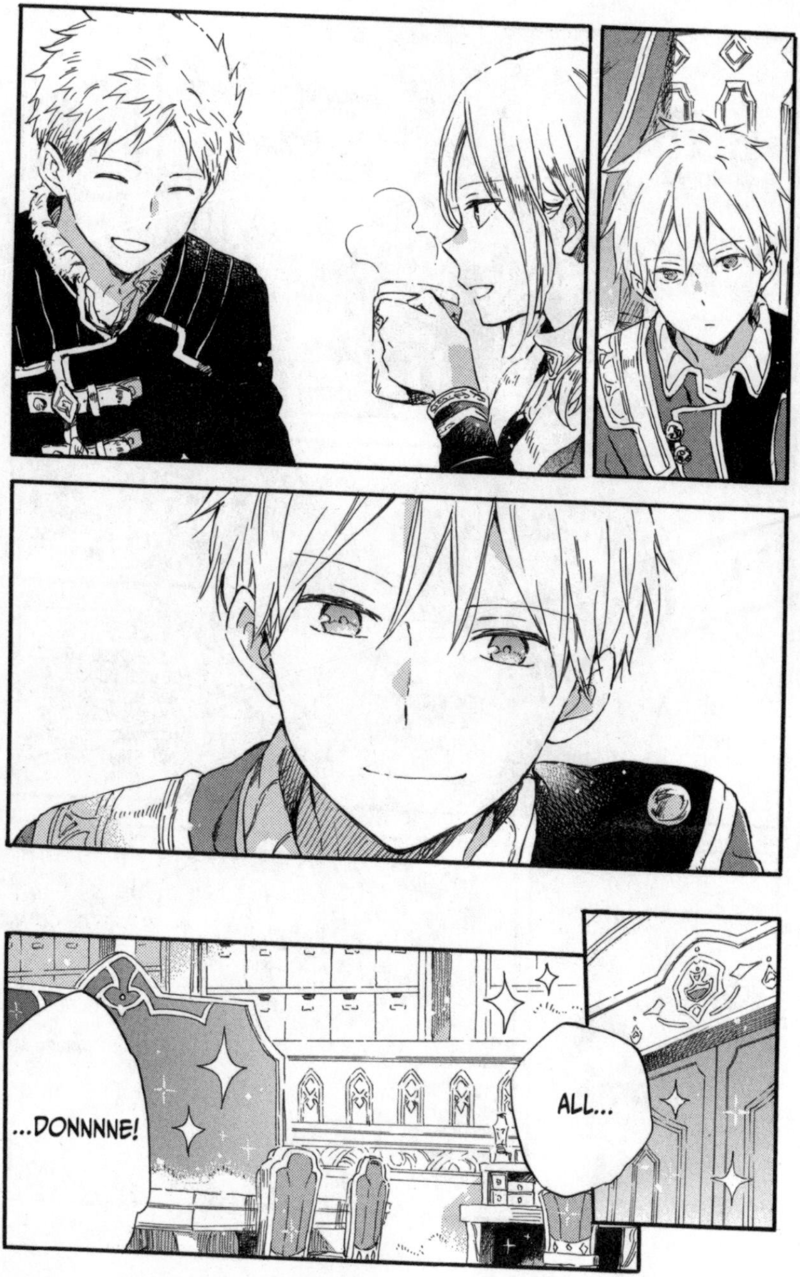
ALL...
...DONNNNE!

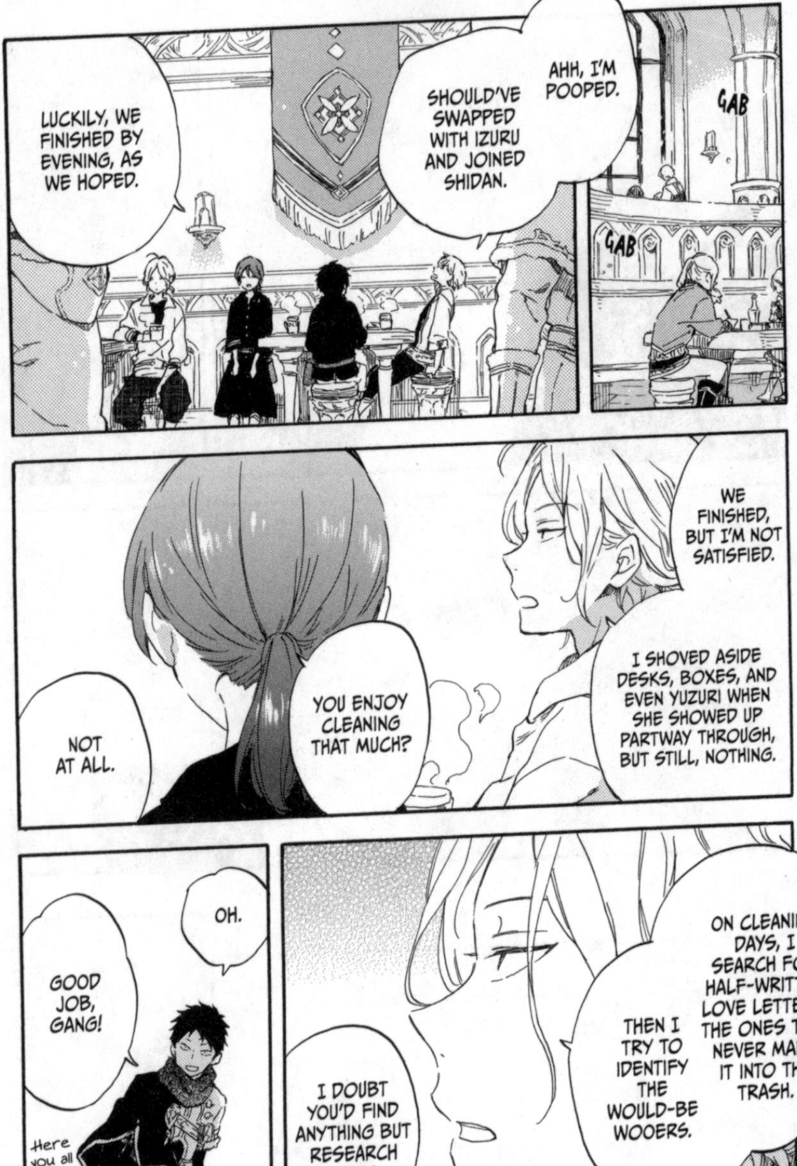
GAB
GAB
AHH, I'M POOPED.
SHOULD'VE SWAPPED WITH IZURU AND JOINED SHIDAN.
LUCKILY, WE FINISHED BY EVENING, AS WE HOPED.
WE FINISHED, BUT I'M NOT SATISFIED.
I SHOVED ASIDE DESKS, BOXES, AND EVEN YUZURI WHEN SHE SHOWED UP PARTWAY THROUGH, BUT STILL, NOTHING.
YOU ENJOY CLEANING THAT MUCH?
NOT AT ALL.
ON CLEANING DAYS, I SEARCH FOR HALF-WRITTEN LOVE LETTERS. THE ONES THAT NEVER MADE IT INTO THE TRASH.
THEN I TRY TO IDENTIFY THE WOULD-BE WOOERS.
I DOUBT YOU'D FIND ANYTHING BUT RESEARCH PAPERS...
OH.
GOOD JOB, GANG!
Here you all are!

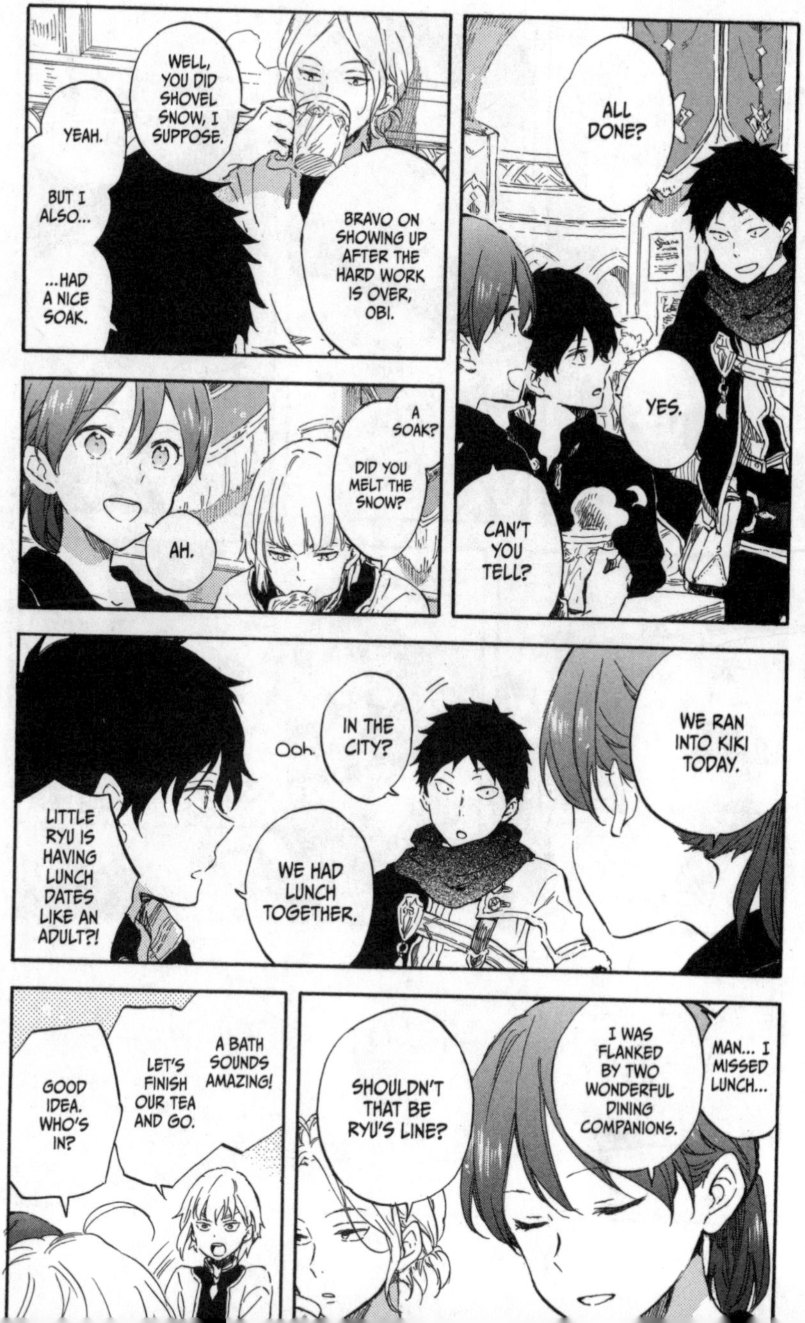
ALL DONE?
YES.
CAN'T YOU TELL?
WELL, YOU DID SHOVEL SNOW, I SUPPOSE.
YEAH.
BUT I ALSO...
...HAD A NICE SOAK.
BRAVO ON SHOWING UP AFTER THE HARD WORK IS OVER, OBI.
A SOAK?
DID YOU MELT THE SNOW?
AH.
WE RAN INTO KIKI TODAY.
IN THE CITY?
Ooh.
WE HAD LUNCH TOGETHER.
LITTLE RYU IS HAVING LUNCH DATES LIKE AN ADULT?!
MAN... I MISSED LUNCH...
I WAS FLANKED BY TWO WONDERFUL DINING COMPANIONS.
SHOULDN'T THAT BE RYU'S LINE?
A BATH SOUNDS AMAZING!
LET'S FINISH OUR TEA AND GO.
GOOD IDEA. WHO'S IN?

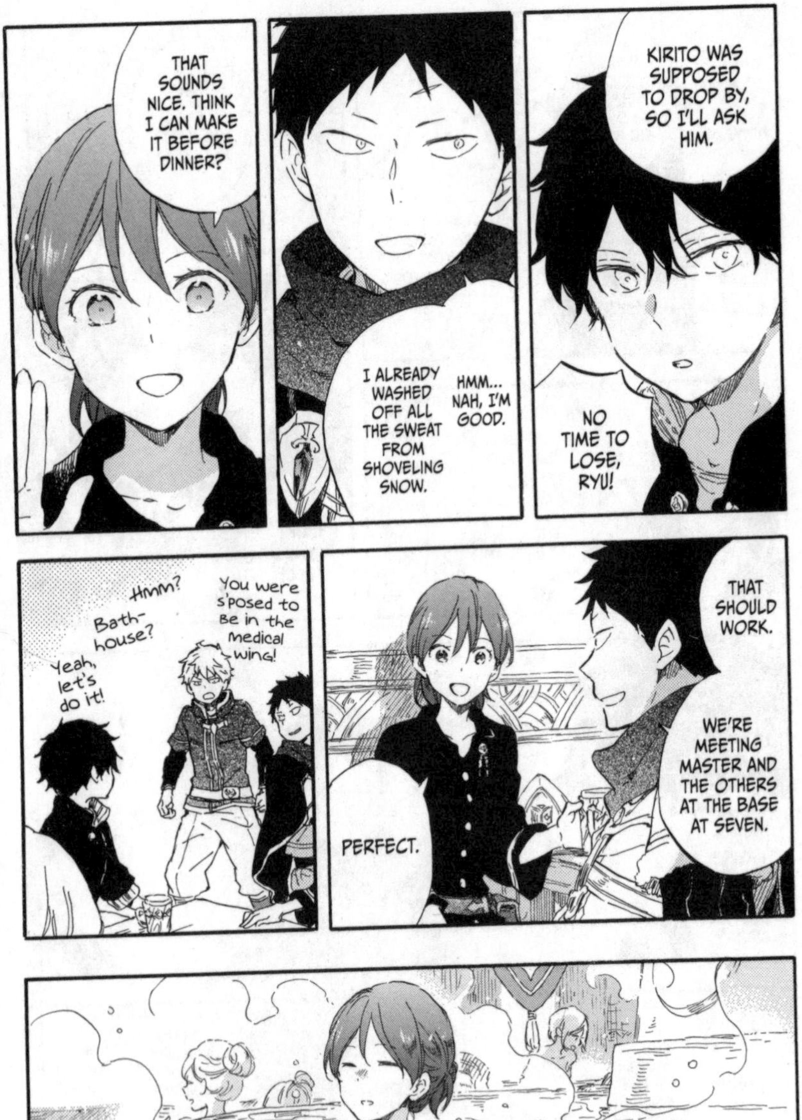
KIRITO WAS SUPPOSED TO DROP BY, SO I'LL ASK HIM.
NO TIME TO LOSE, RYU!
HMM... NAH, I'M GOOD.
I ALREADY WASHED OFF ALL THE SWEAT FROM SHOVELING SNOW.
THAT SOUNDS NICE. THINK I CAN MAKE IT BEFORE DINNER?
THAT SHOULD WORK.
WE'RE MEETING MASTER AND THE OTHERS AT THE BASE AT SEVEN.
PERFECT.
You were s'posed to be in the medical wing!
Hmm?
Bath-house?
Yeah, let's do it!

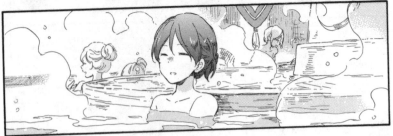

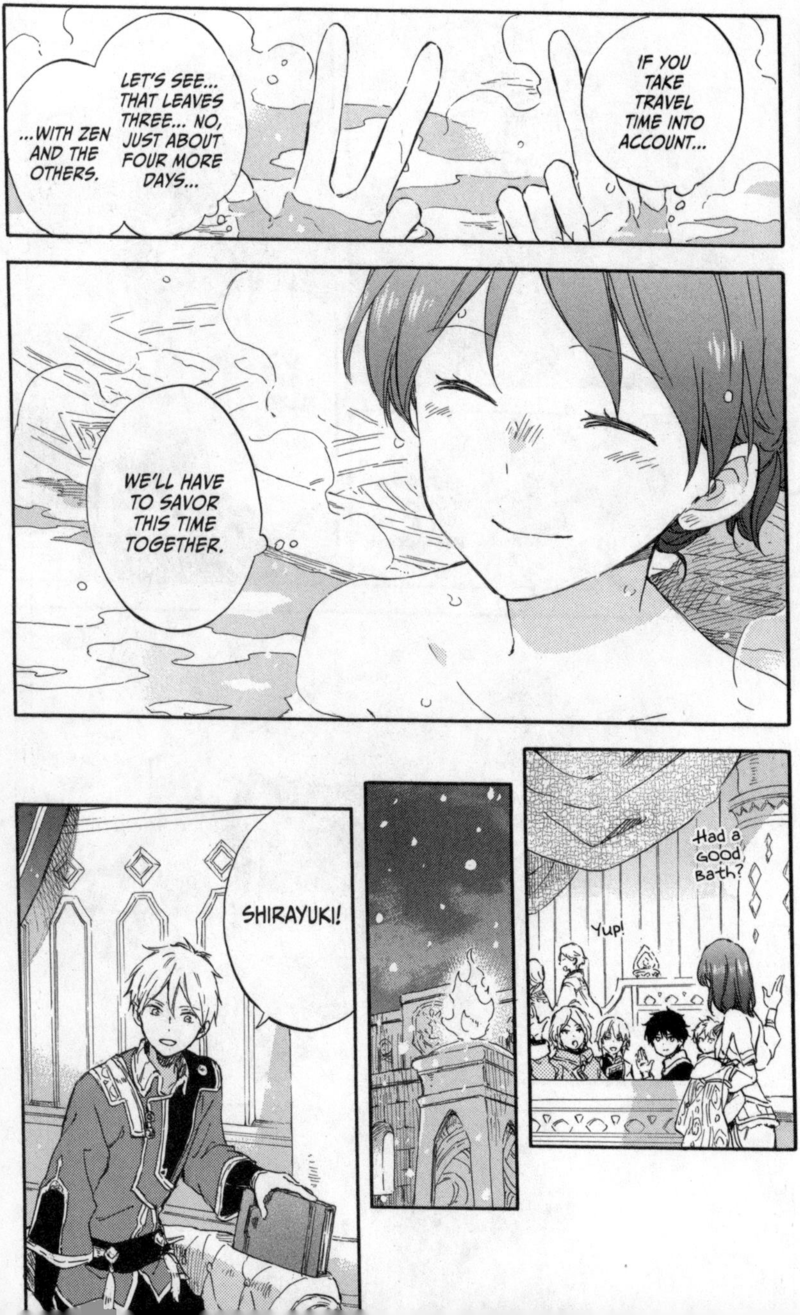
IF YOU TAKE TRAVEL TIME INTO ACCOUNT...
LET'S SEE... THAT LEAVES THREE... NO, JUST ABOUT FOUR MORE DAYS...
...WITH ZEN AND THE OTHERS.
WE'LL HAVE TO SAVOR THIS TIME TOGETHER.
Had a GOOD Bath?
Yup!
SHIRAYUKI!

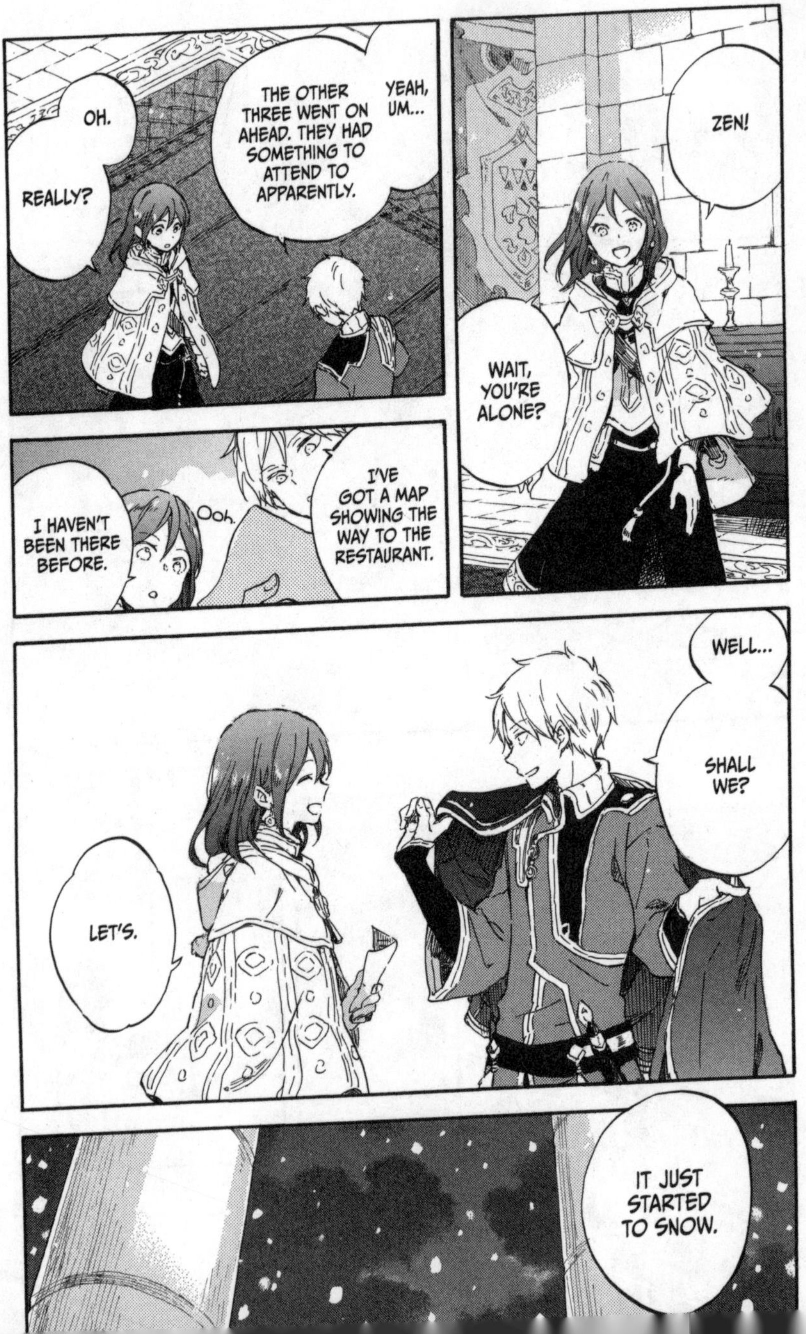
ZEN!
WAIT, YOU'RE ALONE?
YEAH, UM...
THE OTHER THREE WENT ON AHEAD. THEY HAD SOMETHING TO ATTEND TO APPARENTLY.
OH.
REALLY?
I'VE GOT A MAP SHOWING THE WAY TO THE RESTAURANT.
Ooh.
I HAVEN'T BEEN THERE BEFORE.
WELL...
SHALL WE?
LET'S.
IT JUST STARTED TO SNOW.

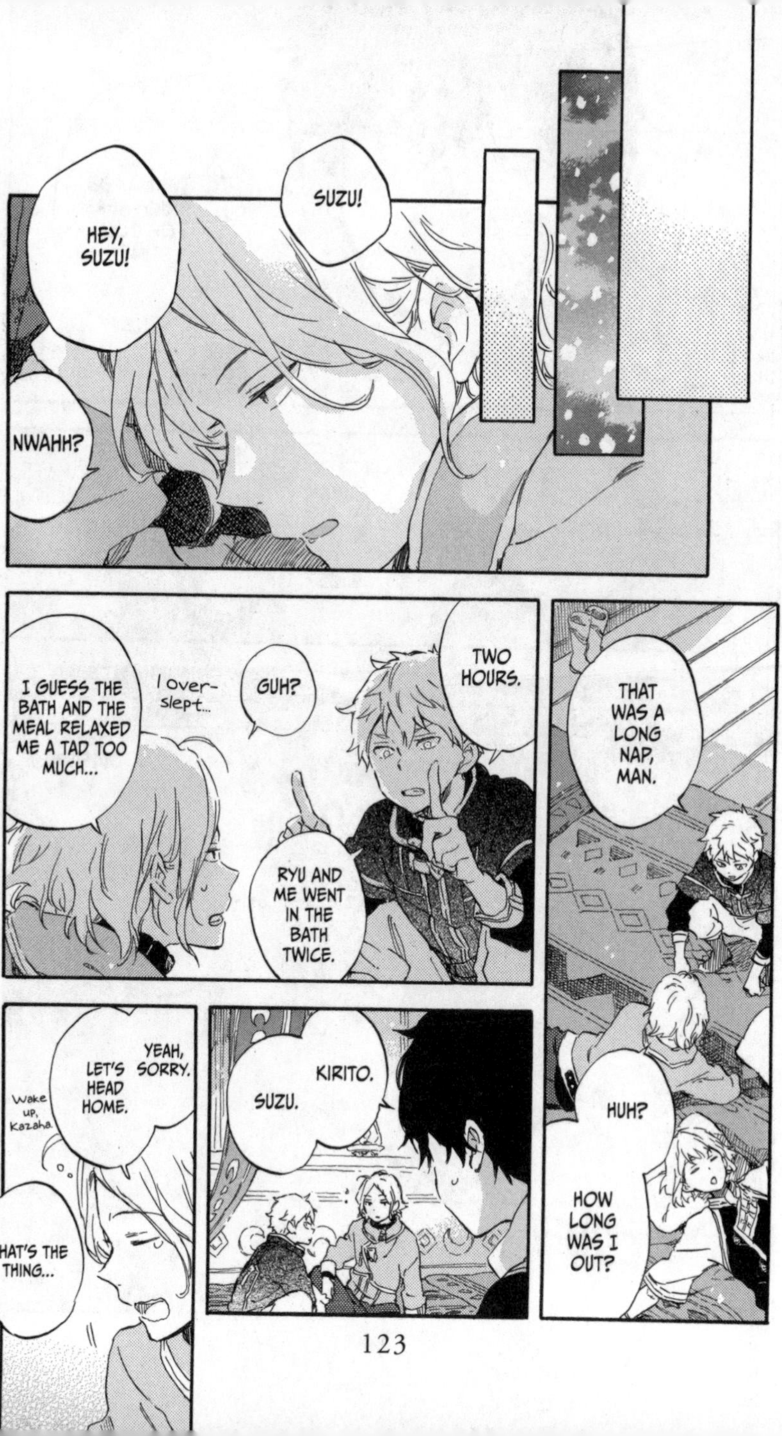
SUZU!
HEY, SUZU!
NWAHH?
THAT WAS A LONG NAP, MAN.
HUH?
HOW LONG WAS I OUT?
TWO HOURS.
GUH?
RYU AND ME WENT IN THE BATH TWICE.
I over-slept...
I GUESS THE BATH AND THE MEAL RELAXED ME A TAD TOO MUCH...
KIRITO.
SUZU.
YEAH, SORRY.
LET'S HEAD HOME.
Wake up, Kazaha.
THAT'S THE THING...

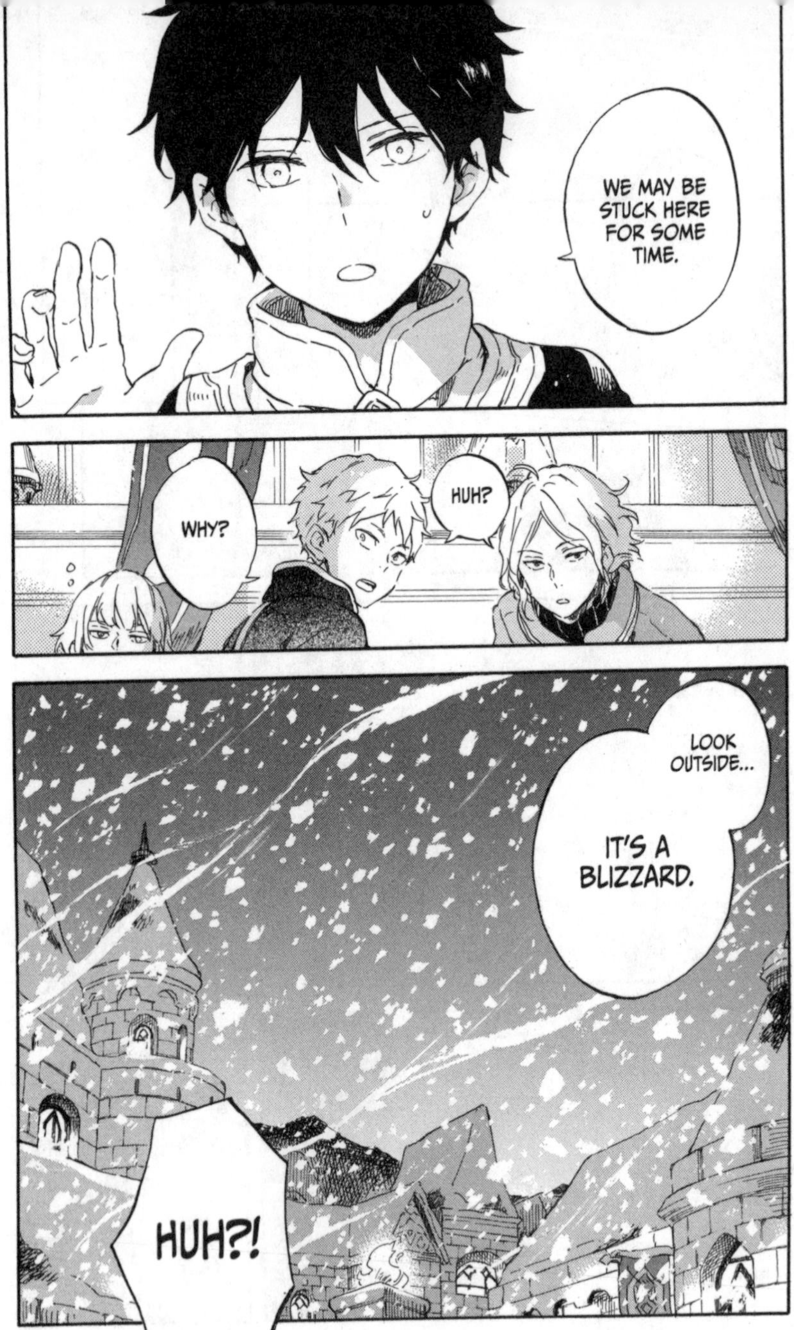
WE MAY BE STUCK HERE FOR SOME TIME.
HUH?
WHY?
LOOK OUTSIDE...
IT'S A BLIZZARD.
HUH?!

Bath #2

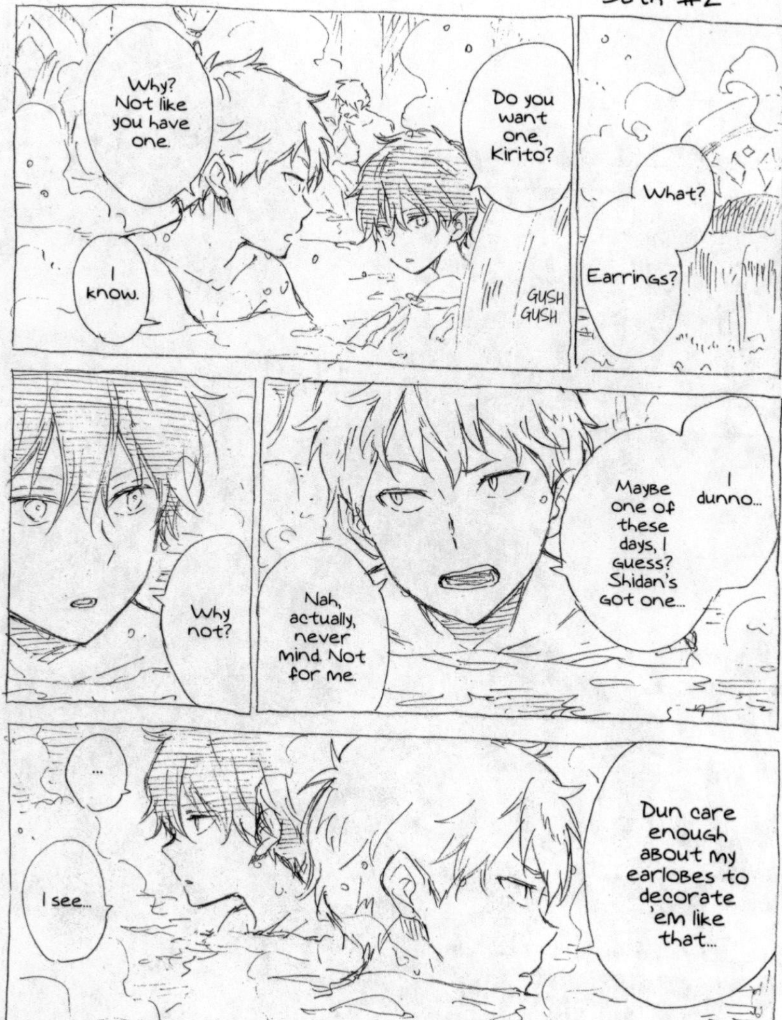
What?
Earrings?
Do you want one, Kirito?
Why? Not like you have one.
I know.
GUSH GUSH
I dunno...
Maybe one of these days, I guess? Shidan's got one...
Nah, actually, never mind. Not for me.
Why not?
Dun care enough about my earlobes to decorate 'em like that...
...
I see...

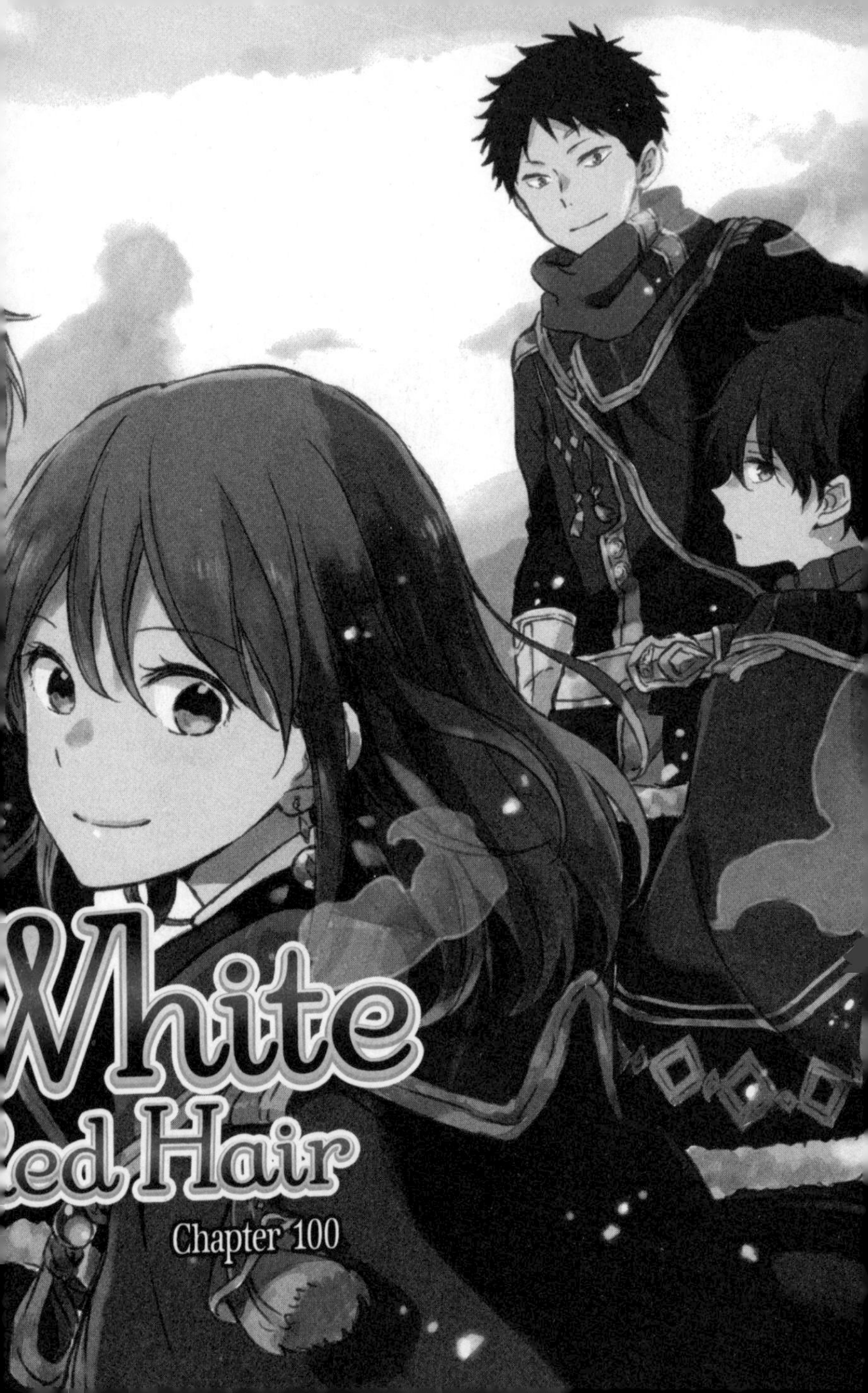
White
Red Hair
Chapter 100

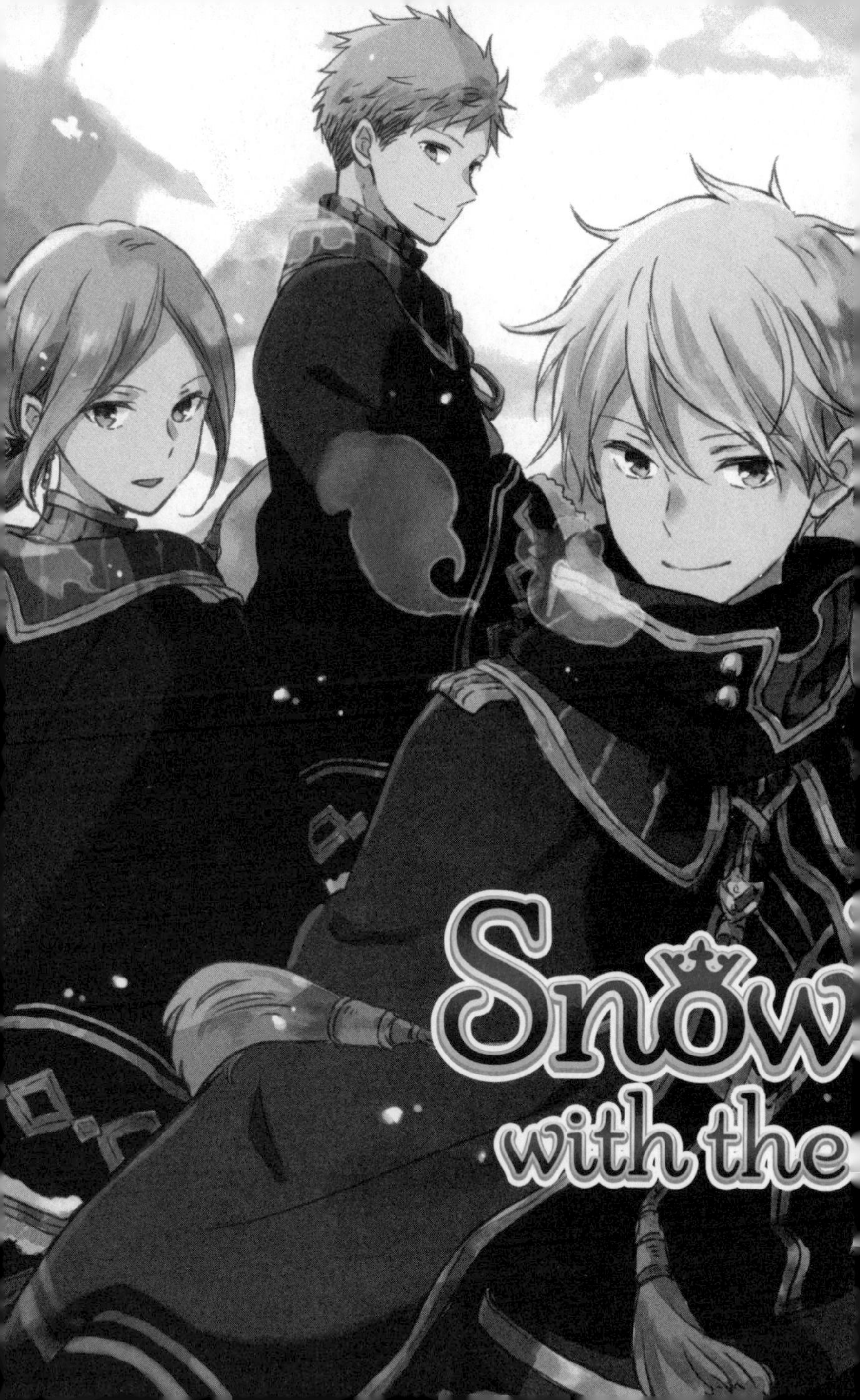
Snow
with the

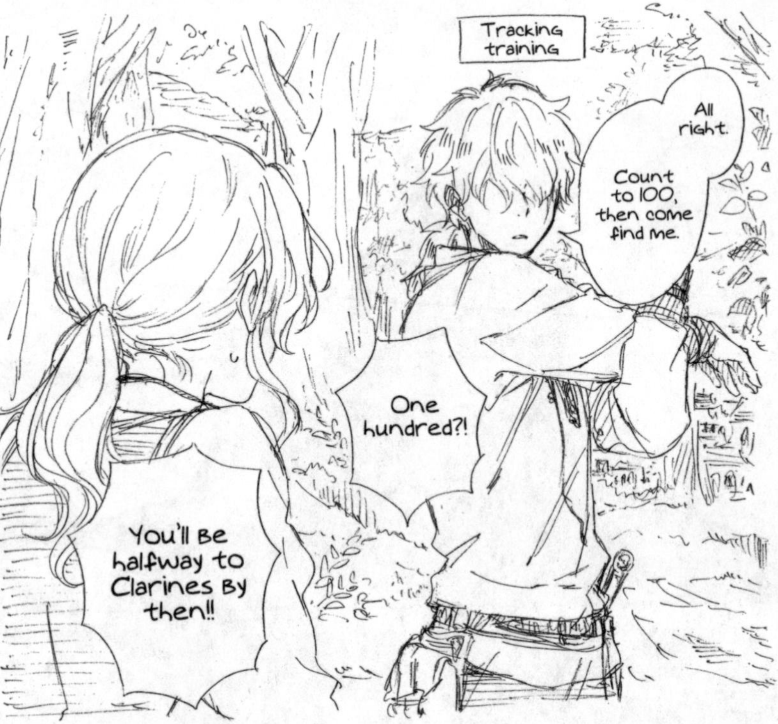
Tracking training
All right.
Count to 100, then come find me.
One hundred?!
You'll be halfway to Clarines by then!!

Special Thanks!!

-My editor
-Everyone in Publishing/Sales
-Noro-sama
-The Drama CD cast and staff
-Kawatani-sama
-Kawatani Design
-Pokkun-sama
-My family

And all the readers!!

I mean, I'd like to visit, but c'mon!

Sorata Akiduki
October 2018

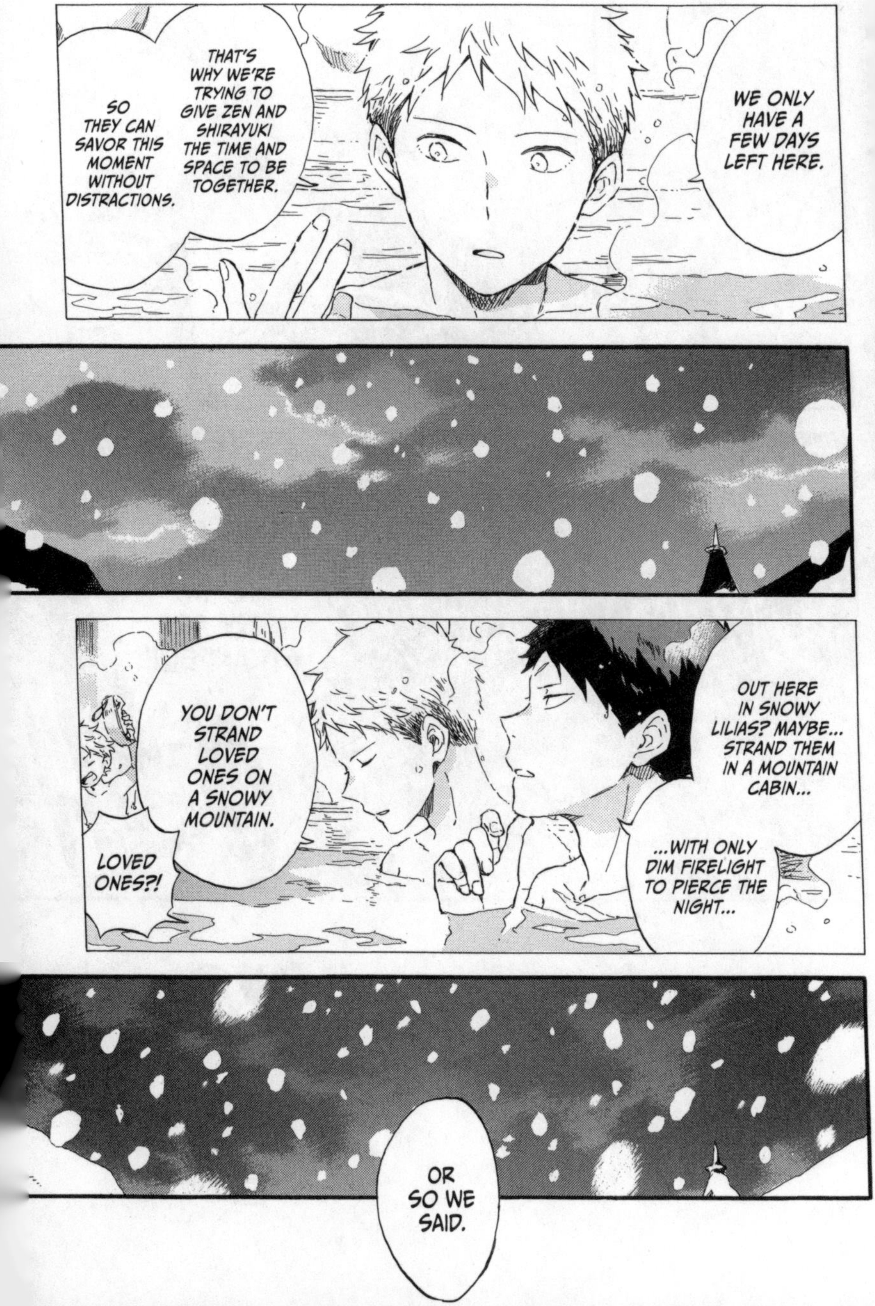
WE ONLY HAVE A FEW DAYS LEFT HERE.
THAT'S WHY WE'RE TRYING TO GIVE ZEN AND SHIRAYUKI THE TIME AND SPACE TO BE TOGETHER.
SO THEY CAN SAVOR THIS MOMENT WITHOUT DISTRACTIONS.
OUT HERE IN SNOWY LILIAS? MAYBE... STRAND THEM IN A MOUNTAIN CABIN...
...WITH ONLY DIM FIRELIGHT TO PIERCE THE NIGHT...
YOU DON'T STRAND LOVED ONES ON A SNOWY MOUNTAIN.
LOVED ONES?!
OR SO WE SAID.

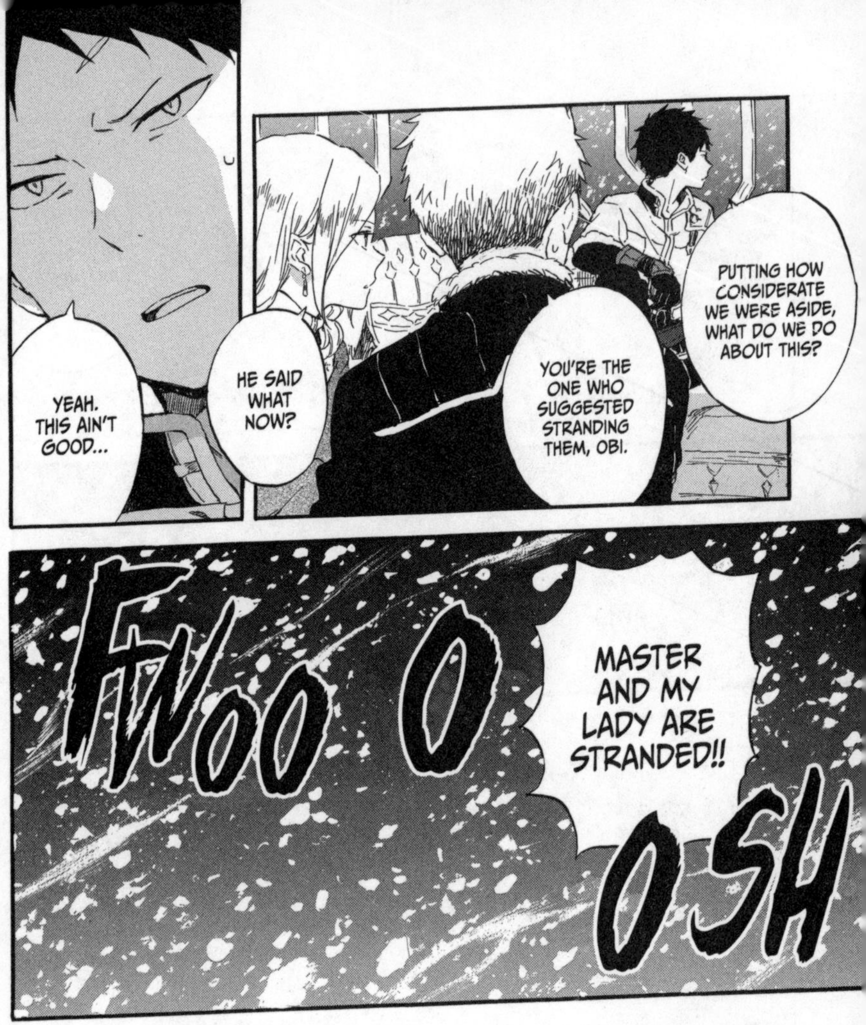
PUTTING HOW CONSIDERATE WE WERE ASIDE, WHAT DO WE DO ABOUT THIS?
YOU'RE THE ONE WHO SUGGESTED STRANDING THEM, OBI.
HE SAID WHAT NOW?
YEAH. THIS AIN'T GOOD...
MASTER AND MY LADY ARE STRANDED!!
FWOOOOOSH

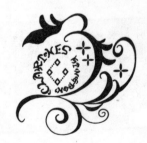

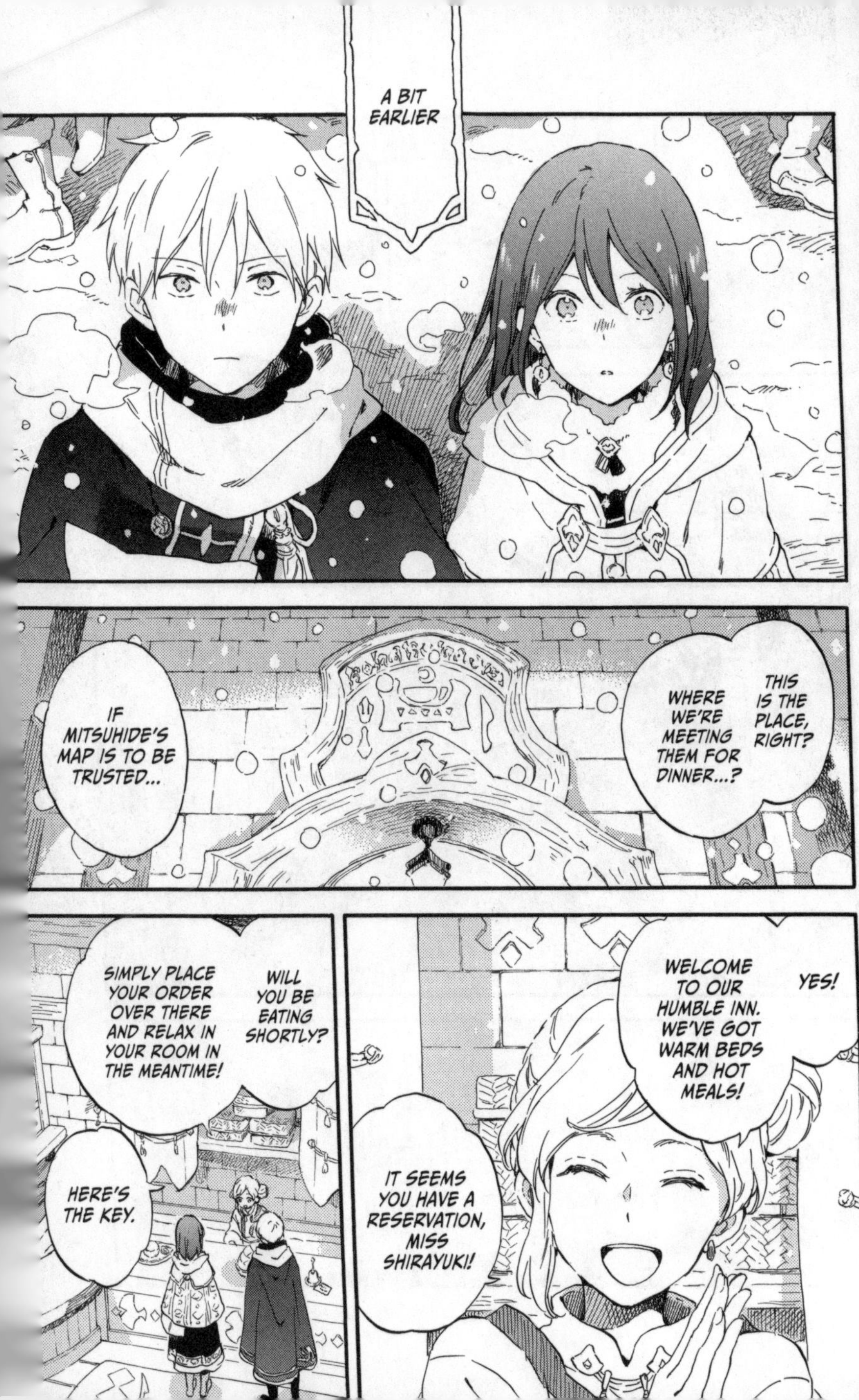
A BIT EARLIER
THIS IS THE PLACE, RIGHT?
WHERE WE'RE MEETING THEM FOR DINNER...?
IF MITSUHIDE'S MAP IS TO BE TRUSTED...
YES!
WELCOME TO OUR HUMBLE INN. WE'VE GOT WARM BEDS AND HOT MEALS!
IT SEEMS YOU HAVE A RESERVATION, MISS SHIRAYUKI!
WILL YOU BE EATING SHORTLY?
SIMPLY PLACE YOUR ORDER OVER THERE AND RELAX IN YOUR ROOM IN THE MEANTIME!
HERE'S THE KEY.

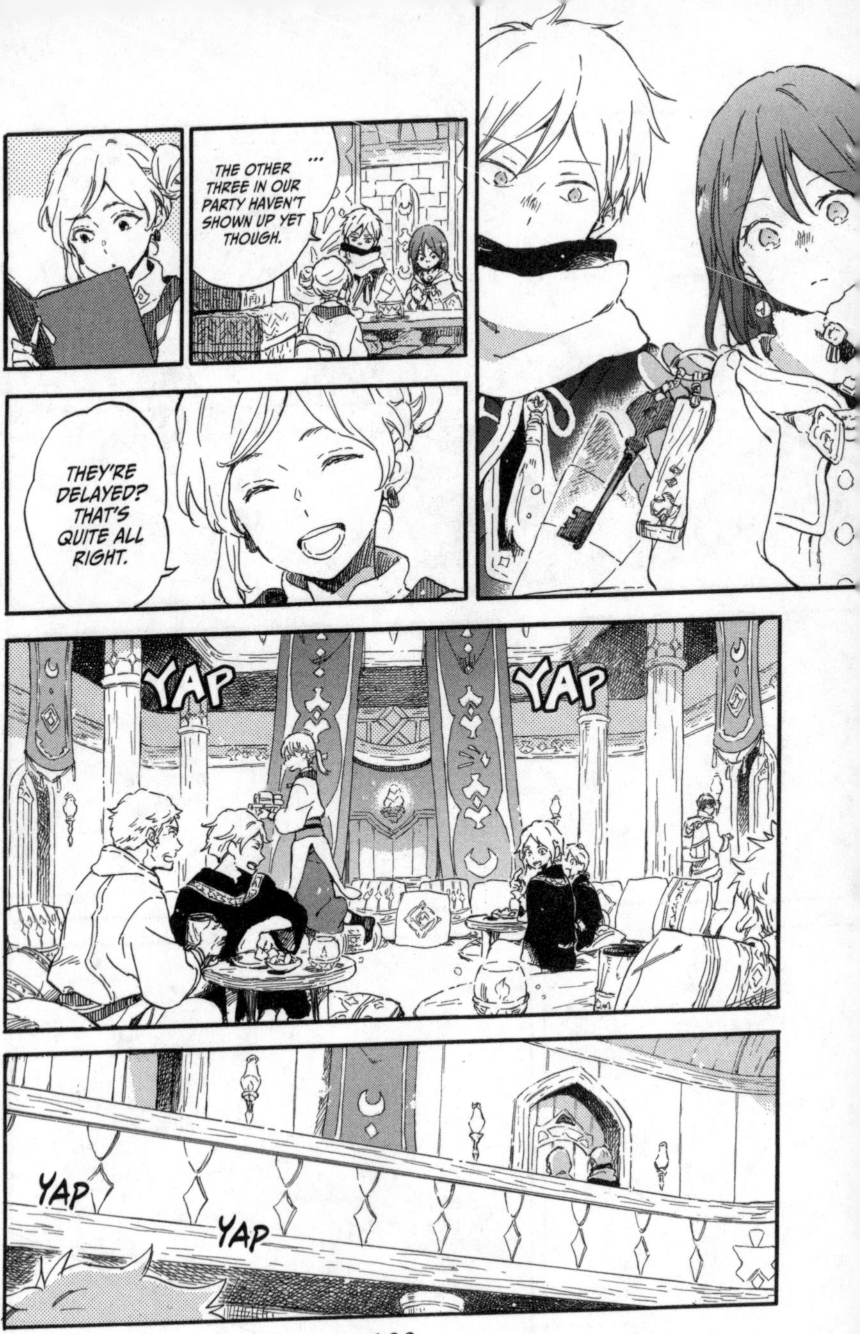
...
THE OTHER THREE IN OUR PARTY HAVEN'T SHOWN UP YET THOUGH.
THEY'RE DELAYED? THAT'S QUITE ALL RIGHT.
YAP
YAP
YAP
YAP

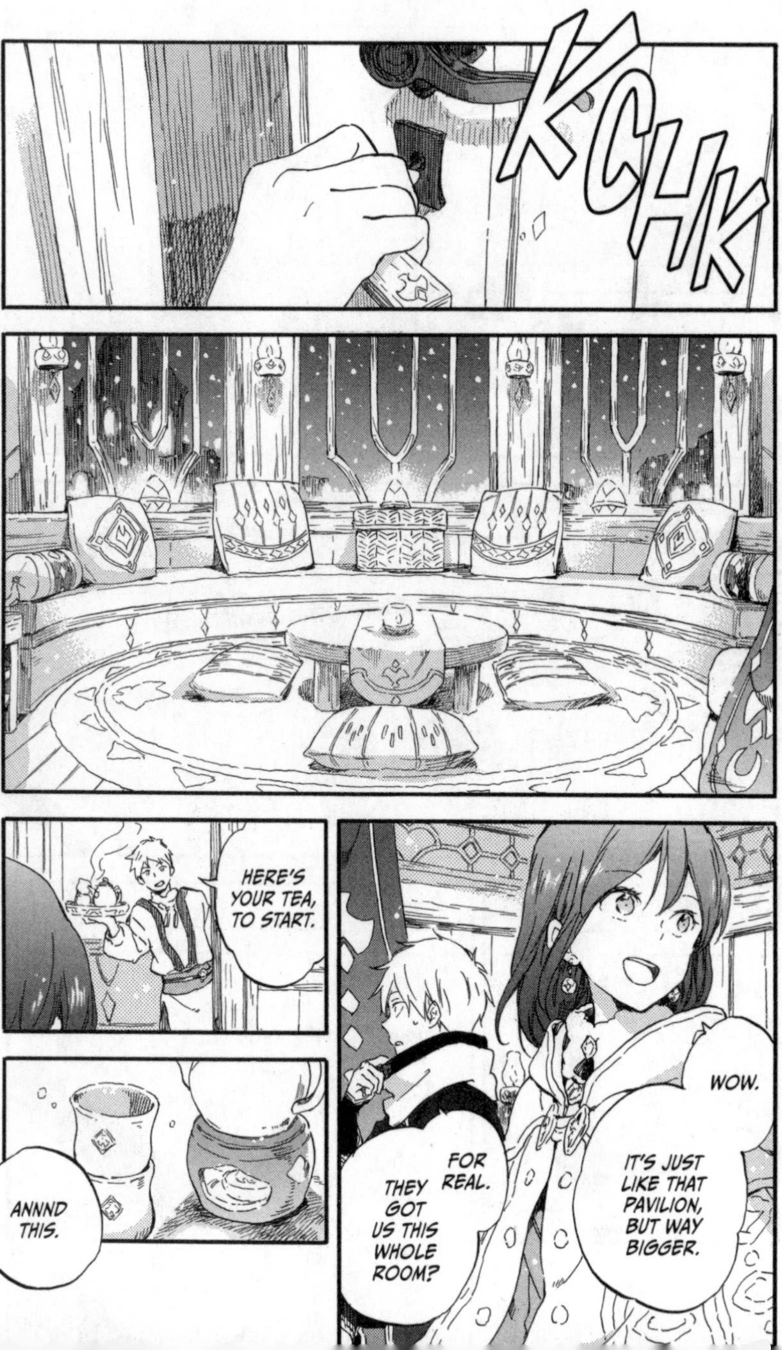
KCHK
WOW.
IT'S JUST LIKE THAT PAVILION, BUT WAY BIGGER.
FOR REAL.
THEY GOT US THIS WHOLE ROOM?
HERE'S YOUR TEA, TO START.
ANNND THIS.

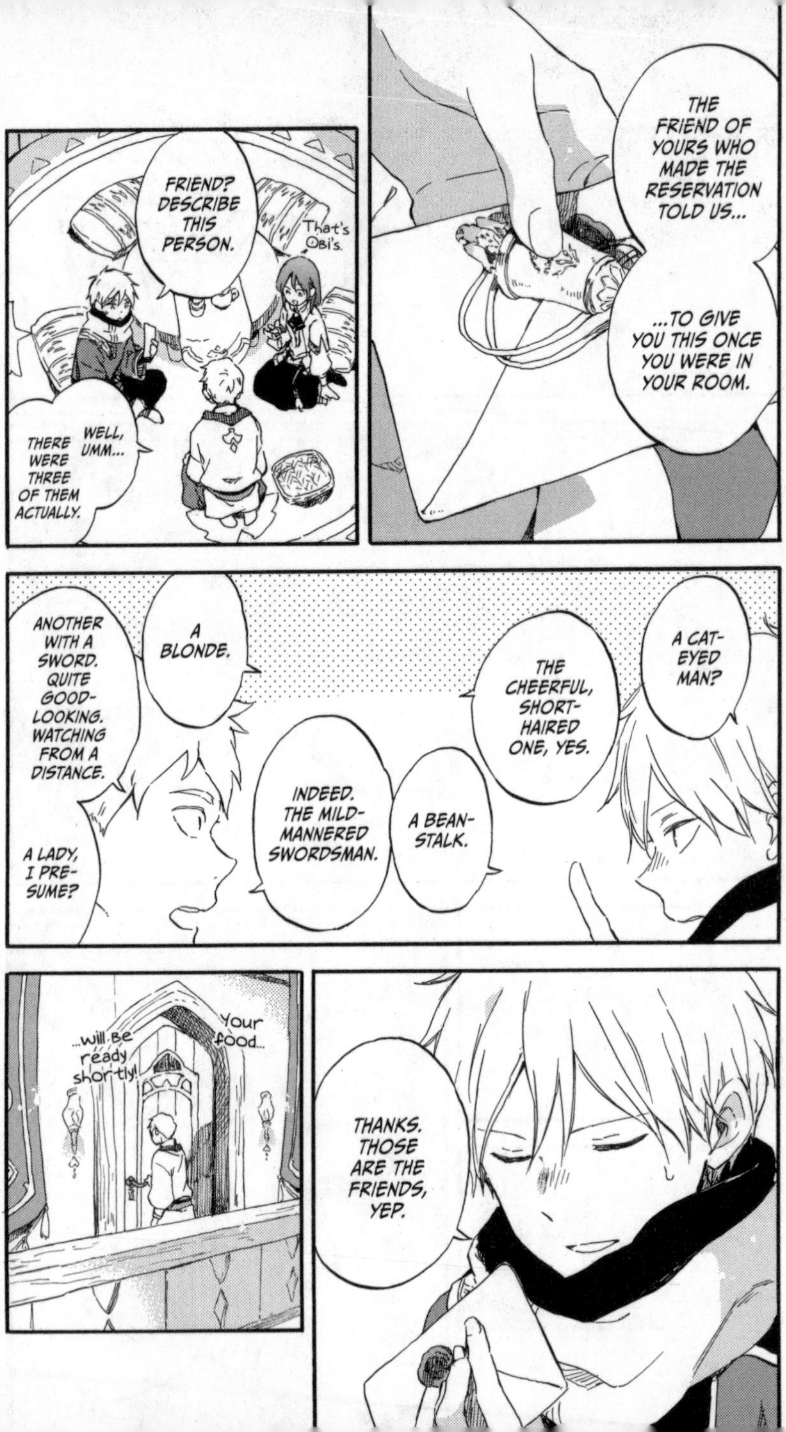
THE FRIEND OF YOURS WHO MADE THE RESERVATION TOLD US...
...TO GIVE YOU THIS ONCE YOU WERE IN YOUR ROOM.
FRIEND? DESCRIBE THIS PERSON.
That's Obi's.
WELL, UMM...
THERE WERE THREE OF THEM ACTUALLY.
A CAT-EYED MAN?
THE CHEERFUL, SHORT-HAIRED ONE, YES.
A BEAN-STALK.
INDEED. THE MILD-MANNERED SWORDSMAN.
A BLONDE.
ANOTHER WITH A SWORD. QUITE GOOD-LOOKING. WATCHING FROM A DISTANCE.
A LADY, I PRESUME?
THANKS. THOSE ARE THE FRIENDS, YEP.
Your food...
...will be ready shortly!

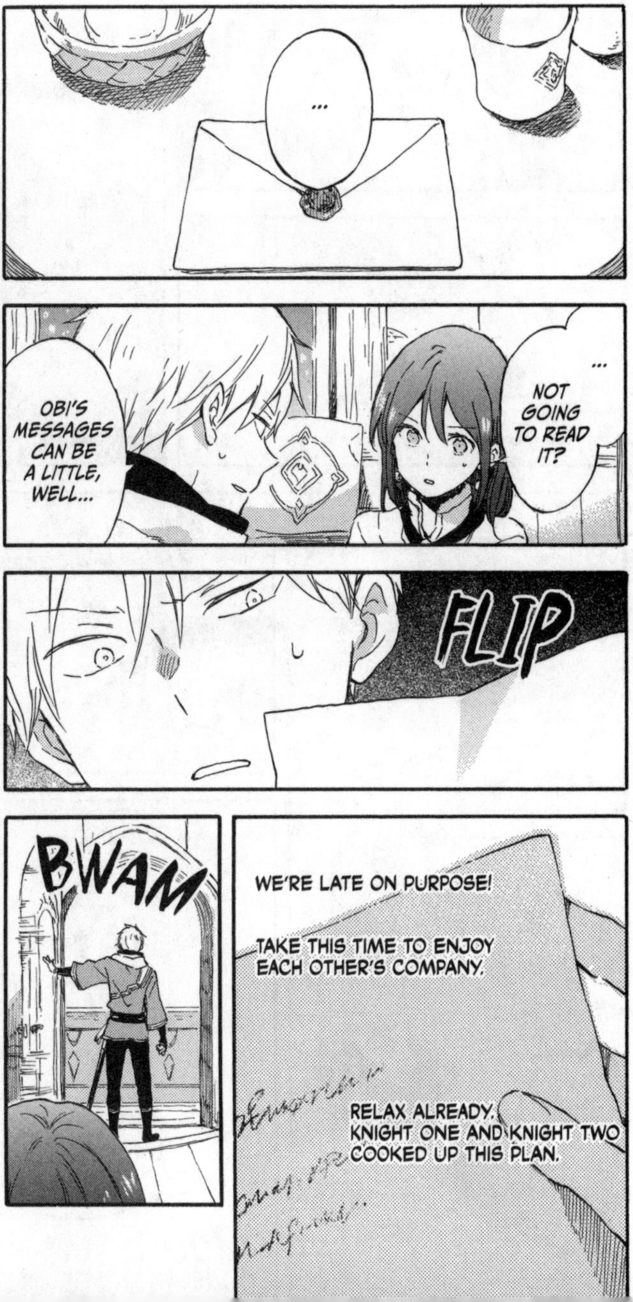
...
... NOT GOING TO READ IT?
OBI'S MESSAGES CAN BE A LITTLE, WELL...
FLIP
WE'RE LATE ON PURPOSE!
TAKE THIS TIME TO ENJOY EACH OTHER'S COMPANY.
RELAX ALREADY. KNIGHT ONE AND KNIGHT TWO COOKED UP THIS PLAN.
BWAM

5

TRIP DIARY, PART 4

At lunch, just as I was wondering if the salad was meant to be so bland...I noticed someone else from our tour, at the same table, putting salt and pepper on their salad. I copied them, and the salad was suddenly fantastic. A mini revelation. A salad-based revelation. From that moment forth, I didn't stop shaking salt and pepper onto every vegetable I found in Malta.

This was also the day when...I went to a restaurant with Hachi! We ordered some pasta and Maltese specialties. Maltese wine is apparently famous, but neither of us drink, so I ordered orange juice instead. There was a previous Euro trip where they brought me Fanta when I asked for orange juice, so I had to wonder what might emerge this time!! A server came out and sputtered, "Orange juice?!" He was checking that the order did indeed come from our table. Yes. You have that right. I ordered orange juice, sir.

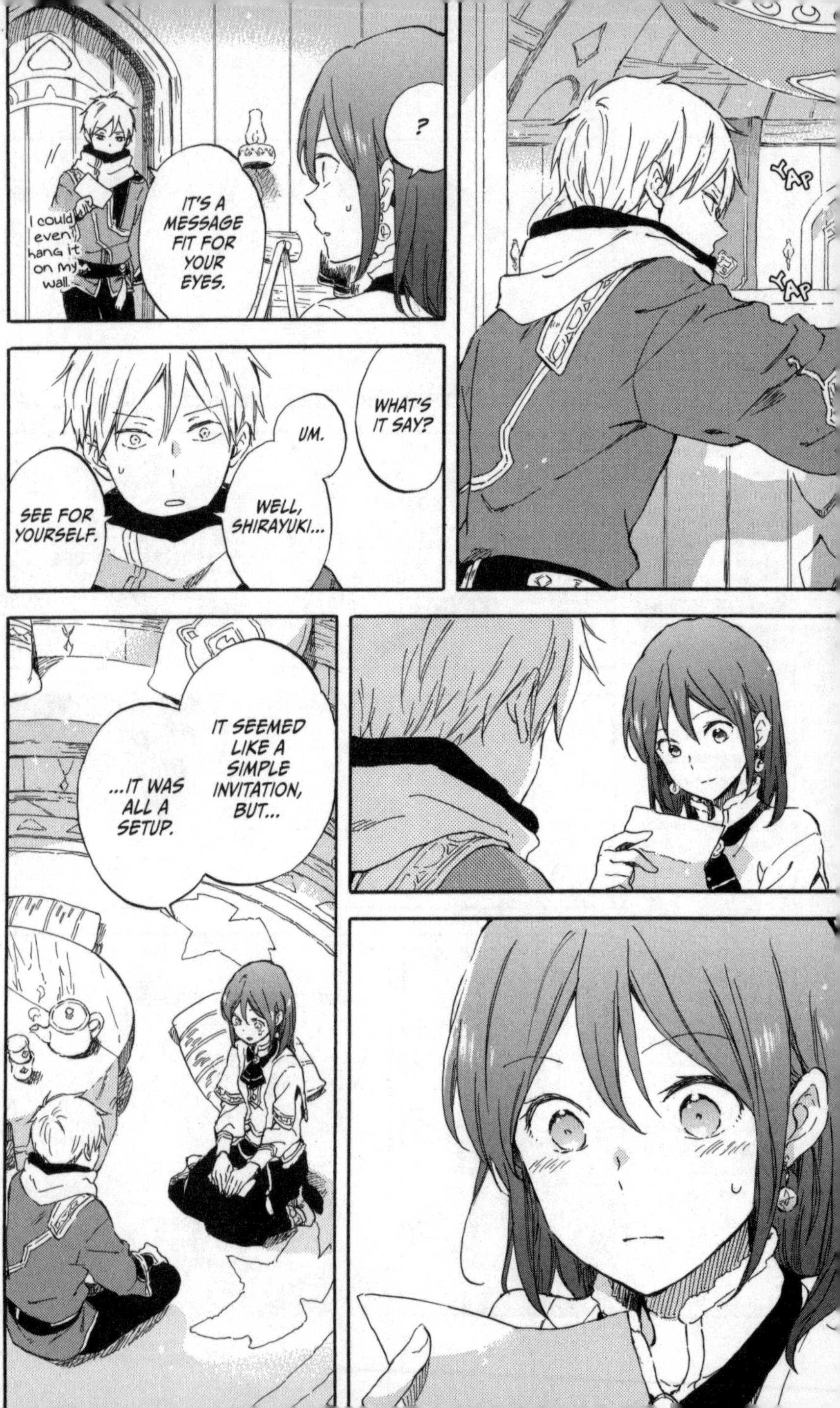

YAP
YAP
?
IT'S A MESSAGE FIT FOR YOUR EYES.
I could even hang it on my wall.
WHAT'S IT SAY?
UM.
WELL, SHIRAYUKI...
SEE FOR YOURSELF.
IT SEEMED LIKE A SIMPLE INVITATION, BUT...
...IT WAS ALL A SETUP.

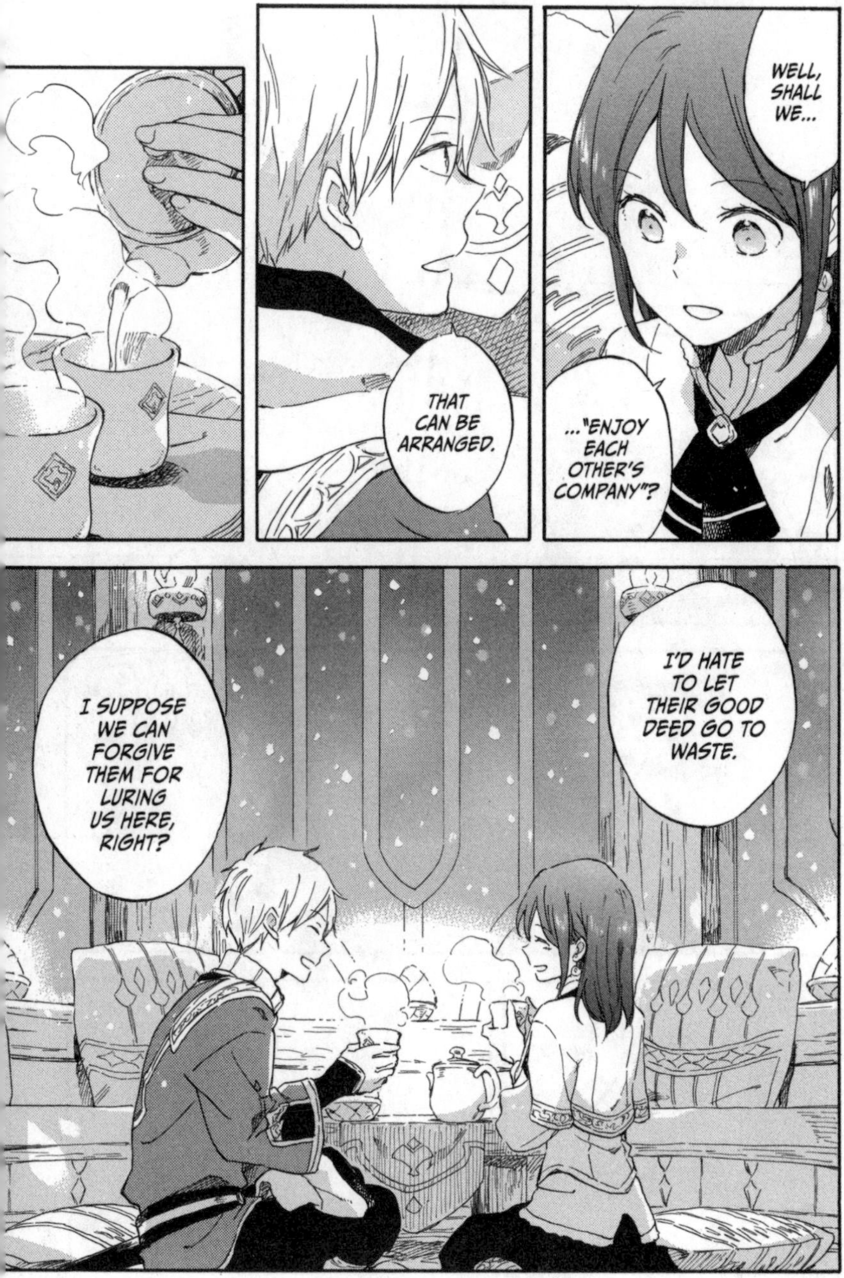
WELL, SHALL WE...
..."ENJOY EACH OTHER'S COMPANY"?
THAT CAN BE ARRANGED.
I'D HATE TO LET THEIR GOOD DEED GO TO WASTE.
I SUPPOSE WE CAN FORGIVE THEM FOR LURING US HERE, RIGHT?

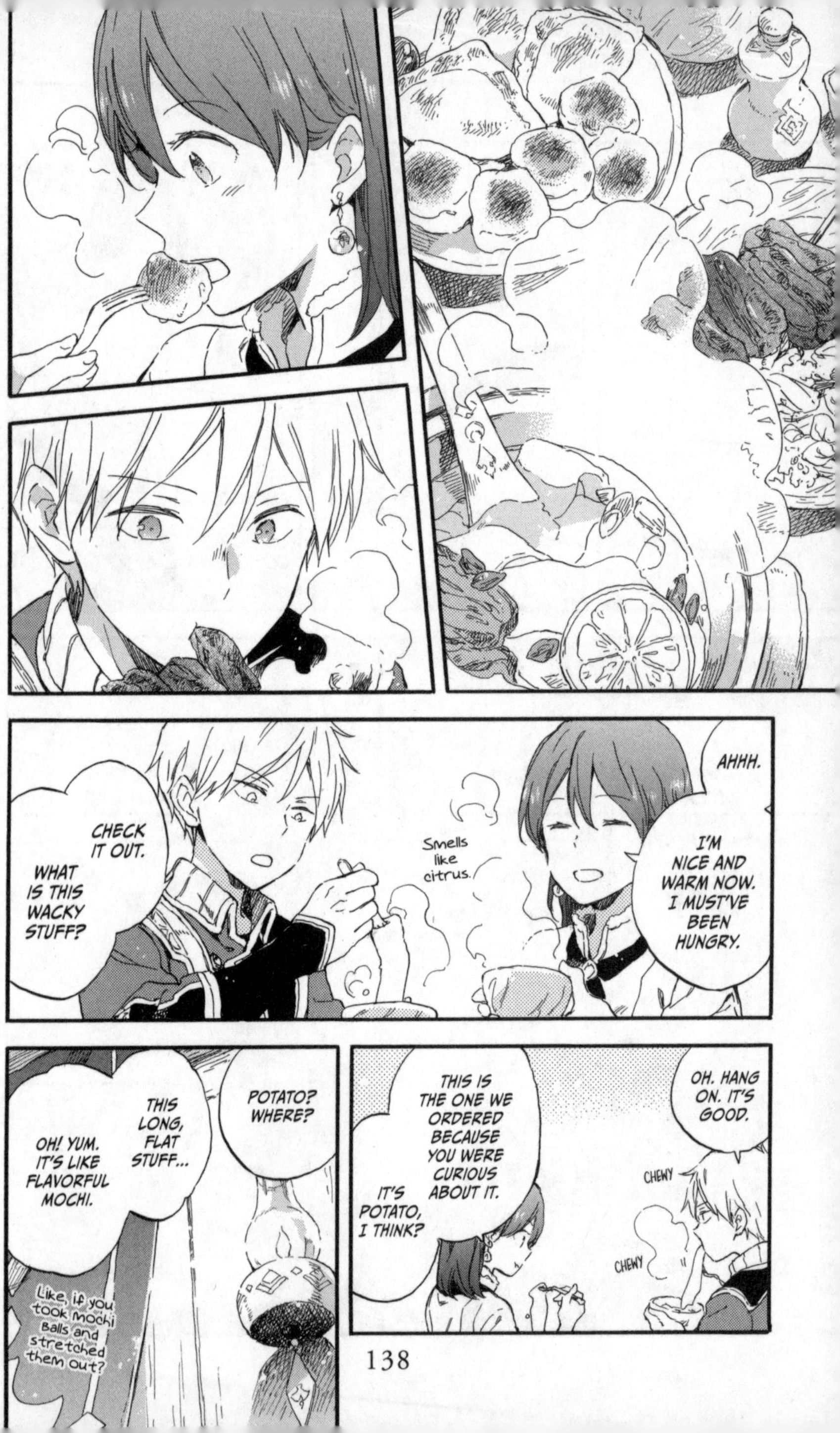
AHHH.
I'M NICE AND WARM NOW. I MUST'VE BEEN HUNGRY.
Smells like citrus.
CHECK IT OUT.
WHAT IS THIS WACKY STUFF?
OH. HANG ON. IT'S GOOD.
CHEWY
CHEWY
THIS IS THE ONE WE ORDERED BECAUSE YOU WERE CURIOUS ABOUT IT.
IT'S POTATO, I THINK?
POTATO? WHERE?
THIS LONG, FLAT STUFF...
OH! YUM. IT'S LIKE FLAVORFUL MOCHI.
Like, if you took mochi balls and stretched them out?

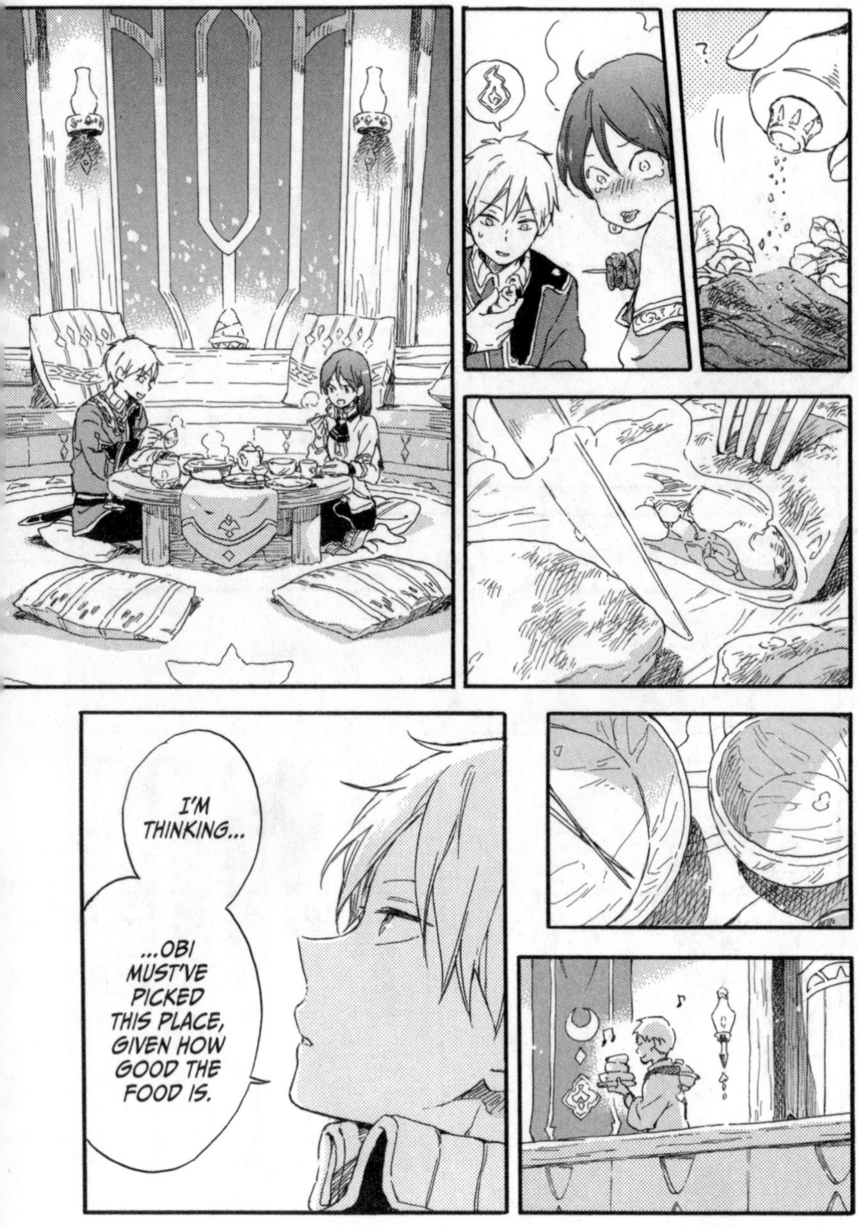

?
I'M THINKING...
...OBI MUST'VE PICKED THIS PLACE, GIVEN HOW GOOD THE FOOD IS.

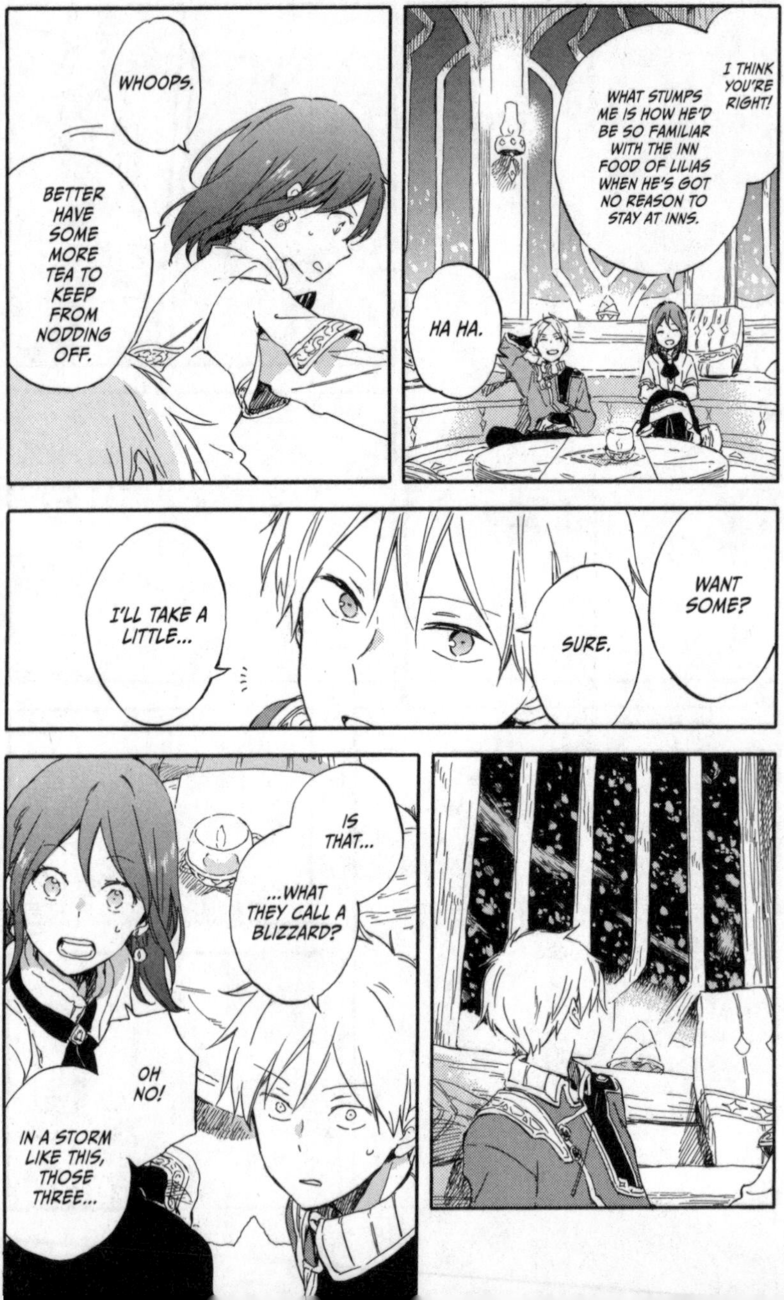
I THINK YOU'RE RIGHT!
WHAT STUMPS ME IS HOW HE'D BE SO FAMILIAR WITH THE INN FOOD OF LILIAS WHEN HE'S GOT NO REASON TO STAY AT INNS.
HA HA.
WHOOPS.
BETTER HAVE SOME MORE TEA TO KEEP FROM NODDING OFF.
WANT SOME?
SURE.
I'LL TAKE A LITTLE...
IS THAT...
...WHAT THEY CALL A BLIZZARD?
OH NO!
IN A STORM LIKE THIS, THOSE THREE...

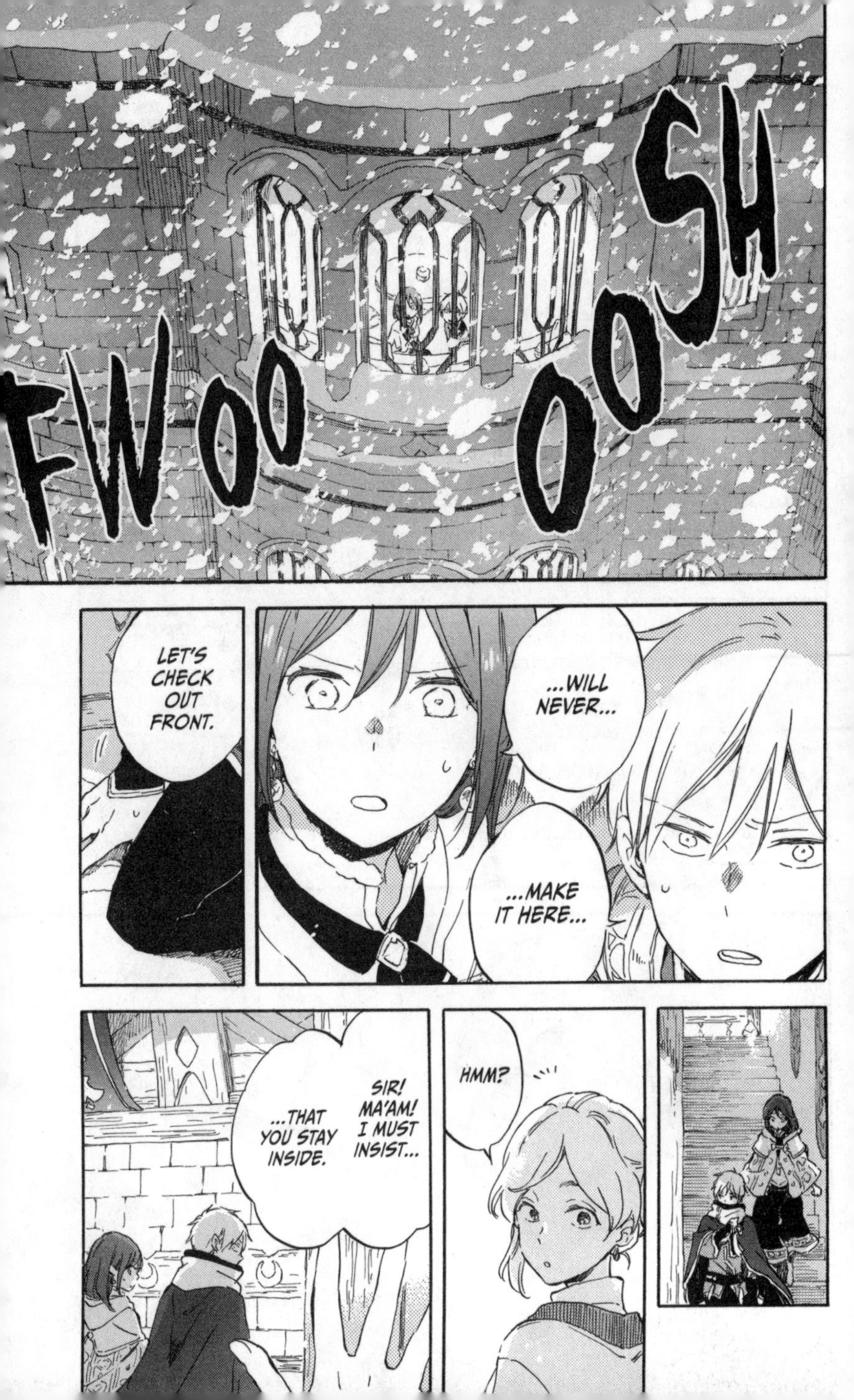
FWOOOOSH
...WILL NEVER...
...MAKE IT HERE...
LET'S CHECK OUT FRONT.
HMM?
SIR! MA'AM! I MUST INSIST...
...THAT YOU STAY INSIDE.

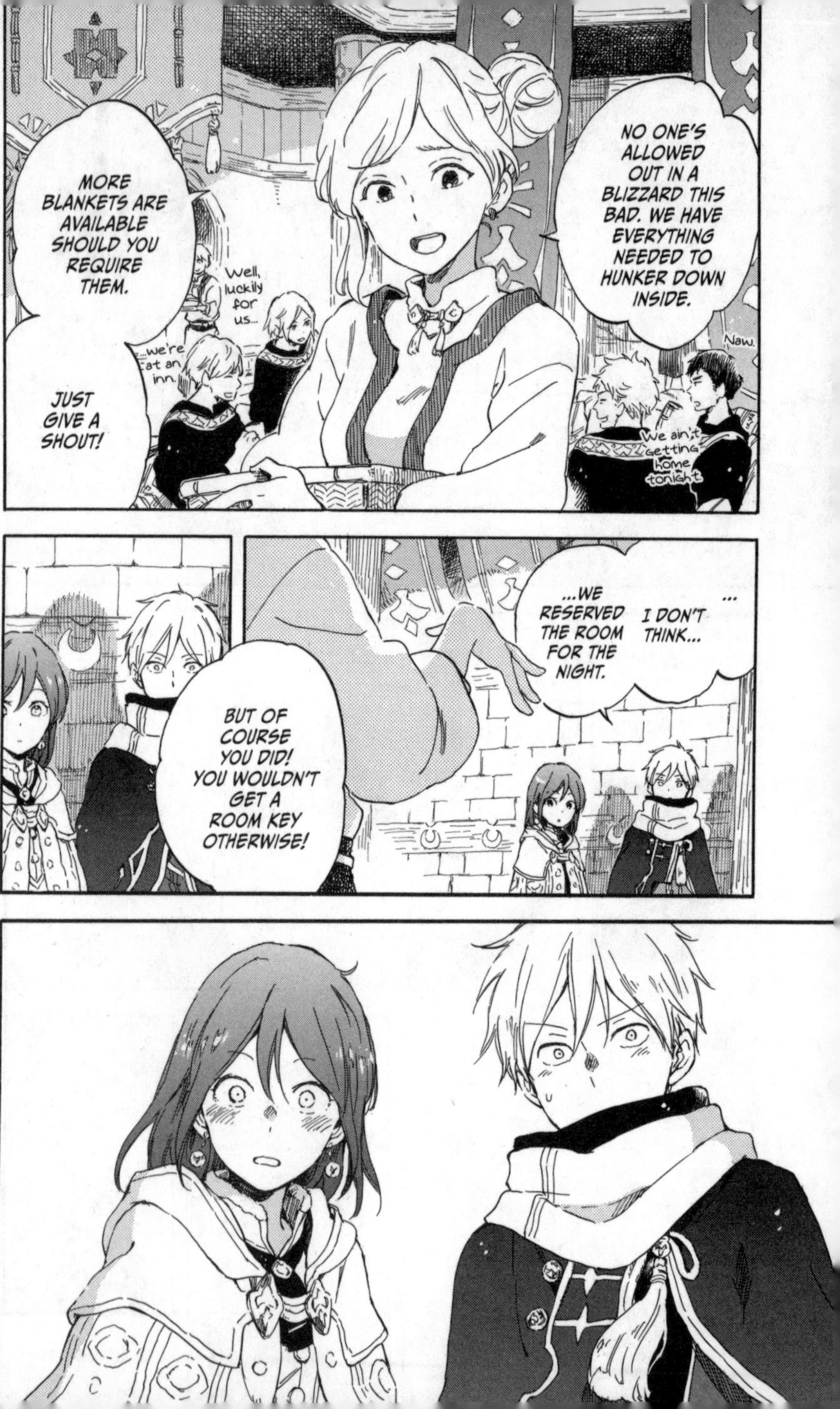
NO ONE'S ALLOWED OUT IN A BLIZZARD THIS BAD. WE HAVE EVERYTHING NEEDED TO HUNKER DOWN INSIDE.
Naw.
We ain't getting home tonight.
Well, luckily for us...
...we're at an inn.
MORE BLANKETS ARE AVAILABLE SHOULD YOU REQUIRE THEM.
JUST GIVE A SHOUT!
...
I DON'T THINK...
...WE RESERVED THE ROOM FOR THE NIGHT.
BUT OF COURSE YOU DID! YOU WOULDN'T GET A ROOM KEY OTHERWISE!

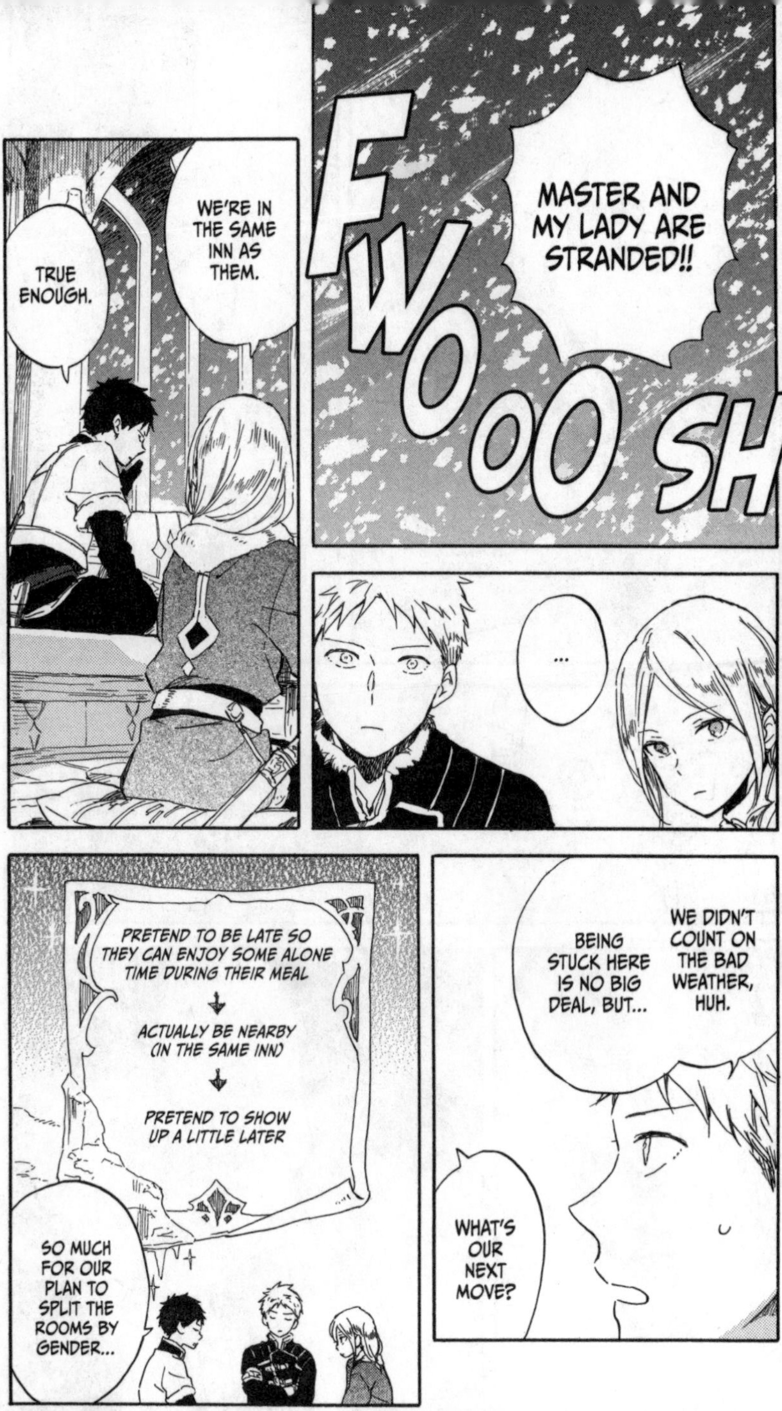
MASTER AND MY LADY ARE STRANDED!!
FWOOOOSH
...
WE'RE IN THE SAME INN AS THEM.
TRUE ENOUGH.
WE DIDN'T COUNT ON THE BAD WEATHER, HUH.
BEING STUCK HERE IS NO BIG DEAL, BUT...
WHAT'S OUR NEXT MOVE?
PRETEND TO BE LATE SO THEY CAN ENJOY SOME ALONE TIME DURING THEIR MEAL
ACTUALLY BE NEARBY (IN THE SAME INN)
PRETEND TO SHOW UP A LITTLE LATER
SO MUCH FOR OUR PLAN TO SPLIT THE ROOMS BY GENDER...

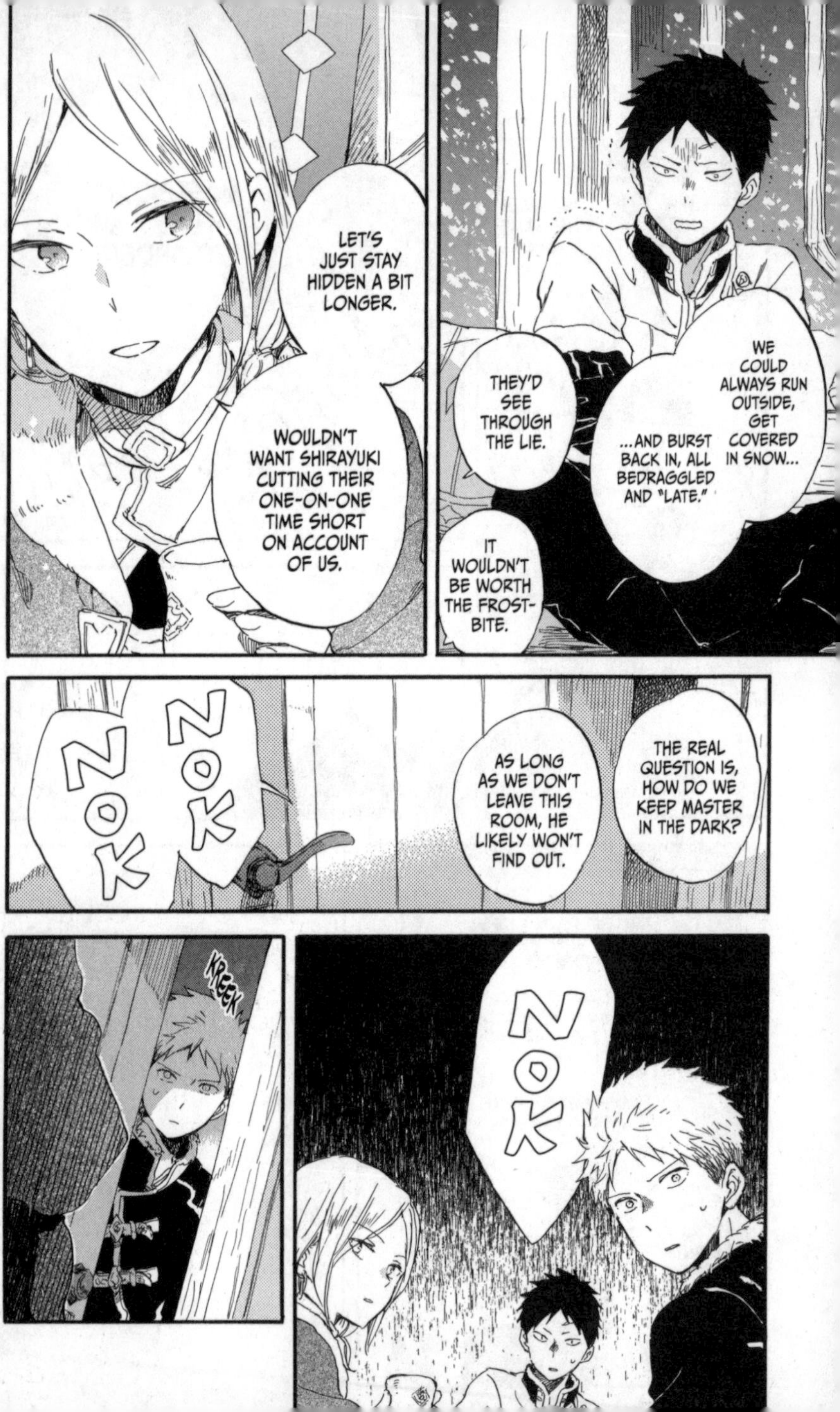
WE COULD ALWAYS RUN OUTSIDE, GET COVERED IN SNOW...
...AND BURST BACK IN, ALL BEDRAGGLED AND "LATE."
THEY'D SEE THROUGH THE LIE.
IT WOULDN'T BE WORTH THE FROST-BITE.
LET'S JUST STAY HIDDEN A BIT LONGER.
WOULDN'T WANT SHIRAYUKI CUTTING THEIR ONE-ON-ONE TIME SHORT ON ACCOUNT OF US.
THE REAL QUESTION IS, HOW DO WE KEEP MASTER IN THE DARK?
AS LONG AS WE DON'T LEAVE THIS ROOM, HE LIKELY WON'T FIND OUT.
NOK
NOK
NOK
KREEK

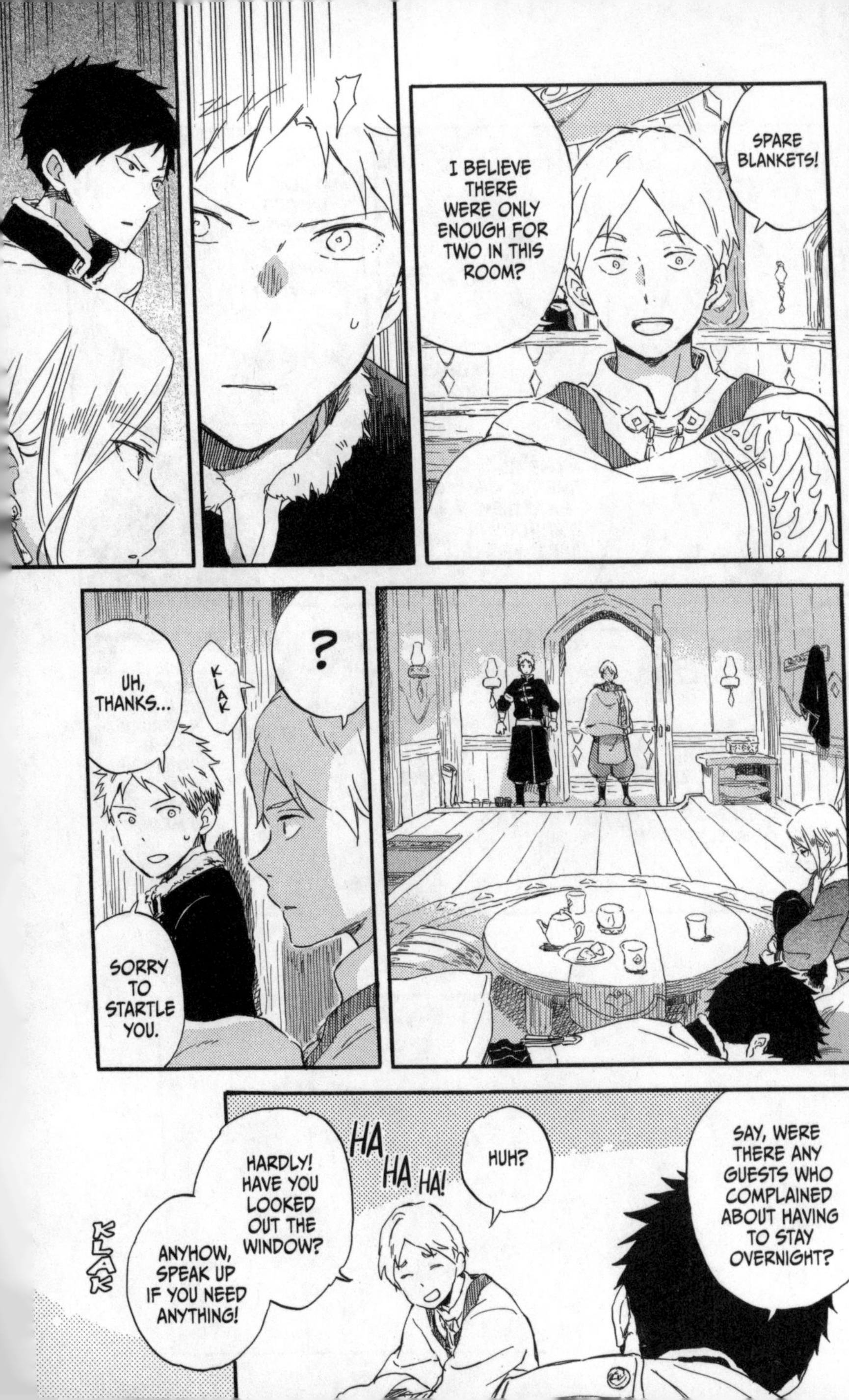
SPARE BLANKETS!
I BELIEVE THERE WERE ONLY ENOUGH FOR TWO IN THIS ROOM?
?
KLAK
UH, THANKS...
SORRY TO STARTLE YOU.
SAY, WERE THERE ANY GUESTS WHO COMPLAINED ABOUT HAVING TO STAY OVERNIGHT?
HUH?
HA HA HA!
HARDLY! HAVE YOU LOOKED OUT THE WINDOW?
ANYHOW, SPEAK UP IF YOU NEED ANYTHING!
KLAK

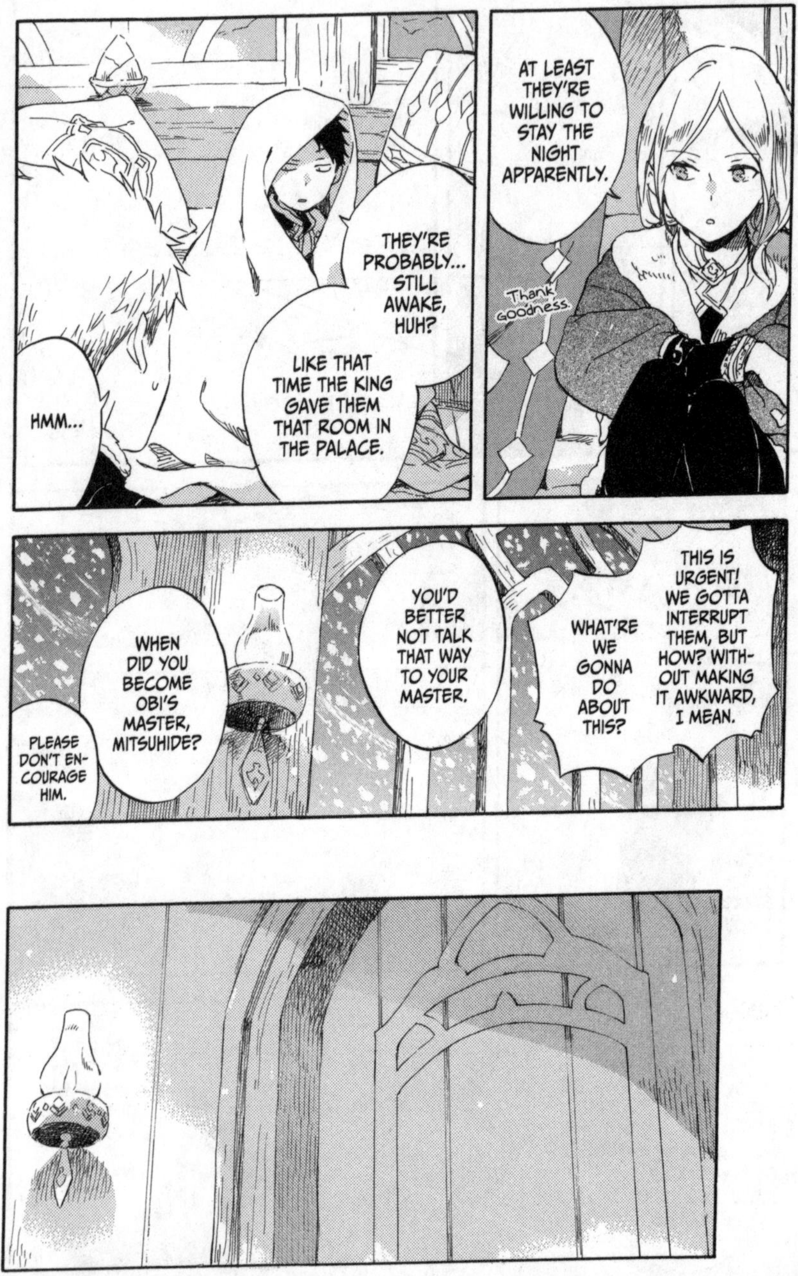
AT LEAST THEY'RE WILLING TO STAY THE NIGHT APPARENTLY.
Thank goodness.
THEY'RE PROBABLY... STILL AWAKE, HUH?
LIKE THAT TIME THE KING GAVE THEM THAT ROOM IN THE PALACE.
HMM...
THIS IS URGENT! WE GOTTA INTERRUPT THEM, BUT HOW? WITHOUT MAKING IT AWKWARD, I MEAN.
WHAT'RE WE GONNA DO ABOUT THIS?
YOU'D BETTER NOT TALK THAT WAY TO YOUR MASTER.
WHEN DID YOU BECOME OBI'S MASTER, MITSUHIDE?
PLEASE DON'T ENCOURAGE HIM.

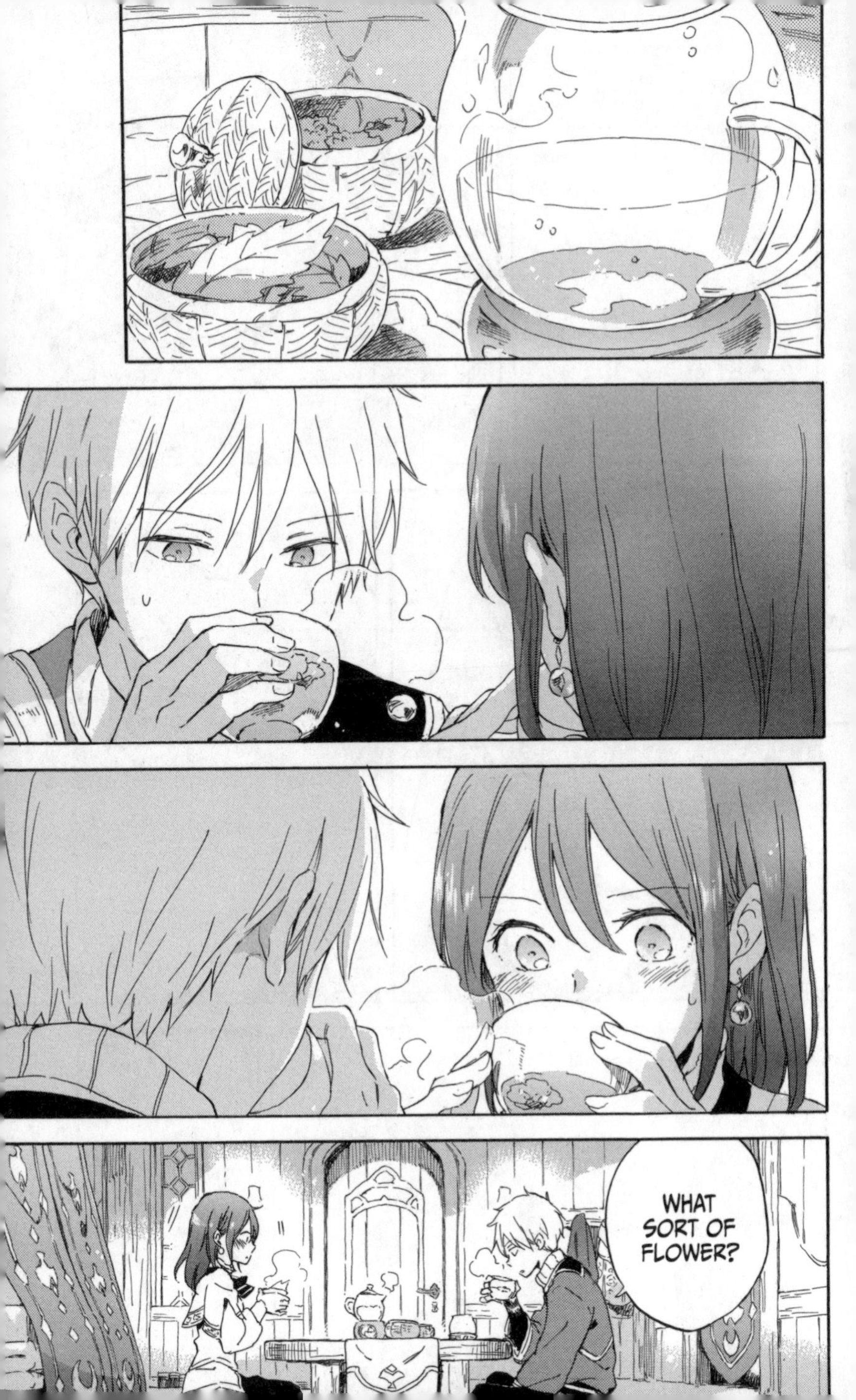
WHAT SORT OF FLOWER?

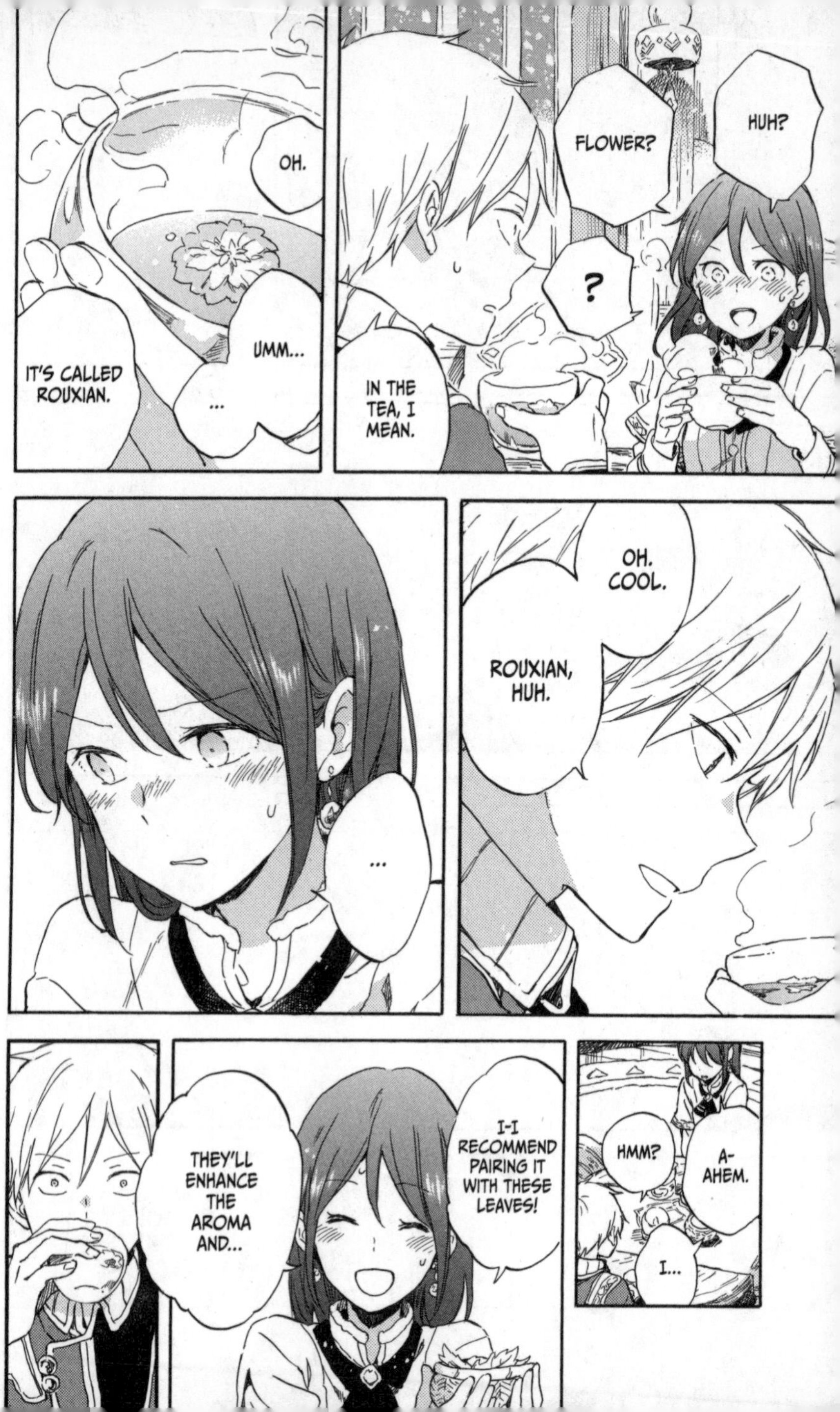
HUH?
FLOWER?
?
IN THE TEA, I MEAN.
OH.
UMM...
...
IT'S CALLED ROUXIAN.
OH. COOL.
ROUXIAN, HUH.
...
A- AHEM.
HMM?
I...
I-I RECOMMEND PAIRING IT WITH THESE LEAVES!
THEY'LL ENHANCE THE AROMA AND...

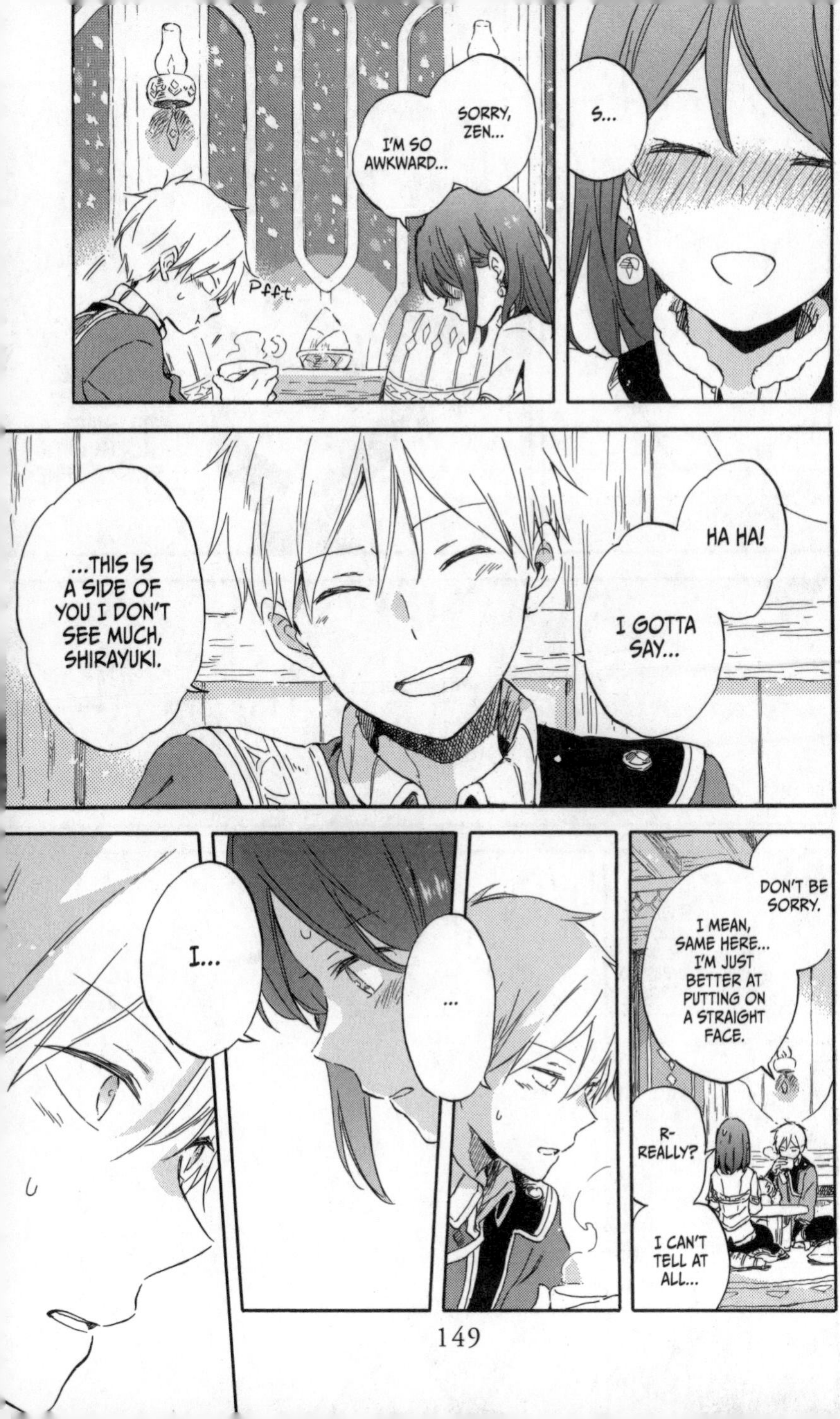
S...
SORRY, ZEN... I'M SO AWKWARD...
Pfft.
HA HA! I GOTTA SAY...
...THIS IS A SIDE OF YOU I DON'T SEE MUCH, SHIRAYUKI.
DON'T BE SORRY.
I MEAN, SAME HERE... I'M JUST BETTER AT PUTTING ON A STRAIGHT FACE.
R-REALLY?
I CAN'T TELL AT ALL...
...
I...

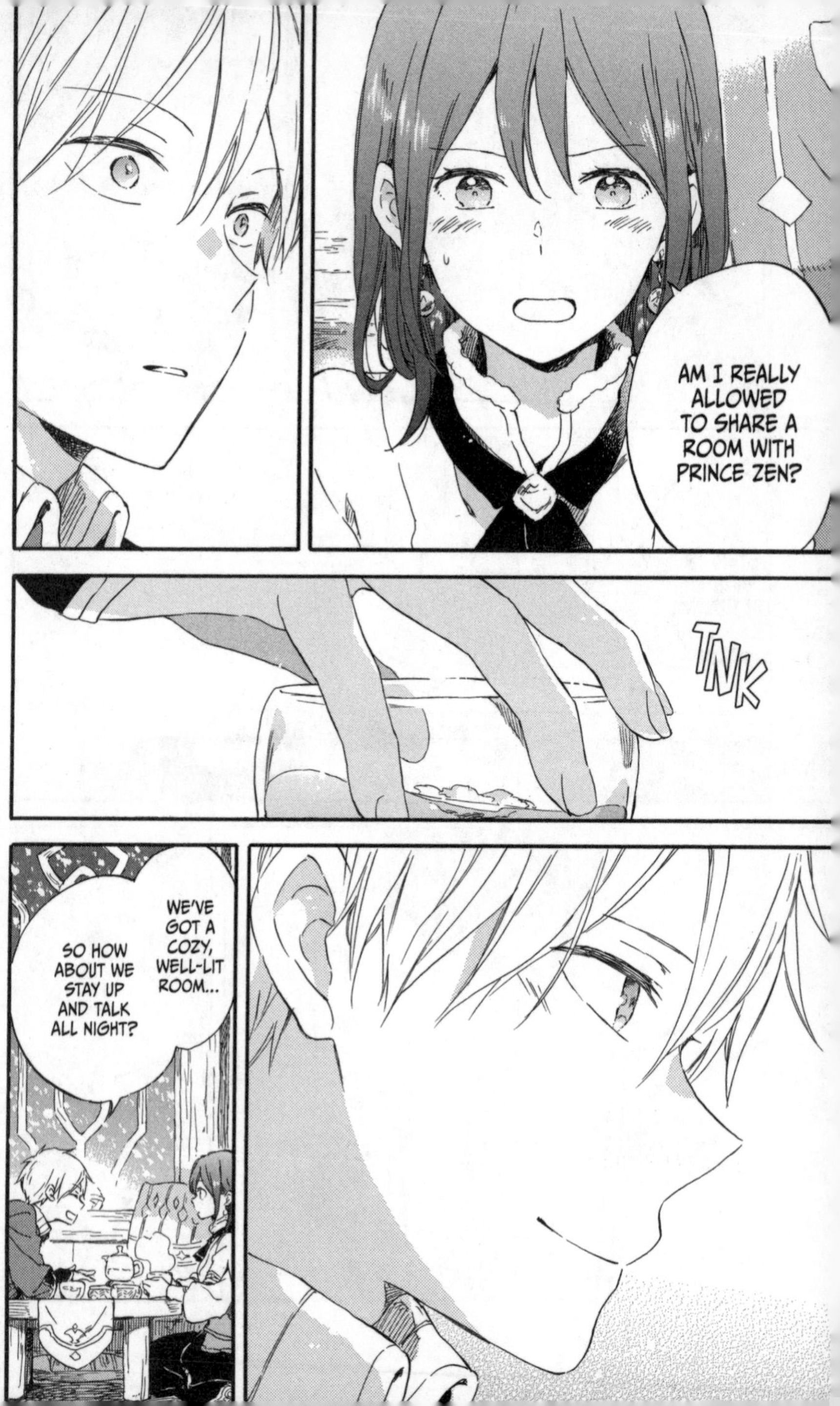
AM I REALLY ALLOWED TO SHARE A ROOM WITH PRINCE ZEN?
TNK
WE'VE GOT A COZY, WELL-LIT ROOM...
SO HOW ABOUT WE STAY UP AND TALK ALL NIGHT?

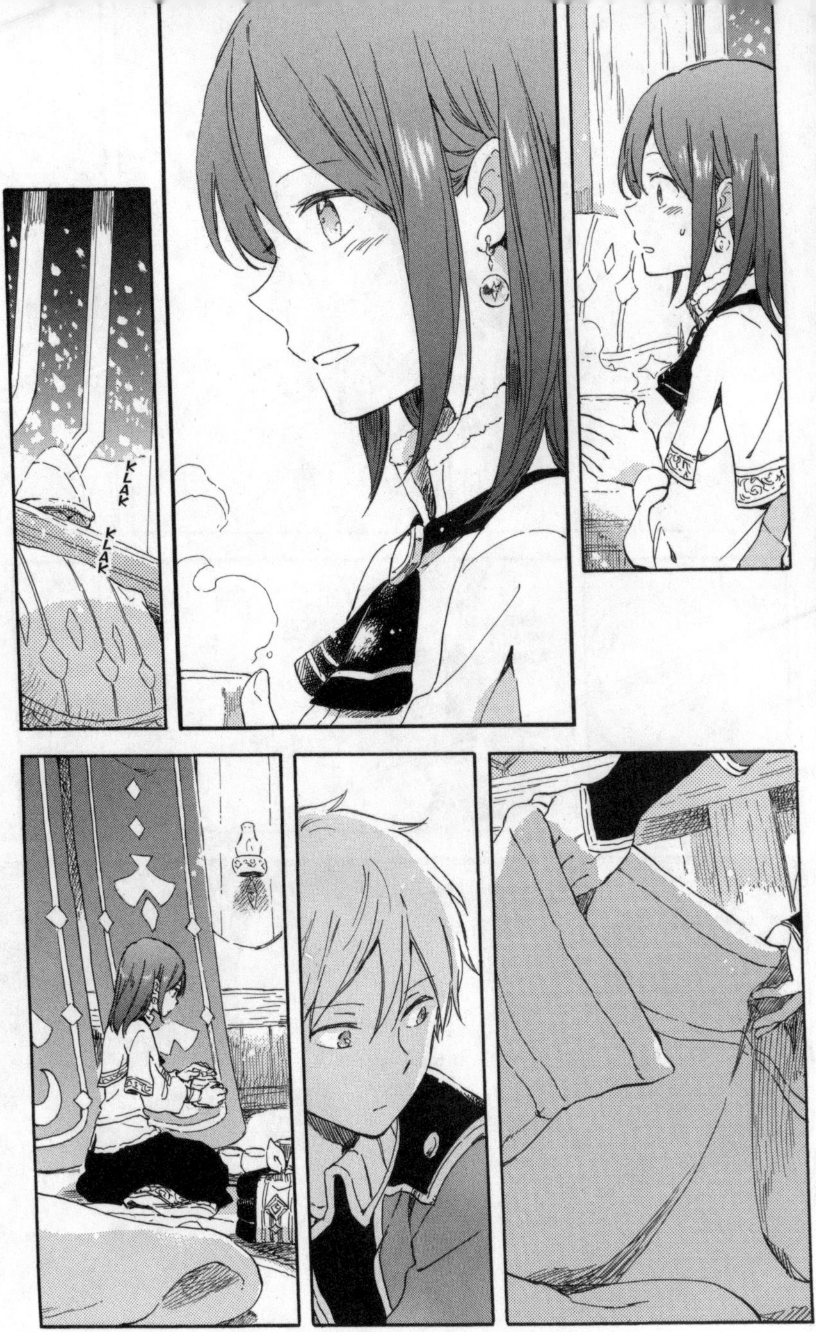
KLAK
KLAK

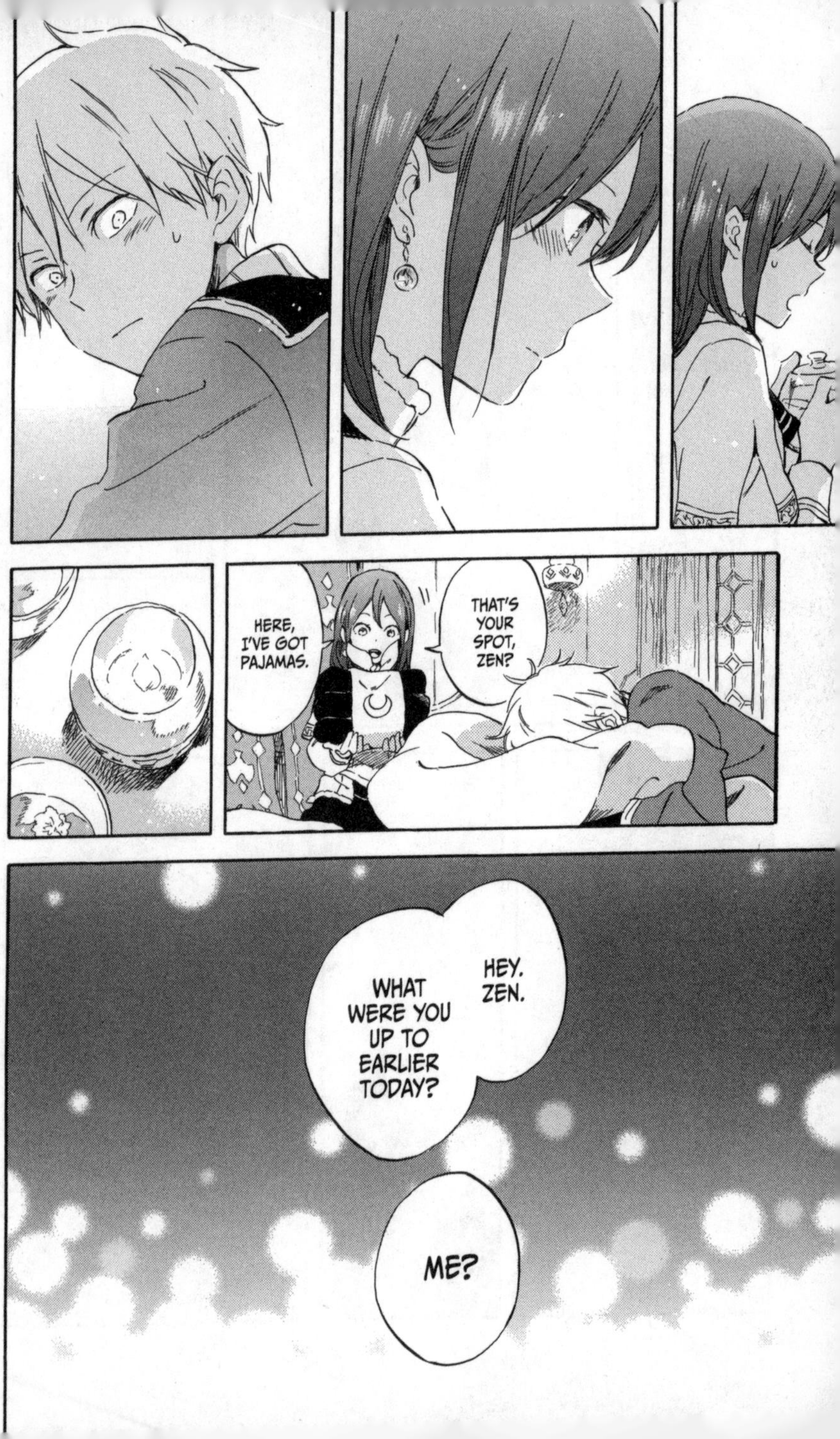
THAT'S YOUR SPOT, ZEN?
HERE, I'VE GOT PAJAMAS.
HEY. ZEN.
WHAT WERE YOU UP TO EARLIER TODAY?
ME?

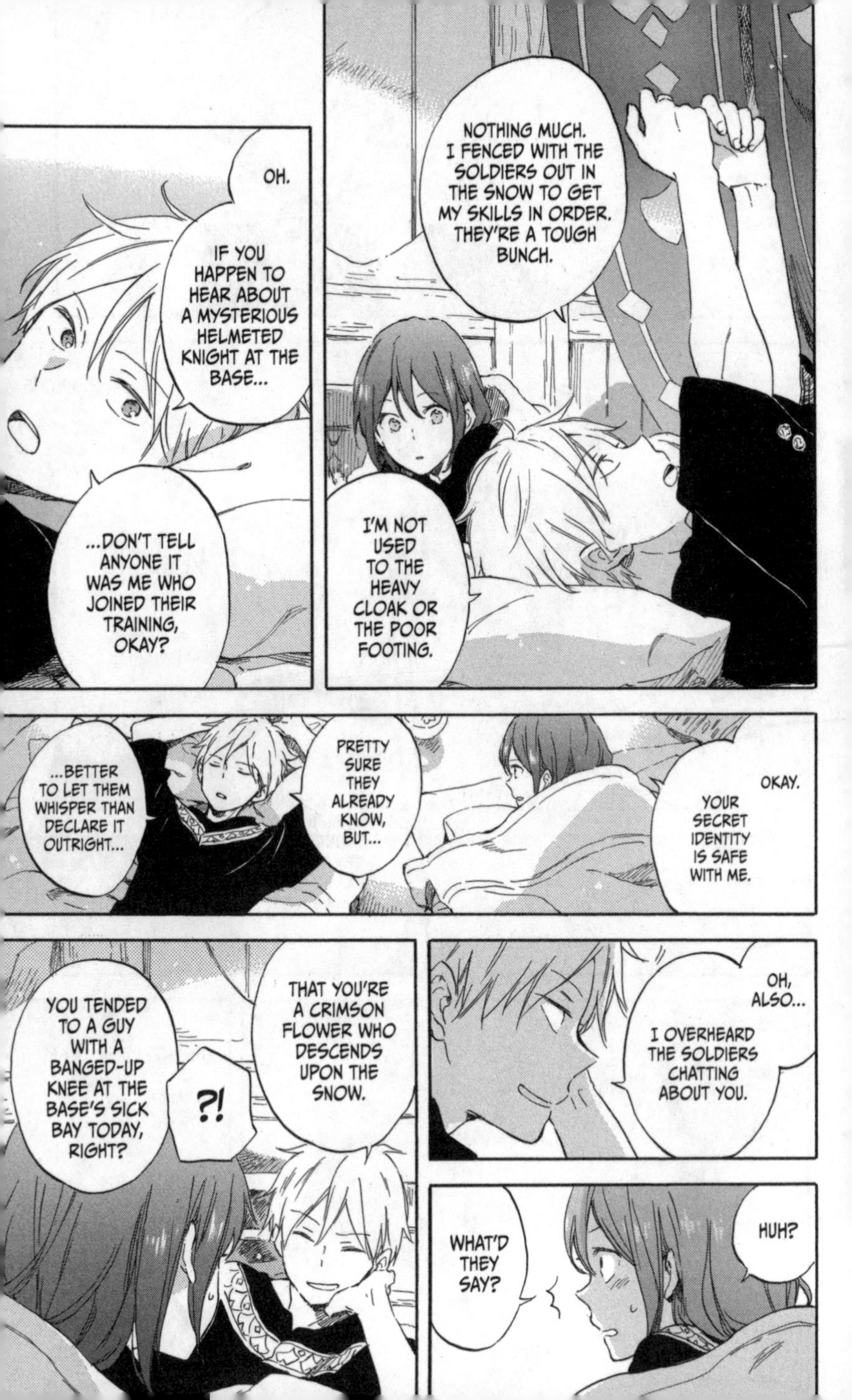
NOTHING MUCH. I FENCED WITH THE SOLDIERS OUT IN THE SNOW TO GET MY SKILLS IN ORDER. THEY'RE A TOUGH BUNCH.
I'M NOT USED TO THE HEAVY CLOAK OR THE POOR FOOTING.
OH.
IF YOU HAPPEN TO HEAR ABOUT A MYSTERIOUS HELMETED KNIGHT AT THE BASE...
...DON'T TELL ANYONE IT WAS ME WHO JOINED THEIR TRAINING, OKAY?
OKAY.
YOUR SECRET IDENTITY IS SAFE WITH ME.
PRETTY SURE THEY ALREADY KNOW, BUT...
...BETTER TO LET THEM WHISPER THAN DECLARE IT OUTRIGHT...
OH, ALSO...
I OVERHEARD THE SOLDIERS CHATTING ABOUT YOU.
HUH?
WHAT'D THEY SAY?
THAT YOU'RE A CRIMSON FLOWER WHO DESCENDS UPON THE SNOW.
?!
YOU TENDED TO A GUY WITH A BANGED-UP KNEE AT THE BASE'S SICK BAY TODAY, RIGHT?

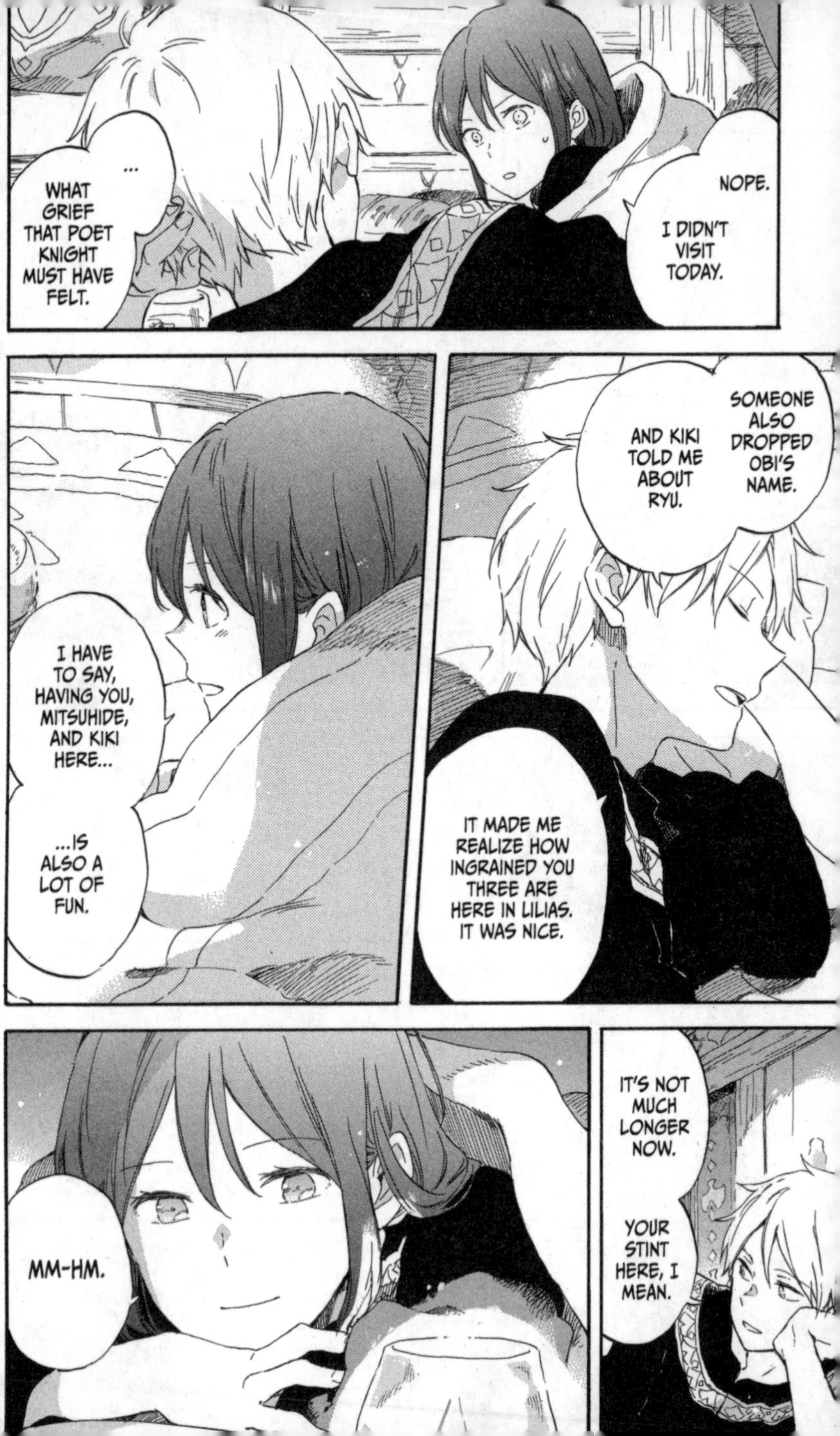
NOPE.
I DIDN'T VISIT TODAY.
... WHAT GRIEF THAT POET KNIGHT MUST HAVE FELT.
SOMEONE ALSO DROPPED OBI'S NAME.
AND KIKI TOLD ME ABOUT RYU.
IT MADE ME REALIZE HOW INGRAINED YOU THREE ARE HERE IN LILIAS. IT WAS NICE.
I HAVE TO SAY, HAVING YOU, MITSUHIDE, AND KIKI HERE...
...IS ALSO A LOT OF FUN.
IT'S NOT MUCH LONGER NOW.
YOUR STINT HERE, I MEAN.
MM-HM.

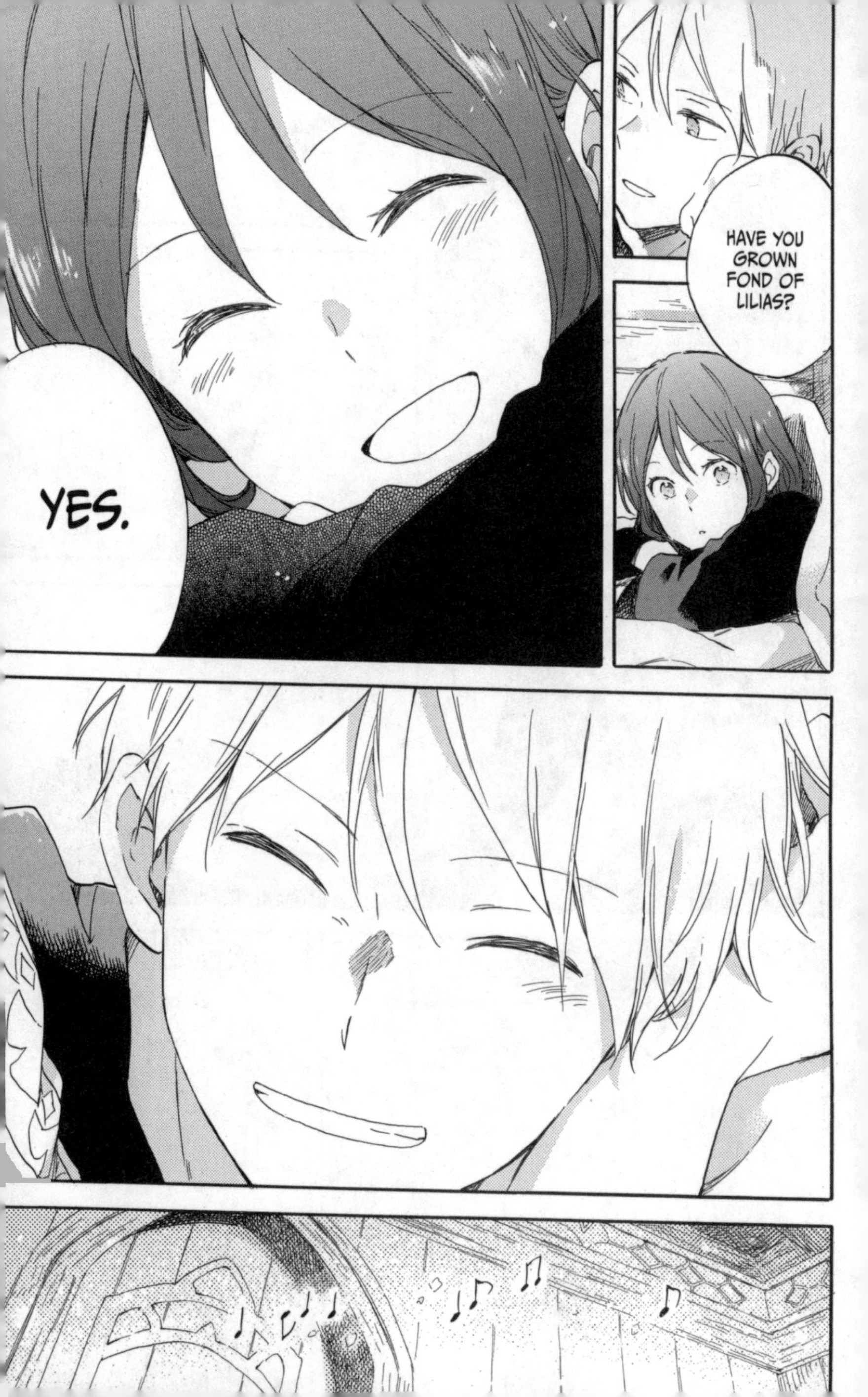
HAVE YOU GROWN FOND OF LILIAS?
YES.

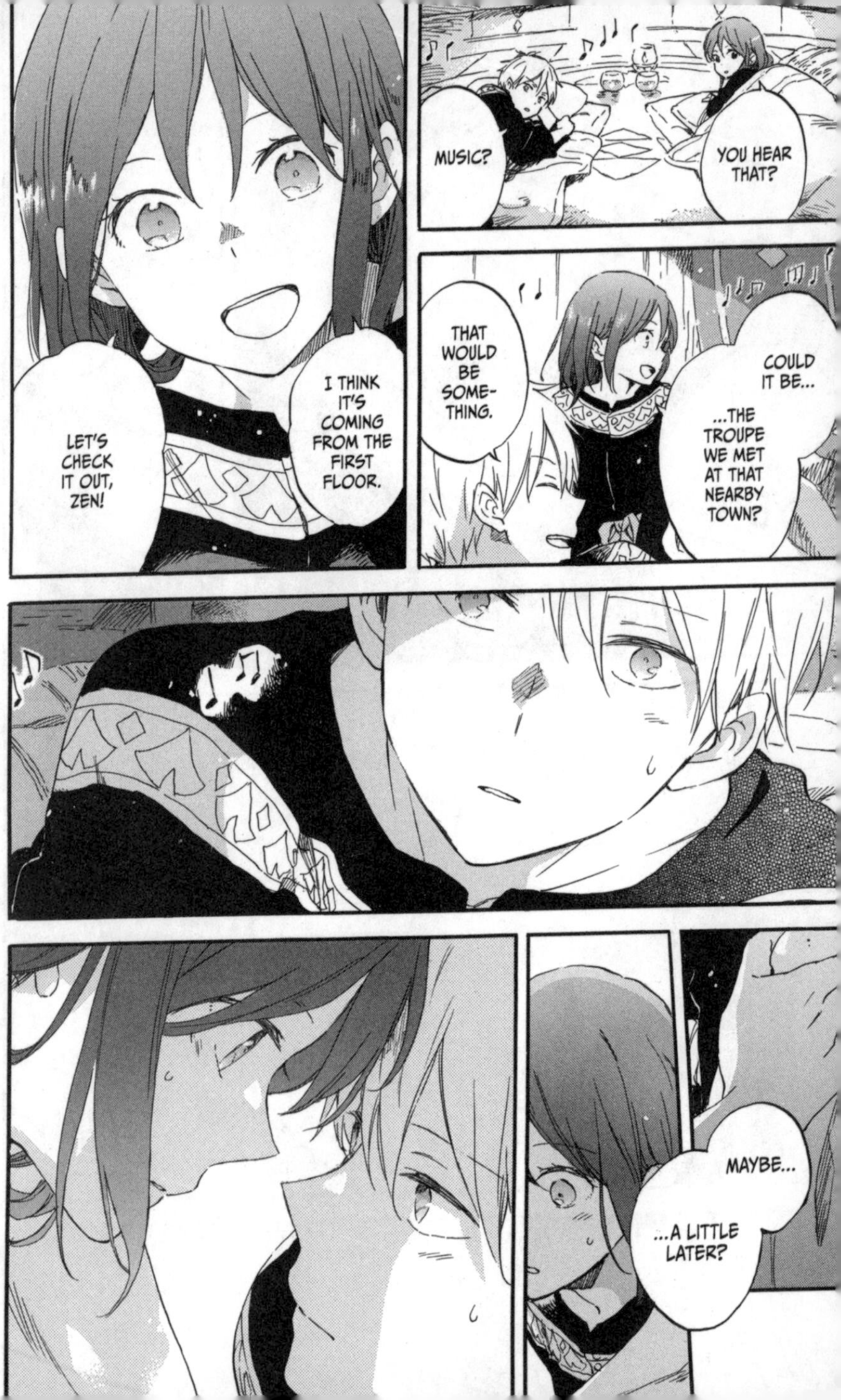
YOU HEAR THAT?
MUSIC?
COULD IT BE...
...THE TROUPE WE MET AT THAT NEARBY TOWN?
THAT WOULD BE SOME-THING.
I THINK IT'S COMING FROM THE FIRST FLOOR.
LET'S CHECK IT OUT, ZEN!
MAYBE...
...A LITTLE LATER?

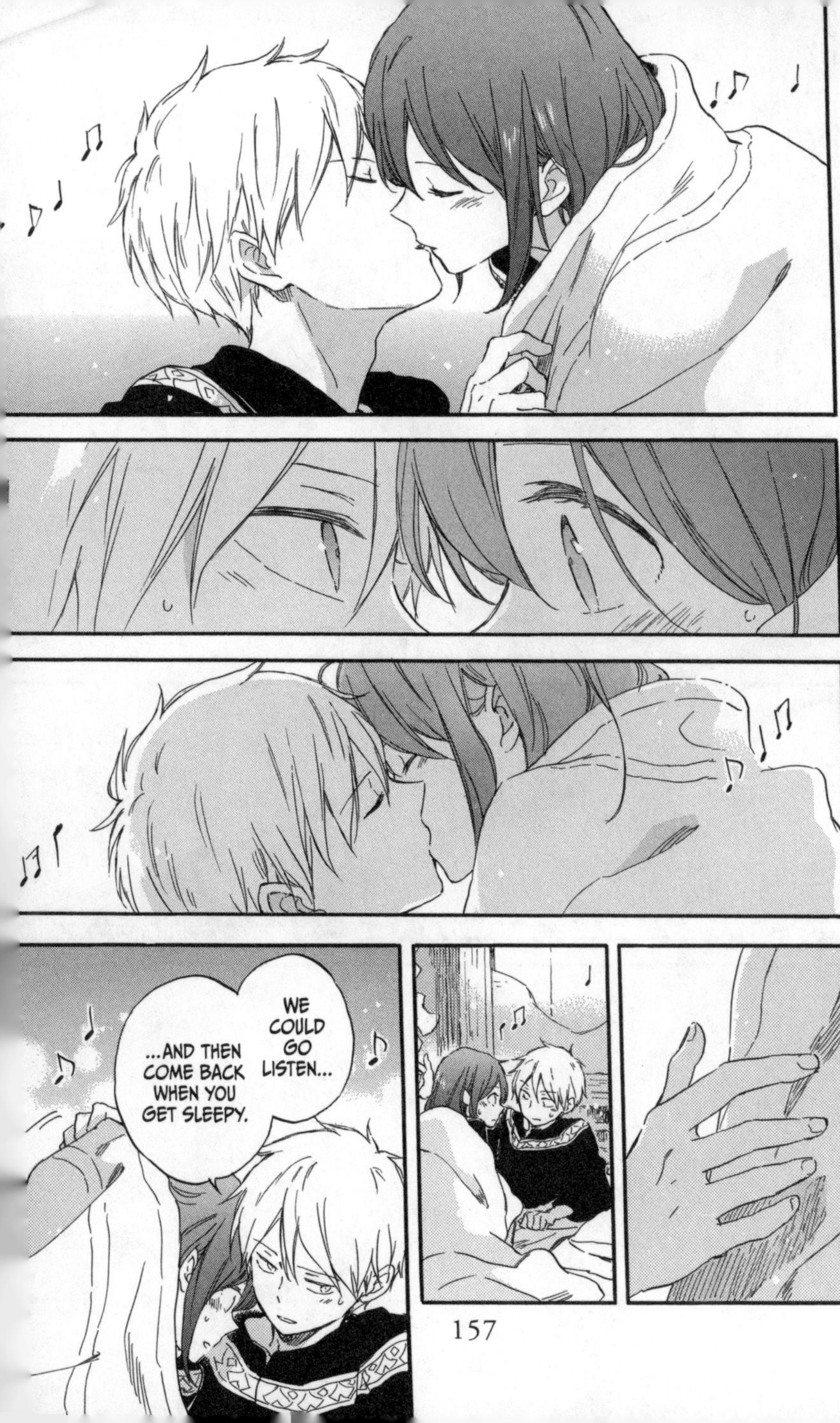
WE COULD GO LISTEN...
...AND THEN COME BACK WHEN YOU GET SLEEPY.

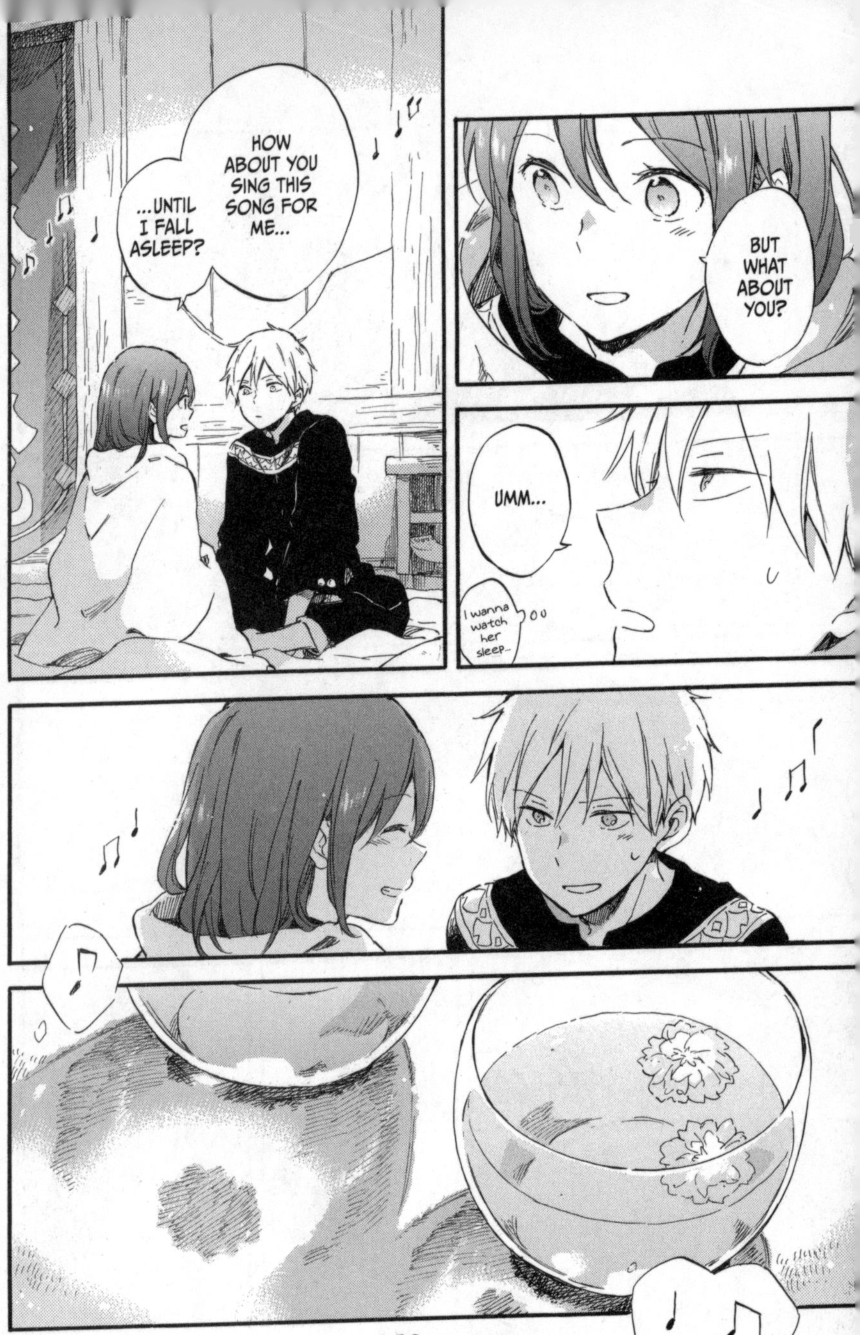
BUT WHAT ABOUT YOU?
UMM...
I wanna watch her sleep...
HOW ABOUT YOU SING THIS SONG FOR ME...
...UNTIL I FALL ASLEEP?

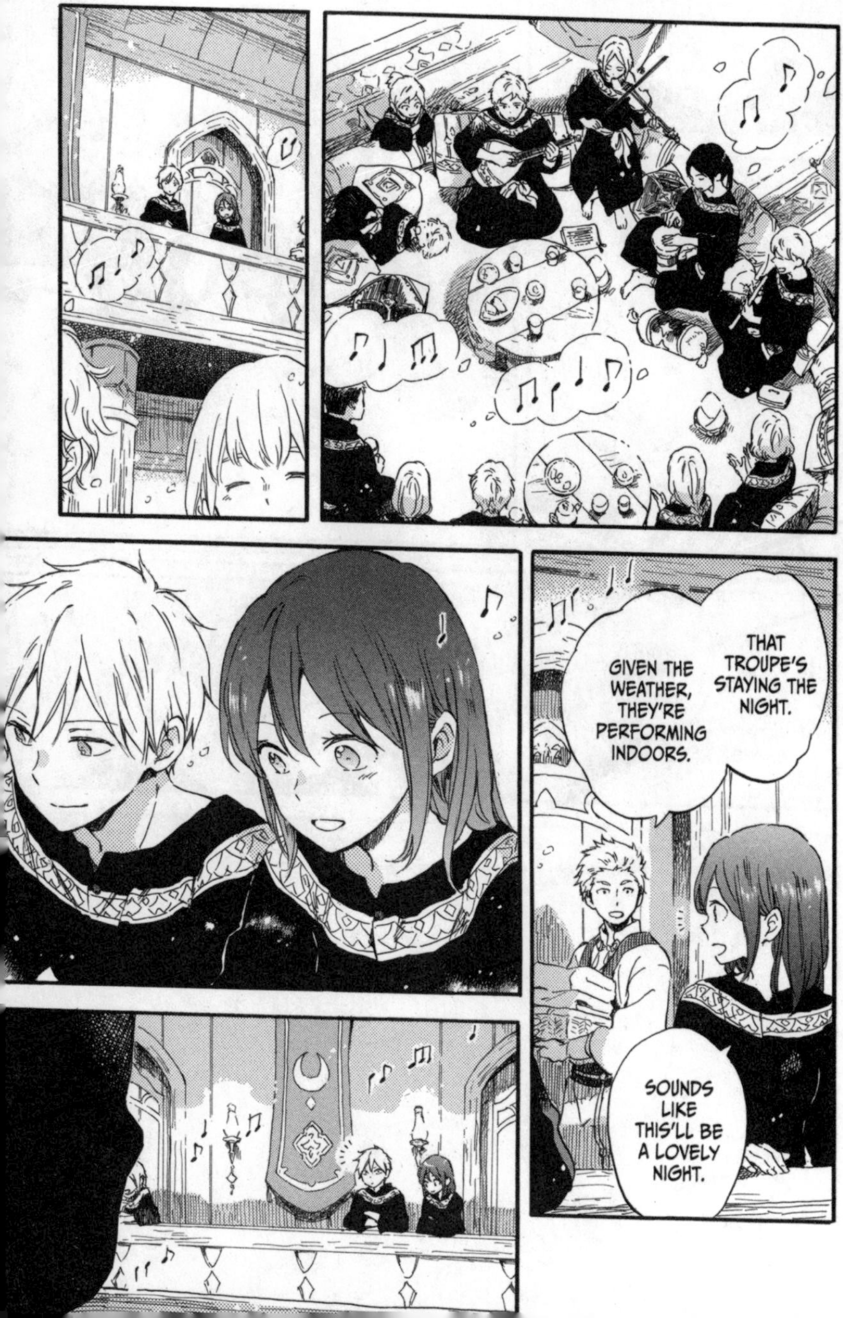
THAT TROUPE'S STAYING THE NIGHT.
GIVEN THE WEATHER, THEY'RE PERFORMING INDOORS.
SOUNDS LIKE THIS'LL BE A LOVELY NIGHT.

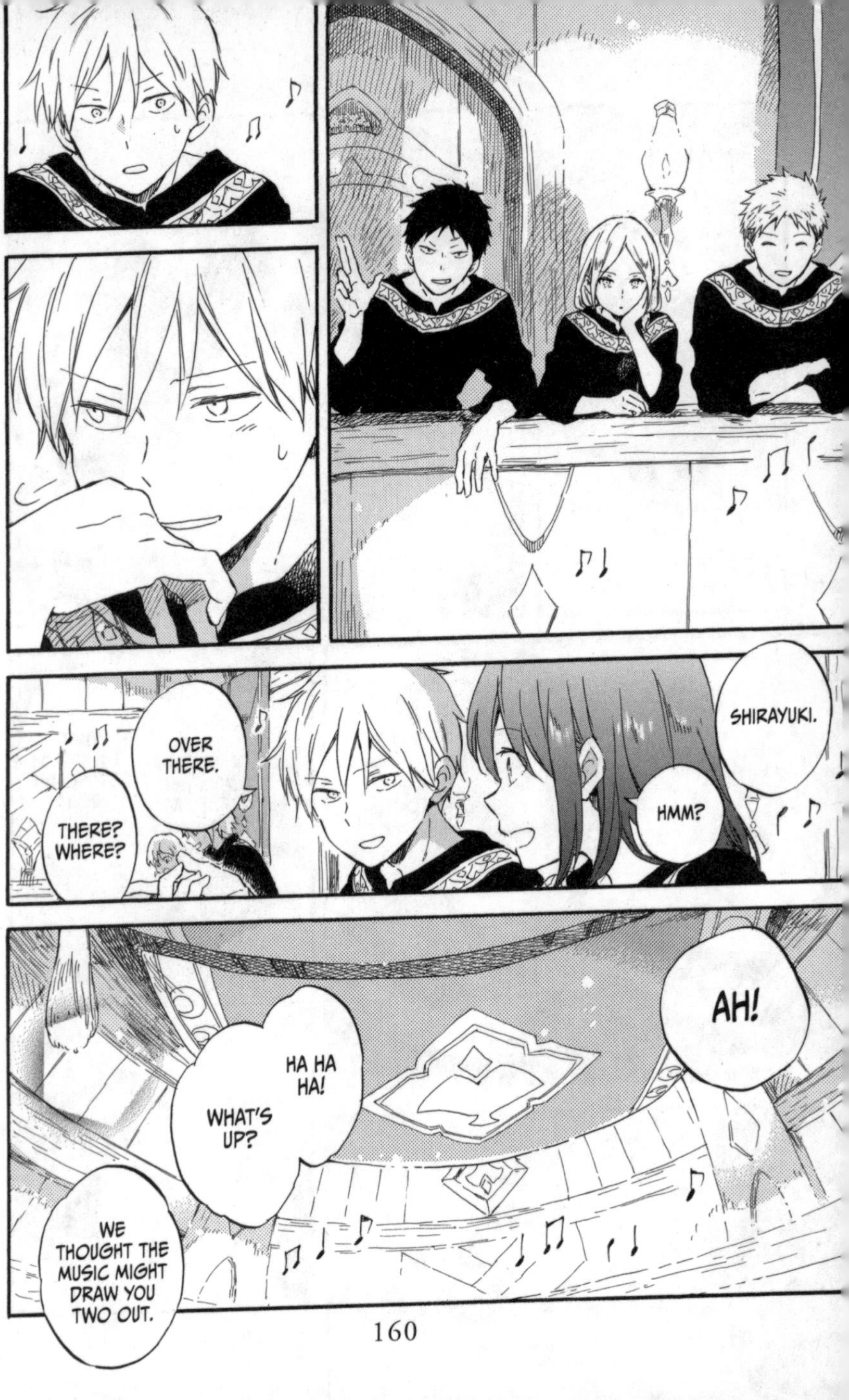
SHIRAYUKI.
HMM?
OVER THERE.
THERE? WHERE?
AH!
HA HA HA!
WHAT'S UP?
WE THOUGHT THE MUSIC MIGHT DRAW YOU TWO OUT.

Chapter 101

A PRINCE IN THE MIDDLE...

AND A DUDE ON EITHER SIDE, SPREAD OUT LIKE A FOLDING FAN...

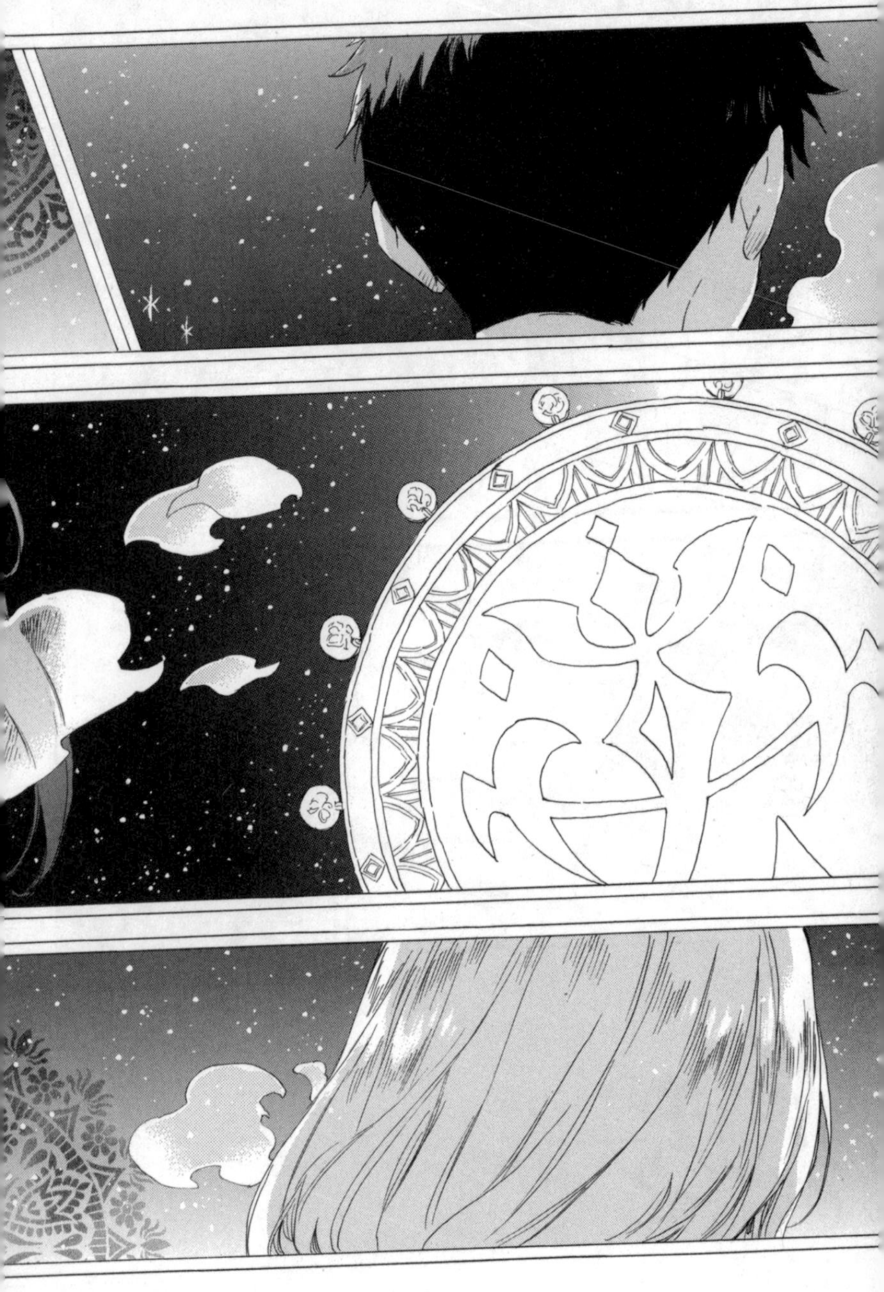

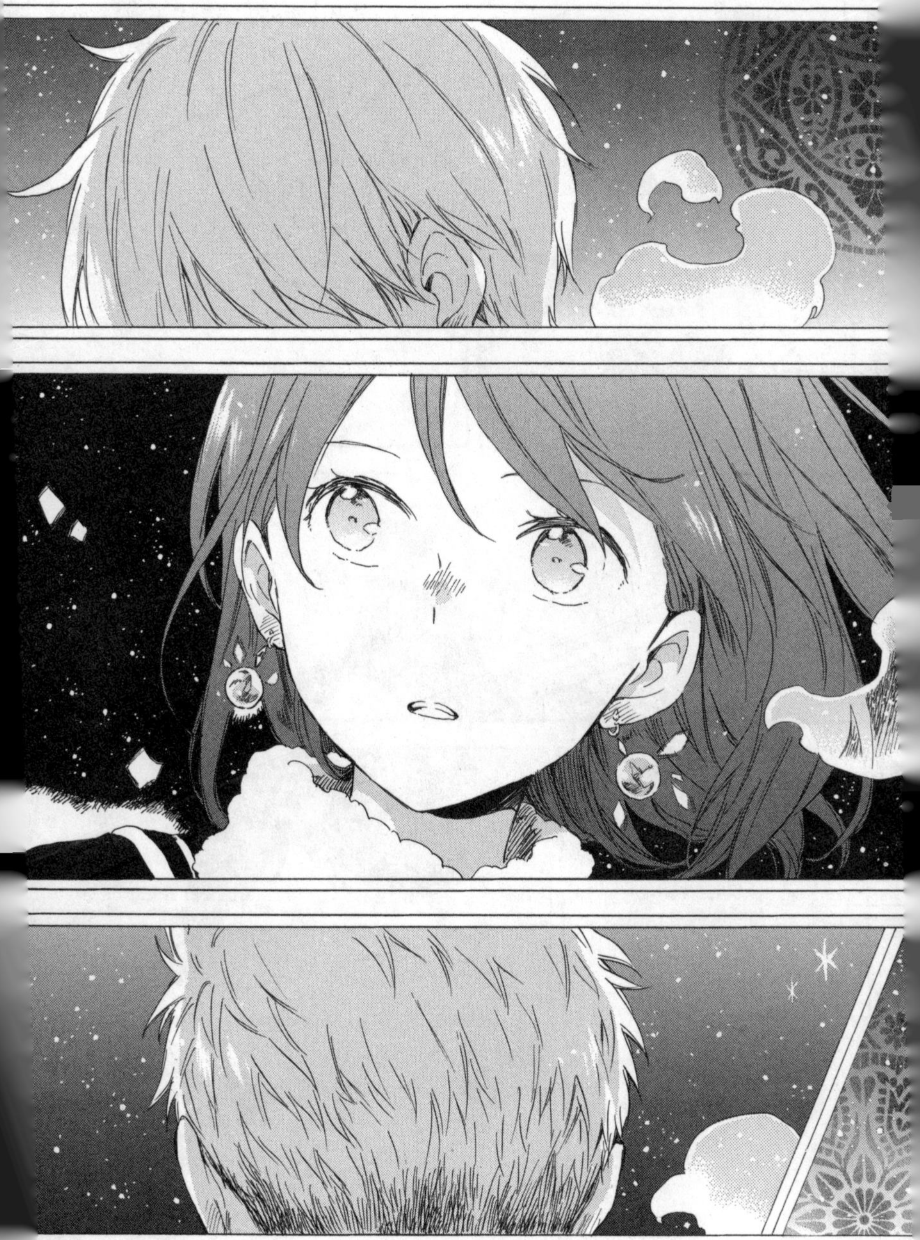

Chapter 101

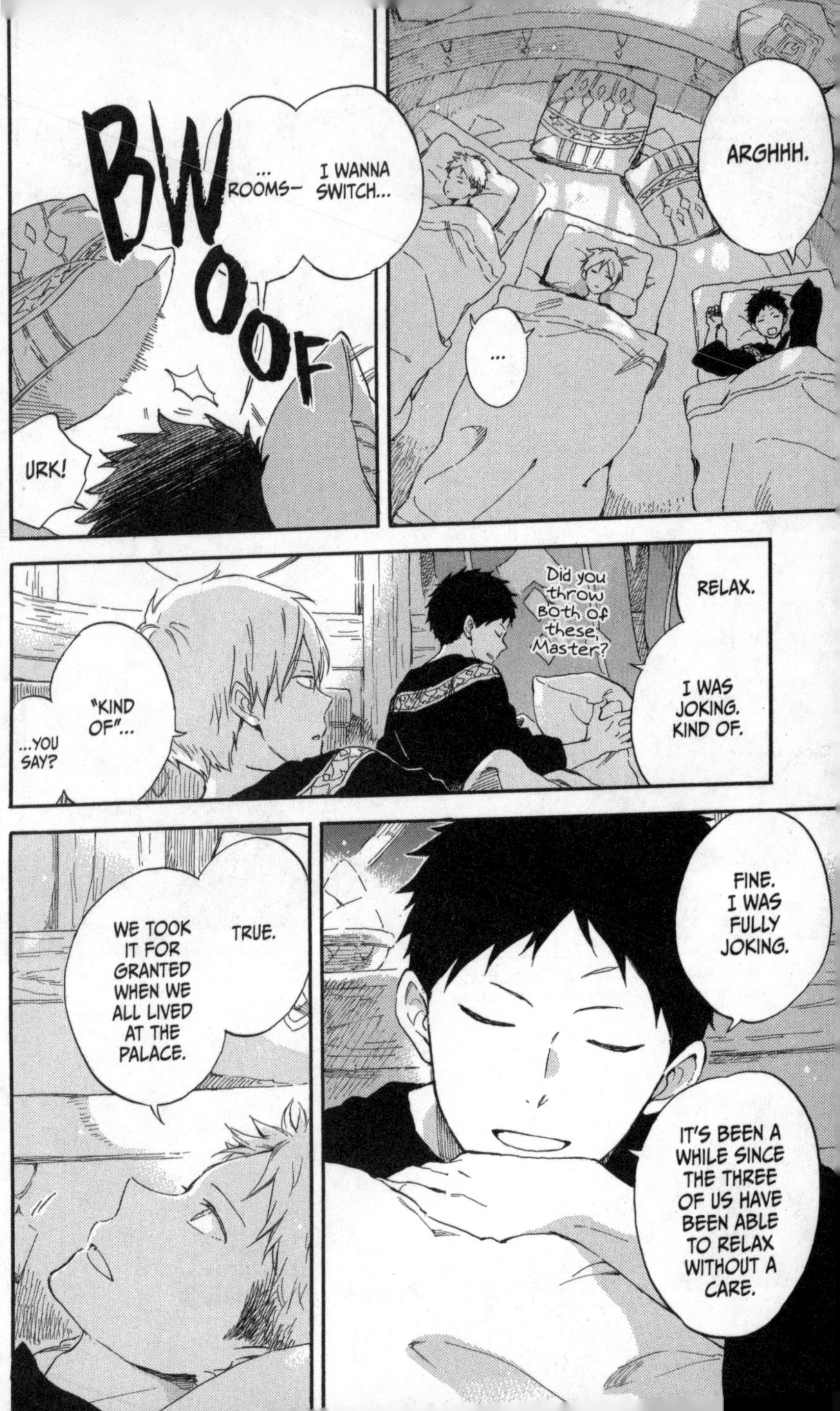
ARGHHH.
...
I WANNA SWITCH... ... ROOMS—
BWOOF
URK!
RELAX.
I WAS JOKING. KIND OF.
Did you throw both of these, Master?
"KIND OF"... ...YOU SAY?
FINE. I WAS FULLY JOKING.
IT'S BEEN A WHILE SINCE THE THREE OF US HAVE BEEN ABLE TO RELAX WITHOUT A CARE.
TRUE.
WE TOOK IT FOR GRANTED WHEN WE ALL LIVED AT THE PALACE.

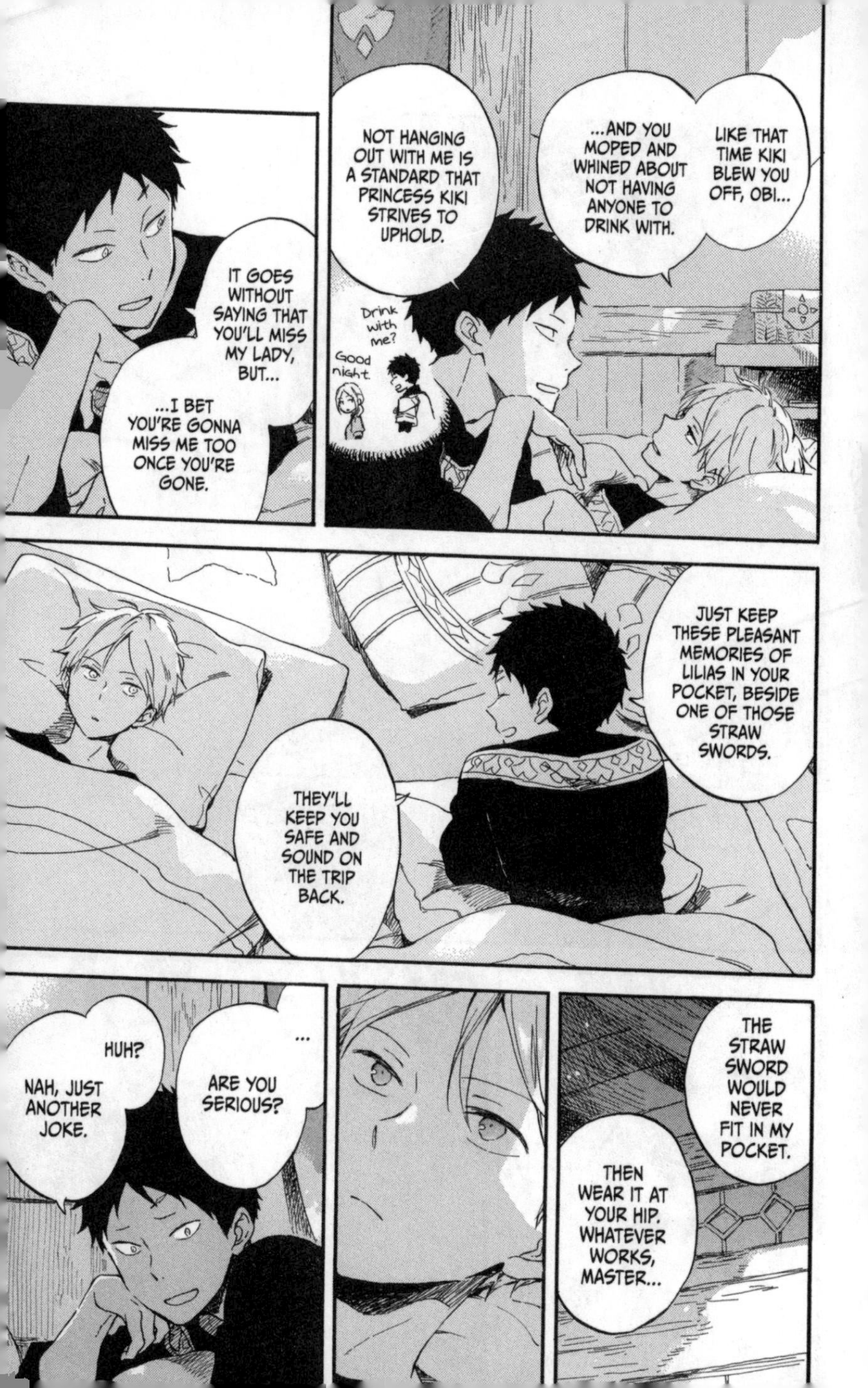
LIKE THAT TIME KIKI BLEW YOU OFF, OBI...
...AND YOU MOPED AND WHINED ABOUT NOT HAVING ANYONE TO DRINK WITH.
NOT HANGING OUT WITH ME IS A STANDARD THAT PRINCESS KIKI STRIVES TO UPHOLD.
Drink with me?
Good night.
IT GOES WITHOUT SAYING THAT YOU'LL MISS MY LADY, BUT...
...I BET YOU'RE GONNA MISS ME TOO ONCE YOU'RE GONE.
JUST KEEP THESE PLEASANT MEMORIES OF LILIAS IN YOUR POCKET, BESIDE ONE OF THOSE STRAW SWORDS.
THEY'LL KEEP YOU SAFE AND SOUND ON THE TRIP BACK.
THE STRAW SWORD WOULD NEVER FIT IN MY POCKET.
THEN WEAR IT AT YOUR HIP. WHATEVER WORKS, MASTER...
...
ARE YOU SERIOUS?
HUH?
NAH, JUST ANOTHER JOKE.

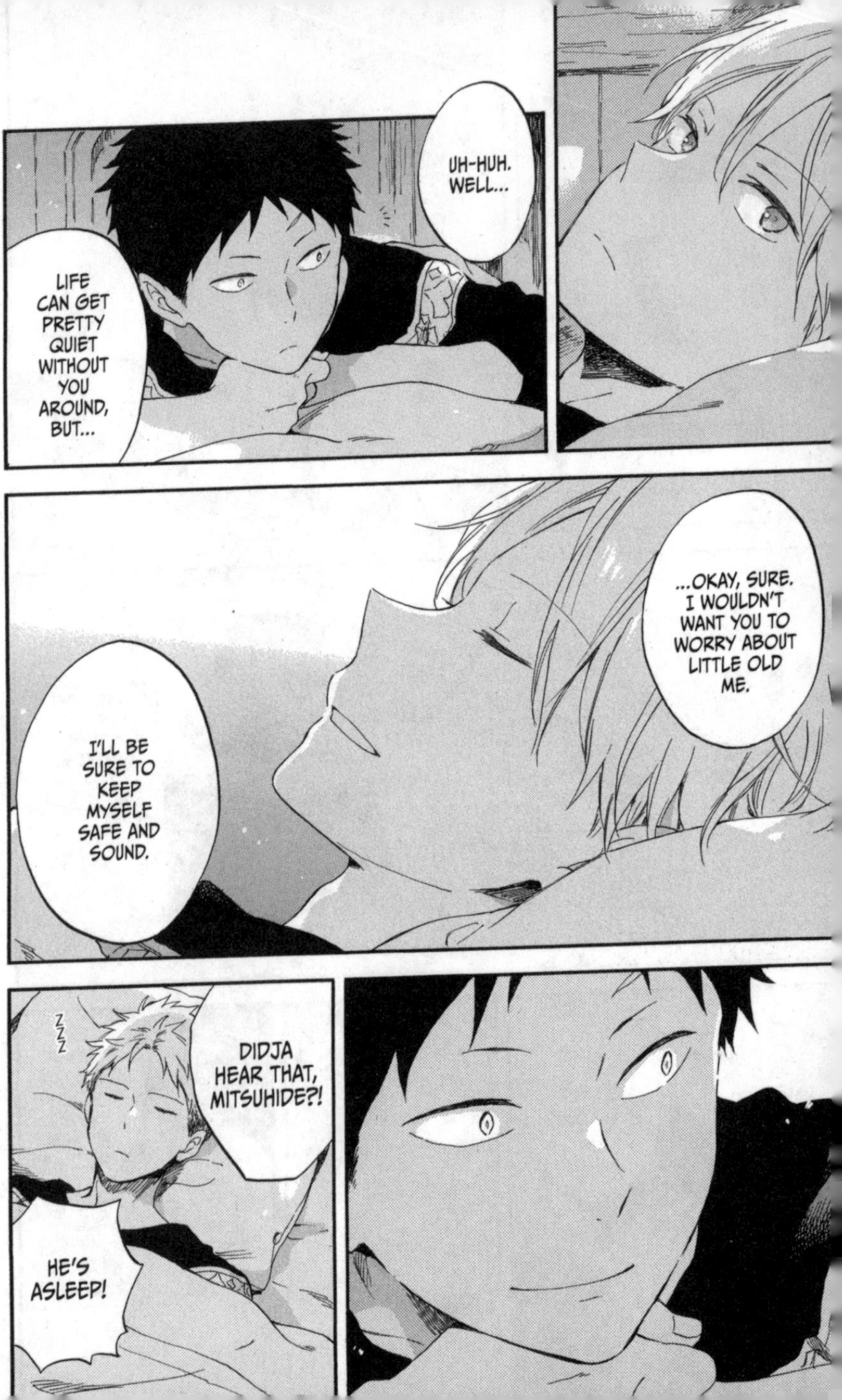
UH-HUH. WELL...
LIFE CAN GET PRETTY QUIET WITHOUT YOU AROUND, BUT...
...OKAY, SURE. I WOULDN'T WANT YOU TO WORRY ABOUT LITTLE OLD ME.
I'LL BE SURE TO KEEP MYSELF SAFE AND SOUND.
DIDJA HEAR THAT, MITSUHIDE?!
ZZZ
HE'S ASLEEP!

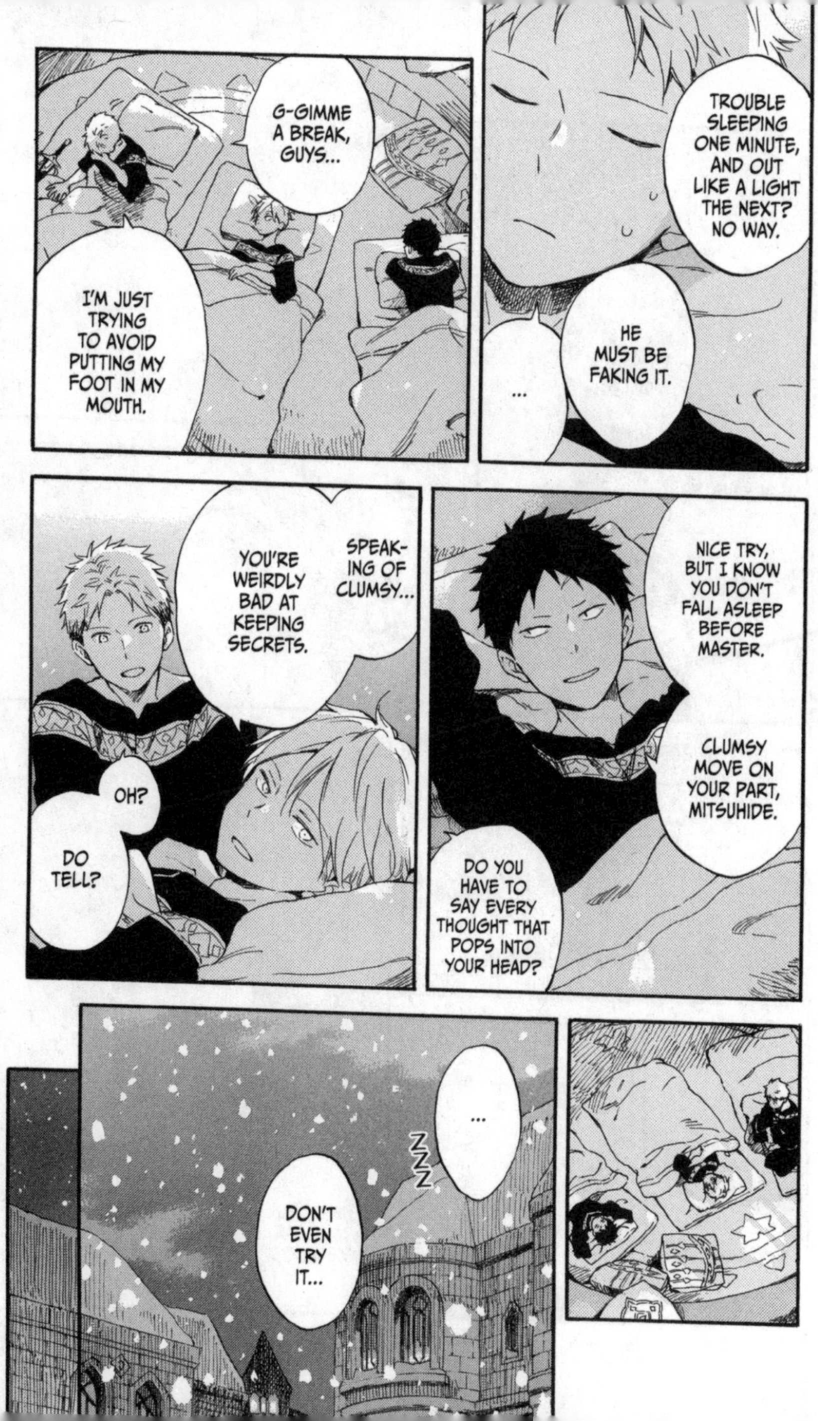
TROUBLE SLEEPING ONE MINUTE, AND OUT LIKE A LIGHT THE NEXT? NO WAY.
HE MUST BE FAKING IT.
...
G-GIMME A BREAK, GUYS...
I'M JUST TRYING TO AVOID PUTTING MY FOOT IN MY MOUTH.
NICE TRY, BUT I KNOW YOU DON'T FALL ASLEEP BEFORE MASTER.
CLUMSY MOVE ON YOUR PART, MITSUHIDE.
DO YOU HAVE TO SAY EVERY THOUGHT THAT POPS INTO YOUR HEAD?
SPEAK-ING OF CLUMSY...
YOU'RE WEIRDLY BAD AT KEEPING SECRETS.
OH?
DO TELL?
...
ZZZ
DON'T EVEN TRY IT...

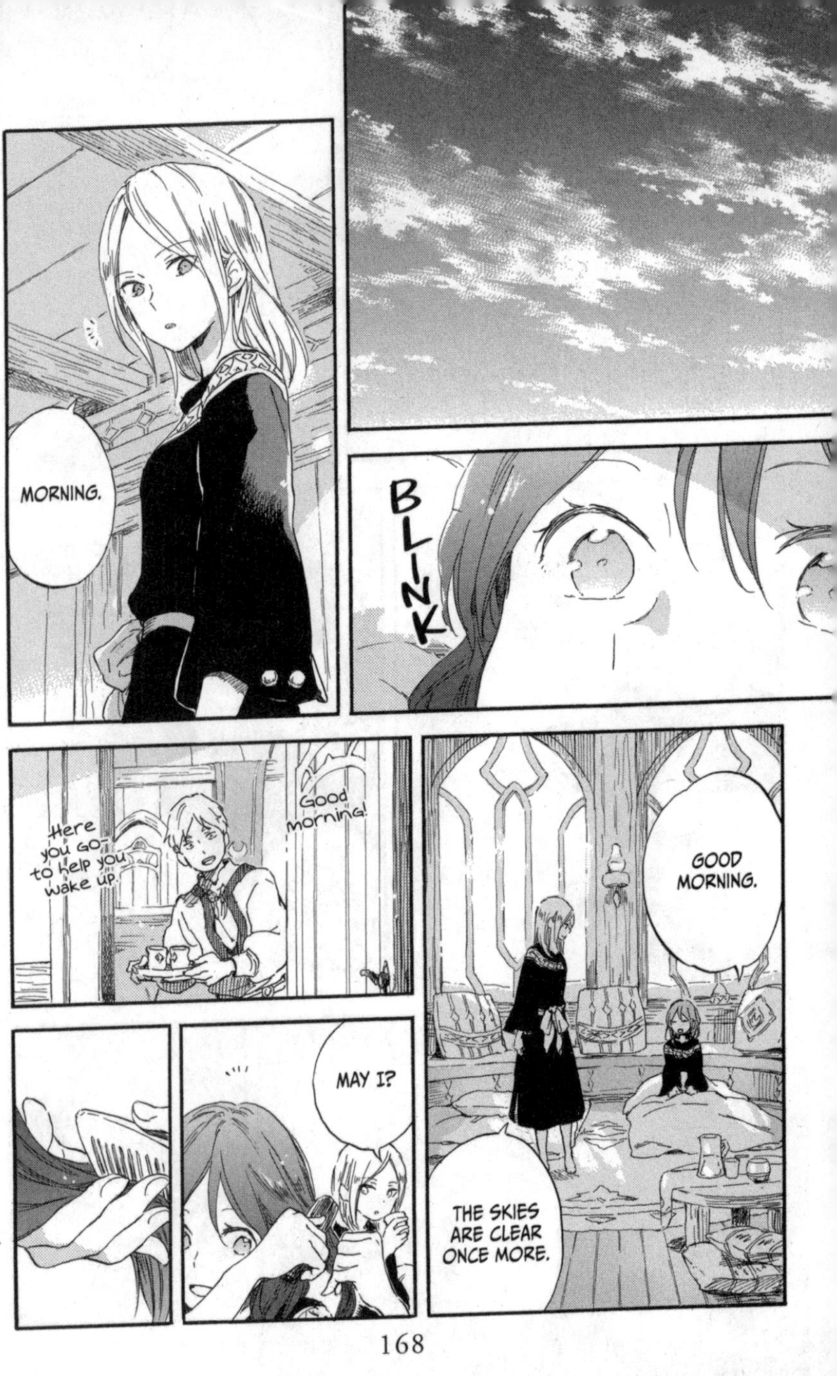
BLINK
MORNING.
GOOD MORNING.
THE SKIES ARE CLEAR ONCE MORE.
Good morning!
Here you go—to help you wake up.
MAY I?

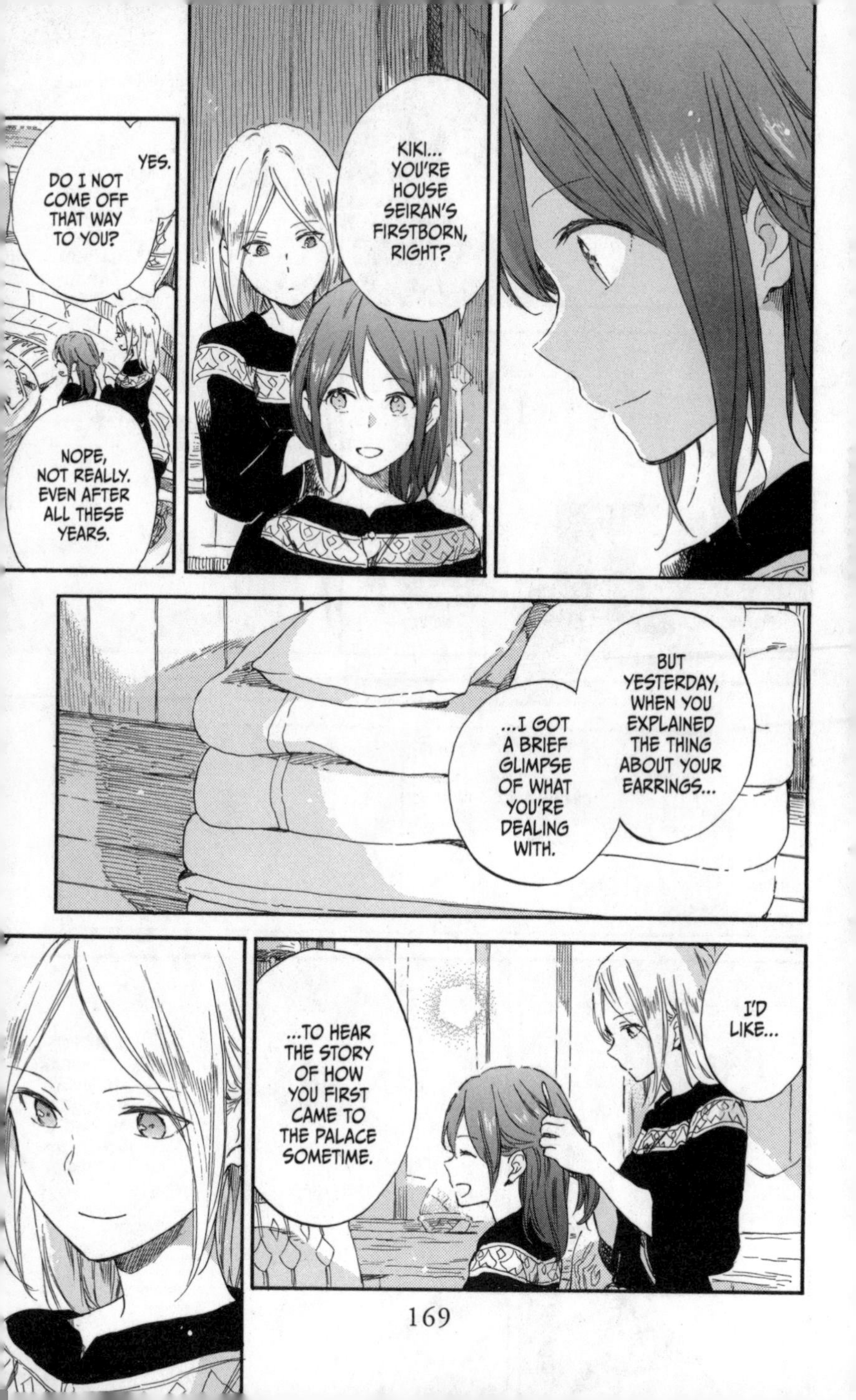
KIKI... YOU'RE HOUSE SEIRAN'S FIRSTBORN, RIGHT?
YES.
DO I NOT COME OFF THAT WAY TO YOU?
NOPE, NOT REALLY. EVEN AFTER ALL THESE YEARS.
BUT YESTERDAY, WHEN YOU EXPLAINED THE THING ABOUT YOUR EARRINGS...
...I GOT A BRIEF GLIMPSE OF WHAT YOU'RE DEALING WITH.
I'D LIKE...
...TO HEAR THE STORY OF HOW YOU FIRST CAME TO THE PALACE SOMETIME.

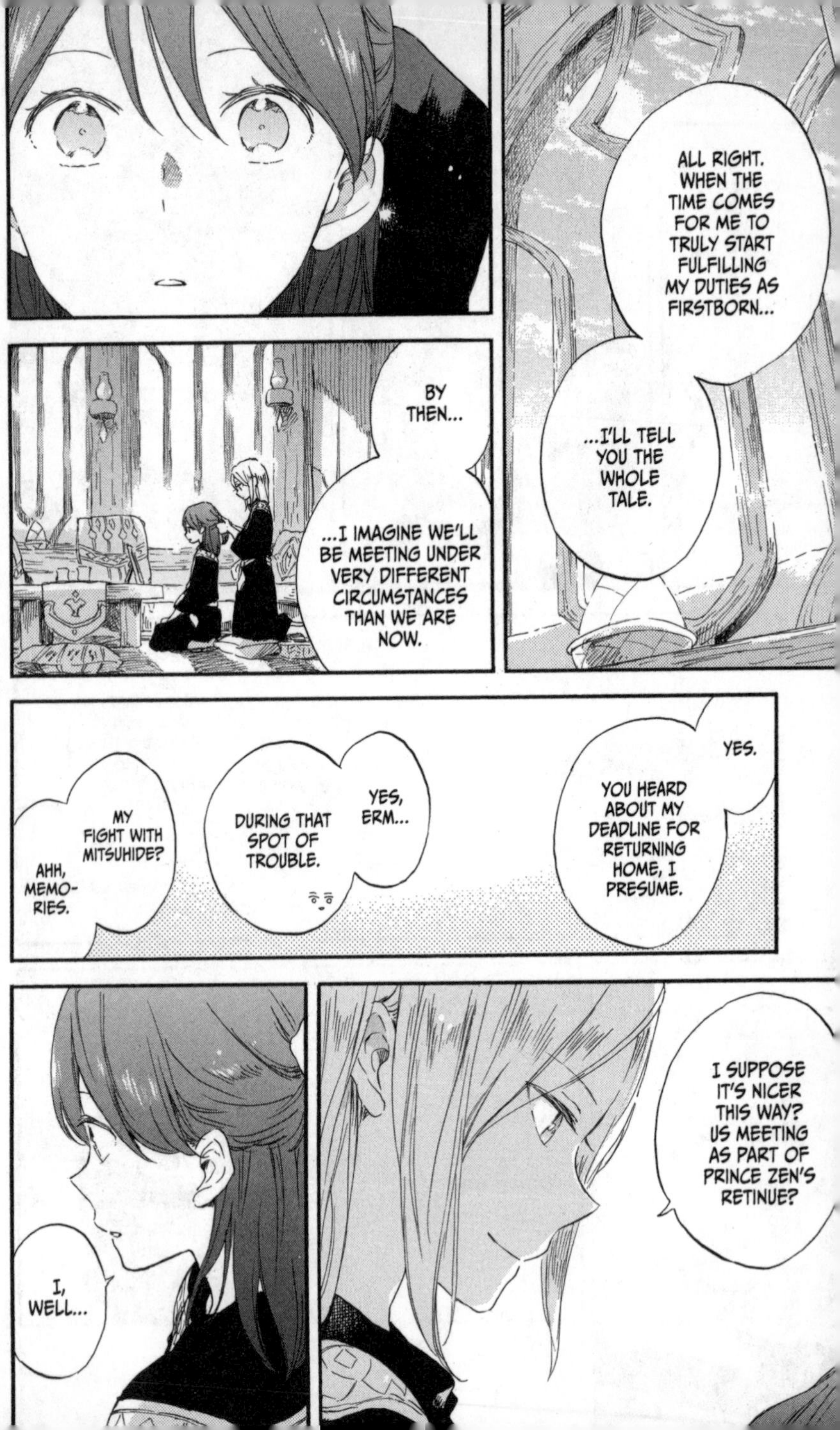
ALL RIGHT. WHEN THE TIME COMES FOR ME TO TRULY START FULFILLING MY DUTIES AS FIRSTBORN...
...I'LL TELL YOU THE WHOLE TALE.
BY THEN...
...I IMAGINE WE'LL BE MEETING UNDER VERY DIFFERENT CIRCUMSTANCES THAN WE ARE NOW.
YES.
YOU HEARD ABOUT MY DEADLINE FOR RETURNING HOME, I PRESUME.
YES, ERM...
DURING THAT SPOT OF TROUBLE.
MY FIGHT WITH MITSUHIDE?
AHH, MEMO-RIES.
I SUPPOSE IT'S NICER THIS WAY? US MEETING AS PART OF PRINCE ZEN'S RETINUE?
I, WELL...

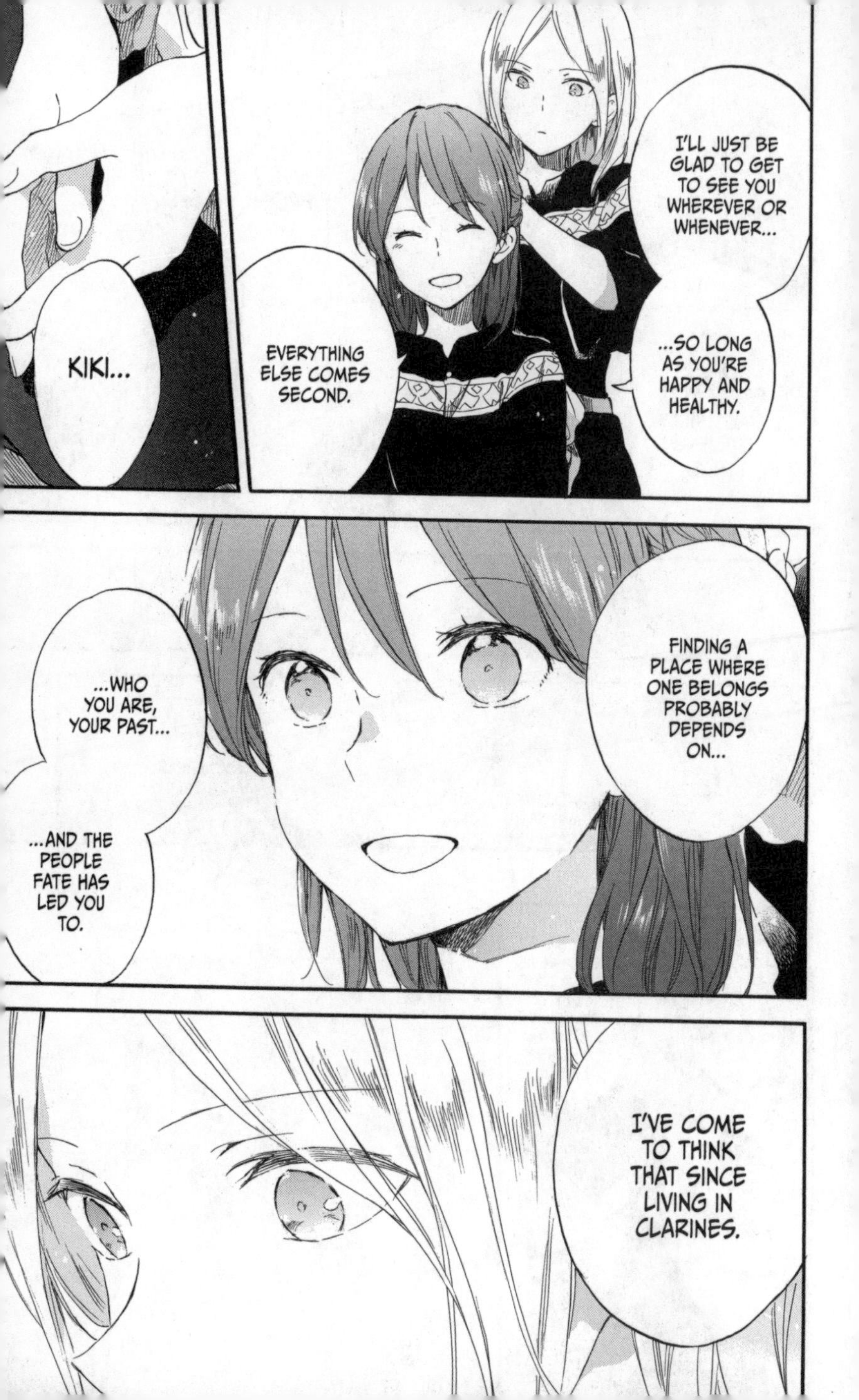
I'LL JUST BE GLAD TO GET TO SEE YOU WHEREVER OR WHENEVER...
...SO LONG AS YOU'RE HAPPY AND HEALTHY.
EVERYTHING ELSE COMES SECOND.
KIKI...
FINDING A PLACE WHERE ONE BELONGS PROBABLY DEPENDS ON...
...WHO YOU ARE, YOUR PAST...
...AND THE PEOPLE FATE HAS LED YOU TO.
I'VE COME TO THINK THAT SINCE LIVING IN CLARINES.

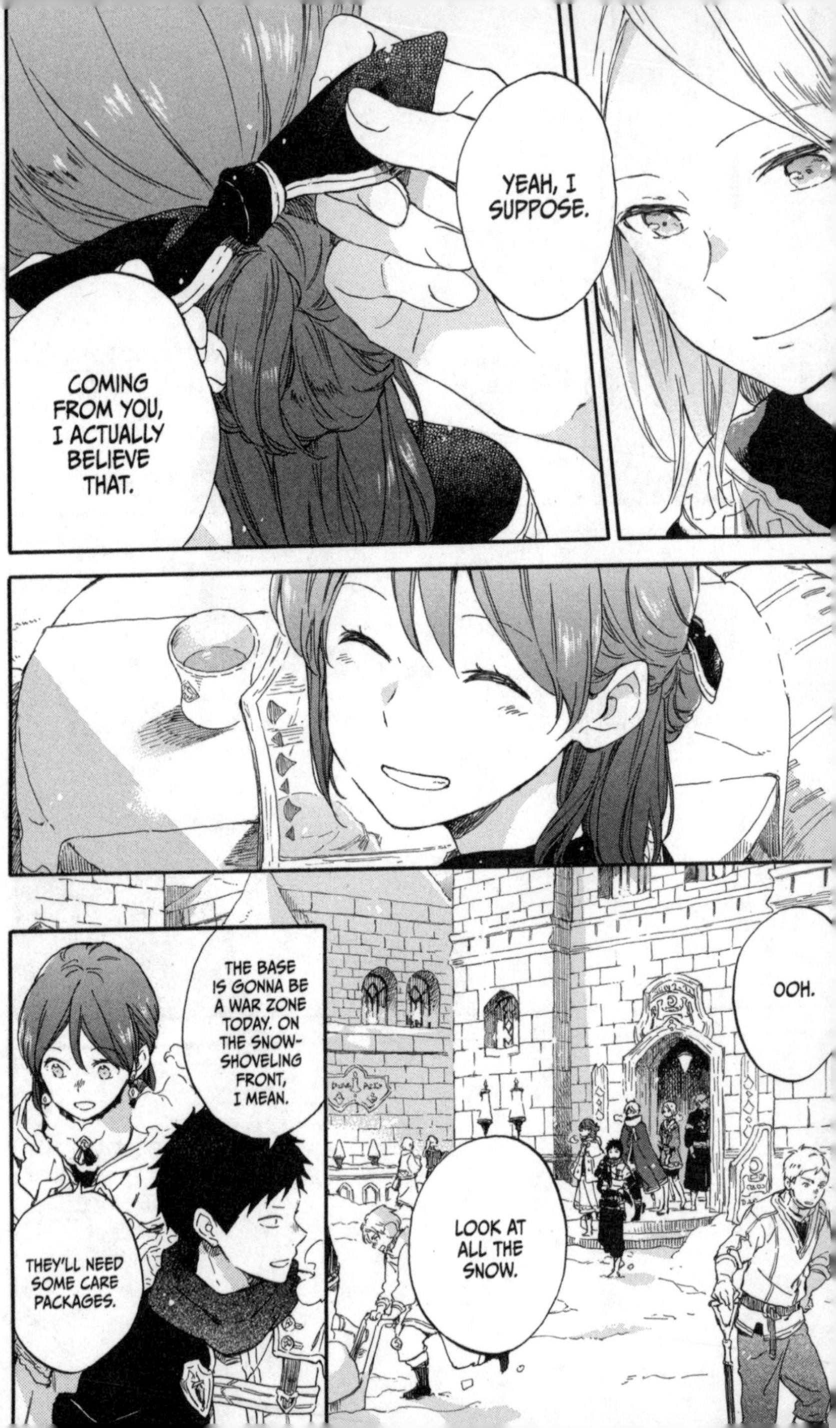
YEAH, I SUPPOSE.
COMING FROM YOU, I ACTUALLY BELIEVE THAT.
OOH.
LOOK AT ALL THE SNOW.
THE BASE IS GONNA BE A WAR ZONE TODAY. ON THE SNOW-SHOVELING FRONT, I MEAN.
THEY'LL NEED SOME CARE PACKAGES.

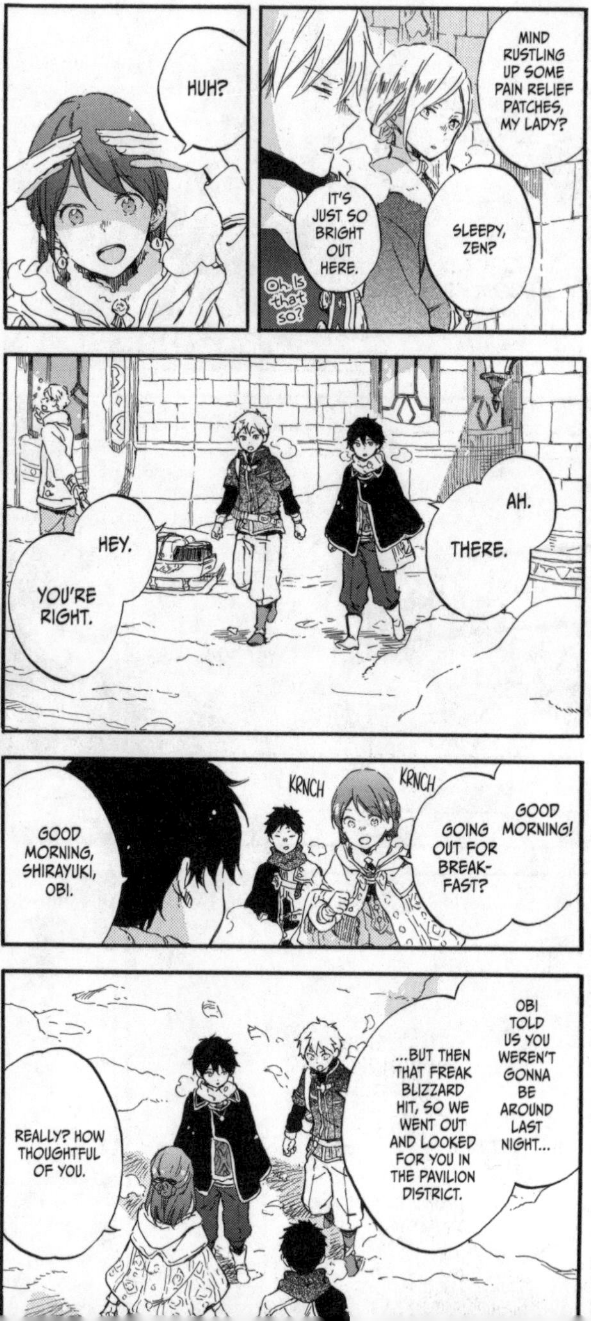
MIND RUSTLING UP SOME PAIN RELIEF PATCHES, MY LADY?
SLEEPY, ZEN?
IT'S JUST SO BRIGHT OUT HERE.
Oh. Is that so?
HUH?
AH.
THERE.
HEY.
YOU'RE RIGHT.
GOOD MORNING!
GOING OUT FOR BREAK-FAST?
KRNCH
KRNCH
GOOD MORNING, SHIRAYUKI, OBI.
OBI TOLD US YOU WEREN'T GONNA BE AROUND LAST NIGHT...
...BUT THEN THAT FREAK BLIZZARD HIT, SO WE WENT OUT AND LOOKED FOR YOU IN THE PAVILION DISTRICT.
REALLY? HOW THOUGHTFUL OF YOU.

Final 6

TRIP DIARY, PART 5

I took up so much space writing about putting salt and pepper on salad that I ran out of room.

So let's tackle all the rest at once! Here we go! Forgive my crossed memory wires!

Ferry to the isle of Gozo!
Epic battle against flies at a seaside restaurant with a gorgeous view of blue seas and the sky.
Buying sandwiches at the supermarket one night.

Heading to the fortified city with Hachi on a bus. Then spotting a nice wine at a restaurant that made my head spin as we ate a late dinner.

Standing around at the fishing harbor and eating a mini mountain of strawberries.

Strolling around the fort on our own.

Hearing about how the Maltese love fireworks, and how it's tradition to bring your special someone to a local fireworks show.

Having instant miso soup back at the hotel.

What a blast it all was!!

The day after I got home, I was laid up in bed with a fever.

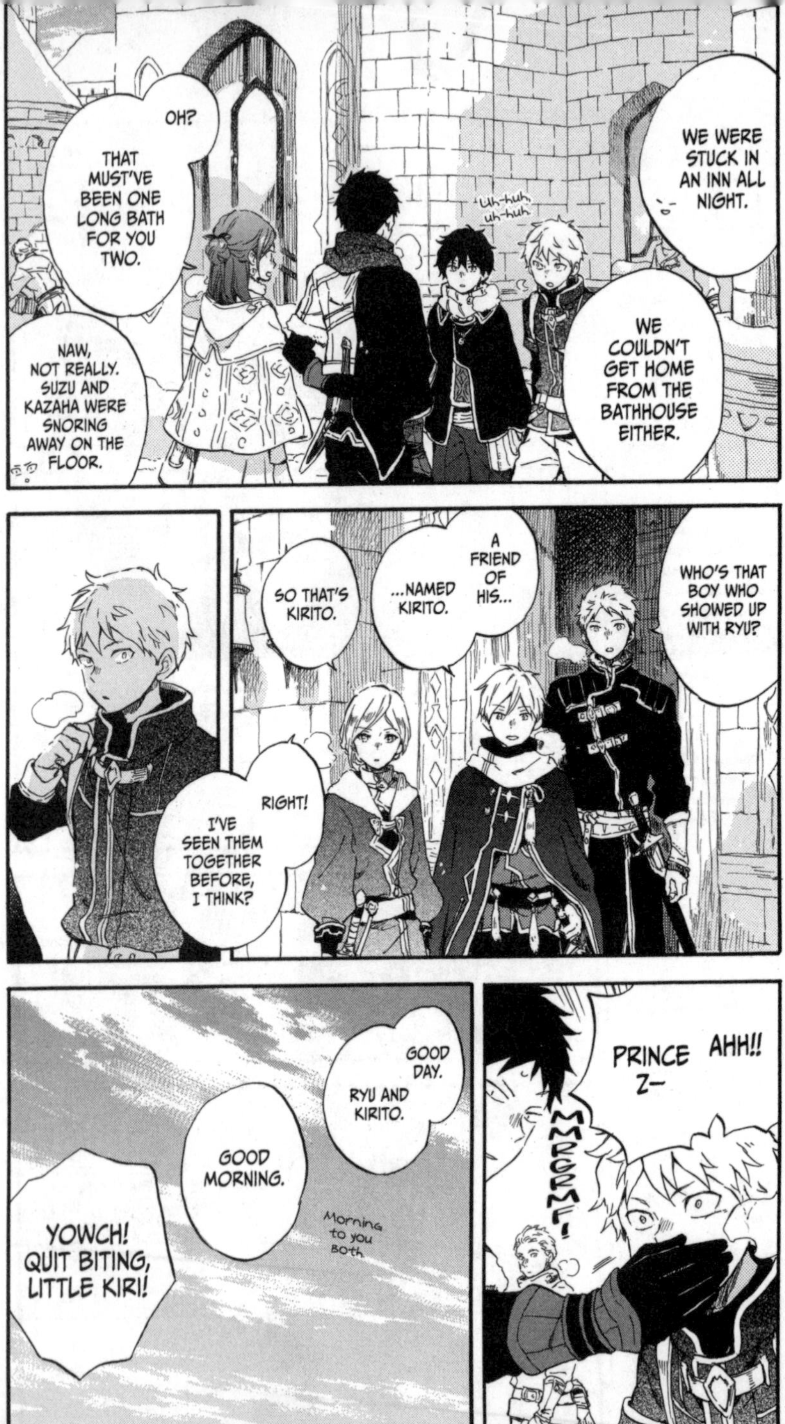
WE WERE STUCK IN AN INN ALL NIGHT.
Uh-huh, uh-huh
OH?
THAT MUST'VE BEEN ONE LONG BATH FOR YOU TWO.
WE COULDN'T GET HOME FROM THE BATHHOUSE EITHER.
NAW, NOT REALLY. SUZU AND KAZAHA WERE SNORING AWAY ON THE FLOOR.
WHO'S THAT BOY WHO SHOWED UP WITH RYU?
A FRIEND OF HIS...
...NAMED KIRITO.
SO THAT'S KIRITO.
RIGHT!
I'VE SEEN THEM TOGETHER BEFORE, I THINK?
AHH!!
PRINCE Z—
MMRGRMF!
GOOD DAY.
RYU AND KIRITO.
GOOD MORNING.
Morning to you both
YOWCH! QUIT BITING, LITTLE KIRI!

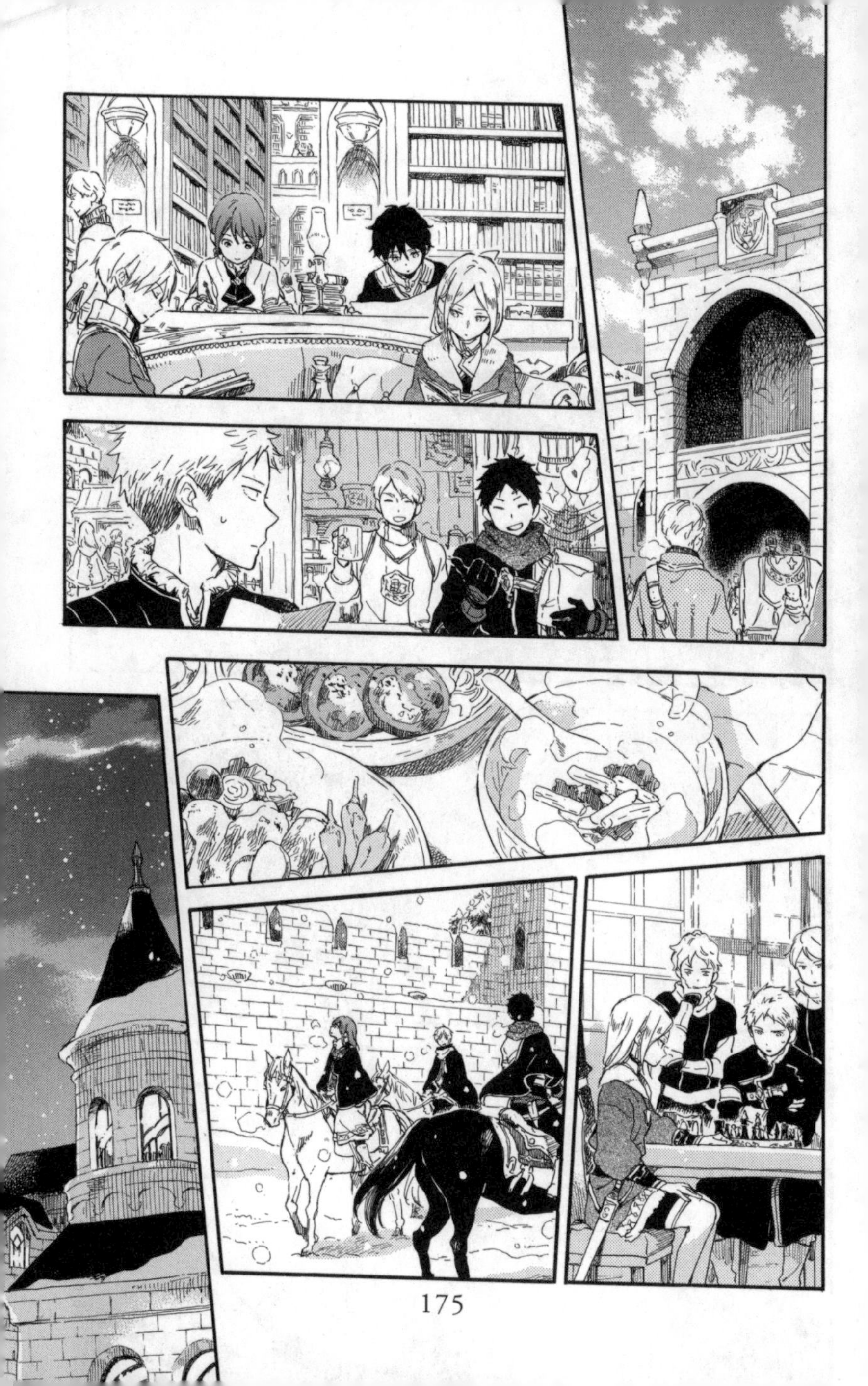

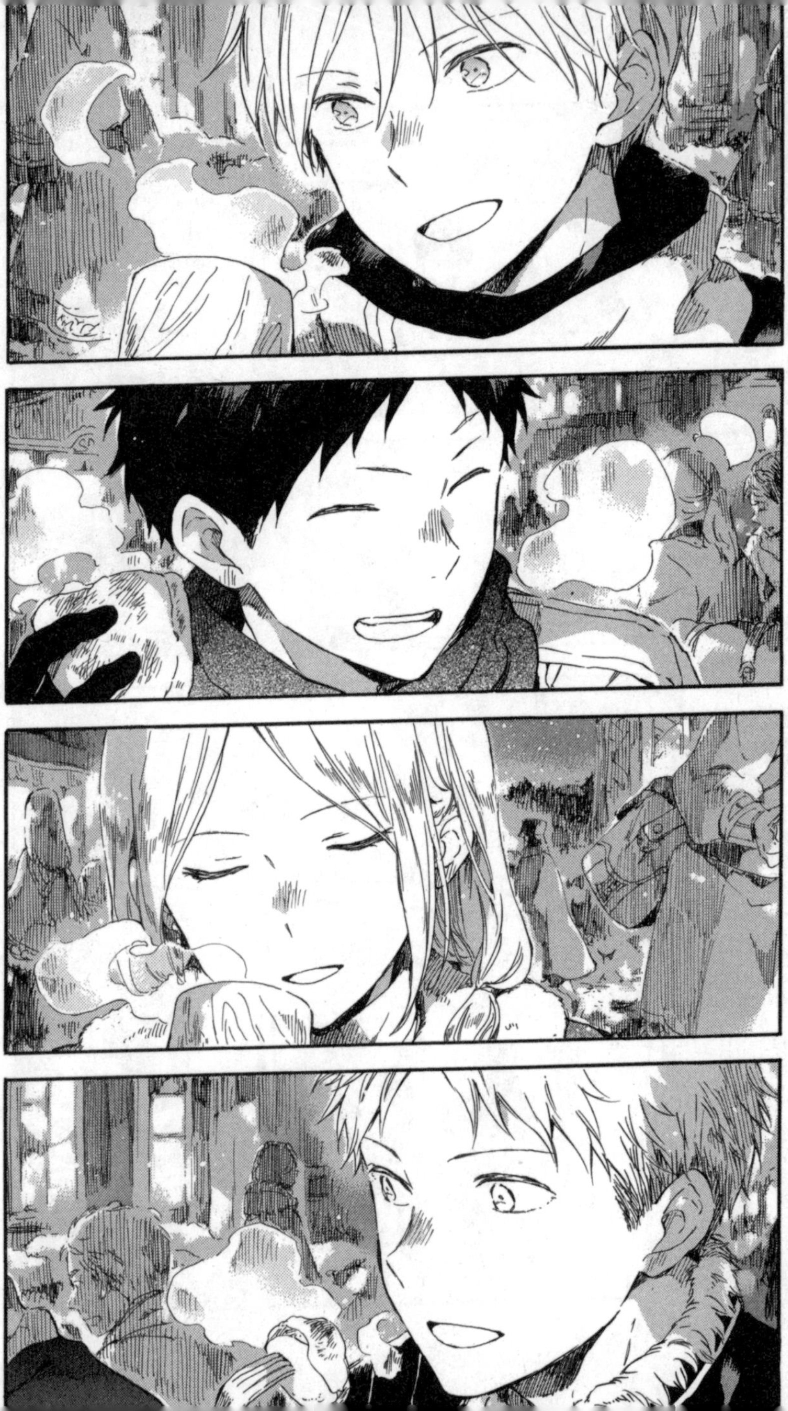

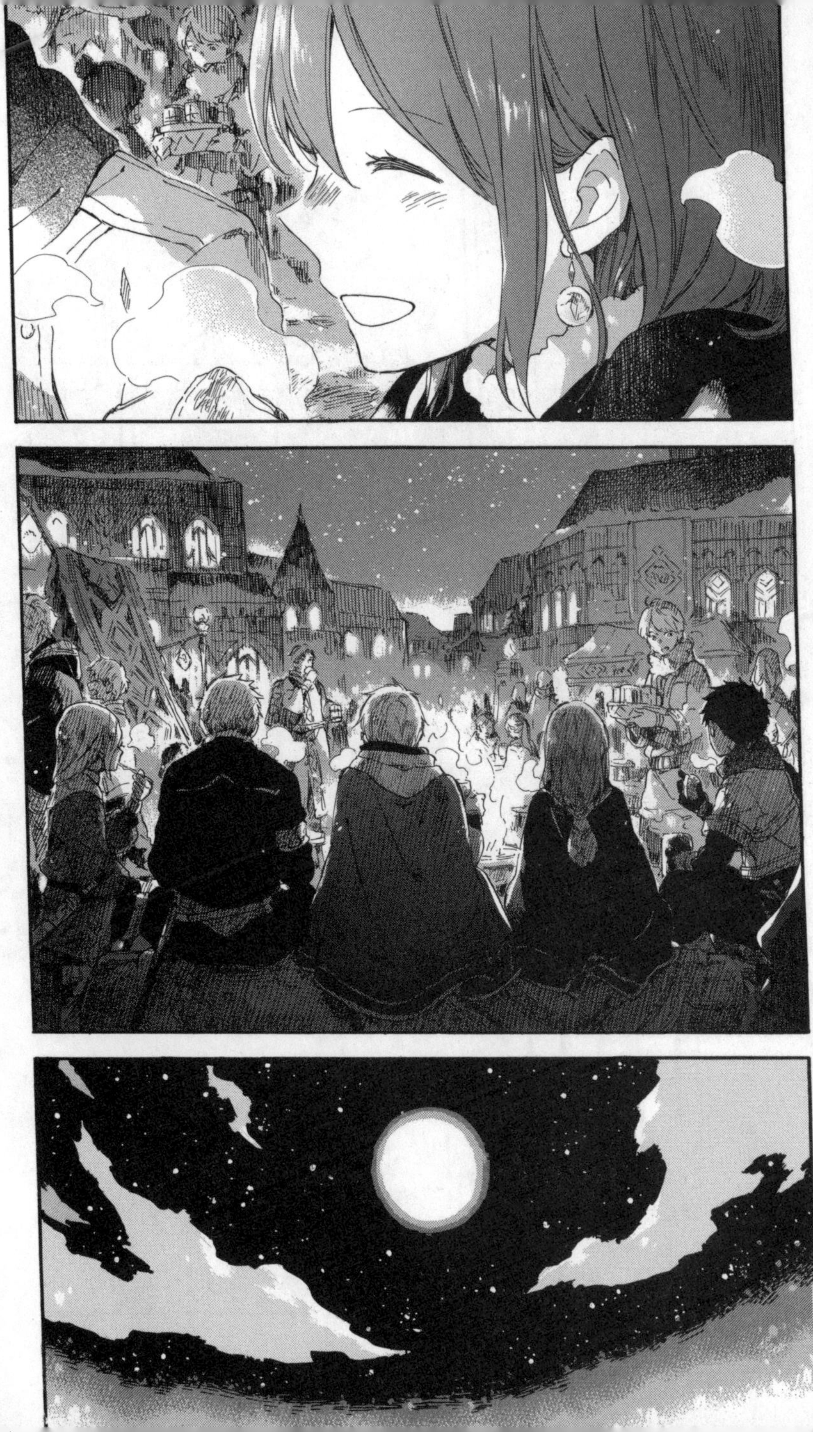

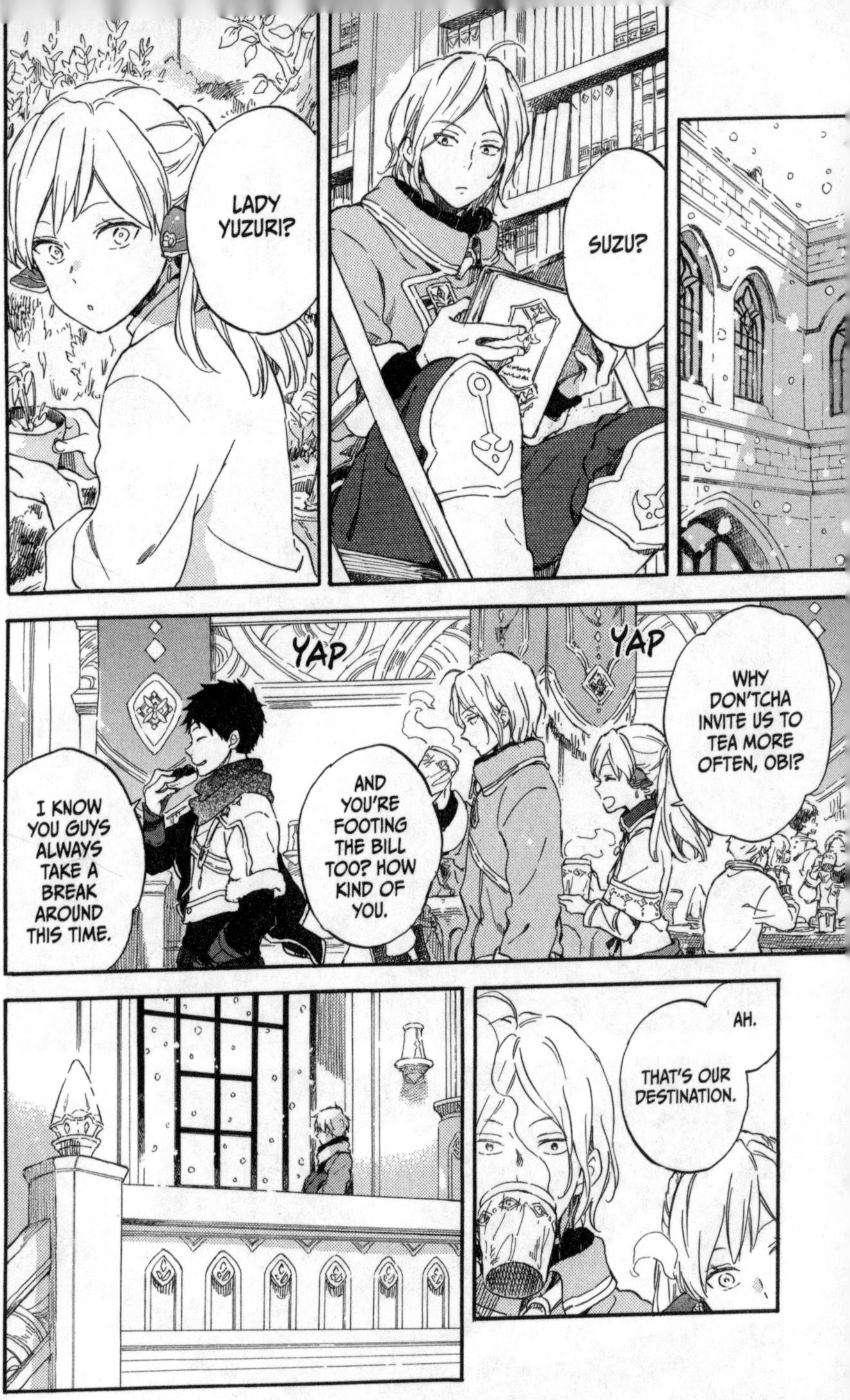
SUZU?
LADY YUZURI?
WHY DON'TCHA INVITE US TO TEA MORE OFTEN, OBI?
YAP
YAP
AND YOU'RE FOOTING THE BILL TOO? HOW KIND OF YOU.
I KNOW YOU GUYS ALWAYS TAKE A BREAK AROUND THIS TIME.
AH.
THAT'S OUR DESTINATION.

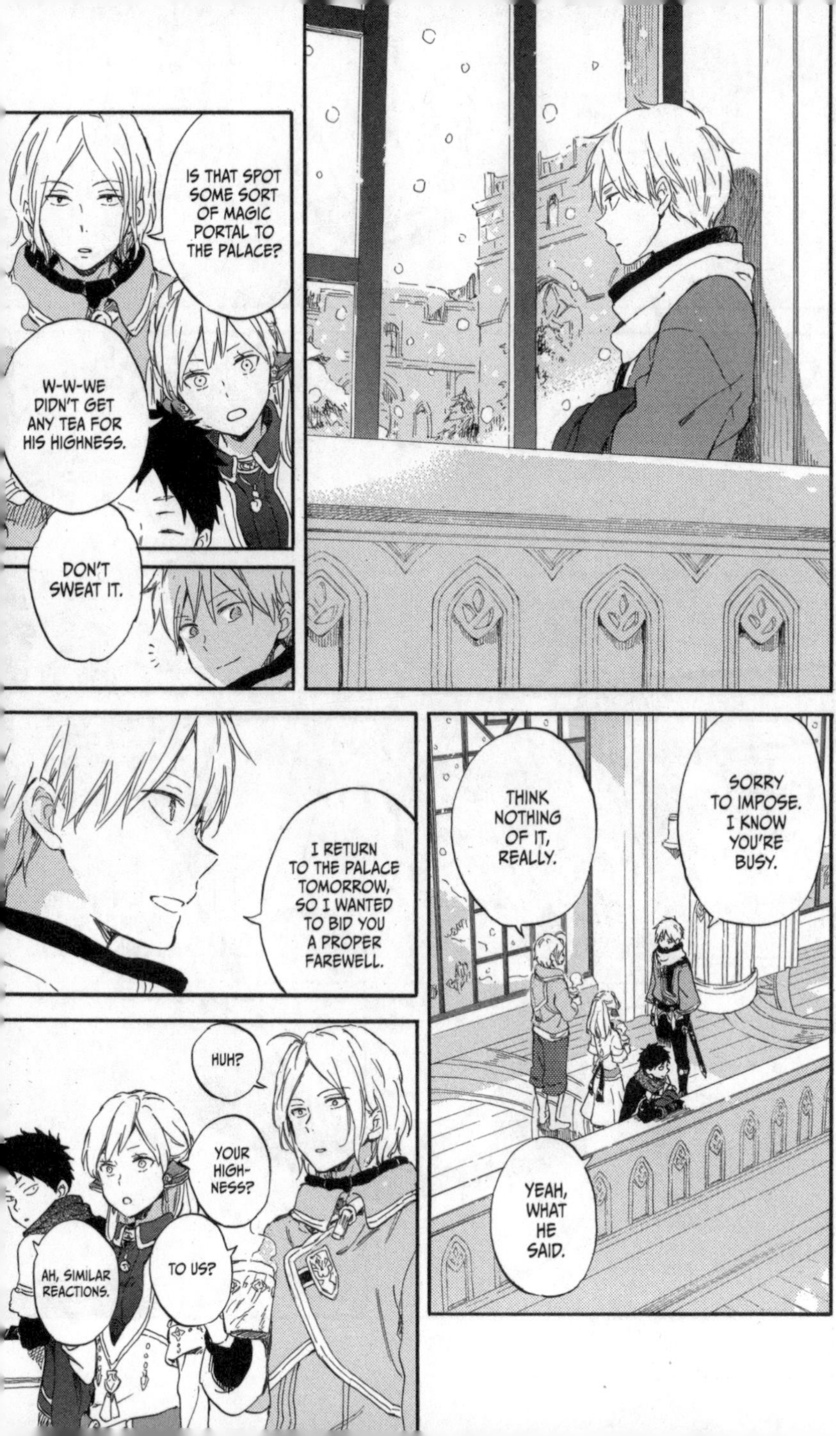
IS THAT SPOT SOME SORT OF MAGIC PORTAL TO THE PALACE?
W-W-WE DIDN'T GET ANY TEA FOR HIS HIGHNESS.
DON'T SWEAT IT.
SORRY TO IMPOSE. I KNOW YOU'RE BUSY.
THINK NOTHING OF IT, REALLY.
YEAH, WHAT HE SAID.
I RETURN TO THE PALACE TOMORROW, SO I WANTED TO BID YOU A PROPER FAREWELL.
HUH?
YOUR HIGHNESS?
TO US?
AH, SIMILAR REACTIONS.

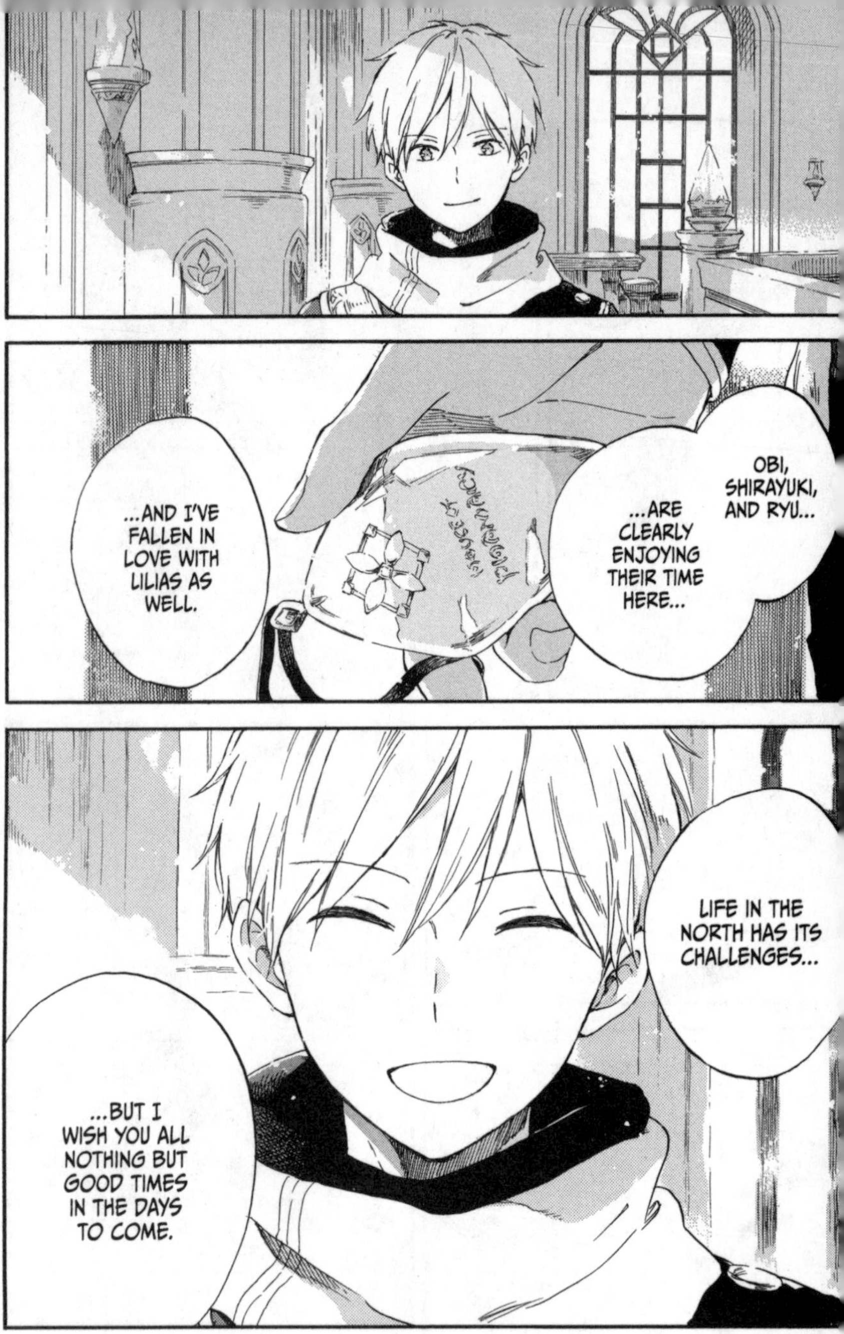
OBI, SHIRAYUKI, AND RYU...
...ARE CLEARLY ENJOYING THEIR TIME HERE...
...AND I'VE FALLEN IN LOVE WITH LILIAS AS WELL.
LIFE IN THE NORTH HAS ITS CHALLENGES...
...BUT I WISH YOU ALL NOTHING BUT GOOD TIMES IN THE DAYS TO COME.

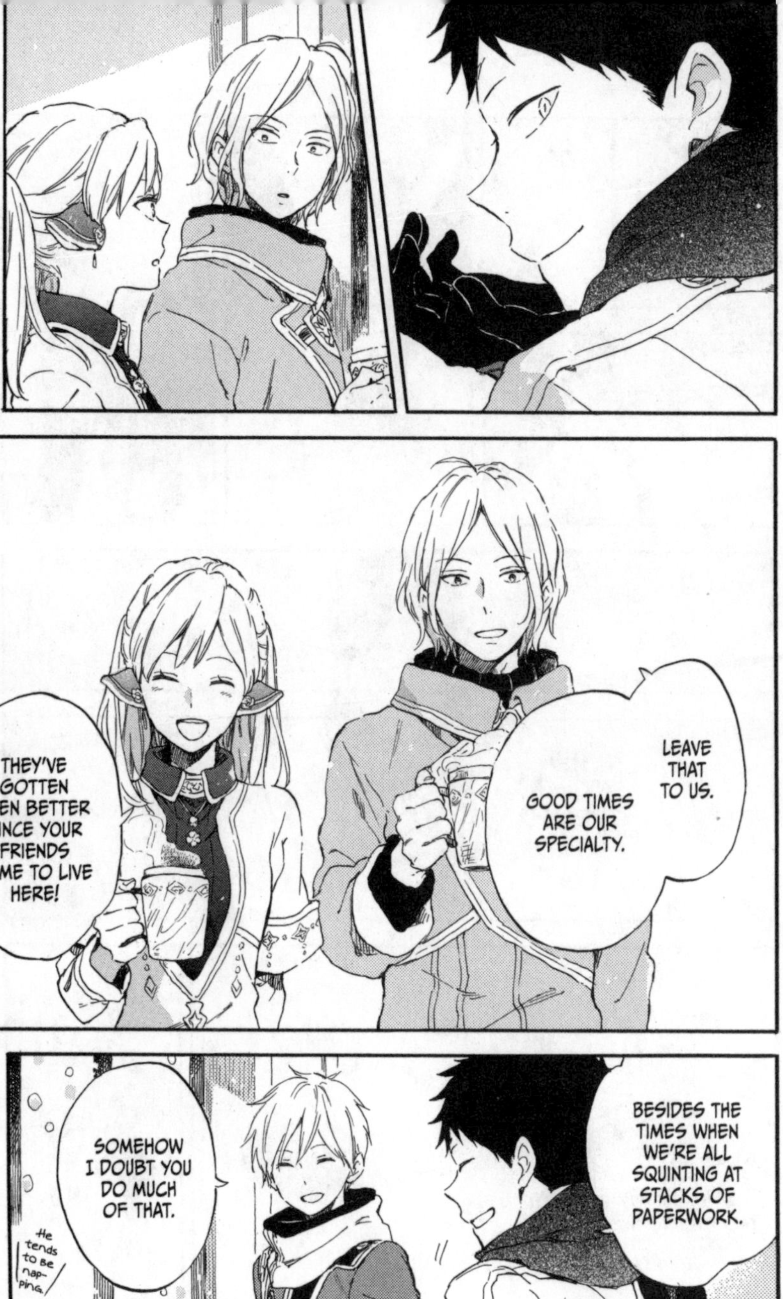
LEAVE THAT TO US.
GOOD TIMES ARE OUR SPECIALTY.
THEY'VE GOTTEN EVEN BETTER SINCE YOUR FRIENDS CAME TO LIVE HERE!
BESIDES THE TIMES WHEN WE'RE ALL SQUINTING AT STACKS OF PAPERWORK.
SOMEHOW I DOUBT YOU DO MUCH OF THAT.
He tends to be napping.

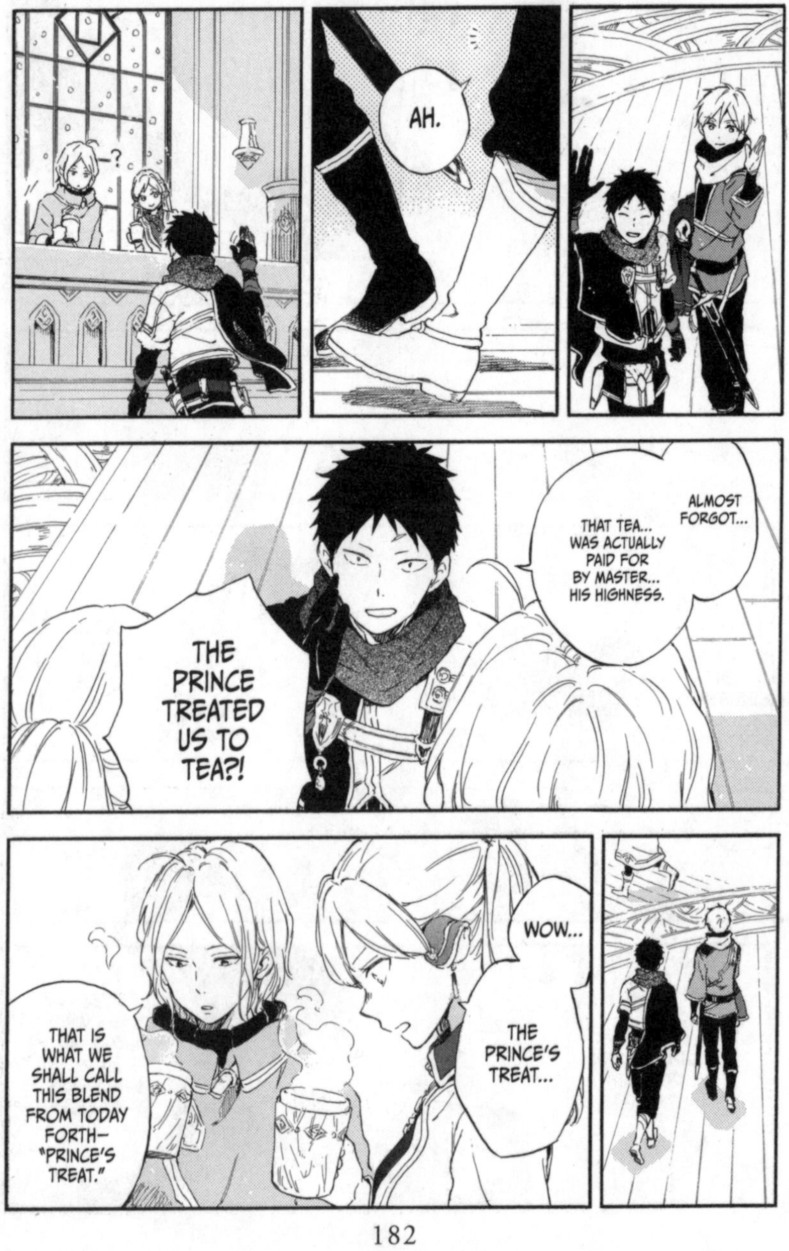
AH.
?
ALMOST FORGOT...
THAT TEA... WAS ACTUALLY PAID FOR BY MASTER... HIS HIGHNESS.
THE PRINCE TREATED US TO TEA?!
WOW...
THE PRINCE'S TREAT...
THAT IS WHAT WE SHALL CALL THIS BLEND FROM TODAY FORTH—"PRINCE'S TREAT."

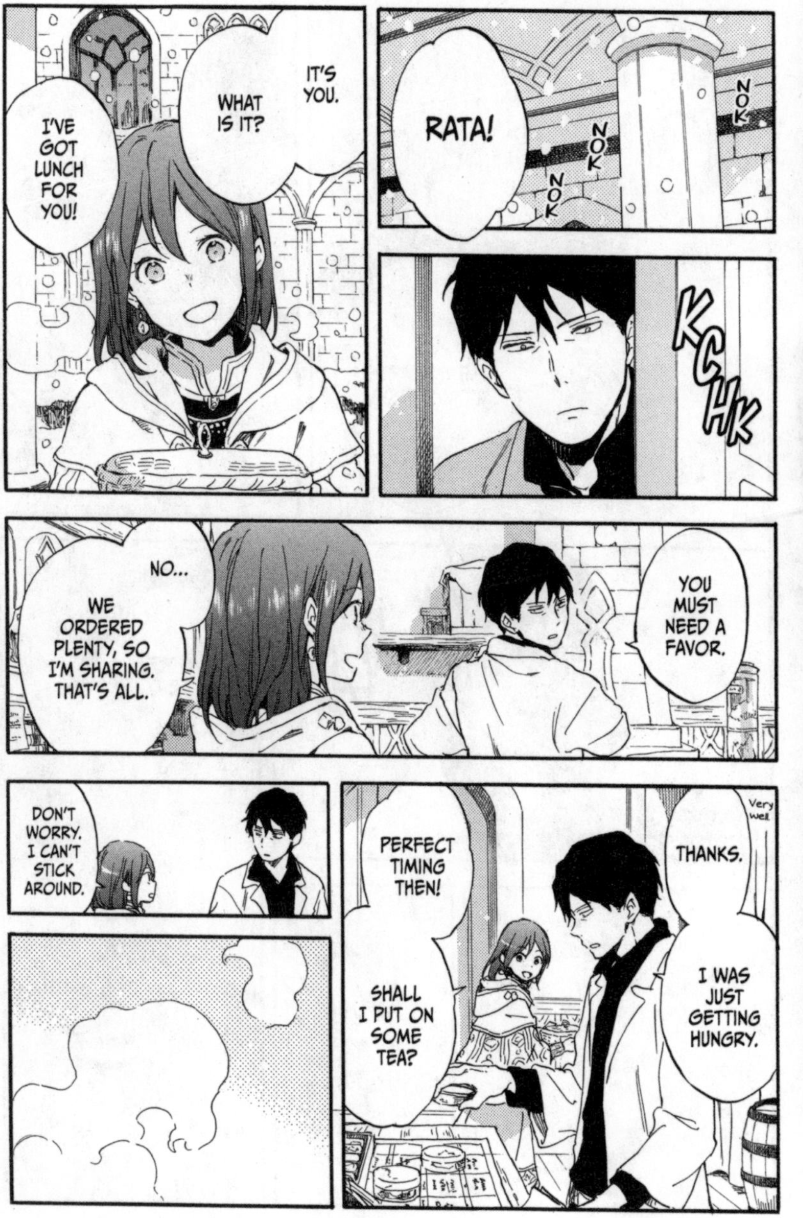
RATA!
NOK NOK NOK
KCHK
IT'S YOU.
WHAT IS IT?
I'VE GOT LUNCH FOR YOU!
YOU MUST NEED A FAVOR.
NO...
WE ORDERED PLENTY, SO I'M SHARING. THAT'S ALL.
Very well
THANKS.
I WAS JUST GETTING HUNGRY.
PERFECT TIMING THEN!
SHALL I PUT ON SOME TEA?
DON'T WORRY. I CAN'T STICK AROUND.

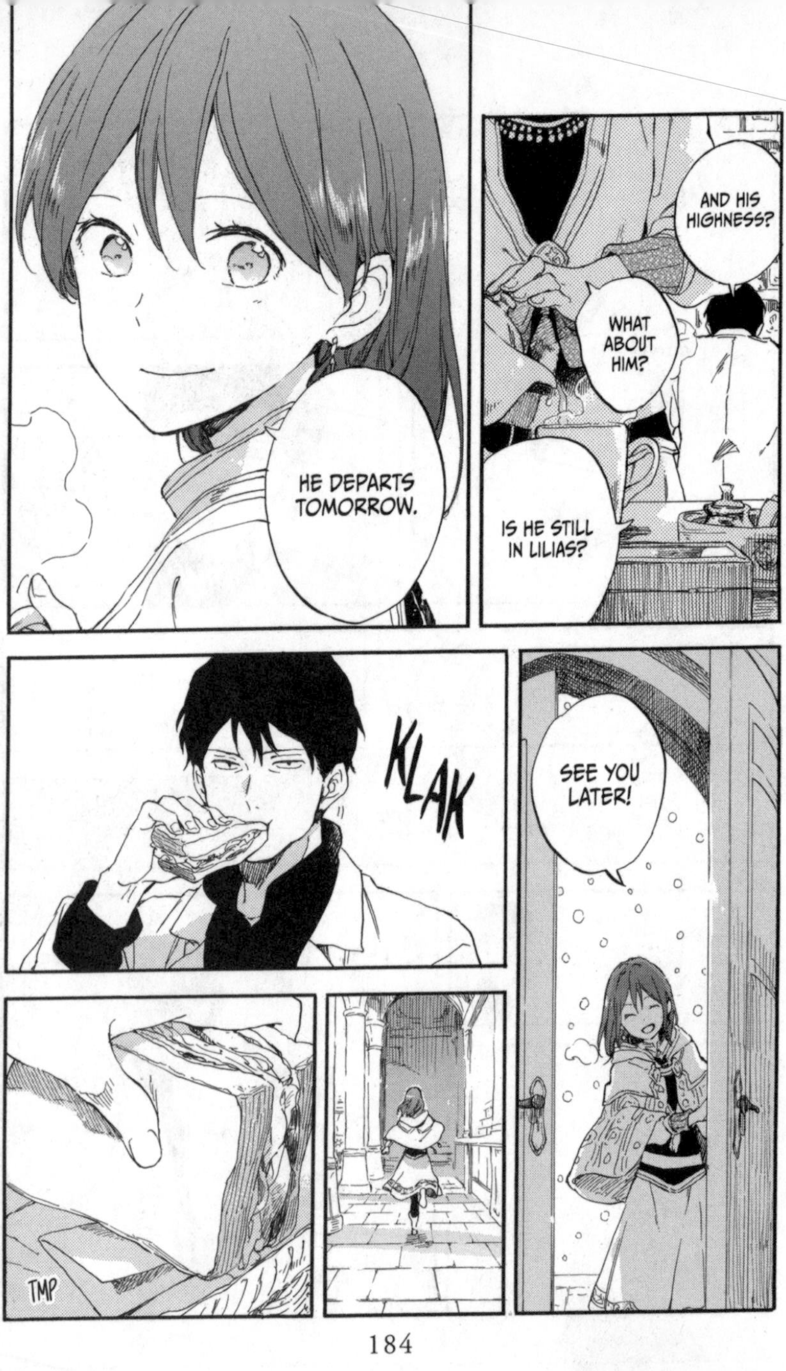
AND HIS HIGHNESS?
WHAT ABOUT HIM?
IS HE STILL IN LILIAS?
HE DEPARTS TOMORROW.
SEE YOU LATER!
KLAK
TMP

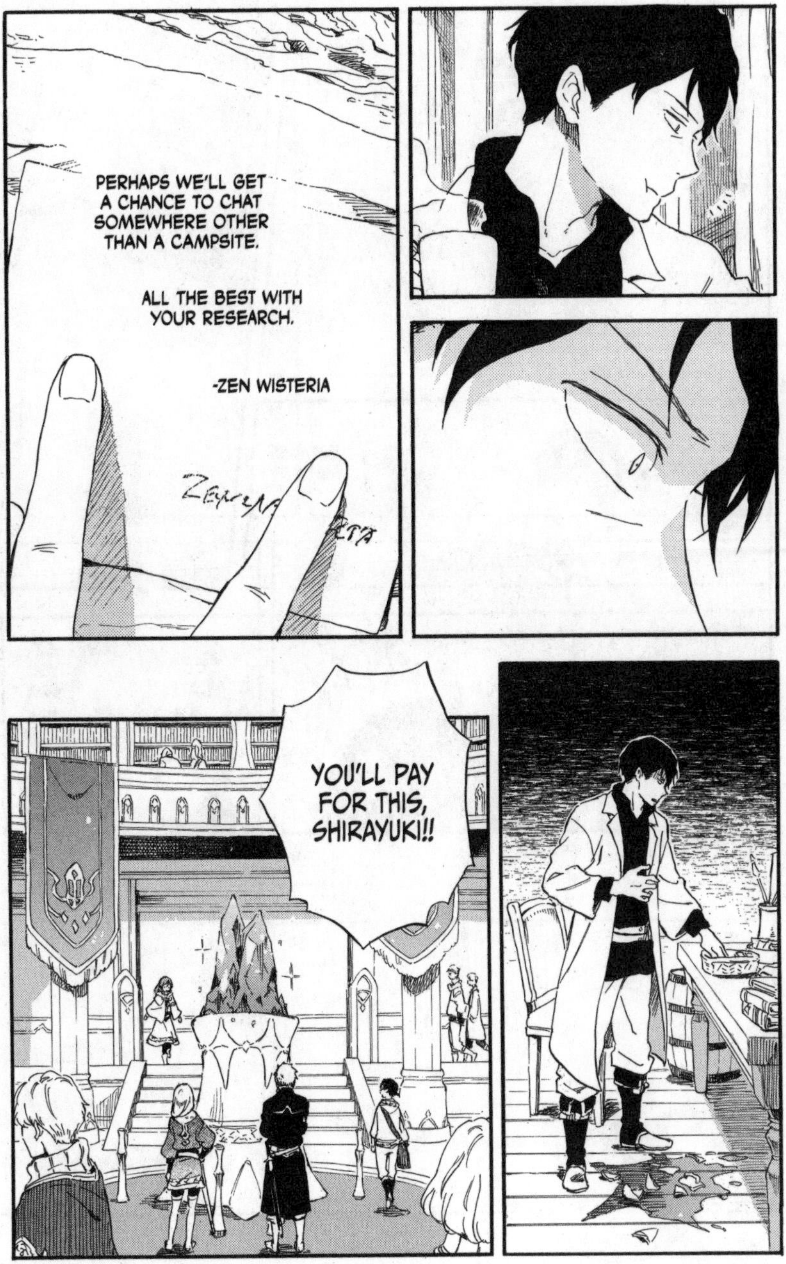
PERHAPS WE'LL GET A CHANCE TO CHAT SOMEWHERE OTHER THAN A CAMPSITE.
ALL THE BEST WITH YOUR RESEARCH.
-ZEN WISTERIA
YOU'LL PAY FOR THIS, SHIRAYUKI!!

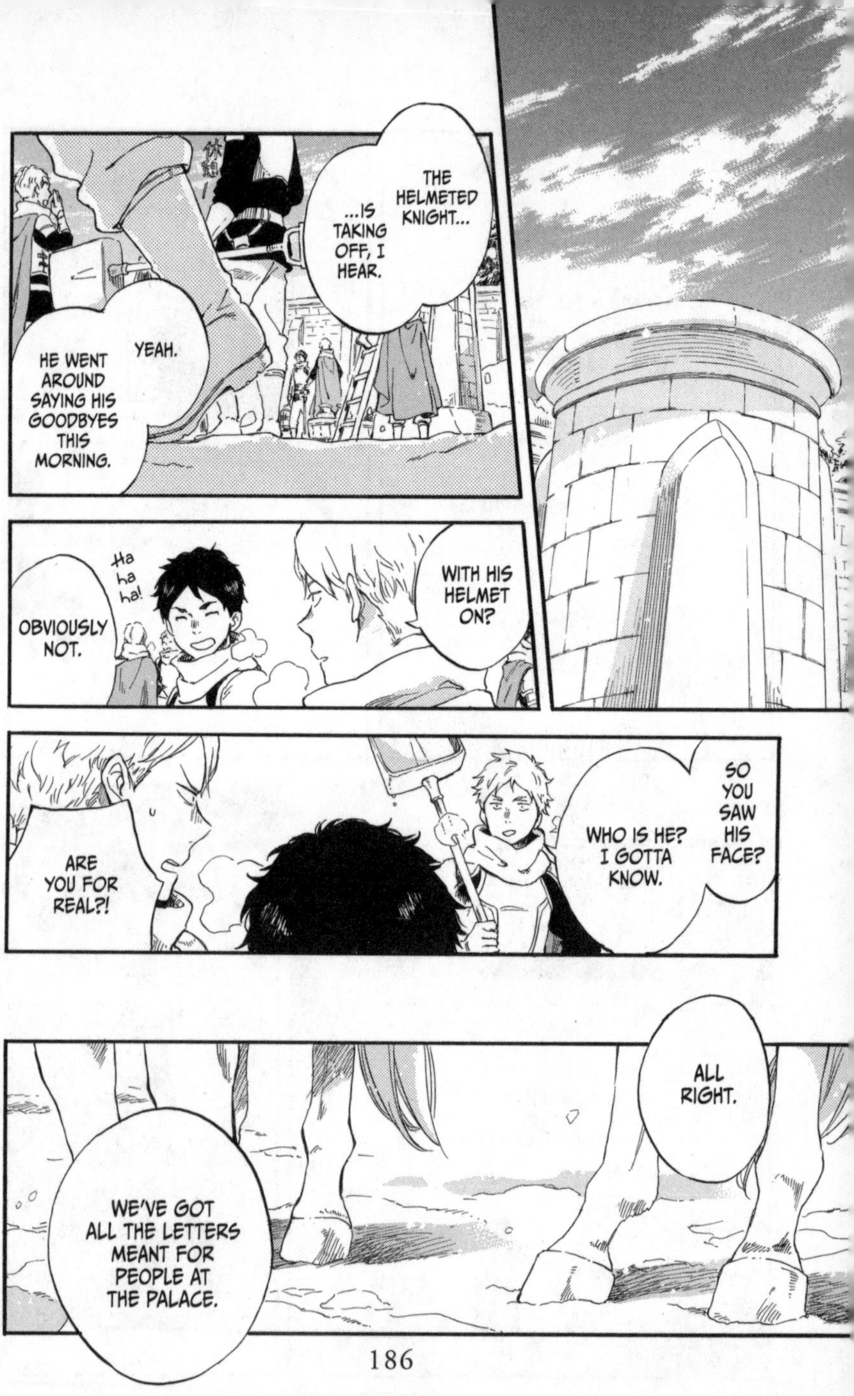
THE HELMETED KNIGHT...
...IS TAKING OFF, I HEAR.
YEAH.
HE WENT AROUND SAYING HIS GOODBYES THIS MORNING.
WITH HIS HELMET ON?
Ha ha ha!
OBVIOUSLY NOT.
SO YOU SAW HIS FACE?
WHO IS HE? I GOTTA KNOW.
ARE YOU FOR REAL?!
ALL RIGHT.
WE'VE GOT ALL THE LETTERS MEANT FOR PEOPLE AT THE PALACE.

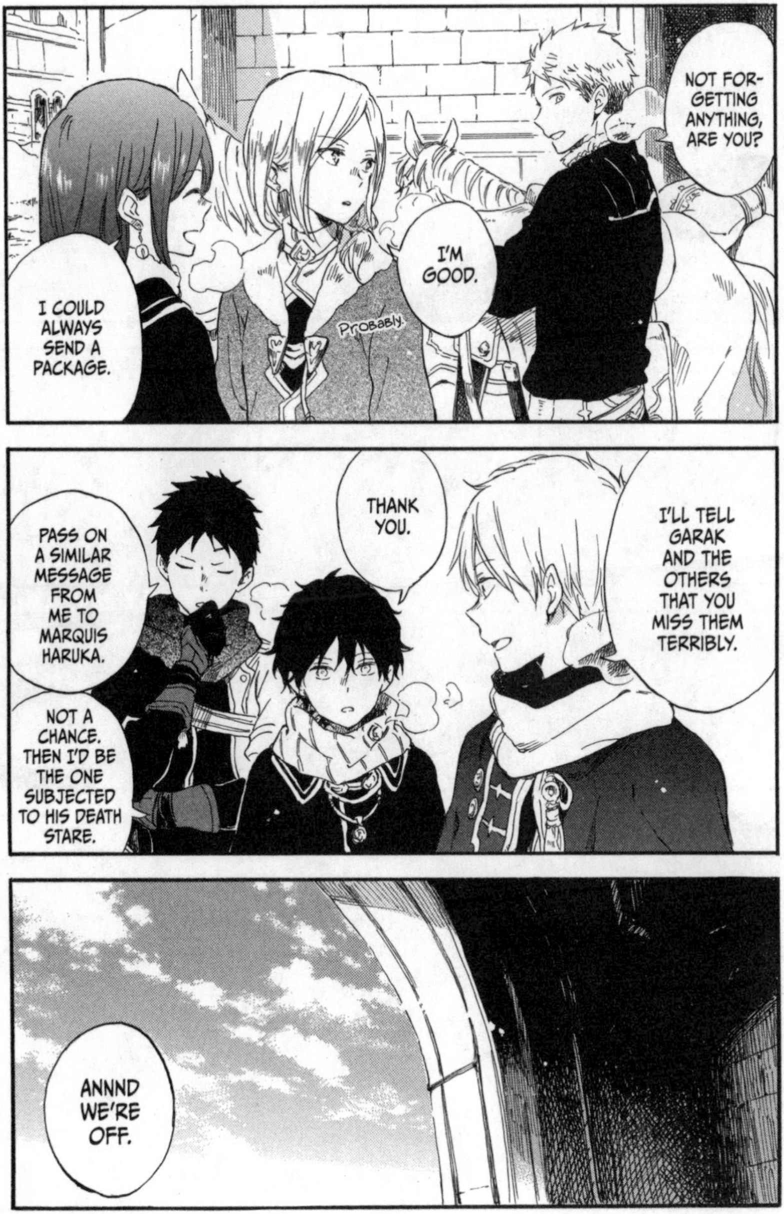
NOT FOR-GETTING ANYTHING, ARE YOU?
I'M GOOD.
Probably.
I COULD ALWAYS SEND A PACKAGE.
I'LL TELL GARAK AND THE OTHERS THAT YOU MISS THEM TERRIBLY.
THANK YOU.
PASS ON A SIMILAR MESSAGE FROM ME TO MARQUIS HARUKA.
NOT A CHANCE. THEN I'D BE THE ONE SUBJECTED TO HIS DEATH STARE.
ANNND WE'RE OFF.

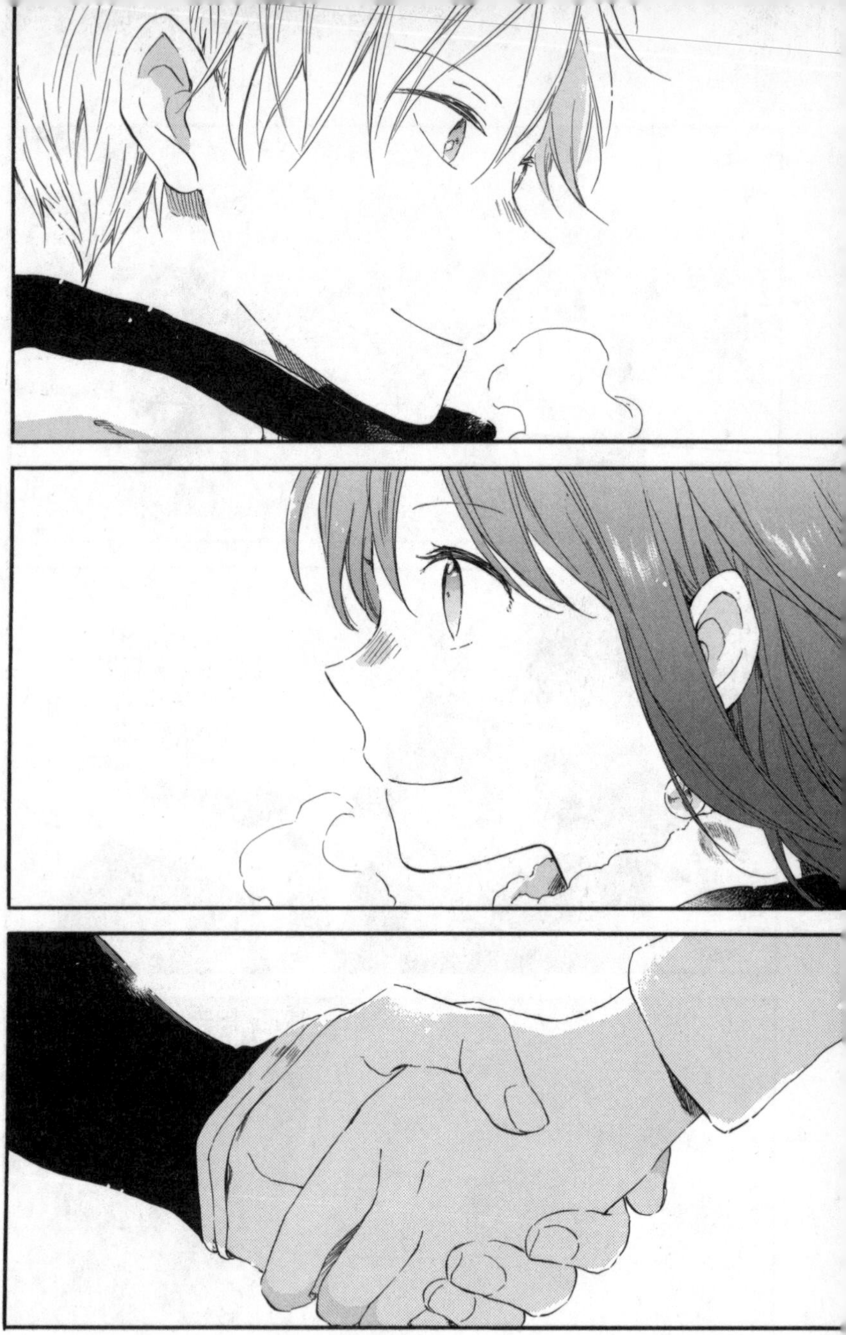

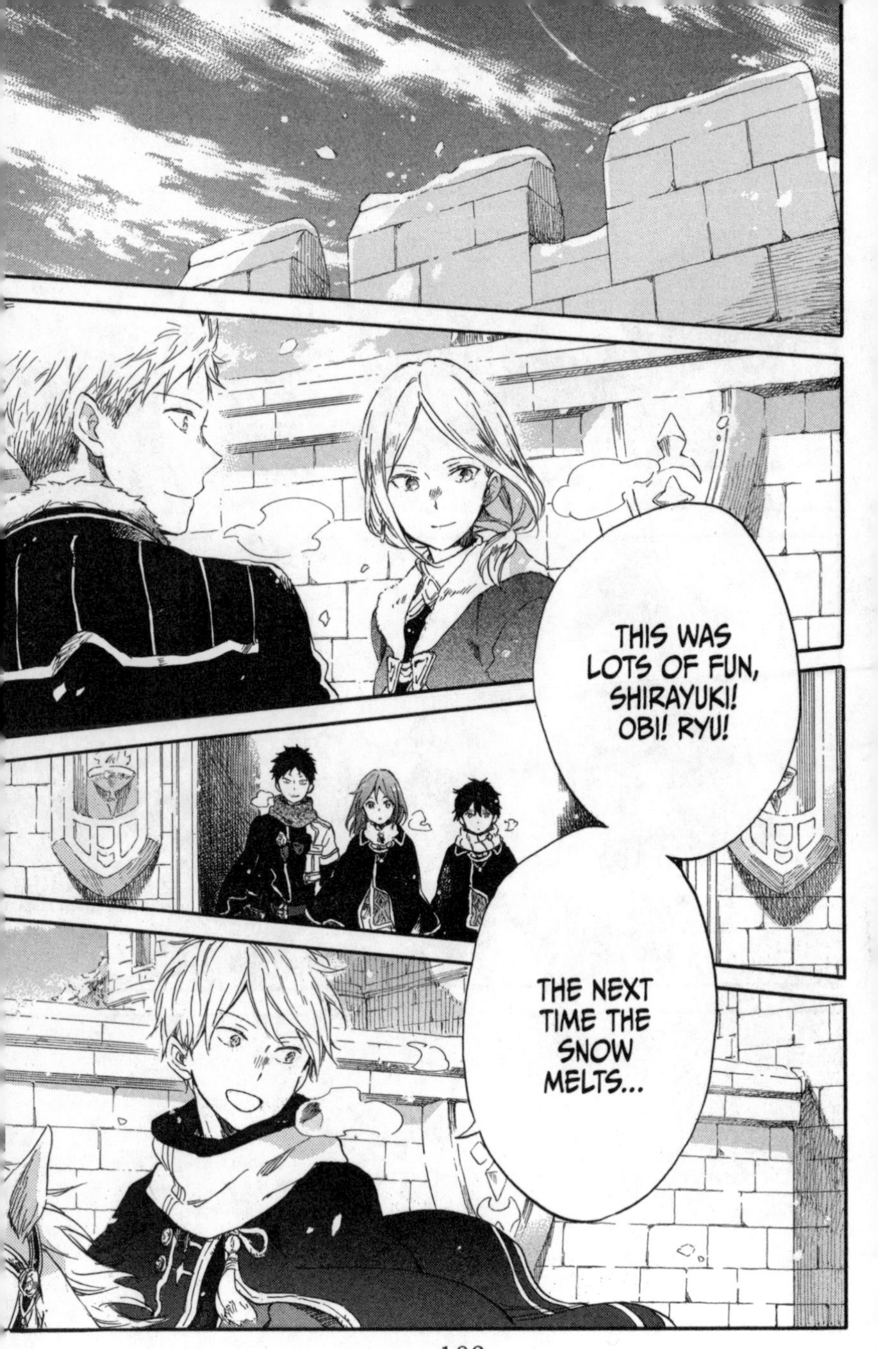
THIS WAS LOTS OF FUN, SHIRAYUKI! OBI! RYU!
THE NEXT TIME THE SNOW MELTS...

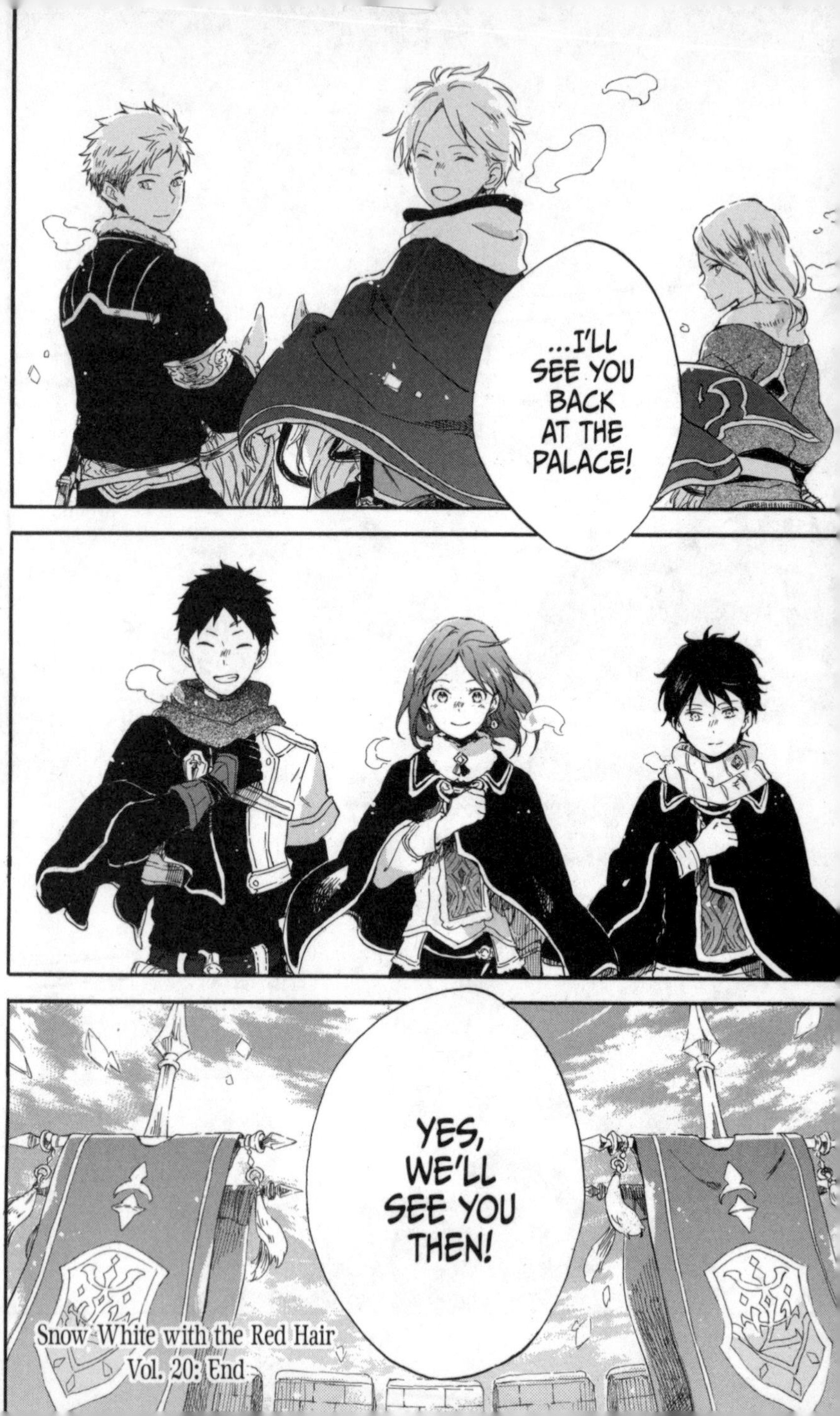
...I'LL SEE YOU BACK AT THE PALACE!
YES, WE'LL SEE YOU THEN!
Snow White with the Red Hair Vol. 20: End